GOD'S OWN SINGER

A LIFE OF
GRAM PARSONS

First edition published in 2002 by Helter Skelter Publishing
4 Denmark Street, London WC2H 8LL

Copyright © 2002 Jason Walker

All rights reserved
Cover design by Paul McEvoy at Bold
Typesetting by Caroline Walker
Printed in Great Britain by The Bath Press, Bath

A CIP record for this book is available from the British Library

ISBN 1-900924-27-7

GOD'S OWN SINGER

A LIFE OF
GRAM PARSONS

by

Jason Walker

Helter
Skelter
Publishing

CONTENTS

THANKS

When I began writing about Gram Parsons in 1993, I had just become aware of Ben Fong-Torres' *Hickory Wind*, a book then recently released in Australia. Having been born about the time that the Flying Burrito Brothers ruled the North Hollywood country music clubs, I was a long way from the epicentre of Parsons' achievements. Still, at 24 years old, I was the perfect age to appreciate in full his ability to hold the listener in his thrall. Having been a fan of his music since I was about 18 years old, I was convinced that I was beginning to understand all that went into his singing.

His singing, then as now, moves me in a way that I have rarely encountered in any other strand of popular music. His voice, like that of his hero George Jones, was the promise – and product – of a broken heart. I had always felt that I knew what experiences he was singing about, but it took Ben's book, and another I discovered by Sid Griffin, to tell me some of what he'd been through. As it turned out, I knew nothing at all about Parsons and when I did find out more, it transpired that I understood his motives even less.

As both Ben and Sid know only too well, he is still a fascinating subject. This book is merely my addition to the collection, and I don't claim that this work is definitive by any means. I am of course indebted to both Ben Fong-Torres and Sid Griffin for their previous works – they remain my favourite reading material, not to mention a valuable resource for my own work. Their assistance in this project is valuable and much appreciated.

I would also like to thank two other people who are directly responsible for the book that you now hold in your hands: Michael Stranges and Sean Body. My friend and fellow music-lover Michael Stranges was my link to Sean Body, the publisher at Helter Skelter in London. Michael passed my manuscript on to Sean for his consideration. Luckily for me, he liked what he read and furthermore, has displayed a great amount of faith in my book, even from a rough draft stage. My sincerest thanks to them both. I would also like to thank Pete Doggett, author of *Are You Ready For the Country?*, who cast a balanced eye over a rough first draft of the manuscript.

This book was written in quite a few different places over quite a long period of time, when I was content to ignore my share of housekeeping duties in exchange for the welcome silence of my all-night writing sessions, as opposed to my all-night music sessions, a much more rowdy affair. Thanks and love are therefore due to my parents, Peter and Elaine, who forever remain concerned about their 'night-owl' son, whose habit of keeping irregular hours since birth probably precluded any chance of him holding down a 'normal' job.

To Steve and 'Sweet' Annie Trindall, my thanks for all hospitality at Beach Road and Centennial Park. Also many thanks to Helen Cobain; Celeste Cunningham, who kindly let me use her PC but took my beloved cat in repayment; Richard Hodge, from whose musical knowledge and compassion I benefited many times over; my brother Jarrod, who continues to berate me for not writing the script of Gram's life before the book – my love forever; Tracy Anne Forrester for enthusiastic friendship, drunken dancing and encouragement; and finally, thank you to my good friend Brian Crouch, for letting me turn you on to Gram.

I would like to thank the following for being encouraging and kind to me while I wrote this book: Paul McIntyre; Jennifer Johnston; Andrew Lay; Michael Carpenter; Kurt Wagner and Mary Mancini for their timely and Nashville hospitality and Joe Pernice, for great music and fun times on the road.

A special round of thanks to Paul Surratt for his hospitality and help in Los Angeles. Also to Frank David Murphy, whose friendship and support of my book have been absolutely invaluable. Thank you to Larry Klug, proprietor of www.gramparsons.com. To Mishy Parker, Mack, Mari, Keith, Jim Beau, Bill Allen, Dr. Zinc, Jolanda Vogood and Romeo Nathan Blue. Thanks to Peggy for sending articles and photos. Thank you to Ed Leimbacher for his reminisces on meeting Gram in 1969. Similarly, a big thank you to Brian Day who added his fine remembrances of seeing the Burritos on a number of occasions.

A special thank you to Peter Kleinow, whose interview with me was one of the high points of my career as a writer. Many thanks to writer Stanley Booth, whose book The True Adventures of the Rolling Stones inspired me to write about music, and Gram in particular. My gratitude is extended to writers Sylvie Simmons and Clinton Walker, both of whom helped me greatly in the writing of the book by way of encouragement and putting me in touch with the right people.

Finally, I would like to thank the one person who influenced me greatly, but who did not live to see me do something more with my life, Shane Peter Allen, who passed away in 1995. His belief in my abilities was exactly what I needed to attempt something like this book.

INTRODUCTION

Across a singing career spanning less than a decade and an involvement in the making of eight albums (of which nearly all are great), Gram Parsons, once a youthful folk singer from Winter Haven, Florida, became one of the central figures of a musical movement that continues even today.

However, Parsons' participation in the construction of this form is not what he is principally remembered for. Rather, he has become the first true mythological figure of alternative country – sadly, it sometimes appears that this mythic status is mostly unrelated to his talent. Instead, Gram is remembered for his prodigious drug intake, his brown-eyed, handsome good looks, his friendship with the Rolling Stones, his premature, drug-related death and, perhaps most tantalising of all, the manner in which his body was cremated after his passing by two drunken friends bent on honouring a promise. As for his musical legacy, it is something that most people like to call either 'country-rock' or in these latter, more enlightened, days 'alternative' country.

Whatever we might like to call his music now, it's worth noting that it was Gram's own presumed influence on that musical form which troubled him more than anything, particularly its rise to prominence in the last two years of his life. It was that selfsame Frankenstein's monster entitled 'country-rock' that so pissed him off. It wasn't about the music itself; it was the fact that people called a band like the Eagles 'country-rock', implying that Parsons had begun what they had finished. Parsons considered that band to be little more than 'bubblegum'. "Life is tougher than they make it out to be," he said, resentfully.

The Eagles – who, it must be said, made some great albums – had casually made off with most of Gram's act, from his hair to his boots, glossed it over and had three hit singles in 1973. That was of course, the same year in which the flowering promise of Parsons' own career, and the recognition that had always been denied him, was cut off at the root. By 1974, the year that Gram's second and perhaps finest album *Grievous Angel* was released, his influence was all but buried along with him. It remained hidden for a time, until Emmylou Harris, Gram's protégé and singing partner, came back to the stage with her Hot Band, comprised mostly of Elvis Presley's live group. She singlehandedly resuscitated Gram's music, and the music that had influenced him. Her repertoire always borrowed from classic rock 'n' roll of the 1950s (Everlys, Buddy Holly, Roy Orbison) and '40s and '50s country (George Jones, the Louvin Brothers), just as Gram had. Furthermore, to honour Parsons' belief in her own talent, she returned the favour by recording at least one of his songs for inclusion on nearly every album she would cut in the next 25 years of her spectacular career.

It is far from idle speculation to suggest that the two of them would have had the fame that Emmylou enjoyed from the outset of her solo career in 1975. Emmylou, through her brief but seminal association with Parsons, has enjoyed the sort of crossover credibility with rock audiences that no other country artist bar Johnny Cash can claim. Moreover, Harris has received all the honours and accolades offered by country music, a genre whose traditions she has fully explored but whose moralistic codes and conservatism she absolutely rejects.

While public interest in most of the '60s rock groups (other than the Beatles and Gram's friends, the Rolling Stones) fluctuates and declines, interest in the work of artists like Gram Parsons is now at an all-time high. This situation is sadly far-removed from the reality of his own lifetime, when the artist sought an audience for the music he had great faith in. While Gram struggled with unappreciative or small crowds and some critical indifference, he would have been overjoyed to learn that the newest audience for his music today were either still very young or had yet to be conceived at the time of his death.

Despite the timing of his exit, we can still profit from Parsons' feelings of loss and melancholy. His music has facets that are not diminished by time, particularly his two solo albums, both of which resonate with timeless qualities worthy of celebration.

As for Parsons, his last hours on earth are covered in the final chapter of this book. But I have not sought to investigate some of the frankly outlandish stories that proliferated at the time of his death. I have chosen instead to concentrate on his life, his musical development, his enduring fascination with Elvis Presley, his love of folk music and his decision to make country music his career, which proved to be of great cost to him.

Gram Parsons was a young man full of contradictory ideas and principles. He was not especially gifted as a musician, but he surrounded himself with the best players. Nor was he blessed with the ability to write prolifically. In fact, his personal gift for writing was sporadic, and occasionally made more so by his lifestyle, and he required the assistance of more experienced writers to bring his songs to completion and thus, life. Once those songs had been written though, boy, he sure could sing them. It was the voice that made him stand out from the crowd. His voice was as expressive an instrument as any that has sung country music, or rock, or pop. His voice is unique in its fragility and I believe, without peer in its ability to move us. I can think of no modern singer who has so successfully married that combination of frailty and beauty – and it's probably better that way.

Jason Walker

CHAPTER 1
THE EARLY YEARS

Inherited wealth can be a real stumbling block to happiness. It is to ambition what cocaine is to morality.

Gloria Vanderbilt

They left Waycross, Georgia, by train on Tuesday morning, 22 December 1959, bound for Winter Haven, Florida, and a warm holiday season. On the train that cool December day was Mrs Avis Connor, accompanied by her two children Little Avis and Ingram Cecil Connor III. Her husband Cecil had bid farewell to his wife and young children at the back of the station.

Though it was winter, that part of the United States rarely sees very cold weather. The children were eager, anticipating another comfortable Christmas spent at the Snively family mansion, overlooking beautiful Lake Eloise. Avis Connor's people were one of Florida's wealthiest families, their citrus holdings, processing plants and shipping concerns earning them millions of dollars each year. Overseen by Papa John Snively and his son, John Junior, Snively Groves shipped 20% of Florida's citrus fruit to the rest of the country. There was only one competitor with a similar-sized operation. There had been setbacks – a fire had destroyed the entire operation in 1953 – but, six years later, they had rebuilt it and were now bigger than ever.

At the enormous white mansion, which has now become part of Cypress Gardens, the family gathered – matriarch Haney and her three children, John Junior, Evalyn and Avis, with their respective spouses and children. Haney's husband Papa John had succumbed to cancer in February that year. Cecil's absence was remarked upon, but Avis explained that he was taking care of the box factory (another part of the Snively business empire) and needed to hand out the employees' Christmas hampers. He would arrive the following day to join in the celebrations. The family celebrated the season, the adults sipping drinks, the children ogling the gift-laden tree in the enormous living room.

The next afternoon, there was a telephone call for Avis from the police in Winter Haven. Her husband, Cecil Connor, known locally as 'Coon Dog', had been found dead in the master bedroom of the family home, the victim of an apparent accidental shooting. Avis's initial reaction was one of shock, but there were no scenes of emotional hysteria.

In fact, her reaction struck some, including her own daughter, as being very cold – she informed her mother, sister and brother that day, but waited until Boxing Day to tell the children. Ingram Cecil – "Gram" – was told the news separately from his sister, although any mention of suicide was avoided, since the Waycross coroner had not yet established the facts of the shooting. The boy became intensely emotional, and spent the rest of the Christmas holidays avoiding the other children and his mother, playing by himself in his room at the mansion or staring off into space. Little Avis was told the news, and her reaction at her young age was confusion. Where was her beloved father? And why was he not here with her at Christmas time?

At least one answer to that question had emerged nearly two months prior to the day Coon Dog's body was discovered with a single bullet wound to his right temple. Connor's youngest brother Tom and his mother Nancy had visited in early November, and Coon Dog had disclosed to his brother the terrible and conflicting feelings and the dissatisfaction that working for his wife's family caused him. But he didn't seem unhappy to Tom. In fact, he informed his brother, he had worked out a way to leave the family business. His mother was concerned for her eldest son. He was a sensitive man, with a great emotional attachment to his two children, and an intense, some said unstable, relationship with his wife.

He had committed himself to this life in Waycross, to working at the Snively box plant 40 miles away in the town of Baxley. He drove the 80-mile round trip every day, but work was not what kept him grounded. Coon Dog lived to hunt and fish, it presented the opportunity to keep away old ghosts and bad memories. He kept a sleeping bag, a fishing rod and a gun in the trunk of his car, just in case he saw a spot that looked like it might offer good hunting.

Waycross is a small Georgia town that rests on the edge of the shaky land of the Okefenokee Swamp, a short drive from the Florida state line and only about 60 miles inland from the Atlantic Ocean. Jerry Wexler of Atlantic Records, who was looking for the name of a town that would suggest a redneck *je ne sais quoi*, once described it as being 'the asshole of the world'. Wexler may not have ever passed through the Waycross city limits, but writer Stanley Booth grew up there. His assessment: "Culture exists there only in the anthropological sense".

The Klan still holds occasional meetings, but race relations are little different to any other Southern town of similar size. Whether in boom or bust, "Waycross hasn't really grown a whole lot," says resident and Gram Parsons historian Billy Ray Herrin. "In fact, it's a lot like it was when he was living there. Now there's an expressway and a few more fast-food joints. It used to be a real railroad town, but the railroad is now even less prominent economically than it was when Gram was a kid. It's just a typical small South Georgia town, that didn't grow like they thought it would."

In America's flourishing post-World War 2 economy, there were certain towns in the South that, because of their location and size, could not and did not benefit. Waycross was one of these towns. Post-war, Waycross did not change. Its founding fathers had always hoped it would be a moral beacon, to do a little better than other towns elsewhere in the United States. "At that time, the country was in the grip of a conformist mindset," says Stanley Booth. "But it was nothing compared to Waycross. In America at that time, well, you saluted the flag and you went to church and you tried to be a good man or woman, boy or girl. That held just as true in Waycross, maybe ten times more true. I was thinking about this only recently, that culturally, Waycross is actually *less* diverse now than it was when I was living there. Now, there are no Jews in Waycross, there is no synagogue even. But there was then. For the most part, Waycross was dominated by white Protestant males who knew 'everything' there was to know about life. They had 'received Wisdom'."

This wisdom and its many permutations were lost on many of the town's young people. There were those who shared with Stanley the sentiment that culture had somehow passed them by, that all worldly experiences had fallen through the cracks. "I was ready to start thumbing to get out of Waycross," Gram Parsons said. "There's an old saying about it: as soon as you learn to walk, you start walkin' out of town."

Before he came to Waycross, to the land that trembled on the edge of the Okefenokee Swamp where the hunting was good, Coon Dog was a *bona fide* war hero, who had seen death firsthand.

Born in 1917 in Columbia, Tennessee to Nancy and Ingram Connor, Ingram Cecil Connor Jr., the scion of a respected, well-to-do (but not wealthy) family, had completed nearly all of his four years at University without incident. By 1939, the rest of the world was already at war, although America remained at arm's length. For Ingram, flying was all he wanted to do. He had not considered fighting in a world war. He just wanted to fly planes. Without consulting his parents, Ingram left college two months before he was due to graduate and enlisted in the army. With his nearly complete degree in aeronautical engineering, regimental brass decided to put him in the Army Air Force, where he trained as a pilot, very much to the satisfaction of his superiors.

After training in Oklahoma and Texas through 1940, Connor rose to the rank of second lieutenant by the time he graduated from his flying cadetship. He received orders to present himself at Wheeler Field on the island of Oahu, Hawaii. Wheeler Field was an enormous Army Air Force base near the US naval port of Pearl Harbour. Connor took a room off base, along with other officers, living in relative luxury in a large mansion that belonged to the Huttons, the family who owned Woolworths. He was still living there when, a year later, the Japanese launched a devastating surprise attack on the United States Navy in 1941. Early on the morning of December 4th, he heard the huge explosions rocking the house. He headed for the Naval base. The carnage he saw there that day he could not speak of again –not to his family, nor anyone close to him.

As America became further embroiled in theatres of conflict throughout the Pacific and Europe, Ingram received his first orders –to ship out to New Guinea in early 1942. He served under the command of General Douglas MacArthur, commander of the US forces in the Pacific, as an air force operations officer and pilot. Within a year, he was promoted to captain.

Captain Connor excelled at flying. So exceptional was his conduct that he was awarded a presidential citation for heroism and was extensively decorated as a result of his bravery in action, during which he engaged Japanese troop ships and dive bombers. During his commission, Ingram flew no fewer than fifty bombing missions out of New Guinea and Darwin, in Australia's Northern Territory. His mission was to cut off Japanese troop and supply shipping and generally monitor US and Allied troop movements through the Timor Sea.

By 1943, the war still raging, Connor was promoted to the rank of Air Force Major. Flying regular dangerous missions between Darwin and New Guinea left him exposed to the tropical diseases that were felling nearly as many men as the Japanese. A serious bout of malaria contracted in the humid, rotting tropics nearly killed the pilot whom some believed was invincible. He left his base in New Guinea on a stretcher, wasting from a high fever and in need of extensive hospital treatment. He was shipped back to Darwin, where he spent several months resting in a naval field hospital. Eventually, after a prolonged period of recuperation, he was flown home to the US.

Connor had left the fighting a long way behind, but the experience would stay with him always. Having sustained mental wounds as scarring as many physical injuries, Connor's personality changed. He had what psychologists today would refer to as post-traumatic stress syndrome, which manifested itself in depression and periods of lengthy personal anguish.

Back in the U.S.A. Major Connor accepted a posting at Bartow Field, in Jacksonville, Florida. Today Bartow is a commercial airfield, but in the war years it was an Air Force base. Connor was involved in the training of combat pilots for missions just like the ones he had served. He was a well-respected and well-liked officer, but his men had little idea of the horrific combat that had scarred him so badly. Gentlemen did not talk of such things in those days.

As part of his recuperation, Connor liked to pick up the musical instruments that he found in the officer's mess and fool around with them. Soon, he took up playing the bass fiddle, mastering the bass line for 'Pagan Love Song', as he proudly reported in a letter to his mother. Connor had always enjoyed music, particularly classical and a little swing, though he also liked the hillbilly songs that some of the enlisted men preferred. While living on the base at Bartow Field he began buddying around with a friend from the service, John Snively Jr.

Today, the Snively clan are more genteel than their turbulent past suggests. In the days before the Second World War they were a very wealthy family with an antebellum mansion, servants and fine cars. They owned many of the citrus holdings in Orange Grove, Florida, where the air is sweetened with the oil of millions of orange and grapefruit trees. The sweet and bitter fruits of America are still grown here and are packaged for a hundred thousand supermarkets. Even during the Great Depression, when it seemed that all of America, and indeed the world, was shaken by poverty and hunger, there was still a need for fruit, however scarce money was. It meant health to millions of Americans to be able to eat citrus fruit, although in California growers sealed millions of tons of oranges in creosote dumps or bulldozed containers off wharves to prevent starving migrant workers from eating them.

Snively was a fellow Air Force man, and he took a liking to the friendly Tennessean major, thinking that he should introduce him to the family. John did just that, bringing Ingram to the family mansion one weekend, taking good care to ensure he was introduced to his 22-year-old sister Avis, a dark-haired, bright and attractive young woman with a feisty personality. Avis fell for the sad-eyed major in his dashing uniform and they began their courtship, which would shortly lead to their engagement. The impending marriage had the Snivelys divided. Papa John liked the young Air Force man but wasn't sure if he should be part of the clan. Avis's mother Haney, however, was adamant that she would marry her major, and she did so in late 1943.

Connor continued with the Air Force and by the end of the war, was decommissioned, having served his country well. Now that his son-in-law was back on Civvy Street, Papa John invited him into his office and offered him a good job in the family firm. He was to oversee the Snively family's processing and packaging factory based near Waycross, Georgia, where the boxes for the oranges were put together. John Sr. made him director of the plant.

In the nervous months following the war, Connor tried to rein in the growing feelings of anxiety, anger and disquiet he had been experiencing. While post-traumatic stress syndrome had not been diagnosed as such in early 1946, the things he had experienced continued to trouble him. The air force doctors had called it 'shell shock' or 'battle fatigue', and told him it would go away eventually. But some days the feelings of anxiety and emotional stress settled down like a fog. The only relief he could take from his days in the service of the family business was to take his hounds out into the swamp and hunt for the weekend. His new bride didn't mind too much. She would organise a get-together at their new home for the local bridge ladies.

In early 1946, Avis announced that she was pregnant. Connor was ecstatic but he kept right on working, fishing and drinking hard. He had not started out as a drinker, but his wife's family liked to booze and he found it helped him to deal with the twin stresses of work and his war experience. As Avis became heavily pregnant, Coon Dog relaxed a little more. Two weeks before she went into labour, Avis had returned to Winter Haven with Connor to await the birth at the family home, surrounded by Snivelys and several members of the Connor clan. His first son and heir was born on 5 November 1946, and was christened Ingram Cecil Connor III. The child was made much of, and highly celebrated, being the newest male heir to the Snively family fortune.

Within the first two years of the marriage, various problems had already emerged. The couple drank heavily – Avis, mostly out of boredom and because it was part of her social regimen, while Connor drank as a means of covering up his ever-growing depression and trying to numb the psychological effects of his war service. Even in the early years of their son's life, there was talk around town that Avis had been having an affair with a prominent local man. True to the social mores of the time, these problems were swept under the rug, aired only as gossip. Also, the couple's fast social life, which revolved around endless parties, began to exert strain on the family. Another problem was the financial disparity between Connor and his in-laws. Although the Connors were a 'solid' family financially, the Snivelys never let Avis' husband forget just who was the wealthier.

It was another pregnancy that rescued the marriage for the time being, and Avis and Connor were happy again with the birth of a sister for Ingram Jr, named Avis after her mother. The new baby was soon known to all as Little Avis. Both of the children took after their mother's dark hair and olive complexion – although young Ingram had his daddy's prominent ears and the same sad, hound dog eyes that led everyone, workers and friends alike, to call his father 'Coon Dog'. Avis and Coon Dog made sure that Ingram attended the Episcopalian Sunday school regularly, while Avis became the director of the women's group at the Waycross Episcopal Church. It was all part of her busy social life. Big Avis was also involved in various community charity organisations, and was president of the women's auxiliary to the Waycross Golf and Country Club, since the club was still 'men only'.

In church, as at home, little Ingram loved to sing and did it often, making the words up if he didn't know them. On many church occasions, like Easter and Christmas, he would sing a song for the assembled adults while the other children looked on. As the congregation applauded, he would bow politely and return to his seat. His sense of showmanship was beginning to develop already, and he loved the feeling of having captured the attention of the adults.

Former Waycross resident Barbara Walker Winge babysat Ingram and Little Avis in the early 1950s, shortly before she married and left Waycross. She can only barely recall the family, but remembered young Ingram well. "What can I tell you about Gram?" she asked. "Of course I never knew him by that name, I just knew an adorable little boy with dark hair and eyes and his pretty little sister, also dark hair and eyes. To all outward appearances, it was a happy family. Money was no worry or seemed so. There was a housekeeper, a yard keeper, two vehicles, and the children had every toy imaginable. Mr. and Mrs. Connor loved baseball games and that was when I sat for them. They paid me well and told me to eat whatever I wanted. I would put the children to bed. The little boy would play his records and then I would sing to him. He loved music."

The Connors were known to be a generous family and regularly gave gifts to friends and family, as well as to their house help, who were often the beneficiaries of the family's kindness. Employees of the Snively box factory also fondly remembered Connor's generosity and even-handed management. In a predominantly working-class town such as Waycross, it was uncommon for families to have help around the house, but the Connor family had black maids, babysitters, and a yardman who looked after the house. When Winge announced her engagement Coon Dog and Avis gave her a "complete set of fancy glassware, very expensive... I still have it."

One day, one of Connor's hunting dogs got loose and terrorised the neighbourhood. The animal went to Winge's house at 1609 Suwannee Drive and chewed up a litter of newborn kittens, which upset the Connor children and Winge badly. Still, such events were rare in Gram's early childhood, a period of time that he would always look back on with mixed feelings. He attended the William Heights School, and his days were mostly uneventful. He was a good student, intelligent but dreamy, often detached from schoolwork. Ingram preferred to live in his own fantasy world and remained there happily.

Because this part of his life was relatively short, Ingram would return there often in his mind as he got older. According to Billy Ray Herrin, a long-time Waycross resident and amateur historian, "Waycross was the only time that he ever had any stability in his life. His mom was drinking real bad. After what took place with his daddy, he never overcame it and it was the only serenity he did have and he held onto that, all through his life. I mean, Ingram and Coon Dog, they loved each other. They did all the father and son things, camping and fishing, the stuff that Dads like to do with their sons."

Another shared father and son activity was the Scouts. For several years, Coon Dog was the Scoutmaster of Troop 80, which he had named after the fighter unit he had commanded in World War 2, the 80th Fighter Squadron. There was also the Indian Guides, a father and son program sponsored by the YMCA. There can be no doubt that Coon Dog sought to be as active a father as possible to his son.

Gram would, in later years, describe his father to his friends as a doomed and romantic figure, an amateur musician whose musical ambitions had been thwarted by the machinations of the family he had married into. Although his dad was not the itinerant country singer Gram claimed him to be in interviews with writer Eve Babitz before his death, neither was he an alcoholic who died in gaol, another story friends can remember hearing.

Coon Dog would often disappear into the woods by himself for days at a time, avoiding contact with the business outside of normal working hours, not to mention his in-laws. Some have hinted that it was a marriage that he had eventually come to regret ever entering into. Avis's feelings on this are unknown, although family friends recall that she treated his frequent absences as normal, using the time to pursue her own social connections and to put her entertaining skills to good use.

When the couple were together, they put on a classy front of sophistication that was unusual for such a quiet Southern town. The Connors entertained often and well and to be invited to one of their frequent parties was quite an honour. The laws governing the sale of alcohol in Georgia were strict and booze was usually sold only in licensed clubs and a few restaurants. It wasn't what you might call readily available, and there were certainly no liquor stores within the city limits. But alcohol would play a big part in damaging both the couple and Gram, as he was now known, and Little Avis.

Gram's dad became a distant but loving figure whose own love for music had been transmitted to his son. Gram fell in love with all kinds of music; folk and rural music forms were his first love, and Child Ballads were among the first songs that friends can remember him singing. Gram followed the example of his parents and threw frequent parties for his friends at the house, usually in the 'Florida room', a name often given to the sunroom of a house in the South. In the Florida room were the musical instruments that Coon Dog had bought for the kids; a player piano, a trumpet and a drum kit – although music was as much a release for him as education for the children. He enjoyed seeing his children playing with music.

There was also a record player, on which Ingram would play his father's many records. He would teach the kids at the party how to dance the jitterbug and slow dances. The Florida room reverberated with childish enthusiasm and music, an escape for the serious-minded Ingram. Music had presented itself as a major influence early in his development and he would sit at the piano and pick out tunes and melodies for himself when no one else was around. Soon, his confidence on the instrument grew and he would entertain his father and mother with little songs that he had picked out by ear.

Gram's interest in the piano led him to take lessons with local teacher Bessie Maynard, who offered treats before and after the lesson, rather than the strict discipline of conventional piano teachers who threatened to smack a child's hands with a wooden ruler when they made a mistake. It was in this unthreatening and warm environment that Gram learned to love music, and his desire to create it grew. He sought solace in tapping out little rhythms on the drums or coaxing a note out of the trumpet, but mostly he sat at the piano and tried to teach himself popular songs, to the disappointment of Bessie. She had noted his ability to improvise quite freely for someone so young. He was able to listen to a record and, with three or four run-throughs, play it close to the original.

There were other influences on him besides his piano teacher. "I've spoken to a lot of guys that worked at the Snively box factory in the '50s and a lot of those workers played music," says Billy Ray Herrin. "They would get together after work in the factory and play country music. When he was a little boy, he would go down to the factory after work and wait for his daddy to finish for the day and he would see these men, playing music. He was fascinated by it – he loved it. And the songs he was hearing were many of the songs that he later recorded, the old '50s country tunes. I sincerely believe that what Gram was doing was pulling himself closer to that sound that he heard then, back in the days when he felt safe."

The songs he heard waiting for his dad at the box factory on weekday afternoons after school, as the workers brought their guitars out to play, would be hugely influential. He would have heard Lefty Frizzell, Patsy Cline and Hank Williams while he sat there politely, a serious look on his face. "I believe that's why he was so emotional when he sang," says Billy Ray Herrin. "People thought he was trying to create a new musical sound, but he was just singing what was in his heart. It all relates to that. A lot of those guys remember Gram being there when they played.

He was a link in the chain and a lot of them thought that he (Gram) would come back and run the company."

While country music dominated the airwaves during Gram's childhood, by the mid-1950s the songs on the radio were beginning to pick up their tempi. He found himself interested in the white outworkings of rhythm and blues, which had been dubbed rock and roll. Although Coon Dog had little interest in this musical development, it proved hugely inspirational to his young son. Under the aegis of boogie-woogie and rock 'n' roll piano players, Ingram even composed his own tune, titled 'Gram's Boogie', a salute to his own ability and something that many instrumentalists of the time did. The fact that at the age of eleven he could compose a song himself amazed his friends and impressed his father no end. But Ingram's obsession with musical instruments didn't end there.

Among the new wave of rock 'n' rollers, Elvis Presley began to emerge as king, flanked by the crown princes like Carl Perkins and Johnny Burnette. The guitar was their primary instrument, a sound unlike any other. The guitar fed rock 'n' roll with a distinctive sound and energy not even the piano could compete with. But it was young Burnet Clarke, a school friend of Ingram's, whose flat-top Gibson acoustic guitar mesmerised the young boy. Watching his friend play it, ringing out a G chord on the resonant guitar, he was captivated by the clanging sound that it made, the collision of metal, wood and flesh setting in motion the desire of his heart. Like so many young men of that generation, he was smitten by the music that would initially point the way forward for him – rock and roll.

In 1955, Elvis Presley was yet to become a worldwide phenomenon. For the time being, he was a regional sensation, and his Sun singles were epiphanic to eight-year-old Gram Connor. He had heard Elvis on the radio and on regional television. Posters advertising an appearance by Presley as part of the *Grand Ole Opry* show began appearing at the Waycross City Auditorium. When the boy heard about it, he begged his parents to let him go. They agreed, provided he was accompanied by a chaperone. Having heard about how the kids reacted to this Presley character, the adults didn't want any part of it. A pair of teenaged twin sisters, friends of the family and a few years older than Ingram, were asked to accompany him.

The girls managed to get backstage after the show to meet Elvis in person. Gram went with them and, as he later recounted to Jan Donkers, bowled right up to Presley and said, "Hello there, you're Elvis Presley and I'm a little kid who buys records and I think you're alright." The young man who would soon be crowned the King was only slightly taken aback. "He said, 'Yeah,' and he shook my hand, put me on, gave me an autograph, sent me out the door, made sure I was with the twins." Gram went home with the twins, walking much taller.

Following this encounter with Presley, Ingram threw himself into music even more. He particularly enjoyed miming to the sound of Elvis's records, and he would often invite his friends over to play with his musical instruments. They would set up on the front step of the house with their instruments, and set up the record player so they could mime along with rock 'n' roll records for the benefit of a gathering audience of kids.

Still, he could be a hard taskmaster to his musicians. He would fix with an angry stare anyone who didn't pay attention to what they were miming. Avis had to fight to join her brother's group, but once in there she wasn't allowed to put a foot wrong or she would be out of the band just as quickly. All the girls in the neighbourhood were smitten with Gram, who was growing to be a good-looking, gangly kid who could comb his hair into a fine pompadour with some help from the maid. He strutted along the front porch, working the microphone. The appreciative front row swooned when he curled his lip and wiggled his hips.

Despite his interest in what many considered a rebellious and evil form of music, Ingram was mostly a quiet, serious boy. He could be outgoing in some ways, but was introspective like his father most of the time. Racism, segregation and classist behaviour were societal norms, all hangovers from the past, when the South was very English in its derivation and manners.

Since Ingram was known as a deeply sensitive kid, he could not help but be influenced by such cultural pressures. During the 1940s, it was unthinkable that blacks should even be considered for equal rights. A federal initiative to give public education to Native American Indians had been greeted with a violent reaction. Not until the late 1950s would the African-American people begin to rise up and demand basic rights, both as human beings and as American citizens. On a personal level, the Connor family had at least one point of contact with black society – the yardman and the housemaid, both of whom were coloured. Ingram liked the maid's kids and they would hang out together after school, stealing Avis' cigarettes from the pantry and sneaking into the woods to smoke a few. He would later claim that the maid's family were his introduction to R&B music.

As he learned to fend for himself at school, Gram also learned to temper his claims about the family wealth, which seemed preposterous at first to those who knew him as a shy, even awkward, pupil. His claims were not lies, and the stories of loading up the family car with toys on Saturday shopping sprees weren't fabricated, much to the dismay of his friends. Ingram didn't seem to be the image of the spoiled brat, but he didn't want for much in the way of material goods. Emotionally, he desired more from his beloved mother, although her upbringing had stilted that side of her. She found it difficult to be the comforter of the children, and was more likely to be responsible for administering discipline to them. As a result, little Avis and Ingram turned to their father for affection, and he was only too willing to provide it.

Connor took his fatherly duties very seriously and tried to be as involved as he could with the raising of the children. But eventually, he began to see that the children were considered heirs to the family fortune, being Snivelys in all but name. While he may not have felt that the kids were being turned against him, he did feel powerless and lacking in influence because of his wife's money. Resentment set in, the inevitable by-product of a marriage where there was much more than domestic harmony at stake. The Snivelys continued to undermine Coon Dog's self-confidence and his ability to run the Waycross packing plant. Some have described their tactics as 'antagonistic'. He should not have taken it so personally. As with many wealthy families – each with much to lose – the Snivelys were prone to infighting, and John Snively Sr. had been known to isolate members of his immediate family, shutting off the supply of money without hesitation.

Gram was about to turn 11 when Avis decided that her firstborn required the discipline of a boarding school environment. Still, she did not want to send him where he would be too far from his immediate family, and while leafing through the private school advertisements in the back of *Harpers Bazaar* magazine, Avis found one for a low-key military prep school in Florida with connections to West Point. The Bolles School (pronounced 'bowls') was located in Jacksonville, Florida, only 75 miles from Waycross as the crow flies. It had once been an upscale hotel and its facilities, combined with its location, meant that it was perfectly situated for all concerned. All except Gram, who made his initial dislike of the school known to his father, whom he missed terribly.

He found the school's military discipline too rigid at first, but the school's teachers tended to reward students with an academic bent and Gram, with his love of learning and of books that were considered more suitable for older boys, was an attentive and intelligent student. After a while, he formed definite opinions about this new situation he found himself in, where he was bereft of close family and found the company of his fellow students sometimes irksome. He penned regular letters to his mother and sister, cheerfully complaining about certain teachers and the school principal.

For his dad, life was just about unbearable. Neighbourhood talk said that his wife had been having an affair with a prominent Waycross citizen. His personal life was sliding out from under him; the quality of life he had known as an adventurous young man was nearly gone. He had married into money and the attendant curses that it brings. His taste for alcohol had increased in proportion to the scars left by his war service. The distraction and joy that he had once taken in fine marksmanship and regular weekend hunting trips with his son, father and brother had gone stale. Worst of all, his depression had insidiously convinced him that life could not improve, and so he chose to end it before it blossomed into something truly unmanageable.

For Gram, that cold Christmas in Winter Haven, at the home of his maternal grandparents, was a turning point. But the changes he felt had begun shortly before the suicide of his father. His 13th birthday, November 5, 1959, was so much more than a simple chronological turning point. It was the exact middle point of his life and the beginning of his markedly early maturity. Not once could he have guessed that he had just 13 more years in which to complete his work, to make his mark.

In his 13th year, Gram grew up suddenly. His puppy fat slipped away and he started to shoot up, becoming tall and lanky. Between his hound dog good looks and his courtly Southern manners, he appeared a little like an adult in miniature. Of course, we all must learn some of life's harshest lessons in our first 13 years of life. We learn that our body develops, that it betrays us and that it even breaks down on us at times. Our bones stretch and we may or may not begin to appreciate the elasticity, the give that our bodies allow us. At this tender age we learn about the things that we can put in ourselves to enhance sensation, fight pain, get high.

Gram learned all these things. With the false security blanket of family wealth and the sudden absence of a father, he was hemmed in by his insecurities. Music was his only outlet. In time, he learned that nothing is ever written in stone, except that which is inscribed upon the stones on our graves. He learned to lie, to mask his emotions and rephrase the past. Still, he took time to learn most of the tricks of being a normal kid, even though one of them – the value of hard work and saving a few dollars – was never drummed into him, despite the fact that his father did try to give him some grounding in reality. His mother simply bought him everything he wanted, and on the rare occasions when she would resist doing so for some reason, she could eventually be manipulated into getting him what he asked for.

The last time Gram saw his father alive was Tuesday, 22nd of December 1959, at the back of the railroad depot in Waycross. "I think that was without doubt the most influential event of his life," avers Billy Ray Herrin. "He spent all his years trying to get back to that moment, to that feeling of security. Coon Dog was drinking real bad, in fact the whole family was, Big Avis included. He was controlled by the Snivelys.

The alcohol, all the affairs that Gram's mother was having, brought Coon Dog to his decision. And it can't have been easy. He loved his children. He lived for them. It was the hardest decision he'd ever had to make. And Gram never overcame that sorrow."

But his death just before a customarily happy time for the family left a terrible and confusing burden for his children, who were not informed of the tragedy right away. Big Avis left off telling her children until a few days after Christmas was over. Perhaps worst of all, she appeared not to grieve openly for him, something that would temper Ingram's love for his mother for many years.

Upsetting the boy further was the fact that his mother held another party just days after his father's death. It had been planned for some time and it went on without Coon Dog, as if nothing had happened. The Snivelys, who some felt had done their utmost to undermine Coon Dog in life, found it in their hearts to bring his body back to Winter Haven, where he joined the departed Snivelys in the family plot. His coffin was draped with the American flag, noting his service to God and country as a war hero.

"He was a real war hero," says Stanley Booth. "He had been on all these combat missions and he had seen some things that maybe had shocked him or caused him real pain. We may never know what caused him to do what he did – it was such an unthinkable thing that someone who was a successful white businessman could do that to himself. I know that even the Waycross paper reported it as being an 'accidental shooting'."

They returned to Waycross after their winter holiday break, and Gram went back to Bolles in early 1959. After the death of his father, things were increasingly difficult for him. His studies suffered further. A letter from his mother during that first year brought him news that he was unsure how to process. A man named Robert Ellis Parsons, a Florida-based businessman who worked for Bechtel Corporation, had been actively courting Big Avis. She had introduced her new escort to her family, who were already fuming; mostly because of her timing, but also because Bob Parsons was the very image of the Errol Flynn-esque playboy. A sharp dresser with a smooth tongue and business interests in South America, he had been conspicuous in his wooing of several young ladies from other wealthy families. The family suspected that he was something of a gold-digger. Nonetheless, he seemed to have some money of his own that he liked to splash around.

Parsons' business dealings involved the leasing of heavy earthmoving equipment for American business ventures in Latin America and Cuba. He had experienced some financial setbacks following the recent Castro takeover, which had made a point of ousting American property developers, including Mob-backed casino owners and hoteliers. As anti-Castro sentiment increased in America that year, Bob was part of the backlash and was known to talk about helping out in the overthrow of the new communist government.

Despite this radical element to his personality, Parsons was mostly talk. He liked women, he liked to drink and he was effortlessly charming with everyone, even the suspicious Snivelys, who considered him to be a real slimeball.

Gram heard all about Bob from his mother and eventually, the two were introduced. Almost immediately, they formed an uneasy relationship, which was to continue for the rest of their respective lives. It was based on two factors; Gram's grudging admiration for the well-dressed charmer, and Parsons' attempts to get the boy to accept him as a possible stepfather. This would involve Bob giving Gram extravagant and expensive gifts, while Gram often treated him with contempt for even trying to take the place of his beloved father.

Meanwhile, the stress of dealing with his father's death continued to affect Gram's schoolwork. In June, Bolles' superintendent Major DeWitt Hooker wrote Avis, informing that her son's conduct at school had been less than exemplary, and the school's discipline committee – comprised of teachers and senior students – had voted not to allow Gram to enrol again in the fall.

After Gram's ignominious departure from Bolles, Avis took the children out of school early for a summer train-trip across the United States. Along with them for the trip was Robert Owens, a young man of Avis's acquaintance who acted as escort and chaperone. The four of them travelled first-class all the way, wanting for nothing, cosseted against all possibilities. The trip took them north to Chicago, then west to San Francisco via the Grand Canyon, where they peered into the muddy Colorado. Then after California it was back east, to New York City, where the children and Big Avis stayed in fine hotels and ate at fancy supper clubs while being entertained by the likes of Nat 'King' Cole and Tony Bennett. Avis made one more trip back to Waycross, to organise the sale of their house and have the furniture moved back to her family home.

Avis was upset with her son for disgracing the family's connection to Bolles, but she enrolled him into St. Josephs, a co-ed non-denominational school in Winter Haven. By the end of 1959, Gram's grades had picked up – a sign perhaps, that the trip with his mother and sister had done much to improve his outlook. Soon Gram was a trusted pupil, and the principal sometimes left him in charge of classes when teachers were ill. His skill at storytelling kept the younger students enraptured, particularly the girls. He was equally as good at infuriating the boys by being too suave, and they would gang up on him in the playground, where they discovered that he was also pretty good with his fists when he had to be.

Avis and Bob announced their engagement to the family, news that had Gram in tears. There was certainly no way that he could protest about the wedding to his mother, although grandmother Haney was less than impressed. Following the marriage, Parsons became an immediate and enthusiastic stepfather to Avis' children. His enthusiasm was perhaps a little too hearty for the comfort of the Snively, family but they stopped short of interfering in the affairs of their daughter. Within a few weeks, Parsons had legally adopted Gram and Avis as his own children, to the extent of having new birth certificates issued listing him as their birth father.

This put him on an awkward footing with the Snivelys, exacerbated when Avis announced that she was taking the family to court, because she believed they were stealing from her. This was not the case. In fact, according to her cousin, Rob Hoskins, the family was moving money around from different areas of the business to make sure Avis had enough. The Snivelys settled with their daughter out of court, giving her a share of the orange groves. As it turned out, Bob Parsons was behind the court case. He fed Avis's insecurity about money with suggestions that, because she was not actively involved in the running of the business, she was most likely being misled about how much she was due. The legal action Avis took would later contribute directly to a downturn in the family's fortunes. In the meantime, Avis and Bob purchased a new home on Piedmont Drive in Winter Haven, an exclusive street that was home to many of that town's prominent citizens.

For Gram, the transition from being Ingram Cecil Connor III to becoming Gram Parsons was never easy, nor were any of the complex issues it brought to the surface ever resolved. Gram grew to resent this adoption more than anything, as even the implied friendship between him and his stepfather gave him cause for grief. The relationship of names between Gram and his stepfather was an emotional issue, as the feelings Gram had for Parsons alternated between occasional flashes of open admiration and complete disdain. Folks said that Gram liked Bob because he was a flashy playboy type. His attempts at fatherhood were mostly borne of his inexperience – Bob had never known his own father.

After a promising start, Gram's grades began to slip at St. Josephs, and further discipline problems emerged. He began to buckle under the strict, but by no means severe, school codes. His interests were many at school, but they did not always include homework. He loved English and literature classes and read poetry and novels compulsively. He also wrote beautiful little poems, expressive for a kid of his age, and these impressed his teachers. Gram's sense of humour remained with him always, despite the trying times at home. He could improvise comedic routines on the spot and made the debating team. Most of all, he loved his music. At home on Piedmont Drive, Gram pursued his interest in rock 'n' roll. He would listen to his favourite 45s on the record player; songs like Ray Charles's 'What'd I Say', and lots of Chuck Berry.

Gram's mother Avis was developing slowly and surely into a heavy drinker. Her life revolved around dinner parties, cocktail parties and a gentle tendency to ignore her children and then smother them with gifts and affection when her neglect occurred to her. Still, music flourished in the Parsons household. Gram would hold band rehearsals and put on plays in the large basement room that was fitted out with a drum kit and amplifiers. Gram's earliest rock influences were Elvis Presley, the Everly Brothers, Rick Nelson and Buddy Holly; all artists with roots in country music who recorded entire albums of country music later in their careers. Also popular was Cowboy Copas (a country singer later killed in the same 1962 plane crash that took Patsy Cline and Hawkshaw Hawkins).

This mature young man attended high school but stuck out like half an adult. He had his own car, despite the fact that he was not licensed to drive. "He was just intrinsically hip," said Jim Carlton, recalling how awed he felt around Gram that January of 1960 when they first met, and slowly became close friends. "He was aware of the world at large. Certainly, he had the advantages: a piano in his room and a private entrance to same, lots of freedom, money and a car before he was old enough to drive legally. However I must say he handled all of this with a real sense of responsibility and was basically considered an adult by his parents.

"When I met him, he was playing piano very casually. As I said, there was one in his room, so it was just convenient. He'd write a song about his latest girlfriend and, later, his current pelvic affiliate and soon realized, as all musicians do, the main reason for doing this is for the female attention. I think the guitar came a year later with the Pacers, not a good band at all."

The Pacers might not have been a professional rock and roll band, but with Gram's coltish good looks and their fair musical ability, their good quality instruments and Fender amps, they looked as though they were. It was, as Jim Carlton noted, "a good place to start."

Chapter 2
SHILOS!
RED COATS NOW TO THE SHILOS

During the summer of 1961, Gram – then just 13 years old – was introduced to a young man named Buddy Freeman at one of his mother's dinner parties at a Winter Haven restaurant. Buddy, aged 22, was a fine horseman who occasionally rode in equestrian events with Gram's little sister Avis. He also worked at his father's plumbing supplies business in Greenville, South Carolina, but regularly attended equestrian displays in Florida. During the course of dinner that evening, Freeman struck up a conversation with Gram, who wasted no time informing Buddy that horses didn't interest him in the slightest. It was music that interested him, he disclosed. Only momentarily taken aback, Freeman didn't at first know how to take this kid. He looked older than he was, dressed well and behaved like an adult in miniature, although you could tell just by looking at the long arms and legs (and those big hands) that this kid still had some growing up to do. Buddy knew a little about music. He didn't play a musical instrument himself, but he liked folk and pop music, and even a little country music as well. Mostly, he liked a good show – the sort in the Las Vegas mold, with singers and jokes. Gram liked folk music too, although in 1961, Gram was still in the thrall of rock and roll. He repudiated singers like Bobby Vinton and Fabian as 'lightweights' but he remained a big fan of Elvis Presley and the Everly Brothers. "I play piano, and I play a little guitar," said Gram when Buddy asked him what it was he could do. In fact, he had a nice little repertoire going of all kinds of songs, not just rock and roll. Usually, when he was at home, in the Snively mansion, he would either pick up the guitar and bash out a three-or four chord rock tune or if his mother was around the place, mixing up a drink, she might request an older standard. A Hammond organ now sat in the parlour, and soon Gram made it his business to learn whatever popular songs he could, buying sheet music and reading through it a few times, then filling in the gaps by ear. It pleased his mother no end that he was so talented and she told everyone about him.

That night at the restaurant, Buddy mentioned that he knew the owners of the place and he was sure they wouldn't mind if Gram went and played the piano in the lounge. With their permission, Gram sat down and picked out a few melodies, then casually delivered a couple of pop songs in his devastating tenor. A little of the dinnertime chatter ceased as patrons began to notice this good-looking, well-tanned individual singing rather emotionally. Buddy began to see the possibilities. While he was obviously not the first to notice Gram's abilities, he was the first to see their commercial potential. Buddy's social movements kept him in regular touch with the Parsons and Snively families and he invited Gram and some of his young friends to stay at the Freeman family home in Greenville during the late summer of 1961. Gram brought his guitar with him on the trip and during a cookout, he started playing and singing for the assembled people. The applause and the repeated requests for more songs was simply more proof of his abilities, and Buddy also took into account the effect Gram had on the young ladies present. A witty, talented young man such as Gram needed a manager, Big Avis exhorted Buddy. Aware of Avis's strength of character, her society connections and her no-bullshit persona, he readily agreed to become the boy's personal business manager. As he had already guessed, he would be paid well for any booking or contractual work that he performed and naturally, that work would be slotted in and around Buddy's work for his father's company.

When Auburndale teen sensation Jim Stafford began to think about forming another group early in 1961, he asked Gram to join as lead singer and rhythm guitarist. Although Jim had some musicians in mind for a rhythm section, Gram also had some guys in mind – a group called the Dynamics. Jon Corneal, who would eventually be involved in two different stages of Parsons' early career (all the while pursuing his own), was the Dynamics' drummer. He was introduced formally to Parsons for the first time in late 1961, although he had seen Parsons around the same teen centres and high school shows for some time before that. "Carl, Gerald [Chambers] and I first met Gram in the early '60s, while we were rehearsing at the Auburndale Teen Center with our group, the Dynamics," Corneal recollects. "Gram had come over to have a rehearsal with a group of musicians he had recently been playing with. He introduced himself and told us he really liked our music – 'our sound' as he put it – so we invited him to come and sit in with us on a gig we were playing at Cocoa Beach, at a sock hop at the teen club they called Tiger Town. He drove his little red sports car – an MGB, I think. Anyhow, he asked Gerald and I to join this group he was putting together with Jimmy Stafford."

Stafford remembers Gram as being a talented and confident young man barely in his teens who was already an excellent pianist and guitarist. "He was grooming himself for stardom when he was 13 years old. He was writing songs, a good keyboard man, he was just learning the guitar. He was an amazing fella."

The group, of which Gram was both the lead singer and the youngest member, was comprised mostly of slightly older teenage boys from Winter Haven and nearby Jacksonville. Stafford already had a name for the group – The Legends. Today, it's a *nom de rock* that seems quite prescient, but one that at the time seemed initially arrogant to anyone not completely convinced of their abilities. The multi-talented Jim Stafford, who could easily have been the lead singer of the group himself, chose instead to be the lead guitarist. Gram took rhythm guitar duties on as well, buying himself a brand new Fender Stratocaster from Casswin Music in Lakeland, Florida. "The one thing that impressed us about him was he was playing this white Fender guitar with gold plate on it instead of chrome," says Jon Corneal. Everybody shook their heads when they saw it. Some were plainly envious, others thought it made them look more professional.

Gram, clearly established as the group's singer, was second in command under Stafford, who arranged all the songs they performed. Gram took on some of the band-leading duties, by all accounts it was another facet of performance that he relished and took very seriously. It didn't take very long for the Legends to earn their name with local high school kids. They were already faithfully covering the songs that most working dance bands of that era did – songs by the Ventures (the staple of many teenage bands then), a lot of straight rock'n'roll and a few soft ballads for the end of the evening, like 'Harbour Lights' and 'Stormy Weather'.

According to Jon Corneal, the setlists were devoted to blocks of Elvis Presley's early rockabilly material, Ray Charles, the Everly Brothers, Chuck Berry and Duane Eddy too. Gram, Jim, Stafford and drummer Jon Corneal would spend hours rehearsing popular songs into medleys (where songs of similar tempo and key segue into each other without breaks) in order to keep the girls and boys jumping and jiving at their shows. Gigs were never too varied, and their youth kept them out of bars. "We played a zillion teen centers, high school proms and the occasional fraternity house," remembered Jim Carlton. "As I said, we were big on the Ventures, also Duane Eddy, as they were popular and easily reproduced. We never much cared about the money. It was just a case of grabbing one of the red blazers, which Gram had a number of, getting in the VW bus and going to the gig. It was great fun." Sometimes the Legends' lineup was further augmented by horns, saxes and trumpets, if the members of their semi-regular horn section, Buddy Canova, Lloyd Morgan or Grant Lacerte, were available that night.

House PA systems were rare in those days, but as always, the family money saved the day. Gram was the proud owner of a Premier 'peashooter' PA public address system, which would accommodate three microphones. "We'd place one of its 10" speakers on each side of the stage, and that was it for the vocals," Carlton says. With good equipment and a rocking sound, the Legends worked just about every weekend. Gram in particular benefited from the regular rehearsals and work in more ways than one. His musicianship on guitar, never a strong suit, developed further, but it was as a singer that he began to hit his stride. According to those who were there, Gram was already capable of mesmerising performances and powerful singing. It wasn't hard for him to hold an audience's attention. Girls had been known to stop dancing with their partners just to watch him do his act. He loved the powerful gospel-style emoting of Ray Charles and also imitated the energetic stage antics of Jerry Lee Lewis. Of course, when Stafford would wring a solo out of his Stratocaster, Gram would start thrusting and shaking his hips, overcome by a fervent need to rock. While he made a point of maintaining his position at the mic, he never held back vocally in any way. The more he worked his voice, the older he sounded. "He loved the image of being the guitarist/singer," says Jim Carlton. "He was perfect for it, and that side of him emerged naturally. Stafford didn't care or compete with him for attention. He didn't have to anyway, because his playing was so good, but Jim didn't care about singing at all. He still doesn't consider himself a singer, even after five or six hit records! So, with me on the upright bass, a sometime horn section, lead, rhythm and vocals, we were a hot rockabilly band."

Of course, Gram had his critics even then. Some of his musical peers (though not the ones he regularly gigged with) found the combination of family money and obvious ability made him insufferable at times. Mostly, he was widely-liked, despite his propensity for the tall stories that are still related by his old friends with no small degree of amusement even now. Only the most churlish individual would have begrudged Gram the opportunities that came his way, even though the doors that opened and closed without warning for other musicians seemed never to have been shut to him.

"We played a lot of really nice gigs in '62 and '63 with that group," says Jon Corneal. "We played on "Hi-Time", which was a teenage TV show on Saturday afternoons on channel 8 – the local NBC affiliate. We even played a number of private schools, including Bolles School in Jacksonville, where Gram spent his last two years of high school; St. Andrews Boys School in Boca Raton and also Lake

Region's Country Club Teen Room. Gram did most of the booking of those places and got us some pretty good gigs."

Gram did in fact handle some of those bookings, using his influence at the Bolles School in particular, while Buddy Freeman would also take an interest in the band and find them some of the more up-scale shows, like the Winter Haven Annual Horse Show banquet and dance. The line-up of the Legends changed several times during the twelve months they were together. New members included bassist Jesse Chambers and Tallahassee, Florida native Roland Kent Lavoie (also known as Lobo). For high school students, the boys also earned decent walking-around money for themselves, although Gram always had enough. Though he never felt entirely comfortable at home with the clannish Snivelys in Florida, he realised that his mother was very much reliant on her father's generosity. He was also aware that his cousins had been cut off from the family money by grandfather John after a dispute with John Jr. Gram wasn't hung up on money. As such, it became an issue for people involved with him, either because they resented his inherited wealth or they thought it made him lazy. As for Kent Lavoie and Jim Stafford, they saw past the wealth and acknowledged his talent. The family money ceased to be an issue, since it had helped the band achieve certain things, like better gigs every so often, which meant better money for them. Gram liked to spend his spare cash on the seemingly endless succession of older girls he was dating. His good looks meant that pretty girls were never far away, and it seemed that they were all completely smitten by him.

The Legends became increasingly popular. There were always plenty of high school shows to do, and when there wasn't a show on, Gram would occasionally play keyboards in Kent's other group, the Rumors. Even as he played rock music for teenagers, Gram was ever mindful of the savvy merger of music and business. As Buddy had pointed out, folk music was making forays into the popular consciousness and soon, his acoustic guitar was with him everywhere Gram went. Gram had always loved old folk songs and when the Kingston Trio had broken through in 1959 with *Tom Dooley*, he was right there, learning to play the song. The Kingston Trio continued with the hits, producing a string of #1 songs, mostly based around tunes that predated their parents. By 1962, Parsons was regularly involving himself in two or three musical side projects, while still a full-time member of the Legends. He continued to sit in on keyboards with the Rumors, while keeping his ear on whatever else was filtering onto the charts. Soon, it became clear that folk music was angling to replace rock'n'roll in the hearts of young people. Parsons had already started dabbling in that genre more and more, and Buddy would book an occasional solo show for him to play. With Legends bassist Jim Carlton, he even worked up a folk and comedy duo in the style of the Smothers Brothers, having purloined some of their routines. Next, Parsons put together the Village Vanguards, a folk trio patterned after Peter, Paul & Mary that featured his girlfriend of the time, Patti Johnson, and high school buddy Dick McNeer. For the most part, the Vanguards played during intermissions at shows by the Legends, although it is evident they played quite a few shows under their own name.

Most influential of all were the groups that didn't quite make it in the same way as the Kingston Trio or Peter, Paul & Mary. In particular, acts like the Cumberland 3 were popular with older kids because they were less 'commercial' and more uncompromising in their approach to folk. Another act that sprung out of this fertile time was the Journeymen. Far from being as pedestrian as the name might imply, they were perhaps the finest folk trio ever assembled. It was John Phillips' group, and with virtuoso banjo player Dick Weissman on board, it seems that the only concrete reason they could not succeed was allegedly because Weissman was too homely-looking for the television audience. John and Dick were amazed at this development, but then you only had to look at the clean-cut blonde Kingston Trio to see what they were up against. On record though, they were practically untouchable, then as now. With Weissman's clear baritone and unusual instrumental phrasing, combined with Phillip's piercing, rough-hewn voice and knack for choosing and writing great material, they should have been the biggest act of the era. However, those in the know said they were the best and Gram picked up on them quickly.

An increasing self-belief pervaded Gram's own work and soon he began to write more of his own material. It wasn't great, nor was it groundbreaking. Some of it showed a heavy reliance on whatever acts were passing through at the time. But his lyrics were always strong, even if the melody was lifted from someone else (fortunately for him, it is one of the great traditions of folk music). Through his own hard work (and mostly at the expense of his school studies), Gram persisted with music, endeavouring to create a sound of his own. Country music, however much he had loved it as a small child, did not always factor in his repertoire. Artists like Hawkshaw Hawkins and Cowboy Copas (coincidentally both killed in the same plane crash as Patsy Cline) were definitely to Gram's taste. They both tended toward the story-telling side of country music and as such, he considered them both great. Rural music, whatever its origins was to be hugely influential on him. But it should be remembering that even though the Legends were a "rockabilly band", Gram had little interest in pursuing anything like country music. "Gram was NOT into country music at all back then," stresses Jim Carlton. "He did not consider it to be hip and had no interest in country at all. Jim was, and Gram never criticised him for it because he knew it was part of Jim's heritage, but it really wasn't for Gram. Once, I learned a few bars of "Steel Guitar Rag" and played it for him and was immediately chastised as he went to the piano and played a mock version of some Floyd Cramer song. It was funny and he asked me what the hell I was doing playing "that stuff?' I never had the heart to remind him of that story later on."

Stafford, on the other hand, remembered Gram as definitely having a good country quotient, even if he sometimes tried to hide it. In a *Rolling Stone* interview in 1973, Stafford recalled his influence on Gram: "I said to him, "you got country roots, y'know, go with country music. There isn't any long haired country group. That's where you oughta be, country music'. I don't really know how much influence I had on that [*Sweetheart of the Rodeo*] but I did tell him he oughta be doing country music."

Gram seemed impossibly worldly to his fellow Legends, as he did to everyone he met. "He was no shitkicker," says Carlton. "He was a most urbane and sophisticated teenager, or young adult. He had a highly developed sense of humour, a love of jazz and good literature. These things were endemic to him and not necessarily the product of formal education."

Meanwhile, Avis Parsons had given birth to a daughter by her new husband, but before long Bob Parsons was spending an unseemly amount of time with their 18-year-old babysitter. Avis Parsons in turn became increasingly dependent on alcohol and on the pharmacopoeia she had accumulated with the help of a neighbouring doctor. Gram began to sample from her medicine cabinet as well. He had left the Bolles School during early 1962, with a scandal brewing over a copy of a letter he had written for the amusement of his schoolfriends, in which he expressed his feelings about certain members of the faculty. Avis, somewhat unamused by Gram's behaviour, grudgingly enrolled him in Winter Haven High School in 10th grade. But he was never going to succeed at that school either with girls (the sweetest fruit of coeducation), music and pills to distract him from his schoolwork, he failed his junior year at Winter Haven High.

Early in 1963, Gram's thoughts had turned to folk music and comedy. Gram loved comedy almost as much as music, and his skewed sense of humour coloured his take on life. He loved Brother Dave Gardner, the cartoonist Rodriguez, Jonathon Winters and the Smothers Brothers.

While he was chastised by his stepfather for his poor performance at Winter Haven High, Gram could not anger him for long. While the relationship between the two was always strained, Bob, in an attempt to curry favour with his adopted son, bought him a nightclub in which to perform. The Derry Down, as it was christened, became Winter Haven's only English-themed folk club. With a menu of non-alcoholic drinks and food named after Shakespearian characters, it soon became a popular place for Gram's mostly female admirers to gather to see their object of affection. Gram was particularly popular because he would take out all the girls on dates; every weekend he wasn't playing, he was out with a girl. Her looks weren't important necessarily, although Gram displayed a bias for blondes. Mostly, he was an absolute gentleman and schoolgirls followed him everywhere. At the Derry Down club, Gram regularly got up to perform and would act as MC so that other performers, including the Village Vanguards, could play. As his voice had accommodated rock and roll perfectly, he set about developing his folk voice. His youthful tenor was described by some as a "delightful voice", almost plummy in its timbre. He used it to good effect and his older, more experienced friends voiced their encouragement for his singing, even as they scratched their heads over this polite, wealthy kid and his personal venue.

Despite his regular dating habits, Gram made time for one girl and one girl only in 1963, Patti Johnson, a Winter Haven High student, pretty and blonde with a love of folk music. She seemed to Gram to be his perfect girl and their relationship deepened as they played music together. Finally, they began to talk about marriage. Despite their age, they were convinced that it would happen and they managed to keep it a secret from all but a few of their closest friends. Talk of marriage was dashed by Patti, who knew her father would never allow it so Gram put another plan into action: "We'll elope," he told Patti one evening. She was shocked and excited by the idea. Again, only their closest friends were involved and plans were made. Gram had both a car and money to do it, so leaving town wouldn't be a problem. They would go to Las Vegas or Reno. But someone close to the young lovers didn't think it was such a good idea. Patti Johnson's father found out about it shortly before it was scheduled to take place and he was able to prevent her attempted elopement with Gram that summer, incidentally putting an end to the Vanguards. Family friends pulled strings, and in the fall of 1963, Avis insisted that Gram returned to the Bolles School, to repeat his junior year. Without Parsons, the Legends dissolved.

Back at the Bolles School, Gram fell in with some old and new friends, some musicians, most not. Most of the time, Gram tended to act like a much older guy than he was, particularly around women. Frank David Murphy, one of his close friends at the Bolles School remembered a fairly serious infraction of the military school's disciplinary codes. On a free weekend pass, Gram had obtained permission to spend the time at a friend's parents house. Instead, he had organised a weekend of teenaged debauchery with four of his school buddies. This involved getting the older brother of one student to buy them alcohol, while Gram, through some connection, brought along the girls, who someone suspected were hookers. The weekend had more or less passed when the stories started leaking out about the hedonistic pleasures these fresh-faced schoolboys had been partaking of. Gram and his fellow students were hauled across the coals by the school's discipline committee, a group of teachers and older students known as 'the DC'. At first, it was recommended that Gram and his friends (hereafter known in Bolles School legend as the DC5) be expelled, but then the enormity of the underage drinking, not to mention the presence of women of ill-repute, dawned on the school. They realised it could reflect as badly on them as on these five students and so, Gram escaped with a warning. No one else was expelled, but he still toned down his behaviour, for the time being.

Classmates found Gram brimming with a certain inner confidence. He kept to himself a lot of the time, but appeared to be in deep need of good friends. Many of the boys in the school came from both middle class and wealthy backgrounds and the Bolles school was well considered as a stepping stone to other military academies like West Point. Gram proved to be an attentive student, not given to over reaching his abilities. Reports described him as being an average student with some disciplinary problems during his last two years in the school. He did excel at a few subjects, particularly Drama and English, where teacher Bob Hubbard, saw and nurtured Parsons' nascent talents. It was not beyond Gram to overstep the mark occasionally. He once turned in Bob Dylan's "Mr Tambourine Man" as an English composition and received an "A" for it. A few weeks later, Bob Hubbard heard it on the radio and Gram's grade plummeted to an ignominious "F', not to mention getting into trouble for plagiarism.

Still, the young man was not incapable of expressing his thoughts in a clear, even precocious manner. This poem appeared in the Bolles School Literary Magazine in spring of 1965. It's clear that this was the genesis for a song many would know.

Prereminescence
Brass Buttons
Green Silks, and Silver Shoes
Warm Evening's
Delight,
Cocoa Hues
Brightly buckled thoughts
Held fearfully fast
Against the clumsy
Crashing truth of the
Present.

"Gimme the old days,"
Squats the
Puffy-eyed old thing
On the last stool,
"Yes, Giv' em back."
The drunken mirror in
Front of him mutters

(slyly through a crack.)
"Ah! The good ol' whenever they weres!"
Those "once upon a time"
Thoughts, reflected on
Only by those old
Enough to remember them.
Those dream drugs
Sniffed with closed eyes and
Raised brows.
Like warm coffee.
Fine coffee.
Old coffee.
Careful! Not too boldly!
You may sneeze and blow away
Your angels of mercy.
Send them scattering
On mildewed wings.

The young also remember.
Clean sharp memories.
Not rusted or
Worn from over-use.

Yes, my Familiars
Wink back at me
Sometimes from brass buttons
Leaving hints
Of the future's endless
Supply of stools
And mirrors.

These are my "good ol' days"
My "once upon a times".
They obviously don't
Compare
With the old man's.
I wonder if,
(when I'm sitting where he is),
They'll be worth remembering
Anyway?

Somehow, Gram was able to mix his burgeoning career as a singer with his studies. It was not always a successful effort but while he was not a professional performer *per se*; he was very professional about his performances in the way that he dressed, spoke and generally conducted himself. Through Buddy Freeman's contacts with the great Southern icon Coca-Cola, Gram Parsons found himself on the bill of the Coca-Cola Hi-Fi Club, a talent show held in Greenville, South Carolina. He was to be both acting MC and the top-billed attraction, not to mention also being one of the judges.

Present at the talent quest that Friday night in Greenville, were two hopeful young folkies, banjo player Paul Surrat and bassist Joe Kelly, both members of the hotly-tipped Shilos. The Shilos were a three-piece folk group that included guitarist George Wrigley. Paul Surratt, leader of the Shilos, picks up the story of the band up until that point: "The first group that I joined was the Shilos. I was about twelve years old I suppose, and our major influence was the Kingston Trio. But it was some other music that we liked that brought us together with Gram, and that was the Journeymen. Now, they weren't what you'd call real popular at the time but Joe, George and I were big Journeymen guys and I'd found this record in a record store near my home and it was the second Journeymen album called *Coming Attractions.*"

As Paul Surratt explains it, there was a greater divide between how 1960s folk music is generally perceived today and the more onerous commercial reality at the time the Shilos had formed. Groups like the Kingston Trio and the New Christy Minstrels had, with an ear towards attracting pop and rock'n'roll audiences, taken traditional folk songs and material by artists like Leadbelly and Woody Guthrie and used them as a basis for quite successful careers. Interestingly, it was artists like Leadbelly and Guthrie whose contribution to folk music has often been downplayed, given that their inclination towards politics made them appear less patriotic to conservative 1960s America. "Folk was very big at the time and it was commercial, it wasn't like Pete Seeger or the heavy-duty American stuff like Odetta, it was really commercial, the Limeliters, the Kingston Trio sort of thing."

"No, we were not political at all" Surratt insists, "We really just enjoyed what we were doing. I think about the most political thing we ever did was 'Bells of Rhymney' and that was just because it sounded good."

As you might expect, Gram came with no such baggage about race relations, civil rights or equality. He certainly had an awareness of the problems that existed in the South, but he also came from money and black servants had been part of his life for as long as he could remember. His friends undoubtedly believed that he was culturally sensitive but Gram tended not to bring these things into general conversation. Some of his high school friends certainly remember him engaging in passionate debates about the topic but Gram, perhaps typically, never gave too much away at the best of times.

George was in hospital but Kelly and Surratt arrived at the talent show ready to perform in any case. Surratt couldn't help but notice the MC, Gram Parsons. This seemingly over-confident, flashy, tanned, good-looking young man in a purple shirt and gold jewellery had young women swooning over him. "This guy was singing that night. He was singing, "You Know My Voice, I've Heard Your Name", the New Christy Minstrels song. He had such a great voice, we couldn't believe it, so when we came down off the stage, we ended up talking for a while."

While the Shilos were enthusiastic about Gram's voice, he was equally enthralled by Paul and Joe's harmonies. Through the course of the conversation, it came out that the three of them shared a love for the New Christy Minstrels and The Journeymen. "Gram was also into the Journeymen and very few people knew who they were, they were not a popular folk group but they were probably one of the best. They were truly a great group – the one John Phillips came out of, and Scott Mackenzie. When we met Gram, George wasn't with us at the time because he'd been in a fight and was in the hospital. That night we were gonna play a talent show and it ended up that Gram was gonna be the judge. And so we met Gram backstage and started talking about folk music and the Journeymen and we all started singing,

Joe, Gram and myself, we all started singing Journeymen tunes. And we had this incredible blend, the three of us, and we just stopped and looked at each other, this magical thing had happened immediately."

The three of them performed an on-the-spot version of "Run Maggie, Run" and were all impressed with the results. "And just... the harmonies!" says Surratt. "We all stopped and looked at each other and said 'Wow, where's that fourth voice coming from?'" Surratt in particular was taken with Gram, who had seemed initially a little too smooth. Now, it seemed that Gram, what with his personal manager and his obvious wealth, was not as removed or as snobbish as he might have initially appeared. Instead, it was clear that behind his polished stage persona, he was a keen, polite and affable 16-year old kid with great connections and a desire to succeed. He was also a great liar, claiming to Surratt and Kelly that he wrote "You Know My Voice" and later on, the Marty Robbins song, "3:10 to Yuma".

The Shilos must have impressed the other judges too, because they made it through to the finals the following evening. Gram had already made his entry into the Shilos in a small way and he promised to call them tomorrow, hinting that he might come and visit Paul and Joe the next afternoon, Saturday. Surratt for one couldn't sleep, he was so excited at meeting this young guy who had made it sound like together they could be the "next Kingston Trio". Despite Surratt's fear that Gram would simply forget about them or just wouldn't call, he did so and punctually. As planned, after a sleepless night for at least one of them, the trio of Parsons, Kelly and Surratt got together to rehearse some songs for the evening's final round. "We got together the next day, made contact and got to singin', I recall. I don't remember exactly but right away there was contact and connections. For a long time, I was afraid that we would never see Gram again, he was so strong, so great."

Buddy Freeman had already been in Gram's ear that morning about this new group he was talking up and thinking about knocking around with, even though the three of them barely knew each other. "When Gram met us," Paul Surratt recalls, "Buddy said, "You know, if you want to make it in music, don't hang around those guys, "'cause they ain't really gonna. They're just hometown boys." And Gram said, No, there's something about them that I really like and he insisted that we get together the next day and Buddy did not want us to get together."

Buddy was angry with him but knew that Avis probably wouldn't object to it. The best he could do was accept the decision for now. How could Gram think about joining a group when he was so clearly made for a solo career? That could potentially sublimate Gram's own desire for stardom, surely as it would leave Buddy less in control of Gram's performing career. He had plans for Gram that did not include a band. Gram, of course, was already decided on how this going to work. As was his wont, he had taken control of this outfit and their destiny and fame was to be his destiny and his fame.

After the afternoon rehearsals, it appeared that Gram had already made his decision about who would be the winners that evening. He went out to cast his vote with the other judges, joined the Shilos onstage and then awarded them first prize of $150. "We won the talent show that he was one of the judges of, and then we got up and sang as a trio with him, which nobody got upset about" Surratt recalls. "I still can't believe it. It was a strange thing."

Surratt was pretty tickled by that turn of events. It also interested Buddy that Gram could so casually redirect his energies from this mostly unplanned solo career he had going for himself. He thought that for Gram to become part of a democratic band unit like the Shilos could somehow be a mistake. But Gram had a plan in mind. He had, as he would do again in the near future, joined a band in order to shape it to his will, even if it meant that the band would forever remain molded in his shape. Although the Shilos were based in South Carolina, Parsons would regularly travel up from Florida to play with them. Through "sheer force of will", Parsons became the driving force behind The Shilos. "It was like nothing bothered him."

In his own colorful way, Gram knew where the Shilos had to go; all the directions were already there in front of them, it was a process of beginning the journey with a single step, as long as that step was in the right direction. Soon, this seemingly worldly young man had bent them to his will, convincing the group without too much effort to play his few original compositions and encouraging them to follow the example of Bob Dylan and his "intellectual" folk stance. "Gram had complete control," remembered Surratt, who had been the original bandleader.

Buddy, despite his initial disapproval of Gram's involvement in the Shilos, came around to the idea and became friendly with his three new charges. As the manager of a group, he took his responsibility to them seriously and when Gram returned to the Bolles school in Florida, he would secure bookings for them in the Greenville area. "He helped us quite a bit," confirms Surratt. "We were just a bunch of kids and he was quite a bit older than us and we had a lot of disagreements. Still, I look back now and think that while there was a lot of stuff that I did not agree with Buddy on, if we had have stayed with him, we could have gone a lot further than we did. A group needs discipline. You think you can make it on your own when you're 15, 16 like we were but you need somebody. As soon as Buddy took over as our manager in Greenville, when Gram would be playing or in school in Florida, Buddy would have the three of us booked all over town, working constantly, playing steakhouses, fashion shows just to be ready when Gram got back up. We were playing once or twice a week, little shows here and there. He just kept us booked. Buddy was a good influence on us in many, many, many ways."

By personality, Freeman was a gentleman and not given to any kind of outrageous behaviour, but he knew business. As a college graduate and seasoned salesman with his father's plumbing supplies company, Buddy became managerially hard-nosed for his clients and negotiated many deals for them despite his own inexperience in show business. "He's a very gentle person. He's still alive, you know. It was hard sometimes for him to control a bunch of kids but he was not a tough person. He would be a tough manager for us. In other words, he was able to get us good jobs, because no other group in Greenville, South Carolina had a manager, and he was able to negotiate good deals. It was small time but all of a sudden, we had a manager. It's so different than to when the group is doing all of that stuff. It gives you an edge. Buddy would have been a great manager if we'd have kept going with him. He had that ability that great managers have."

There was plenty of television opportunities available to the Shilos in the South. In 1963, folk music was a commercial prospect and the hottest groups of the day were folk rather than rock. After the flashpoint of 1956, when rock'n'roll was birthed noisily from the loins of the South, there were five good years for it, to be followed by three lean years. In the interim, folk music flourished where the seed of rock'n'roll kept falling on fallow soil. It was the right time to be a folk group in the South and Buddy knew it. In all, Freeman got the group onto local and syndicated television shows like *Shindy*, a local version of *Hootenanny*, throughout the South nine times in one year, a huge amount of exposure for a group of high school students. No footage of the Shilos' numerous TV appearances remains but the impact it made on the members of the group was obvious, both on a personal and financial level. The Shilos usually earned around $25 a show, $75 occasionally – good money in 1963. After Buddy went into pitch for them, that amount had increased dramatically to $300 a show or more. Even with Buddy's percentage deducted, it was still substantial earnings.

Gaining in confidence with every right business move made on their behalf, Buddy attempted to press on the boys the importance of professional presentation. No more jeans and tab collars onstage – it was suits or pressed trousers and collared shirts. Hair had to be kept tidy. Gram needed no such encouragement in this area, since he already had fine taste in clothing and jewellery. "Gram was very well-groomed," commented Paul Surratt. "I think that his stepfather had kind of groomed him from an early age, he was very mature for his age and dressed well. Had a great tan too. His hair was a little bit longer than most people's at the time, you know, even before the Beatles and he was always impeccable, had a great style with the ladies and everywhere he went, he just impressed people. Even the mothers of the guys in the group were impressed with him. He was just a real ladies' man. He just had a way about him that was extremely charismatic, he was sort of a frontrunner. Really outgoing and really a good-looking dude, you know. All the ladies just went nuts for him."

While Freeman made all the right moves for the group in managing them as a local act, there was the question of the big time. Dreams of stardom dogged Surratt much as they did with Parsons and both of them talked openly and often about fame and what it might be. It was what the two of them wanted, and George and Joe might have had reservations about those desires but they too wanted to succeed. One night, Gram and Paul were driving around in Gram's car, talking about the future. Gram turned to Paul and said, quite out of the blue, "You know Paul, you and I are the only ones who are ever gonna make it in music because the other two don't care like we do. They don't feel the same as you and I do about this."

Paul could only sit there and agree with Gram. At that moment, Paul knew that Gram was destined for something great and knew only that he wanted to be part of that greatness more than anything else in the world. Gram's gift of self-confidence and self-belief was only matched by what he inspired in other people; loyalty, faith and a willingness to hitch their dreams to his. Gram articulated many of Paul's fears about the life he had barely begun living. Gram was a star already, a magnetic figure in the lives of the people who knew him. Some didn't trust him necessarily, some were wary but all were captivated by his finer qualities, which were for the most part only offset by his occasional flashes of selfishness and ambition. Paul was certainly captivated by Gram. As the youngest member of the group and the most impressionable, Gram was proving to be a positive role model and influence for him. "He was like a brother figure to me. I never had a brother and we just spent time together. Like when I was in high school, he was a grade further along than I was, he would say stuff to me like, "Come on, you're a musician, grow your hair longer, don't worry what anybody says. You're different than they are. Feel free to dress different, be yourself. Don't worry what anyone else tells you, believe in yourself, believe in what you believe in." And as time went on, we just grew to be like brothers."

Buddy Freeman knew that the Shilos would have to expand out of the Southern folk circuit if there was to be any shot at success. Gram knew this too, and doubtless so did Joe, Paul and George. There was of course every chance of success for this group of young men. They were all talented and in Gram, they had a fine frontman. However, in harnessing the group's potential there was a danger of setting one member against another, particularly if one member was now writing all the songs, rather than the egalitarian folk music tradition of using standard ballads and songs. "We did have that, you know," says Surratt. "[Buddy] felt that Gram had the voice, the looks and that we were the backup group. Gram was the one who was the star. He changed it from the Shilos to Gram Parsons and the Shilos but any group, no matter who they are, has one person who is the frontperson. But I see also that management make the mistake of thinking that one person is more important than the rest of the group; it's even worse when the frontperson starts thinking that. But even Gram didn't necessarily buy into it. It's like any band; you take the lead singer out and make him or her the star, you'll fall down. But Gram *was* the goodlooking one, he was the best singer, he was the best dressed one and Buddy would sell him as the drawcard. He was the drawcard, there's no doubt about that. Even though we were all a group, we were the backup. But we all shared equally in the vocals. Gram would sing solos, George would do a solo and I would do maybe do a solo. Gram and Joe would also sing together."

Buddy had monitored the entertainment press for ideas as to what he could do to bring a further professional edge to the show. One of Buddy's problems, if it could be described as a problem, was that he had a "clean view" of popular music and wanted the group to present a clean-cut image. Gram's stage banter didn't ever veer towards profanity, although some of his jokes were clearly lifted straight off Jonathan Winters' records. There was no doubt that Gram had an original and humorous way of looking at life and his attitude towards the group showed that. George, the group's equal to Gram both in outlook and intelligence thought that the group was getting all too serious in it's approach to shows. However, Buddy was increasingly interested in fashioning the image and presentation of the band and accordingly, drafted in two young women, one of whom was his cousin, Marilyn Garrett and Kathy Fowler. It was a Vegas showband idea that Buddy had, the girls would sing with Gram backing them, then Gram would solo, then the Shilos would perform to close the show. "We eventually rejected [the idea] because it was getting too much like the New Christy Minstrels and that's when we started fighting Buddy. He didn't understand music so much, well, he understood the clean version of pop music, he understood that so he had these two girls. They did sing with us but they didn't end up as permanent. Buddy wanted to do a self-contained show, the girls with the Shilos, the girls separately, the girls with Gram, the girls by themselves, us by ourselves, thank you very much. Well, that's not the way it ended up in pop music but it was kind of like, the show did work."

One of the key components of the group's success, according to Paul Surratt, was the vocal blend. The New Christy Minstrels' chart success was at least in part due to Barry McGuire's gravelly voice, while the rest of the group harmonised sweetly behind him. "George had a good voice and we all blended together real well. You pick a group that's all got the same kind of voices, like the Lettermen or something, where all the voices are kind of soft and you get this blend that's a little, I don't know, bland or something. You need voices that are hard and soft, like Lennon and McCartney. You had Lennon with the rough edge and McCartney with the smooth edge. That makes for a great blend. And you had Gram with this incredibly strong, yet smooth voice, Joe had come from a gospel background and sung in church so he had this incredible powerful voice and I was like a medium voice and George had a rougher voice and it just really worked."

Musical prowess was a strong point in the group, although Gram's abilities on the guitar were less than excellent, a fact that he himself admitted. He was stronger melodically on the piano but could convincingly hold down the necessary basic folk rhythm patterns. "At the time, he was not a great guitar player," says Surratt. "He was good but he wasn't great. He was a hard guitar player. If you saw my guitar, you would see where he actually scratched the varnish off it, he was a real intense player. But his voice was just incredible for his age, for any age and like you said before, you should hear his voice on the Shilos record before he got into country and some of it was absolutely great, very strong. We'd all be singing together and we'd just stop sometimes and look at him like, 'Whew. Where's that coming from?' He knew how to use it."

At that time, there weren't many traces of country music in Gram's voice. His bandmates confirm, and the *Early Years* recordings demonstrate, that Gram's voice was textbook smooth, carrying with it few traces of either the rocker or the young child who loved to listen to workers at his father's factory play country songs. It is interesting to note that Gram's early vocal style, which can mostly be gauged from early rehearsal tapes, did not possess anything in common with country stylings at all. It was classic folk with a slight jazz inflection in some of his phrasing. That said, Gram had a natural affinity for older style country tunes, which he liked to include in the set once in a while. "We'd do a concert and he would do a solo spot like 'Kickin' My Dog Around,' 'every time I go to town, somebody's always kickin' my dog around', he'd always want to do one of those kind of songs. He definitely liked that kind of song. I know he liked Fred Neil, he liked Josh White... I've been told about Elvis too and how he loved Elvis, but we never talked about Elvis when we were with him. It's funny, we were mostly talking about or singing folk music but I never heard him mention other stuff that he liked. He even did some New Christy Minstrels stuff, but country was sneaking in there, it was even coming through at that time for sure."

Gram's grandmother Haney Snively was also a supporter of her grandson's music group and she hired them to play at a political fundraiser. Haney was sponsoring a gubernatorial candidate for Florida and held a number of parties and events at the Cypress Gardens mansion. The group was generously paid for their efforts but even they were shocked when Haney passed a bowl around for donations, with a note reading: "Please chip in for the boys". That raised an extra $1,000, which the band put into a joint bank account to be administered by Buddy. The money would pay for suits for appearances, travel costs and for Gram to get further singing and guitar lessons.

During a break in the band's schedule, Gram, Buddy and Avis travelled to New York for a short holiday. Gram had designs on the city's folk clubs in the Greenwich Village area and talked his mother into purchasing a new guitar for him, a Martin D-28. When he mentioned to Big Avis that he might also need a Goya 12-string as well, even she initially baulked. Buddy cleared his throat and suggested that, as the boy's manager, it might be a good idea to get him the 12-string, as it would assist in the development of his career. Avis thought it over then took out her chequebook, adamant that one guitar would be his birthday present and one would be for Christmas. Gram readily agreed, knowing that his mother would forget making any such proviso by the time his birthday and Christmas rolled around.

While in New York, Gram went to many of the major folk music clubs, and networked himself into a number of parties and hoots. He got up and sang some songs in a few clubs, to which many people responded favourably. He was introduced to Fred Neil at this point, who was encouraging.

While the musical development of the group continued at a good pace, the band weren't quite up to speed as far as Buddy was concerned. He had been asked by the boys to enquire about the possibility of getting on Ed Sullivan's show, a move that, if successful, would undoubtedly land the group a record deal. Buddy duly sent the talent bookers at NBC the Shilos promotional pack with their basic four-song demo and its polite covering letter, with photographs at their well-dressed toothy best.

With an impressive array of local television appearances under their belts, and glowing references from nightclub managers and talent scouts right across the South, the boys looked like being the sort of group that Ed Sullivan could certainly help. The talent manager at NBC sent back a letter enquiring whether the boys were available for an appearance on the show soon. But Buddy had decided that the group was not pulling their weight, either in rehearsals or as a live act and he summarily rejected the offer from Sullivan, saying that he believed the group was not yet ready for such prestigious exposure.

Joe, George, Gram and Paul were gutted. Gram in particular was shocked by what he considered a betrayal. Buddy had been hired by Avis as a manager to guide his nascent musical career and this was the result? The chance to appear on this nationally popular television show would not return again for them, the band knew. Gram would later see it as a turning point in his musical career; a turnpike that led him continually away from a shot at the big time. Throughout his career, he would return to that feeling, that glimpse of the elusive nature of stardom. The road seemed a little more rocky but Gram was ever the professional about it, besides, he didn't want to upset the other guys too much as they were all equally devastated by the news. In private, the group met to discuss how they would counteract this setback.

One of Buddy's final acts as manager of the Shilos, although he didn't yet know it, was to secure the group a booking at Fort Caroline, a popular resort in South Carolina. It was a summer gig, which meant long, hot days. As it turned out, the Shilos were expected to play six shows a day, seven days a week. They would be well remunerated for it but it was hard work. Still, there were only a few grumbles about the hours, since the exposure would do them all good.

As that summer progressed, the boys were able to take the occasional day off and they would often simply stay at home, relaxing with friends and girlfriends, whoever happened to be around. Buddy began to begrudge the band their sometimes raucous offstage behaviour and tired to exert some pressure on them to behave. George and Gram didn't take kindly to it but let it slide a few times. But towards the end of the summer of 1964, they were tiring of coming home from a hard day's work only for Buddy to get upset about something that one of the group had said or done. All the tension and resentment came to a head one Saturday night when the guys were relaxing with friends at Buddy's house. A group of noisy fans were also hanging out and some of the older ones, who had been around before, Buddy considered a nuisance and a bad influence on the band. Finally, he lost his temper and told the group of kids to leave immediately. Joe Kelly was incensed by Buddy's behaviour toward their friends.

Finally, Joe snapped. He told Buddy, "All you've done all summer is bitch and complain. You haven't gotten us any more shows, so that's it. We can't work with you."

Buddy was shocked. He returned to his father's plumbing business feeling the terrible pinch of failure. Whatever judgements he had recently made on behalf of the Shilos, he had worked hard for the band and furthermore, had boosted their profile in the southeast region enormously. The Sullivan rejection had more or less been the final nail in his coffin but because of his efforts in other areas, the guys had voted to keep him on as manager until his final outburst. Freeman never managed another band again and kept to himself, running the family business until he retired.

With a question mark hanging over the future of the group, Gram was now convinced that he could manage their affairs in the interim period, if the rest of the guys were prepared to put some time into helping him. They all agreed. Together, they drafted another letter to send to bookers and got some new photos taken that better suited the newfound looseness of the Shilos. But without Buddy's mature business head prevailing, things could and occasionally did get a little out of hand. The fulfillment of Gram's ultimate vision lay far beyond the South, in Greenwich Village, New York. It was the spiritual home for the Shilos and they all hoped it would be the peak of their aspirations and achievements. "Gram had been to Greenwich Village before," explained Paul Surratt. "And he wanted us to come up there with him when he went back, so in the summer of '64, we went there."

While the rest of the gang found themselves staying in the attic of a friend's Village apartment, taking turns at sleeping on a mattress, Gram had found himself a more comfortable place of rest. He had the spare room at another folk singer's Village apartment (belonging to either Texas John Estee or Odetta) and it was during this period that Gram began listening in earnest to what Dylan was doing with his music. The godhead of modern folk that summer was Bob and Joan Baez, who were also at this time romantically linked. Together, they were expected to achieve great things, but as history has shown, Dylan used Joan's great mainstream success as a toehold for the success of his far more intense visionary music. The album *Another Side Of Bob Dylan* had just been released and within a few months, it was seen as the most momentous outpouring of the *zeitgeist*. Moreover, it was the driving force behind a new and more personal version of folk music that acknowledged openly the influence of rock and poetry. While Dylan had been one of Gram's big influences, he was now like a god to him. No other popular artist Gram admired was so honest, or so coruscating.

Gram took Dylan's lyrical influence on board first. One of his first originals, 'Zah's Blues', started as a poem dedicated to a Village folk singer, Zahariah Ryan. It took on a life of its own some weeks later as a bittersweet song, with some jazzy changes supplied in part by George Wrigley. The lyrics, however earnest they might seem in retrospect, are full of the passion and soul that Gram always added to anything he recorded, even if its sentiments sound a little twee thirty-five years later.

The other Shilos were captivated by their New York experience, where it was possible to be invited to one of Albert Grossman's famous parties and even see Bob Dylan being his challenging and confrontational self. Gram met Bob at one of these parties but was too stricken to say much more than "hello" to one of his new heroes. "We had a lot of things going on for us," remembered Surratt. "We played for John Phillips [future leader of The Mamas and The Papas]. We saw him walking down the street one day with the Kingston Trio and he saw me and we started talking. John knew me because we'd played with the Journeymen a few times. He invited us over to his apartment and we played some songs for him. We played for an agency that wanted to sign us. [John] got us an interview with an agent. We sang live in the agent's office and they wanted to book us. It was a very exciting time."

The group were once again frustrated and disappointed when the agency learned that the group were all under eighteen and unable to sign the full contract without parental approval. Joe, George, Paul and Gram decided that they should go ahead and get their parents to sign the contract on their behalf, reasoning that inside a year, they would just about all be of age and able to re-sign any contracts offered to them. They were encouraged when the bookers at the Bitter End invited them to participate in Hoot Night and both the crowd and the management were impressed with the witty and talented young men. They were invited to appear again as soon as they were able to return to New York.

As the summer of 1964 wound down, the group was faced with the reality of having to return to the South and complete their final year of high school education. Even though no one wanted to confront parental expectations, it was generally known that both Gram and George were expected to start applying for university entry in the upcoming year. Paul, who had not ever considered attending university, could not understand why the band wouldn't just continue in the meantime.

With various futures to consider, the band kept moving, kept working when schedules permitted. Back at the Bolles School, Gram began knuckling down to his studies. On a personal level, he was continually concerned by his mother's declining health. Her alcoholism was taking a real toll on the family, while her husband and her parents seemed unmoved by her problem, her children were all too aware of the ways in which she had changed. Big Avis had always been supportive of her children's activities, musical or equestrian and she had willingly spent money on both of them. But her ill health continued and in early 1965, she was diagnosed with cirrhosis of the liver. Avis was treated by the best doctors in Florida for the disease but the sad fact remained that there was no cure for her sickness. She was advised to stop drinking, a move which would at least prolong her life span but Big Aviis would find it difficult to control her lifelong habit. The consumption of liquor was a familial curse and was causing problems for the entire Snively clan in one way or another. Whether the true nature of his mother's illness was ever fully revealed to Gram is not known. The family had conspired to keep the truth about Coon Dog Connor's death from the children and it's possible that they acted similarly when faced with Avis' life-threatening illness. Gram, who had himself made night time raids on Bob's liquor cabinet regularly, tried to accept his mother's decline.

The Snivelys opinion of Bob Parsons was not helped when they learned that Bob did little to discourage his wife from drinking. He often laughingly tempted her to drink, surely aware of the damage he was doing to her. His callousness in this matter was exacerbated by the newest rumour around town, that Bob was having a sexual relationship with the young nanny Avis had hired to take care of Diane, Gram and Little Avis' four-year old sister. Bonnie, as the babysitter was affectionately known, was a laidback young lady with supposedly "relaxed" morals. Avis tolerated her and even liked her, although she was well aware that Bob was making his feelings for the babysitter known to his friends.

Despite her illness and his infidelity, Avis and Bob continued their regular round of parties and socializing. Their parties were the stuff of legend; beautifully pressed white napkins, the finest liquor, needles of crushed ice in all the drinks and well-presented hors d'oeuvres that remained mostly untouched at the end of the night. Gram often performed at these gatherings to the satisfaction of his parents and would even debut his self-penned songs on piano or guitar. His mother's friends were always generous in their applause and Gram's bearing at these affairs was always impressive. His own pals would often be around during these parties, sneaking alcohol out the back and they would be surprised at how maturely Gram conducted himself, so like an adult at 17.

But Gram's maturity came at great cost to him personally. The death of his father at a young age, never fully or honestly explained to him by his mother or grandparents, weighed heavily on him. He had been told the truth of his father's death by members of his father's family but remained uncertain of his feelings for his mother's side of the family. Knowing that they had worked hard to keep the truth hidden did not make him angry necessarily. He understood that there were reasons why they had chosen to hide the truth from him. Gram's level of tolerance in these kinds of situations was legendary; his facility for laughing in the face of adversity was well regarded by his friends.

While many who did not know the workings of this complex family suspected that this rich kid had it all going easy for him, nothing could be further from the truth. Gram treasured all of his close friendships, although he had plenty of hangers-on who were keen to see how the other half lived. Sometimes he scared some of his friends with the power of his boastfulness and ego, but this was reasonably rare, more so now that he was a teenager. He had learned as a child, as had Little Avis, that boasting that you had a chauffeur and servants didn't always endear you to folk.

Gram's closest friends, Frank David Murphy and Gerald Chambers, understood where he was coming from, even though they didn't come from particularly wealthy families. They bore his occasional boasts and outright lies with good humour, little caring about the family money, Gram's MG sports car or his fine clothes. They had managed to do what few would do in Parsons' lifetime, to get through the protective layer of mystery and celebrity that Gram continuously projected. As a result of this self-protecting veneer, Gram often appeared either immune to the feelings of others or at best, ambivalent about things which concerned others. It was not intended spitefully and he sometimes found himself having to point that out to people.

Gram kept up his regular correspondence with Paul and his typed, single-spaced, lower-case letters kept Paul either in stitches or deep in thought. Surratt, as the youngest member of the group, was very much their emotional barometer and changes in the temperament of the others made him anxious. In early May, 1965, he gleefully forwarded to Gram the results of a photo session that had recently been done in Greenville. Gram viewed the results happily, it seemed a little more modern than the publicity shoots that Buddy had directed. The shots were moody and the group wasn't too dressed up. In short, it seemed to hint at a change in latitude, which was yet to happen musically. During April, the guys had gotten together to rehearse new material and Gram brought along some more of his original compositions. The few that he had submitted previously, *Zah's Blues* and the not-completely original *Surfinanny*, had been well-received by the others but there were now doubts about these newest songs, which seemed alarmingly different to what had gone before. Paul was keen but George, who had university on his mind at the time, wasn't so enthused. Gram was disappointed and returned home to Florida, steadfast in his belief that if the Shilos were to go anywhere, it would be with his music rather than the cover versions they had persisted with for close to two years.

Even as Gram wrote songs from his new and rapidly maturing viewpoint, he was also penning his entrance essay for Harvard University, where he hoped to study theology at the college's renowned School of Divinity. Hatching plans for the future was difficult, even more so when he began to acknowledge the possibility that there was no foreseeable future for the Shilos. He knew the Shilos' days were numbered. In a letter to Surratt dated May 5, 1965, Gram hinted at some of the changes he was feeling about music. "Like it or not, we're always going to associated with this thing that Dylan's started."

He wrote Paul in early June, expressing his doubts about the group. Surratt, who more than anyone believed in Gram and his impending fame, was devastated by the news. Paul's father was taken aback at the change in his son's mood and after a while, he offered to pay for the group to do another recording. The rest of the group thought it through and agreed to do it, even though there was now little chance of saving the band from its fate. The sessions, recorded at the radio studio of Bob Jones University in Greenville, South Carolina, yielded twelve songs, which were not released until they were collected together on the Sierra Records imprint in 1982 as *Gram Parsons: The Early Years, Volume One*. The session cost $33.70 and was paid for in full by Paul Surratt's father. The rest of the band momentarily forgot about the pressures conspiring to break them up and relaxed into the sessions. Gram was in fine voice and George, Joe and Paul handled their instrumental and vocal contributions with a poise that belied their age.

On record, *Zah's Blues* came out sounding very late-night in its mood. Over changes that bear a small similarity to the old 40s swing tune 'Scotch And Soda' (which was itself covered by the Kingston Trio), Gram imbues the song with irresistible emotion, his youthful, warm baritone only faintly resembling his later and more familiar cracked tenor. The material that makes up the rest of this collection relies on the folk standards of the day that had always been part of the Shilos repertoire, such as *Oh, Didn't They Crucify My Lord* and *Bells Of Rhymney*, a song later covered by The Byrds. The band were sharp on record and their ease in playing, the way in which they step up to the mic to take solos then carefully step back, suggests that had they access to a more professional recording environment, they might have achieved at least a little commercial success. But in the weeks following that session, George was heading off to college, as was Gram. The loss of those two made Paul inconsolable. He was momentarily buoyed by the offer of a show later that summer at a fraternity beach party. It was to be their last show.

True to the kind of conjecture that follows comparisons or links to Dylan, there is an-oft quoted rumour that the Shilos even "went electric' and recorded some sides for a major label (supposedly RCA). The rumours have it that these sessions were presumably lost or destroyed, but if released could have led them down another, more lucrative path entirely. Not so, says Paul Surratt. That story was possibly engendered by the Cypress Gardens sessions where The Shilos recorded with a drummer and a bassplayer, but they remained, in that instance, steadfastly acoustic.

After the sessions Gram mentally prepared himself to leave the safety of Florida for Boston and Harvard. Only a few weeks of high school remained until his graduation. Around this time, his mother's condition worsened deteriorated and she was admitted to hospital in a case of near-collapse. On doctor's orders she managed to stay off the booze, but on his regular visits, Bob Parsons started bringing her little airline bottles of scotch and gin to drink on the sly. Her doctors were perplexed at her relapse – Bob was stricken with guilt and stayed away from the hospital, instead seeking out the company of his young lover while his wife lingered close to death.

On the morning of Gram's high school graduation, his English teacher Joe Dyess took the phone call from the hospital, Big Avis Parsons had passed away that morning, succumbing to the effects of alcohol induced cirrhosis of the liver. Joe passed on the news to Gram, who took it oddly well, Dyess thought. His mother was not old, just 38. It was a tragedy and in the photographs taken that day, Gram is smiling dazedly. In one, he stands flanked by his paternal grandparents, an unknown school friend and his pretty sister, Little Avis. His arm is tight around Avis's shoulders and his school friend has her arm on his shoulder with a concerned look on her face. Gram's smile is that of someone who has just been punched hard in the gut by life and despite being severely winded, chooses to grin hard and take the blow without complaint.

Little Avis was devastated and the Snively family reeled, although they chose to soldier on, giving friends the impression that they were not so shocked. Those who were familiar with Bob and Avis Parsons' social calendar knew them as drinkers but even they were shocked that such a young and vital woman could have fallen down so hard. Gram put his customary brave face on when friends came by the Snively home to pay their respects. Sat on his bed, strumming a guitar and drinking, he brushed off any appearance of grief with that tight, crooked smile now affixed, saying that he did not hold with making a show out of his mourning. "I believe in getting on with life," he told his shocked friends. He answered calls from friends of the family with cool detachment. "She had been declining," he said, dealing with one concerned caller in the presence of Jim Carlton, who was taken aback by Gram's strength in the face of his loss. Gram chose to get on with his life. "Death is a warm cloak," he elaborated to one interviewer in 1973. "An old friend. I regard death as something that comes up on a roulette wheel every once in a while. It's sad to lose a close friend. I've lost a lot of people close to me. It makes you a little bit stronger each time. They wouldn't want me to grieve. They would want me to go out and get drunk and have one on them."

His friends in the Shilos all sent their condolences to Gram but it wasn't long after the funeral that Gram arrived back in Greenville to rehearse for their final show together. He talked little about the funeral, which was muted and attended only by the Snively family, Gram's aunt Pauline and Bob Parsons, who appeared shattered. Gram's mood was mostly upbeat although he would lapse into long silences in the middle of a conversation, as though preoccupied with some point on the horizon invisible to others. The Shilos' final performance was on a South Carolina beach in the late afternoon sun. The fraternity guys were appreciative, if a little preoccupied with their girlfriends and volleyball.

The Shilos seemed to end so quickly and without much fanfare. No one beyond family and friends seemed to have noticed that the group, the sum of all their hope, was over. They were all facing the age of 18 and it was the hardest thing that most of them had ever had to deal with.

On their last night together as a group, they hung out and drank a few beers and smoked cigarettes. Gram got a little drunk and confessed to his buddies that while he was looking forward to university, he felt sad about the Shilos' having to break up. Paul understood how Gram felt. "George had gone to college too, Joe had gone to college and I wasn't going to go to college. I had a totally different outlook on things and I had never been a college person. I was destroyed because I really thought that we were going to make it and all of a sudden it came to an end and I thought my life was over."

Paul was the only member of the group not going on to higher studies and after that last show, he went home to his parents house and moped. A deep depression seized him for six months and he could only hope for something more to happen for him. It was that or wait for Gram's letters to arrive.

As for Gram, the future was the only light held up to him and he ran toward it, caring no more for the past and all of the heartbreak it had held.

CHAPTER 3
HARVARD AU-GO-GO:
From The Like to the International Submarine Band

With the end of the Shilos, Gram had consciously attempted to move away from what he saw as the "failure of childhood", a period which naturally followed on from the sudden death of his father and culminated in the death of his mother. By dismantling the poignancy of the memories of his young life, both sweet and bitter, he sought to end the fear and the disillusionment that by now constantly tortured him. His life up to that point seemed to rest on the cyclical (but not necessarily diminishing) returns of heartbreak and pain, almost like the refrain of a country song.

Each evening, he would take his guitar, sit on the lawn of his grandparents' home and look at the stars. He dreamed of possible futures and tried to fantasise about what lay out there for him in America, the land whose opportunities were beyond the limits of even his adventurous imagination. He had little awareness of what life really meant. But he had experienced the most terrible losses. His father and his mother were dead. Fear of death and visions of her late mother tortured his little sister Avis, and their stepfather was using whatever monetary influence he could muster to buy their love. As their legal adoptive parent, he had the right of guardianship, but his current interest in the family babysitter Bonnie consumed him. Gram and Little Avis were of no great importance to him, until it became clear that he would need to curry favour with them in order to maintain his access to the Snively fortune.

The endless machinations of the family over money would remain beyond Gram's control until after his 21st birthday, still three years away. Bob Parsons, as the legal adoptive father of Avis Snively's two elder children, had the potential to snaffle up a $28m fortune should anything happen to either of the kids. But the money was only partially a safety net for Gram. His requirements and needs were met as was deemed necessary. Money was not of immediate interest to him (other than the security of knowing that the family money would keep opening the necessary doors). It was only a tool with which he could place himself closer to people who would want to make music with him. But even music was not his ultimate goal.

Gram actually wanted to study theology, to approach God from all possible angles. Gram was "into God", and had been for several years. His belief had blossomed mostly out of longing; the desire for a father figure and his need for solid parental guidance, which he found lacking in Bob's throw-money-at-the-boy approach to surrogate fatherhood. As he struggled to accept the cards that fate had dealt him, Gram sought refuge in God. While much of America's youth were abandoning traditional religions for uncharted spiritual terrain, Gram found the idea of God comforting. God represented a real spiritual alternative to the alcoholism and bitter rancour over money that characterised the troubled Snively family. Again, his concerns about the legacy of these problems made the promises of familial unity under God seem attractive. Perhaps most of all, Gram desperately wanted to be loved.

"He was a good kid, with a good heart," remembered future musical collaborator Chris Hillman many years later. "If you delve into his background, it's pure Gothic. Very sick, lots of old and new money combined, greedy relatives. Gram's stepfather was a disgusting, evil, manipulative person. I mean, he bought Gram a club to perform in when he was a teenager! How can you ever get a full open vision or goal in your mind if those things occur in your life?"

Gram's short life seemed to perish for the lack of just such a vision. He did not have solid goals, and one of the things that dogged him his whole life was his inability to commit to a task and complete it. As he sought to process and rationalise everything that had happened in the previous ten years, certain themes kept recurring. The fact that his father had strummed a few chords on the guitar was parlayed into a new mythology. His father became Coon Dog Connor, the itinerant country singer whose musical career was stymied by the expectations of his wealthy in-laws, who forced him into a job in the family orange grove business.

Many friends heard the story that his father was a country singer who'd died drunk in jail, a too-perfect fabrication borrowed and reshaped from many an unfortunate tale about the end that singers and guitar players often seemed to meet. The story that Gram told of Coon Dog seemed as powerful and primal in its Southern imagery as those told about the death of Robert Johnson, on all fours howling like a coyote, poisoned by a jealous husband. It was a devastating tale, whatever the truth, and Gram was known to shed tears as he retold it.

Another story that Gram told was that the family mansion in Florida was used in the movie *Gone With The Wind*. Gram's facility for the finely-told tall story was legendary among his friends, and this habit continued throughout his life, although his lies never seemed to offend anyone terribly. It was as though his very sweetness and kindness could negate the impact of any uncovered falsehoods.

Gram told a magazine interviewer in 1972 that he had been accepted into Harvard University on the strength of an essay written on the nature of God. Tall tale or not, Gram started at Harvard in 1965, concentrating initially on studying Divinity. His freshman advisor was the Reverend James Ellison Thomas, known colloquially around the campus as Jet. Jet worked as assistant dean in the freshman dean's office while he completed graduate studies at Harvard's Divinity School.

Nearly seven years Gram's senior, he was a Baptist from Virginia. The connection between the two was made fast by shared Southern roots, and Gram frequently visited Jet at his apartment. The two would hang out and talk about God. Sometimes Gram would bring his Martin guitar along and sing Jet hymns, country gospel songs and spiritual songs. As their friendship became more firmly planted on the solid ground of shared interests, Jet's influence was apparent to those who knew Gram. He became a spiritual father figure to the young man, fulfilling the need for direction and advice that he had never received from his real father, and which Bob Parsons had not provided either, far from it.

Among the students who entered their freshman year at Harvard in 1965 were Al Gore (Vice President to Bill Clinton, later Presidential candidate for the Democrats) and actor Tommy Lee Jones. Asked years later by *Rolling Stone* reporter Judith Sims why he thought he had been accepted, Gram replied: "I guess they had enough class presidents and wanted a few beatniks."

Gram's interest in Kerouac and Ginsberg was well known; he was a voracious reader of all kinds of poetry and prose. And like any young person his age, especially those anticipating entering that prestigious university, he would have read with interest the *Time* magazine reports on the activities of two former Harvard professors, Timothy Leary and Richard Alpert. The choice of Harvard as his alma mater was supposedly related to a personal interest in their controversial testing of LSD on consenting students. Leary had been gone from Harvard Yard a while – he had already disappeared to the West Coast and Mexico in those intervening years, and was still on the run from the law. His credibility on campus was shredded for the most part – only a few students still spoke of him openly.

"At Harvard," said Gram confidently, "you don't major – you concentrate. And one thing I was hellbound to concentrate on was what Alpert and Leary were up to with LSD. But they'd left."

For Gram, the consumption of drugs, legal or otherwise, was a worthwhile hobby. He soon discovered that acid was freely available, despite its *pharmacia non grata* status with Harvard academics. He made several connections on campus during this time, and would always have a supply available for himself. He wasn't evangelical about his drug habits; in fact, he tended to moralise against drugs, although it was from the standpoint of one who had frequently made raids on his mother's sleeping pills and uppers.

LSD proved to be part of Gram's undoing at Harvard. He confided in Jet about his desire to be a novelist, even as he spent most available weekends off-campus with either a few acquaintances or by himself, using acid. According to Jet, Gram's LSD usage had already reached its peak the afternoon that he dropped another tab and found himself in the grip of what experienced LSD users would call the death trip. At the beginning of it, he experienced strong pessimistic feelings and he arrived at Jet's door in a highly wound-up state. His emotional state fluctuated with the usual introspection of the classic bad acid trip, during which he became terribly worried for the wellbeing of Avis and concerned about his own fate. Soon, he was in tears, telling Jet that he "felt helpless in the face of his family history".

Little Avis was struggling with her life and its lack of substantial foundation. She was living in Audubon Park in New Orleans with Bob Parsons, Bonnie the barefoot babysitter and sister Diane, who was still only a very young girl at the time. Avis corresponded regularly with Gram, her letters infused with her feelings and emotions, her confusion obvious in the way she begged for guidance from him; he was, after all, the only family member she felt she could trust. She had spoken with her adoptive father about attending high school in Winter Haven, but Bob wouldn't allow it. He was afraid the Snivelys would turn her against him permanently, although in his uncaring, self-serving manner, Bob himself was doing a good job of estranging her. She disliked him and they fought continually.

In the midst of his own privation, Gram continued to write letters to his sister encouraging her to read poetry and dream. Like him, Avis suffered terrible nightmares and fears about loss and death and Gram, the doting big brother, took charge, trying from a great distance away to provide the love and comfort he knew she needed (and which he needed himself). For her part, Avis found Gram's letters of reply to her cries for help perplexing: they were by turns "generous" and "puzzling". Sometimes his correspondence sounded terribly adult and sensible, but some letters were casually worded and seemed to loop the loop, never resolving. A letter to Avis dated November 8, 1965 showed Gram's obvious concern, not to mention his disregard for punctuation.

"I wish there was some one thing I could tell, some clear advice or magic spell to whisk away all the things that are bothering you right now – the problem is obviously not entirely a growing pain. Besides, they're not just your concern they're our concern, yours mine and Diane's and I'm afraid they will continue for some time yet. The best thing we can do is learn from the past and live our lives the right way so, in time, when we can do something to change things, we will be real people. Not sick and haunted by what life has done to us. Above all – believe in yourself and other people – they're the one thing that is real. I'll try to write as often as I can. Until then – live your life as you see it – as best you can – give it a solid foundation for the future."

While life seemed strange for Gram at such great remove from his sisters and his grandparents, he did not wallow in misery. He was content to skip most of his classes and sit strumming his guitar or writing poems, either in his apartment on campus or outside under the trees, in the cool autumn air. Besides his intense experimentation with LSD, Gram gained great enjoyment by riding his BSA motorcycle around the yards of the university, with an acquaintance from Harvard Law School on the back, cruising for girls.

Stories differ as to how long Parsons remained in one of the world's most prestigious universities. He himself variously claimed that it was five or six months; or at other times, a few days. "Just long enough to hang up my clothes," he smiled. His academic records show that he entered the university in late September 1965 and officially withdrew, with the consent of campus administration, in February 1966.

University was not the open door Gram had hoped for, or needed. He was effectively part of the social order that defined the Ivy League, and perhaps the family money had spoken loudly in the circumstance of his enrolment, but he was a Southerner adrift in a town full of the scions of wealthy Yankee families. Once again, the quiet Southern boy escaped from his alienation and the drudge of school life into private fantasies about music. His dreams were slowly being fulfilled as he drifted away from his studies and into the bars and clubs of Boston, where he sought out like-minded musicians and friends.

In the mid-1960s Cambridge, Massachusetts was well known as a hotbed of fervent folk activism. The club scene was alive and well, pulsing with a number of different interlocking and overlapping strands of music. One was the full-tilt folk movement, comprising hootenannies and folk nights at small local clubs; another was the rock 'n' roll scene. Yet another was the jazz crowd, fed each year by an influx of bright students to study at the prestigious Berklee School of Music, the institution that educated the more cerebral side of the genre.

In the era of The Beatles' *Rubber Soul*, beat music was seen as a style that could be taken beyond both folk and rock 'n' roll, while maintaining the credibility of the former and the raw power of the latter. Some preferred to couch more basic messages in the oeuvre of rock 'n' roll. Gram was firmly in the grip of folk music at that time but, like so many his own age, he had come up on rock music and wasn't averse to the idea of Dylan and other folkies going 'electric'. It seemed like such a good idea at the time, a movement that would colonise the outer reaches of modern music.

Within hours of finding himself inside the ivied walls of higher learning, Gram felt the compulsion to make himself part of something, some movement. Since he didn't feel at home anywhere any more, he did not want to miss a beat(nik) anywhere. His accent put him at odds with the traditions of this Yankee institution, but his ever-inquiring and constantly turning mind endeared him to many of the New York intellectuals in training at Harvard. However, Gram was unsure this was what he had envisioned for himself. It didn't seem to matter that his education had been bought for him, because he already knew he wanted no part of it.

Gram's answers and his future lay in music, and he began to realise this more and more as his studies became increasingly irrelevant. In order to feed his dreams, he began by seeking out musicians of any kind. Gram was not intimidated by anyone musically, not even the bespectacled jazz students with their sheets full of mathematical scales and two-handed chords. He had dabbled fairly successfully in folk and rock 'n' roll, his guitar playing was reasonable, his piano playing was better and his enthusiasm, coupled with his financial backing, were the impetus for several of the groups he had been involved in.

The first step Gram took was to form a band called The Like, a short-lived affair that got him some column inches in his hometown newspaper ("Havenite Brings Go-Go to Staid Harvard Yard") and more interest from other musicians. He began his next musical leap forward by placing an ad for "Musicians Wanted" in the campus newspaper and on poster boards around the university. This way, he came across aspiring jazz musicians from the Berklee School.

Gram's taste for jazz had certainly been developing. He tended to listen to whatever he could get his hands on and his eclecticism was well known (and not unappreciated) among these musicians. It scarcely mattered that his attempts at piano playing weren't quite to the standards of the Berklee students. He was a beginner as far as they were concerned, but none of them had his burning desire to write and create original music.

While The Like were just a rock 'n' roll group, Gram found the jazz musicians he was using lacked the authenticity and feel he was looking for. Gram continued his dilettante approach to music and life, taking hints and ideas from all sorts of music, drawing on influences unconventional and even unhip. "Gram was, I would say, a moderate piano player," avers Ian Dunlop, whom Gram had first met while at Harvard. "Not what you'd call startling. He had a good feel for it and could fake stuff nicely."

Gram was under no illusions about himself and his talent, but his projection of ability was staggering and other musicians, even the jazz musicians whose ability and technique were much more formidable, found that he had a way of convincing them to go along with his ideas and songs. Tom Snow, a saxophone player, was one such jazz player who contributed to Gram's vision. He was the only one who hung around for longer than a few weeks and several shows, staying long enough to record with the next lineup. "You have to remember, these were serious young musicians, obviously with their sights set on jazz and composing," says Dunlop. "It wasn't going all that well – it was a bit too serious for him. When I met him, he had expressed a certain desire… well, let's say he was desirous of other approaches to music. The ISB were people who had come out of rock and roll."

The meeting with Dunlop took place almost by accident, in his girlfriend's apartment above an antique store near the university. Dunlop had been out at a gig that night with his rock band, the Refugees, a band mostly based in nearby Providence, Rhode Island. He arrived back at his girlfriend's house well after midnight, to find Gram sitting in the lounge room with a guitar, picking songs. His girlfriend's best friend had a crush on Gram and had brought him around to introduce him to Ian. Dunlop had seen Gram around and the two started talking, then jamming on old rock 'n' roll tunes. The son of an English judge, Dunlop was very perceptive and had an intellectual bent of his own that stretched across all kinds of knowledge. Finding someone this hip, a musician and a smart, well-read guy to boot, was a godsend for Gram. Based on their love of offbeat humour, the two began a close friendship that endured until Gram's death.

The meeting with Dunlop seemed to lead Gram to the realisation that a new environment could very often be a creative stimulus. The new band, as yet unnamed, began to take shape. The next to join was folkie John Nuese, who was playing in local group The Trolls, who would eventually become better known as the Youngbloods. By November 1965, Gram had lured Nuese into his fold. Dunlop and Nuese had already worked together in a band called Happy Pantaloon and the Buckles, a name that Dunlop, with his ear to the English beat scene, had come up with.

The disparity in musical backgrounds was the key to the new band. Dunlop explains: "Several of us came out of completely different backgrounds – John Nuese was primarily folk and country in the old sense, not Country and Western, that sort of Appalachian bluegrass, Doc Watson-type of thing. Mickey Gauvin too was way ahead of a lot of people. He was from the mid-South and was into that hard soul type of music, funk if you like. James Brown hadn't broken through at that time but that was the sort of thing."

Barry Tashian agreed: "Mickey was a really funky drummer who was into Bernard Purdie." Ian and John discovered Gauvin playing in a band with local James Brown imitator Roger Paice, one of the few white artists working in the New England area who had been influenced by the Godfather of Soul. Gram, Ian and John were knocked out by Gauvin's abilities, and he was equally keen to play straight rock and pop stuff. The band set about working on covers but they dedicated more time to hammering out original tunes, mostly Gram's – although other band members felt comfortable enough to submit their originals too. The fate of most of these songs remains unknown, although the chronology of songs written by Parsons during this period suggests that tunes like "Brass Buttons", "Apple Tree" and "November Nights" were being rehearsed, or may even have been in the set list for gigs.

Gram was revealed as quite the musical autodidact, having schooled himself in any number of genres. His songwriting was characterful and considered. The band realised quickly that they were not just in a fun group but that their prospects were very good. They began working seriously under Gram's influence, setting aside their own songwriting talents for the most part. "We approached songs that were like set lessons," says Dunlop. "We didn't submit material, didn't write stuff. We worked on [Gram's] songs, learned the changes, made modifications."

Gram often referred to the management contacts he had in New York. The rest of the band may have begun to suspect that there were some fabrications in his stories; eventually, they all started to wonder whether the whole Gram Parsons deal was a kind of myth. Characteristically, Gram would prove, as he had done as a child, that his seemingly idle boasts were mostly true. He had connections to a personal manager in New York, name of Marty Ehrlichmann, whom he had gotten to know from his time in Greenwich Village. Ehrlichmann was best known for being Barbara Streisand's manager, and at one point had taken both Gram and a former child star named Brandon De Wilde under his wing. Gram maintained contact with Ehrlichmann, keeping him appraised of the various musicians he had met and how his original compositions were coming along.

Gram's actor buddy De Wilde had already enjoyed a stellar career as a child actor.

He had first come to prominence as the boy in *Shane* with Alan Ladd, then later made appearances in films like *Blue Denim* and *All Fall Down*, and put in a star turn in the 1963 film *Hud* which starred Paul Newman and Patricia Neal. De Wilde had enjoyed notoriety for his performance, which stunned many critics with its visceral power. Nonetheless, by this time he had slipped into semi-obscurity, languishing in the farmhouse he owned in Vermont when he wasn't out in California doing low key film work.

Brandon contacted Gram and then Marty, saying he wanted to make some records. De Wilde, unlike most actors, could really sing and wrote great songs of his own. There was no reason not to work with him; John Nuese considered De Wilde's talent to be at least equal to Gram's, and the two of them harmonised well together, with a sound not unlike the Everly Brothers. Gram offered to bring his new band to New York to work with De Wilde. Ehrlichmann agreed and so did the band, but in the meantime Marty set about trying to get Gram some other work, if not recording dates then at least club shows.

None were really forthcoming, but it was obvious that the band were well rehearsed and had talent to burn. If they were to relocate permanently to New York, they would immediately be offered gigs on a regular basis. Still, Gram had elevated himself to the leader of the band, and while his songs were being showcased, the band had the feeling he was selling them short. "He would refer to us as his backing group in later interviews. Some of those involved don't appreciate that," said Ian Dunlop. "Anyway, his previous group, the Shilos, had established management contacts in New York who saw him as more of a singer/songwriter/performer. These people were of course Tin Pan Alley types. They suggested that he get together a backup group."

At Christmas, Bob Parsons sent for Gram to join him and Bonnie during the university's Yuletide break, calling him down to Ponte Vedra in Florida, where the wealthy shut out the snow for Christmas. Gram went, accompanied by friends Frank David Murphy and Tony Hendra (later editor of *National Lampoon*, the Harvard university humour magazine), along with Tony's current sidekick. The four of them sat around the bar at the Ponte Vedra condo and tried to outdo each other with ridiculous tall stories.

The lazy atmosphere was laced with some Brazilian absinthe that Bob had procured from a South American business contact. The wormwood alcohol ripened the talk, then rotted it. Greased with cheesy food and plied with smuggled alcohol, it was plain to observers that Gram had begun to loathe his stepfather for being both sleazy and charming. Gram stopped by at his paternal grandparents' home for a real Christmas dinner before he returned to Harvard.

The band was by now working through a choice of names. They had been christened the International Submarine Band by Ian Dunlop, a name that he had supposedly taken from an episode of the TV show, *Our Gang*. The name did carry all the hallmarks of being one of Dunlop's random and funny ideas. The other name that they occasionally used was the Tinkers. Together, the gang rehearsed endlessly for the time when they could regularly commute to New York to fill studio dates and live shows but, as always, the goal was to develop original material. "The idea was that we would go to New York because we had recording time there that winter," says Dunlop.

Between occasional studio dates, the band laid down some of their original material on unused portions of other people's master tapes during studio downtime.

The regular shows came thick and fast, and soon the ISB were playing dates around New Jersey, Manhattan and Greenwich Village. There was a slightly surreal sojourn to Gram's old stomping ground of Central Florida, where the band played to crowded bars during spring break at Daytona Beach. Naturally, they played Winter Haven. They were also guests in a parade in Cocoa Beach, where they were conveyed by limousine through the streets before arriving at the local Holiday Inn, where a crowd of six people awaited them.

Soon they were working shows with Freddy 'Boom Boom' Cannon, a singer whose last hit had been the 1962 song "Palisades Park" ("It swings all day and after dark. Come on over!"). As a result, there were several shows at Palisades Amusement Park in Fort Lee, New Jersey with Cannon. Most of the big bands from every era of popular music, from big band swing to '50s doo-wop and '60s pop, had played there at one time or another.

The band had been offered a chance by RCA to record some sides, with a view to a record deal, part of Ehrlichmann's management plan. But Marty was perhaps too involved in the Tin Pan Alley/ Brill Building songwriting scene, since the songs they were already presenting did not have either the power or fashionability that modern pop fans were after.

"After some disappointment with the original plan involving Marty, we used this as the impetus to point us in a different direction than we were going in at the time," said Dunlop. John, Ian and Mickey agreed that while Marty had been extremely helpful to them, it was time to look at securing different management. Several of the band members had been introduced to managers Monte Kay and Jack Lewis, who handled the Modern Jazz Quartet and Flip Wilson, among other popular black acts.

The band recorded some material for RCA on October 28th 1965, under the name Gram Parsons and the Tinkers but the results did not inspire the record label and were buried in the RCA vaults. According to Ron Maharg, the man who discovered these long-lost reels: "In early 1997, I had been working in the BMG North American Vault, located underground in a secure facility in a small town in Pennsylvania believe it or not, for almost a year. While cataloguing some miscellaneous RCA reels, I was absolutely shocked to come across a reel clearly marked 'Gram Parsons and the Tinkers audition tape' dated 10/28/65.

"There were multiple takes marked 'Just Can't Take It Anymore' and 'Remember' (perhaps a misprint for 'November Nights'). Thinking this was too good to be true to stumble upon purely by chance and looking at it from a historical point as the date was 1965, our Archives department in the New York City home office was contacted and requested the tape for further review."

Ron didn't hear anything from the NY office until some months later, when he was in London, England on a business trip. Through the introduction of a co-worker, Tom met Keith Munro of BMG/Camden, formerly a subsidiary company of RCA that once released the works of Hank Snow and David Bowie, among others. "Several pints later, I discovered Keith is as big a Gram fan as I, and he tells me about this reel containing some unreleased material he had heard through the company. I was again shocked at this chance encounter. So after we suspend our disbelief after telling him I was the one who found it, he tells me of his plans to pursue the rights to release this material.

"It was soon thereafter I had the opportunity to hear the entire reel and I was in heaven. There is some fine studio chatter as well as some drastically different, although incomplete, takes of the songs. We kept in contact as he finalized the rights for their appearance on the compilation he oversaw and more information surfaced. Apparently the tracks were recorded around the same time Gram and the band were playing behind Brandon De Wilde in the RCA studios, according to Glenn Korman who is with the NYC Archives Dept. After months of legal matters, the songs finally saw the light of day, which I was so personally pleased to see happen, being a huge fan and having been blessed with the grace of stumbling upon the material to begin with."

It transpired that these tapes, discovered by Ron Maharg, were the very ones that had caused such disappointment within the band. Ian Dunlop confirms this: "We spent several months going back and forth to New York, backing up other people, such as Brandon De Wilde. We did some sessions with him, which were an attempt on the part of his management to squeeze him into the pop music area. We finally moved to New York lock, stock and barrel and we became more of a band. We were there for maybe a year, just gigging. We did a lot of gigs in New York, we worked quite hard. We played at Trudy Hellers, Ondine's, the Village Vanguard. The Eagle too."

Gram was still clearly embarrassed by the failure of the RCA deal, but the new managers came through with some more ideas and managed to deliver something the band had been holding out for: an actual record (or more correctly, a single) deal. The deal in question, once a popular arrangement for record companies to dangle in front of the many hopeful acts that came through their doors, came about through Monte Kay and Jack Lewis. The International Submarine Band were offered the chance to record a single for Ascot, which was to be used as the 'alternative' instrumental theme for the Norman Jewison film, *The Russians Are Coming, The Russians Are Coming*.

The film could be described as a Cold War farce, which might also well describe the attempts Ascot made to promote the single itself. Theme music for the film was scored by Johnny Mandel, but the Ascot single release comprised the ISB's instrumental version of the theme tune backed with "Truck Driving Man", a cover of a Buck Owens song. The synthesis of country and rock had begun but, interestingly, the song had been suggested not by Parsons, but by John Nuese.

Gram was naturally agreeable to the idea. During his friendship with Nuese, Gram was learning again to dig the country music that he had loved as a child in the 1950s. Records by George Jones, Merle Haggard and Buck Owens were just some of those that he began to purchase. He threw himself into the study of country music, while not neglecting Ray Charles, Jerry Lee Lewis and soul artists like Otis Redding, Percy Sledge and Aretha Franklin. This was very much the manner in which he began to knit the two styles together to suit what he wanted.

By fusing country music and soul (not necessarily an original idea, as Dan Penn or Arthur Alexander could have told him), Gram and the International Submarine Band had the opportunity to push beyond the current restraints of popular music and forge ahead. In theory it sounded good to the band, even though Ian and Mickey were personally not so enthused about 'straight' country music.

A single cut for the Columbia label seemed more promising – "Sum Up Broke", a song that John Nuese and Gram co-wrote, b/w "One Day Week". But the single went nowhere fast – surprising, given that "One Day Week" was a brash little pop song that owed a small debt to the Beatles and so should at least have been given a chance. "We found that we had become like a computer card in the great huge file at Columbia Records," recalled Nuese. "And although they had us signed and had something in the can, they really didn't do anything with it."

The group continued to work at a multitude of clubs and discotheques in boroughs near and far, pushing their barrow harder than ever. They managed to boost their public profile with appearances on television, including a two-song slot on one of the Zacherly TV shows that beamed out of New Jersey. Perhaps the high point of the year was a show in Central Park with the Young Rascals, in front of an audience of 15,000 teenagers. But the winter of 1966 dragged on too long for Gram and, although he found New York an exciting town, he knew that California was where it was all happening for bands not even half as good as the ISB.

"It came to the point that these things had happened," says Dunlop. "We'd made a certain amount of progress. New York at that time was seen as slightly second-rate compared to the West Coast. One or two people that we knew had decided to make the jump. Gram took a trip out there late 1966, flew out there and stayed with Brandon De Wilde. He came back pretty soon, saying: 'This is the place. Come on, let's go.'"

Indeed, Gram's trip out west had been eye-opening, to say the least. He took the opportunity to sample the best that the West Coast had to offer – beautiful girls, famous friends and freely-available LSD and pot. It was a short trip – only three weeks – and in that time, California worked its magic on him. He had been introduced to David Crosby by De Wilde at a party one night, and took a shine to Crosby's lissom companion, Nancy Lee Ross. Nancy had grown up in the same social circle as David Crosby, and had, among other things, been married to Franklin and Eleanor Roosevelt's grandson Rex.

The marriage didn't last long and she moved out on her own. She had a brief affair with actor Steve McQueen before David Crosby came back into her life. She was in fact engaged to marry Crosby when Brandon De Wilde showed up at her place the same afternoon that Crosby had set off on a trip, either a tour with the Byrds or a road trip with Peter Fonda. Brandon had with him a handsome Southern boy whom she had never seen before. Brandon left in a hurry and Gram seduced Nancy, much to her confusion and delight. He had appeared out of nowhere and, just as quickly, he brought her back to New York. In his 1998 autobiography *Don't Tell Dad*, Peter Fonda noted that Crosby had cut short a trip with him in December 1966 because he was worried that this Parsons guy was likely to leave town with his old lady. Fonda takes a certain wry pleasure in noting that that was exactly what Parsons did.

Gram had returned to New York elated, convinced that the band would fare better out West. As proof of how rich the pickings were in California, he brought Nancy with him to the Bronx house. The ISB were somewhat surprised by all of this carry-on involving the Byrds, but they agreed with Gram that they'd be better off in California than continuing their thankless slog through the NY clubs. So in February 1967 the International Submarine Band decamped to California, leaving behind the uncertainty and bad weather of a New York winter, and arrived in the uncertainty and clear skies of Los Angeles.

Through De Wilde, Gram had been introduced to hip young actors Peter Fonda, Dennis Hopper and Jack Nicholson, who were part of the whole Ciro's scene. It seemed like everyone he met knew everyone else. Peter Fonda knew all of the Byrds and shared a business manager with Roger McGuinn. It was all too irresistible to Gram, and the elusive notion of fame grew a little more firmly in his mind.

One of Gram's reasons for wanting to come to California in the first place was that he truly believed his musical vision would be better served in a place like LA, where rock bands and country bands frequently worked the same clubs throughout Hollywood, and out into the San Fernando Valley. LA was home to the big bands of the day, Love, The Byrds and Buffalo Springfield, while further out, in Bakersfield and Palmdale, Buck Owens and Merle Haggard ruled the honky-tonks. Gram wanted a slice of this action – in fact, he wanted to bring the two audiences together.

The rest of the ISB were keen to renew their commitment to the group. Moving to LA seemed like the right thing to do, at least as far as Dunlop was concerned. "We were quite ambitious and we certainly were willing to go anywhere. We'd been putting in an honest amount of effort into cracking the East Coast and New York but we looked at this as a trial. We didn't terminate the lease of the house we had rented together in New York."

One by one, the band began to arrive in California. The International Submarine Band guys made their home in Laurel Canyon at a house on Beverly Glen Avenue that was quickly dubbed the first 'Burrito Manor'. Laurel Canyon was a natural choice for musicians new to LA; this low-key, wooded bohemian area was where the rest of LA's successful and up-and-coming musicians lived.

At this point in the band's development, the guys kept coming back to two albums – Ray Charles's 1965 release *Country and Western Meets Rhythm And Blues* and Buck Owens's *Roll Out the Red Carpet for Buck Owens and his Buckaroos*. Brother Ray was, of course, no stranger to country music, although he performed it in his own inimitable way with overtly pop arrangements. But the 1965 album had more of a rough-and-ready soul feel to it with a definite mouthful of 'R&B grit'. With its accent on R&B material, the Owens album was pushing the Nashville sound out of country music fans' minds. Despite initial fears that all their East Coast groundwork would come to nought, it turned out that record companies had heard about this four-piece group and were interested. True to form, Gram wanted to play more of this country-inflected rock music, which sat fine with the rest of the group. Dunlop recalls: "Shortly after arriving, we were met with a lot of interest from A&R people and record companies. We were doing gigs at various venues, doing mini-tours through California."

Gram and Nancy took a place together on Sweetzer Avenue, and it was through his regular visits there that Peter Fonda got to know this Southern boy who had stolen David Crosby's lady. Fonda took a real shine to Parsons, and they talked a lot about music and movies. The two of them would often sit down in the dark room of Fonda's place on 3rd and San Vicente in Hollywood and trade on old Everly Brothers and Buddy Holly tunes, harmonising beautifully together. Like De Wilde, Fonda wanted more than anything to be a singer and he was good at it, not to mention being a good guitarist. Moreover, he was simply impressed with Gram's fine manners and his cultured ways, figuring that this Parsons guy was hardly starstruck and therefore a cool fellow to hang out with.

Fonda mentioned that he was working on a film with Roger Corman and Jack Nicholson called *The Trip*, which was supposed to deal realistically with a man who tries LSD for the first time. Corman's interest in the LSD thing was mainly prurient; he wanted a film that would shock viewers. Consequently, the original script was watered down and was much less effective than Fonda and Nicholson (who wrote it) had anticipated. But Fonda still had high hopes for the film, and even hinted later that he had expected it to be the project that made his name.

That would come later, with the enormous cult and crossover audience success of *Easy Rider*, but for the moment Nicholson and Fonda were under a watertight contract with Corman. The actors held their breath and agreed to complete the film, despite their objections to the script changes. Gram mentioned that his band had already recorded a song that was used in a movie – perhaps there was a place for the Submarine Band on the soundtrack to the film? Fonda agreed, and through his double connection as producer and star of the film got the ISB onto the soundtrack.

Gram wrote an R&B rocker called "Lazy Days", which was produced by trumpeter Hugh Masekela. However, Corman wanted something that was less like R&B/pop and more straight-out psychedelic. Finally, the decision was made to excise the ISB from the soundtrack and replace them with the Electric Flag, a new band comprised of well-known musicians like Mike Bloomfield, Nick Gravenites, Buddy Miles and Barry Goldberg, playing a more acid kind of rock. The decision stunned Gram. It was the latest in a long line of "could-have-been" breaks. The band were somewhat mollified when Peter offered them the chance to appear in the film's nightclub scene.

To make up for the disappointment of not being on the film's soundtrack, Fonda spoke to Gram about pursuing a solo career as a singer. Fonda was looking for a song to release as a single, in the hope of expanding his horizons as a performer rather than just an actor. Gram obliged and helped give Fonda another feather in a cap that was already getting crowded. Fonda picked "November Nights", a song that had been recorded by the International Submarine Band when they were backing Brandon De Wilde.

Fonda recorded his version of "November Nights", and covered Donovan's "Catch The Wind" as a b-side, for the Chisa label, owned by Hugh Masakela. Gram was very pleased to have one of his songs recorded by someone else, particularly such a high-profile movie star. However, while Gram hung out with Fonda, the ISB was, more often than not, going without regular shows. Gram and the rest of the band began to drift apart.

The ISB had a new Hollywood-based manager, Steve Aldberg, who was also De Wilde's manager and a show business scenemaker – just what the band needed to establish vital musical connections. Gram would make the effort to get together with the band once a week to rehearse for the regular A&R auditions that Aldberg was lining up for them. The rest of the time, when they weren't gigging live, the ISB (without Gram) would spend jamming with other musicians who came around to visit their Laurel Canyon place.

Barry Tashian and Billy Briggs had dismantled the Remains and relocated to LA to live and work. Soon, a lineup of musicians had formed independent of Parsons' input. "The music got a little too… diversified, I guess," said Dunlop, speaking of the different directions the ISB was being pulled in. "Country and Western seemed to jar even more with the West Coast crowds. We were also getting into certain music that was way more experimental – it was too many different directions at once and we were meeting with resistance from A&R guys. I mean, these were people who were totally flummoxed by country music."

There are other explanations for the lack of interest in country music. Capitol Records, one of the biggest labels for country music in America, was in the process of dropping many of its country acts as it prepared to deal with the shift in public tastes occurring at the time. People no longer necessarily wanted just country; their tastes had expanded to include pop styles, and even acts as talented and pop-oriented as the Gosdin Brothers were shown the door. But, according to Jason Odd, Australian writer and authority on Los Angeles country music of the 1950s and 1960s, it was still a healthy scene.

"Buck Owens and Merle Haggard were both charting," says Odd, "and quite well. Buck's group, the Buckaroos, had their own albums on Capitol Records, but it's important to note that you had very little chance of seeing them live in Bakersfield or LA; they were too big for all the Bakersfield clubs, especially Buck.

"There was quite a bar band type scene out in towns in the Mojave desert like Bishop, Ridgecrest, California City, Lake Isabella, Lancaster (Zappa's old stomping ground with Captain Beefheart), Trona and I guess Bakersfield too. Fresno had a pretty strong music scene and there was a lot of live country music there plus some pretty whacked-out psychedelic and garage punk bands came from there in the mid-1960s.

"There were a lot of pickers around the scene: drummer Henry Sharpe who played on TV shows and had even been on early Haggard sessions, guitarist Gene Moles, fiddler Jelly Sanders, performing with DJ Larry 'Shotgun' Daniels and his group the Buckshots. Steel player Larry Petree, Tommy Ash, Gil Deleal, Leo LeBlance, Bob Galardo, Dennie Payne, Sonny O'Brien. A lot of bar bands were interchangeable; some groups were informal – bar the bandleader – and would gig where they could, while others stuck to one bar as much as possible."

The LA country music scene of 1967 that Gram and John Nuese immersed themselves in regularly was based around the Palomino, surely the predominant country music club of the time. For Gram, it was something of a first, since he wasn't yet 21, the legal drinking age in California. He made do with a fake ID some nights, while at other clubs he was never asked for proof of his age. Gram also visited the other, smaller clubs in the area, like The Bandera in Ventura, where Delaney Bramlett worked in 1967, the Rag Doll in north Hollywood, the Corn Crib in Monrovia, the Foothill Club in Long Beach, the Hitchin' Post in Gardena and Fred Maddox's Play House in Pomona.

Gram would regularly enter the Palomino's house talent contest every Thursday night, when the house band Red Rhodes and the Detours would and could play whatever contestants requested. Gram would usually attempt George Jones or Merle Haggard tunes, and it was in this atmosphere that his phrasing and ability to sing were tested. His nerves were occasionally jangled by the presence of tough, crew-cut country music fans who were somewhat suspicious of this longhair in satin bellbottoms. Still, his sure voice won them over and he even befriended some of them in a small way. Whatever Gram attempted to sing, he gave the songs everything he could, even if sometimes he had sought beforehand to calm his nerves with tequila.

Gram would often venture outside the Hollywood area to a club called the Aces, out on Valley Boulevard in the City of Industry. The club band at that time consisted of luminaries like pedal steel player Jay Dee Maness, country piano player Earl Ball and bass player Don Holiman. Singer Eddie Drake would perform a vast range of songs and Gram went there to drink and observe, make connections and take on ideas for performances.

Gram would also make it along to a club called Chequers on Lankershim in north Hollywood, where two of the hottest young pickers, Clarence White and Bob Warford, could occasionally be spotted. Clarence White was playing in a hot band called the Roustabouts with steel player Dennis Mathes and Richard Arlen, a singing bass player. They gigged at the Jefferson Bowl, a bowling alley near Culver City, but by November the group had moved to the Nashville West club in Palmdale.

Singer Johnny Paycheck, author of country classic "Apartment #9", made La Puente club the Blue Room his home during the latter 1960s, and Gram visited both here and the Brite Torch, another local club. San Fernando clubs like the Sky Star,

Walt's Place on Sunset Strip in Southgate and further along, Tockers, Miller's Cave and the Bell Gardens Inn also presented live country music six nights a week. While Gram searched out the hardcore honkytonks and bars, Mickey Gauvin and Ian Dunlop "got involved with a bunch of people, friends of mine, like Barry Tashian for example. We were playing popular music. Soul, late forties-early fifties-type of stuff, western swing, early R&B, jump. It was a good fun area to be involved in. We could have gone a lot further with that band but I was personally burned out on playing six nights a week in really crummy bars, 9 until 2, 10 until 2 – those kind of hours."

Ian, who had the best band names of anyone, called this new band the Flying Burrito Brothers. Briggs and Tashian joined forces with Ian and Mickey Gauvin and soon they were making all the clubs; Snoopy's Opera House, The Red Velour, the Hobo – jamming into the night with the many musicians who had gathered in LA from all over the US. Bobby Keys and Junior Markham, Delaney and Bonnie and JJ Cale were all there by then, having left behind dead or dying music scenes in their Southern and Midwestern hometowns for something new and freaky. Living as a poor musician in Hollywood playing the sort of music you wanted to play was still better than battling it out in the Midwest, where no one wanted to hear you play at all. Gram would often come and sit in with the group, putting on a jewelled turban and getting on the piano or the organ to play Jerry Lee Lewis songs.

Gram's musical agenda, far from being definite, was changing and developing all the time. By April 1967, he was regularly visiting as many clubs as were holding talent contests and open microphone nights where singers could get up and play their new songs. At the Palomino, Gram often found himself struggling to get a hearing while another guy singing "El Paso" was getting all the applause. Gram even booked himself into a few shows as a duo, with help from his friend Bob Buchanan. All the while, the ISB withered on the vine, the richness of its promise the very thing that would destroy that first lineup.

"The Sub Band split was a slow, agonising, inevitable thing," Barry Tashian said sadly. "I think Gram had his sights set on a different place after a while, and realised these guys weren't going with him." It had only been a matter of time before something like this happened. Gram had not applied himself to the original International Submarine Band and the others developed their own circles of musicians without any input from him, but thanks to Aldberg's connections, Gram got a much-needed break – an introduction to inscrutable industry man Lee Hazlewood. Gram confronted Hazlewood at a Hollywood party and struck a deal with him. "I had to go to Hazlewood and say, 'OK, just let me record an album,'" Gram told interviewer Chuck Casell in 1971. "'I won't take any money for it,' was pretty much what I was saying 'unless it's a Top Ten album.' And he said 'OK, but my old lady has to produce it.' I said, 'Yeah, great. Anything.'"

The deal with Lee Hazlewood's LHI label was finally struck. Gram took some time to reflect on what he felt was a major, yet pyrrhic, victory; he had scored a deal with the name of the Sub Band, even though the name was Ian's and the original lineup had since broken up. Still, the split had been reasonably amicable. Since it would fall to him and John Nuese to capitalise on the Hazlewood deal, Gram knew there would have to be further compromises made with the now-nebulous International Submarine Band.

He rang John Nuese and told him the good news. John, who had always been into the idea of performing country music, happily stuck with Gram's vision of a young band doing country music for a label that had up to now been home only to Nancy

Sinatra and Duane Eddy. Hazlewood's genius lay in the production field, although his tough-talking manner dissuaded any musician from fucking with him. Troublemakers received short shrift from the Okie industry maven, but Gram wasn't entirely convinced by Lee's front. Judging by comments made in later interviews, Gram never had a high opinion of him, and it appears that the feeling was mutual.

John and Gram started compiling a list of possible songs they could record, and Gram started working on some tunes of his own. "We had a basic style where we would get into a circle and play flat top guitars," said Nuese. "Gram and I had developed a very good rapport doing this kind of thing. This was the basic style in which we were to record." Before recording began, it was time for Gram to go back to Florida, to see the family firm that administered the Snively trust fund. Gram took a three-week vacation from Los Angeles, taking the train back to Florida.

While spending some time with the Snively side of the family, Gram ran into his old drummer friend Jon Corneal. Corneal had, in the years after the Legends, moved to Nashville, where he worked for many of the big Opry acts, like the Wilburn Brothers. "I also worked for Kitty Wells for a short while, then Connie Smith, then I came home for a spring visit to Central Florida. I ran into Gram while I was there and he told me about this recording opportunity in California with the International Submarine Band on Lee Hazlewood's label."

Back in LA, with a drummer to complete the project, talks began with Hazlewood's girlfriend, Suzi Jane Hokom. She had an affinity with country music and thought she could do something with this kid and his songs. Almost a month went by before Suzi Jane got back to Gram about doing some recording, but he remained calm about it all. Gram didn't initially mention that the International Submarine Band (as he had sold the concept to Hazlewood) no longer existed except as an entity in his head, but what did it matter? He knew the music was there.

Work commenced on the album. Chris Ethridge, a Hollywood-based musician, was invited on board as bass player for the sessions. Ethridge had been at the first Monterey Pop Festival, talking to Mike Bloomfield about country music, when Bloomfield happened to mention that there was this guy everyone in Hollywood was talking about – some longhaired kid from Florida who was playing country music. Ethridge knew a little about that, having been raised in Meridian, Mississippi, the hometown of Jimmie Rodgers, country music's earliest hitmaker. He contacted Gram, and the two of them bonded over a mutual Southern heritage and tequila.

Gram, Ethridge, Nuese and Corneal did most of the work, which was to take place in two sessions, split between late July and November 1967. The album was recorded piecemeal; that is, every track was recorded separately, with some exceptions when bass and drums were recorded together. The results of the July sessions were put forward for a single. Suzi Jane suggested that since Gram had written two new songs, "Luxury Liner" and "Blue Eyes", they should be used as a double A sided single. There were also covers that were planned as singles, like "Millers Cave".

As for Gram's originals, they were all good quality, straightforward songs, although "Luxury Liner" was somehow different to traditional country in its arrangement. Barry Tashian was one of the first people to hear it, and he was struck by the propulsive rock/ country feel of the song – it seemed to encompass several different styles of music, but comfortably so. It rolled along at a fine tilt, yet it was somehow earnest. When Gram sang "I've been a long lost soul for a long, long time," it was easy to believe the edge of sincerity in his voice. The other original songs, "Blue Eyes" and "Do You Know How it Feels To Be Lonesome?", veered more towards Merle Haggard in their styling, although there was a healthy dose of jump in the tunes. The sentiments of "Blue Eyes" were entirely modern, eschewing the traditional country notion of drinking to deal with your problems. Instead, the singer states his intention to "get... stoned".

The songs Gram penned during 1967 spoke volumes about his ability to update purist sentiments and make them contemporary. It is also clear that even at this point, Gram was encountering resistance to his ideas, at least in the technical and production sense. He did not necessarily have a lot of studio experience prior to recording with Hokom. His experience with De Wilde in the RCA New York studios was mostly as a bandleader, rather than producer, and the Shilos had not done much recording, and then only in basic two-track studios. He had good musical ideas but he may not have been able to communicate them well to a producer.

As for Hokom, she was something of a perfectionist and tended to take control of recording situations quickly. She had possibly assessed Gram as being somewhat inexperienced, perhaps because of his age. Many people during this period had already assumed that he did not know all that much about recording, but she was wrong if she thought he did not desire to have more control over the sessions or to engineer the sort of sound he wanted. She and Gram did not always see eye to eye, but for the most part the two remained on friendly terms during the first round of sessions.

She was pleased that Gram dedicated himself to endless rehearsals of the songs in order to get the tempos right, before Ethridge, Corneal and Nuese would go in to lay down bass, drum and guitar parts. "There were hours and hours of rehearsals Gram and John and I did at my house in Laurel Canyon," says Hokom. "We pretty much cut the album live. It was, 'Let's go for that pure, raw sound that comes without too much fiddling around.' Only John insisted on doing his tracks separately." Nuese contradicts Hokom's recollection, saying: "She and I disagreed on how to do things. She was into piecemeal recording, doing basic tracks then building stuff over them. I was into a thing, as Gram was, of recording the whole thing live."

A steel player was a necessity for these sessions, so Gram and Nuese asked around the session players and one name in particular kept coming up – Jay Dee Maness, whom Gram was already aware of from his work at the Aces club in the City of Industry. Jay Dee was the steel guitarist for Buck Owens and his Buckaroos, a 21-year old whiz kid on the pedal steel who had a duck's ass haircut and winklepicker boots. Nuese and Parsons arrived at a club in Ontario, in Orange County one evening to see Maness in action with another band. Parsons was impressed by both his skill and his youth. Seeing his potential employers standing out so wilfully among the club's more conservative clientele with their longish hair and 'wild' clothes meant Maness was polite, but wary. They offered him the opportunity to work on the LHI sessions, which he took up immediately, since it paid well and Maness was frankly tantalized by the idea of longhairs like these two taking such an interest in country music.

During the first lengthy layover in recording the album, which lasted the best part of four months, Gram continued to look for new musical partners with whom to co-create and jam on ideas. All the while, he kept trying to write more original tunes, but he found himself foundering between fighting with the forms of country music and writing more pop-oriented tunes which gave him the freedom to experiment. Now that the sessions were over, Gram was pleased with the results – the songs seemed to sound how he had envisioned them, more or less. But there was one problem – it appeared that he had compromised his own musical vision of welding styles, because the album, as it stood, sounded very 'straight' country.

After the July recording sessions were over, it was time to start playing live. Almost immediately, Gram and Jon Corneal began to clash. It was due mostly to a personality conflict, (which friends say had existed for as long as they had known each other), but soon the music became their biggest issue. Corneal honestly felt that he was a better singer and player than Gram, and hinted that he had been lured out to California under false pretences, since Gram had promised that they would record some of Corneal's songs as well. That hadn't happened in the summer sessions – would it happen as promised in the sessions planned for later in the year? Gram tried not to tie himself down, but he did promise Jon that there would be more recording in the new sessions where he could put some stuff down. Having allayed Corneal's concerns, Gram confessed to Nuese that he had been having serious second thoughts about inviting Corneal to LA in the first place.

Gram also had his own personal problems to deal with. Nancy was pregnant, and there was a fairly heavy emotional scene revolving around that. During the late summer months of 1967, Gram fell out of contact with nearly everyone except Steve Aldberg, his personal manager. Beset by various problems, Gram lamented his lack of profile. When Aldberg heard Nancy was pregnant, he was thrown into a tailspin – how could he continue to promote Gram as an artiste when he had a wife and child to support? It almost certainly tied him down to the life of working musician.

During one unpleasant encounter at the Sweetzer Avenue house, Aldberg insisted that Nancy terminate the pregnancy immediately. Peter Fonda was present and was shocked that Gram would let his manager say something like that to his wife, without standing up for her. "All this time, I thought you were different and here you are, acting like a... punk!" He spat the insult out. Gram was so shocked, he nearly fainted. Fonda's admonition proved valuable, since no more was said by anyone about a termination. However, Nancy's faith in her young husband was shaken to the core, and she began to wonder whether the same stars that had brought them together would soon force them apart.

Meanwhile, Gram's behaviour started to deteriorate – not because of drugs, as has been suggested, but simply because the responsibility proved to be too much, especially for someone so young who had never had to commit himself to anything. He had proposed to Nancy, who was overjoyed and the wedding plans were going ahead. In the meantime, Gram left his pregnant girlfriend at home while he hit the clubs, and threw all his energy into singing. As for Nancy, Gram had drunkenly told some friends that he suspected the child wasn't his. This nasty slur got back to Nancy, and only made their domestic situation worse.

At the end of the fall, Hokom contacted Gram about the next round of sessions. The rest of the songs were recorded in November with additional input from Jay Dee Maness, Joe Osborn and Chris Ethridge on bass, Glen Campbell on some guitar and harmonies and studio session player Earl 'Les' Ball on piano. Using the best LA country players gave the album a very upbeat sound that owed more of a debt to Bakersfield than Nashville. Gram openly enthused about the album to several interviewers, no doubt aware that, despite the Hazlewood dramas, he had managed to turn out something that sounded close to what he heard in his own head.

"I was thinking about it the other night" he later told one reporter, "that's probably the best country album I've done, because it had a lot of really quick shuffle, brilliant [snaps his fingers]-sounding country. Once in a while with the Burritos, I'd run into some freak that had nine copies of it or something. Nobody else had ever heard of it. It had a lovely black and white album cover and I had like, four songs I had written on it that were some good ones. I was real young and I got real carried away. I did some Arthur 'Big Boy' Crudup, things like 'That's Alright Mama,' and 'Miller's Cave' and 'Folsom Prison Blues'. But it was all recorded in a week, mixed in one day. If you have everything at your disposal, your own recording studio or even a house full of sound equipment and you're in the right town and things aren't driving you crazy, or you can put up with it long enough to get an album out and make the bread, then you got it made. We wanted the big money so bad, needed it."

Gram also recorded a supple and poignant version of "Satisfied Mind" for the Submarine Band album, a song mostly associated with Porter Wagoner and more recently covered by the Byrds on their album *Turn! Turn! Turn!*. Of more interest to Hokom were the originals, which she found to possess a certain life of their own. She sent rough mixes to various friends and acquaintances like Phil Everly. Phil thought was that the album was fantastic and he offered his encouragement in the form of liner notes, as did Hazlewood's buddy Duane Eddy, who was also taken by the almost-rock feel of the songs. "The Glen Campbells and others I knew were very excited by this," says Hokom, "because this wasn't some guy who thought, 'I'm gonna do a parody'. It was his love for the music that they saw."

The soon-to-be-released *Safe At Home* featured another exceptional and emotionally pivotal song, 'Do You Know How It Feels To Be Lonesome'. This song was co-written with Barry Goldberg, a member of the Electric Flag, the group to whom the ISB mimed in Fonda's film, *The Trip*. He had helped Gram write the song in early 1967, shortly after being introduced to Parsons at a Hollywood party to celebrate the completion of the movie.

Gram was never averse to asking other writers for help with his songs. He valued more experienced songsmiths' opinions on his self-penned material, and then when they made suggestions as to how the song might be improved he would insist on crediting them. Many believe that Gram's co-writes with other artists count among his strongest material. While solo self-composed material like "Brass Buttons" is unequivocally strong, Parsons' lyrics seemed to find illumination with other writers. People like Chris Hillman and later Chris Ethridge, both supremely skilled songwriters in their own right, assisted in the creation of many nuanced, beautifully arranged songs with Parsons.

While he may not have actively sought out the kind of songwriting relationship which flourished between Lennon and McCartney, Parsons gravitated toward writers who, with their superior experience, could nurse his wordy creations into a greater life of their own. As later evinced on *GP*, Gram could veer between the lyrical free association of "A Song For You" and the strictly metered economy of the confessional "How Much I've Lied", a co-write with Pam Rifkin.

"Do You Know How It Feels" was a truly touching song, even with the near-parody of its prefacing statement, "Polka Varieties Farmer John Sausages presents Jon Corneal answering the musical question: Do you know how it feels to be lonesome? Take 22." Its dramatic canter, accented by Earl Ball's strolling piano bass line, brings this treatment on home to Bakersfield, while a later rendition on *Gilded Palace of Sin* veers closer to Hollywood.

A creation of Cowboy Jack Clement, the renegade Sun Studios engineer/

producer of Elvis and a true Memphis eccentric, "Millers Cave" parades all the touchstones of great country music: infidelity, jealousy, madness (however short-lived), murder and, finally, a comforting lack of regret on the part of the song's protagonist. Having shot his girl (who is never named) and the presumably bear-like Big Dave after catching them out, the guilty party removes the bodies with some difficulty to a hole in Tiger Mountain, known as Millers Cave. The murders are shortly to be avenged, as the protagonist is forever lost inside the mountain cave.

Bringing to mind the fascination that Gram had for R&B is "Strong Boy", a country soul tune that evokes considerable machismo and awkward sensitivity, as the singer gamely asserts,

"You may be her boy but I'm her man".

The implication is that any guy wanting to muscle in on Gram's action had better watch out. Gram didn't even have to resort to threats, he just delivers this killer denouement,

"Stick around and watch my love roll by"

That's about as much cracker bravado as you're ever likely to uncover in one of his songs. "Luxury Liner" was a different kettle of fish. Barry Tashian was stirred to hear the casual way in which Gram raked the strings in this lissom number, even as he wrote it. Tashian swears that this song is part of the same lineage as Ray Charles's take on country. Listen as Gram moves onto more familiar ground, what Stanley Booth describes as "not feeling at home anywhere".

Safe At Home the album title might be, but Gram was anything but. He was lost in the canyons and hills of Los Angeles, drifting through fuggy Hollywood bars and colliding with other confused, scared souls along the way. As *Gilded Palace of Sin* would later delight in rhinestone pageantry and the antics of midnight cowboys, *Safe At Home* has a fine vantage point over Sin City, watching it through a telescope, peering into its heart through the smog and hoping, no, *praying* to find a good bar and a sweet blonde girl.

Despite Gram's claim that the album had been recorded in a week, it was cut in two very distinct phases of three full studio days each time, the equivalent of ten sessions, stretching over a five-month period.

"Suzy was a nice person who got the job done," says Jon Corneal of the experience. "I thought she was classy. I found out many years later that Suzy had played our album for George Harrison when Apple Records was happening and George was interested in her producing another album on us for Apple, but Lee Hazlewood wouldn't let her do it."

As Jon Corneal remembered it, John Nuese remained committed to the band, but was losing interest in spending the nights in honky-tonks and the mornings in bed, as he still had rent to pay. "In the early days in L.A., Gram and I would go sit in with the band at the Palomino but we couldn't talk John Nuese into doing it with us. So basically, when we played live around L.A. it was Gram and me and whoever the house band was. One time we did that and the house band was the Byrds."

CHAPTER 4
GROWING UP WITH THE COUNTRY
From *Safe At Home* to *Sweetheart of the Rodeo*

"If it weren't for the rocks in its bed, the stream would have no song."

Carl Perkins

"Folk music is the only music where it isn't *simple! It's weird, man, full of legend, myth, Bible and ghosts ... and chaos? Yeah, chaos ..."*

Bob Dylan

Folk music and in particular, folk-rock, that lazily-named conjoining of musical styles, were not so far away from rock music, especially not in 1967. Every rock band that ever had a credible musical voice was protesting. Even those without a credible musical voice were trying to make some stand. Against what, it wasn't always obvious. But the Byrds? They weren't a *protest* band, man. One of the reasons McGuinn and Crosby had fallen out was because Crosby had started ranting onstage about the Warren Commission into the assassination of John F. Kennedy.

The Byrds were a rock 'n' roll group – based in folk music, sure; melodic, occasionally sour and angry about a thing or two, but they weren't into social protest. That wasn't their milieu. That was all in their collective pasts. The heroic, Homeric Dylan was now a distant figure. Since the motorcycle accident, it appeared that he wasn't interested in protesting about anything and some wondered if in fact he ever had been. Moreover, he was now prone to making a peculiar 'pre-folk' music of the early-twentieth century kind in the cellars of Woodstock, putting it down on tape for his own amusement, with the Band mixing up the medicine. It was, on the whole, a time of clashing ideas. Musically speaking, it seemed that 'anachronism' was the watchword.

Anachronistic or not, the Byrds had had enough in January, 1968. Things weren't going great for them – their newly recorded album of space-country-folk-rock *The Notorious Byrd Brothers* was going great guns with the critics, but the audiences *hated* it or, worse, were ambivalent. Those enlightened children couldn't dig what the Byrds had to say after making one of the most interesting albums yet in their five-album career. Even at that time, The Byrds were in danger of splitting up altogether. In that troubled twelve-month period of 1966-67, McGuinn and Hillman had sacked David Crosby and the airplane-phobic Gene Clark had left the group, rejoined and left again. He had returned to the Byrds' nest for just three weeks. To cap it all off, drummer Michael Clarke left the group just weeks after the release of *Notorious*. Already the movement towards space-country-rock had been hinted at with the inclusion on two tracks of the Palomino Club's celebrity pedal steel player, LA session maven Red Rhodes.

By a turn of events, some deliberate, most of them unexpected, the first day of 1968 saw The Byrds reduced to just two original members, founder-member Roger McGuinn and Chris Hillman, after the dismissal of David Crosby. The band had been playing more and more to college audiences, a group that Crosby in particular had been disdainful of, saying that rock music should not be intellectualised. The band now fought for a chance at continuing their career and retaining their market against the passionate onslaught of acts like the Jefferson Airplane and Moby Grape, as well as their old friendly rivals, the Rolling Stones and The Beatles.

The Beatles had lain down a gauntlet with *Sgt. Pepper's Lonely Hearts Club Band*, the LSD-influenced album that had in turn prodded the Stones towards the troubled *Their Satanic Majesties Request*. That album was recorded "under the influence of bail", according to Mick Jagger, who had seen the inside of courtrooms and jail cells too much that year. The result was a stilted but occasionally glorious album. Still, the results were far-reaching. Richards and Jagger were making it in rock music as bandleaders who wrote and arranged more and more on their own terms, with the once-heavy influence of blues and R&B enthusiast Brian Jones dissipating album by album.

Notorious Byrd Brothers was a complete, wide-ranging take on English psychedelia through the opposite end of the cultural telescope. English rock in 1967 was tempered by lysergics, but it was also about girls in mauve maxi-skirts, the influence of English writer Edward Lear (of whom John Lennon was an admirer) and a certain sense of tranquillity that was mostly untouched by the underlying anger and cynicism of American psychedelia, which had been filtered through the harsh reality of Vietnam and the scores of acid casualties already drifting through Haight-Ashbury.

The Byrds themselves weren't immune to the LSD experience, but they chose not to glorify it overtly, preferring a kind of backhanded approach. There had been conjecture about their song 'Eight Miles High', as most observers and more than a few critics called it a 'drug song'. Of course it was actually about Gene Clark's fear of flying and his feelings on landing in a foreign, unfriendly country. The new album was aimed to showcase a certain sense of the *zeitgeist*, capturing it with a song that Crosby had submitted for inclusion – 'Triad', a song about a three-way affair. Reflecting the promiscuity of the 60s didn't sit well with the rest of the Byrds and McGuinn vetoed the song, bringing about a series of internal feuds that culminated in Crosby leaving the band. Still, the album featured a Chris Hillman composition, 'Artificial Energy', a paean to the use of speed, with the curiously vicious sentiment, "I'm coming down off amphetamine/and I'm in jail 'cause I killed a queen".

Notorious... also included the country stylings of one Clarence Eugene White, a fine guitarist who had begun his career playing bluegrass with The Kentucky Colonels while in his early teens. Clarence's approach to playing altered radically when he took up the electric guitar. By the age of 22, he had become a fluent jazz- and rock-influenced guitar player, treading a similar path to session guitarists like James Burton and Jimmy Bryant. White was the LA scene's superpicker, having mastered bluegrass, country and even, to a degree, blues-rock. He was one of the many musicians of that period who was interested in merging country and rock and refining the results. White, throughout his lamentably short career, redefined all the possibilities for electric guitar in country music.

Clarence White was born in Madawaska, Maine on June 7, 1944. His French-Canadian family name was originally LeBlanc. Eric White, Sr. played a number of instruments, including fiddle, guitar and banjo and his four children Roland, Eric Jr.,

Joanne and Clarence all took up music at a young age. The Whites, as the family had now anglicised their name, moved to California in the early 1950s, where Eric took a job with the Lockheed company.

Clarence picked up the guitar and soon developed a close interest in bluegrass through his elder brother Roland. They formed a bluegrass group called the Three Little Country Boys, which due to their extraordinary talents became very popular, the trio frequently appearing on television. Through the group's regular local shows, Clarence came to know rated country guitar player Joe Maphis, also a Los Angeles resident. Maphis turned the young guitarist onto his favourite non-country players, in particular Charlie Christian, who played with Benny Goodman, and French Gypsy jazzman Django Reinhardt.

By 1958, the group had been joined by banjo picker Billy Ray Lathum and dobroist LeRoy MacNees, also known as LeRoy Mack. With the folk movement gaining momentum throughout America, bluegrass groups were included in the boom and the Country Boys, as they were now known, had begun to include the Hollywood folk coffeehouses and clubs in their itinerary. They then were invited to appear on the Andy Griffith Show on television, which boosted their profile as musicians.

Eric White Jr. left the group and got married in 1961 and Roland was drafted into the army in 1962. At that point, the group became The Kentucky Colonels, one of the best and certainly one of the most youthful bluegrass groups in America. Clarence saw legendary blind guitarist Doc Watson play at a Hollywood club that year and experienced something approaching epiphany. Watson turned out to be the most significant country music influence on Clarence, whose approach to flatpicking guitar (as opposed to fingerstyle) deepened and took on aspects of swing and jazz. Most importantly, his phrasing became much more distinctive.

The Kentucky Colonels recorded one seminal album, *Appalachian Swing*, which showcased Clarence's strong lead playing and his commitment to a marriage of styles outside bluegrass or folk. During a 1964 tour of America, he befriended a young San Francisco-based bluegrass banjo and guitar player named Jerry Garcia who became a close friend.

By 1965, the folk boom years were over. Many of the more established bluegrass artists forged ahead with their music, regardless of prevailing trends. But Clarence was the same age as the young rock artists who were enjoying much success on the back of the Dylan-led 'electric folk' movement. Younger acts like the Dillards started to buy electric instruments to meet their commitments, a move which attracted much criticism from purists. The gigs were becoming sporadic, so The Kentucky Colonels, keen to keep a regular paying gig at a bowling alley, hired a drummer and began playing more straight country. Clarence was personally looking for more inspiration, and found it outside of bluegrass and straight C&W. "It wasn't so much that I was getting bored with acoustic bluegrass," he said in an interview. "I could feel so many new things in the air. I wanted to get in the stream of a new kind of music that combined what you could call a 'folk integrity' with electric rock."

In later interviews, Clarence explained how he saw the music scene in 1965, the year that he bought his first electric guitar, a '54 Fender Telecaster: "[It was] as if [bluegrass] had reached a peak at that time and the only thing that could have happened was what happened – electrifying folk music, or even electrifying bluegrass music, which could have still been called 'folk rock'. But a lot of it had to do with the material, too – Dylan's songs; everything was timed just right, I think. With his material and the Byrds – all previously folk musicians. It was just a great idea." White's ideas of amalgamating styles literally emerged at the same time that Gram's did.

Turning now to the guitarists he knew through the folk and country scene in LA, he called in and got some lessons from James Burton, then one of the premier session guitarists in town. But input from others hardly seemed necessary. Clarence's style on the electric was already remarkably mature. Within a year, he was trying to imitate the sound of a steel guitar – one of his favourite instruments. Recognising the similarity between the two instruments, Clarence attempted many moves in order to replicate the distinctive pedal bend. Anyone who heard him play in the early days of his love affair with his Tele was amazed by his playing.

His work with seminal country-rock band Nashville West in 1966 had attracted the attention of many musicians, particularly Hillman, who had been acquainted with White since the early 1960s, when their paths crossed in bluegrass circles. White could play rock with a striking tone that straddled the stinging attack of Bakersfield and the shimmering glass sound of San Francisco. Jerry Garcia by now considered White to be one of the greatest guitarists in America.

White worked regularly as both a session and live musician at World Pacific Studios in Bakersfield, in between working live gigs around LA and Bakersfield. He first became involved with the Byrds when they asked him to play on their version of the Goffin-King composition 'I Wasn't Born To Follow'. Clarence's picking was lively and fluid and the band augmented it with phasing during post-production, a relatively new studio trick that the Byrds were sold on.

Clarence also worked on another track on *Notorious...*, a Hillman-McGuinn philosophical ramble through Eastern mysticism called 'Change Is Now'. "It was another one of those guru-spiritual-mystic songs that no-one understood," McGuinn said about the song. Writer David Fricke noted that the song was the only one to "feature the contrasting talents of both David Crosby and Clarence White". The country picking stands proudly alongside the mystical bent of the lyrics, an interesting and unusual combination.

Now that Crosby was out of the band, the remaining Byrds could see no problem with accepting further bookings to play at college campuses around the nation. The only real problem was that the band was struggling along in the trio format. Roger McGuinn, in an interview with author Johnny Rogan, said, "We were playing these little gigs and it was terrible. It was really not a good time with the three of us. We needed someone."

The band was about to find itself a new direction and a new way of looking at music. It had come about prior to the climactic sacking of Crosby. In 1967, Chris was standing in a queue in a West Hollywood bank when he spotted the young man whom he knew had stolen Crosby's old lady, Nancy Lee Ross.

"We had on the same kind of jeans and the same looks on our faces," said Gram of the chance meeting. The two struck up a conversation and both found the rapport easy. Hillman was only a few years older than Gram but he'd already seen a lot of the world in that time. Gram was impressed with Chris's reaction to him, and pleased with himself. Chris Hillman seemed like a cool, down-to-earth guy, and Gram was all too aware of his reputation as a direct sort of person.

Hillman was a scenemaker *par excellence* and one with an impeccable country and bluegrass pedigree. He hailed from the San Diego area, where as a young man he was turned onto folk music by the likes of the Weavers and Pete Seeger. While other kids got their kicks from the buttoned-down likes of The Kingston Trio and the New Christy Minstrels (of whom Barry McGuire was a member), Chris got lost in bluegrass. Flatt and Scruggs and the Gosdin Brothers were two of his favourites, and he was inspired enough to pick up the mandolin. By age sixteen, he was good enough at it to join the Golden State Boys, a Southern Californian phenomenon that happened to star Rex Gosdin and singer Vern Gosdin. When the Gosdins made their foray into folk music, they even went so far as to name themselves the Hillmen. Chris was also, at various times, a member of the Scottsville Squirrelbarkers and the Greengrass Group, who, according to Roger McGuinn, played a "horrible, watered-down Disneyland kind of version of bluegrass".

Hillman was already aware of Parsons' reputation in certain circles as something of a prodigy (he was only 22) and, knowing his taste for things country, folk and rock, kept him in mind as someone to keep an eye on. When it came time to find someone to replace at least one of the Byrds valuable departed members, Hillman's mind turned to Gram, so he contacted Larry Spector and requested Gram's telephone number. Parsons was invited down to audition at a rehearsal with new drummer, Kevin Kelley, who had played with LA cult musicians Taj Mahal and Ry Cooder in Rising Sons, one of the most talked-about groups of that period. Kelley was an ex-Marine and a former composition student, who also happened to be Hillman's cousin.

The Byrds were looking for a multi-instrumentalist, preferably a keyboard player who would sing tenor. As Ben Fong-Torres points out in *Hickory Wind*, what they got was a "monster in sheep's clothing," a lead vocalist and a so-so rhythm guitarist. McGuinn was still thinking fondly of Coltrane and the subsequent raga-rock stylings that had evolved on 'Eight Miles High'. He has claimed a number of times that he was looking for someone who could handle jazz piano. Hillman, on the other hand, cannot recollect anyone saying anything to him about the Byrds trying to find a jazz pianist in early 1968. It may be that McGuinn did not tell anyone else about his interest in finding a jazz pianist at the time. Even so, Gram faked a pretty nice McCoy Tyner-style blues, sang well and played some okay guitar. Better still, he was a sweet kid who didn't seem ego-crazed (but whose ego was still *healthy*) and he seemed to fit in nicely with the band.

McGuinn felt the urge to continue in the experimental direction set out on *Notorious*... with the continued use of Moog and electronic instruments as well as the more obvious jazz leanings. Having had Moog musician Paul Beaver (of Beaver and Krause) play on that album had made more of an impression on the critics than it had on a broad audience, but McGuinn was convinced that a keyboard player would suit the band. Now that Parsons was on board, ostensibly as a keyboardist, changes to the sound were imminent, although not in the manner that McGuinn had anticipated.

By the time Parsons had been in the band for a week, he was already singing country songs, as if to prove a point. Gram was never meant to follow, was never meant to be a sideman to anyone or any band. His thing was moulding bands to his own specifications. So while Parsons was singing the Buck Owens tune 'Under Your Spell Again', Hillman hit the tenor part and sealed the country music fate of the one-time folk-rockers. As Hillman recalled wistfully: "Gram was the first person I had come across since leaving country music and entering rock & roll that understood what country was, understood how it felt to play it."

Gram had only been a member of the Byrds a matter of weeks when he received word from LHI that the International Submarine Band album *Safe At Home* was finally to see a full release. It was frustrating for him that it had taken so long to see the light of day, particularly since he had given up hope of the record ever being released and he was now in the process of furthering his career in an entirely new direction. He was called on to give his approval to the final cover artwork, which was a black and white impression of John Nuese, Gram, Jon Corneal and Bob Buchanan. No photographs of this short-lived, studio-only lineup of the ISB ever existed and so the artist took the liberty of doing a fine line drawing from a series of shots of Gram, Jon and John dressed like the Southern gents they nearly all were. A photograph of Buchanan was adapted and added to the group, all of them now seated on a couch.

On hearing that the album was to be released, Gram and Bob Buchanan again hooked up in Florida, where Gram made another trip for more funds. The pair took the train up to Nashville to call in on John Nuese and Jon Corneal, who had both moved back to Nashville to work on Music Row, selling their substantial abilities as musicians for hire. Gram and Bob stayed for a few days, visiting bars and outraging the locals with their floppy fringes. Buchanan and Parsons were about to get on the train to return to Los Angeles and Corneal, with Nuese riding shotgun, drove the LA-bound duo to the station.

"John Nuese and I had the opportunity to go on the train and check out their room," said Corneal. "And Gram said, "Well, you all are welcome to go with us!" But we couldn't because I had driven my car to the station and I didn't have anywhere to put it. So we declined the free train trip out to LA and brought up the rear by driving my car out to LA a few days later. That was in early '68."

On the return train trip to Los Angeles, Gram and Bob sat in their cabin with their guitars and fooled around with country songs. Gram produced one of his notebooks, which accompanied him everywhere. In them, he recorded lyric ideas and aimless doodles, all in his backward-slanted, looping longhand. He asked Bob to help him with a little song he had put together. The song had as yet incomplete lyrics but it had a central recurring theme – nostalgia.

Gram explained to Bob about the hickory and oak trees near his grandparents' Tennessee home and the box pines of South Georgia that he had climbed as a child. Bob understood perfectly; he had climbed the same trees of childhood. The peaceful whisper of a soft summer breeze moving through the boughs of a hickory tree brought about in Gram some unnameable yearning. This feeling represented a central *motif* of Gram's youth. Something about the serenity of that scene, wherever it had taken place, had left its mark. Rather than fall back on the device of unrequited love, he brought forth a yearning for an innocence lost too young.

The poetry of the lyrics was so potent, so evocative that Buchanan immediately began to suggest more lyrical ideas. Framed as a delicate waltz that clattered along as sleepily as a train along its tracks, 'Hickory Wind' began to take shape. Gram and Bob wisely chose to balance the sentimental with an almost world-weary eye on this new life they found themselves living.

> "I started out younger/ at most everything
> All the riches and pleasures/ what else can life bring?
> But it makes me feel better/ each time it begins
> Calling me home/ Hickory Wind"

Those lines are as essential a distillation of the sadness that comes with the accumulation of adult knowledge as have ever been written. Having had to relinquish his hold on childhood at such a young age tore him internally, producing such powerful emotions as he found himself articulating with the helpful input of Bob Buchanan. The only song the pair wrote together, it was the first in a long line of confessional and moving songs that Gram would pen with other collaborators.

✣ ✣ ✣ ✣ ✣ ✣

Safe At Home failed to make any impression upon its release. Despite its current status as a minor saint in the church of country-rock, there would be no further action taken with the International Submarine Band as an entity until the late 1980s, when Jon Corneal and Ian Dunlop made a misjudged attempt to release an album using the name. Gram had made an album about which his feelings were initially mixed. It didn't matter; he had gotten what he'd wanted out of LHI and it hadn't achieved what he had hoped for. So began his tenure with the Byrds. With no group left to promote the album, Hazlewood and Gram both lost interest. The Sub Band went down with all hands.

Of course, it's not like the Byrds had never played country before, either. Like just about every band at the time, they had tooled up a few country-flavoured songs of their own. Hillman's 'Girl With No Name' and 'Time Between' on *Younger Than Yesterday* present evidence of a viable flirtation with country music in the context of a beat group. Hillman had long wanted a group along the lines of the Gosdin Brothers, who were now backing up the newly solo Gene Clark, playing country with a noticeably rock attitude. The Stones and The Beatles had both done country songs, but it didn't necessarily mean that everybody suddenly thought country was hip. It had a certain cachet, although it was more popular among musicians than it was among listening audiences, most of whom thought it reactionary.

Captivated by the new kid's attitude – Parsons was quietly confident without being overly arrogant, but he had a particular kind of youthful rock cool – McGuinn was working on some serious ideas for a new album. His idea was to work chronologically through 100 years of American musical history in a 'concept album' format, taking a cue from works like *Sgt. Pepper's Lonely Hearts Club Band* and the Beach Boys' *Pet Sounds,* which could themselves be conceived as miniature histories (if not affectionate pastiches) of English and American music styles. The new Byrds album would be a bold step for the band; a move that would shift them out of the musical doldrums they were in.

It was certainly a brave idea, one that gave the record company executives and accountants heart palpitations. It would, claimed McGuinn, encompass bluegrass, jazz, ragtime, blues, purist folk, Dylan (now a category of his own where the Byrds were concerned) and country. It would begin as mountain music and end as space-rock. McGuinn's Moog finger was getting itchy. He had envisioned "a chronological album starting out with old-time music … not bluegrass but pre-bluegrass, dulcimers… nasal Appalachian stuff, and then get into like the 1930s, advanced version of it, move it up to modern country, the 40s and 50s with steel guitar." The record would thus conclude, as David Fricke noted, "with a jump cut to the future" and "electronic music … a kind of space music".

But this adventurous trawl through the yellowing back pages of folk music was not to be. The rich seam that was the 'concept album' was left for the likes of Pink Floyd to mine successfully while the Byrds forged ahead in search of a direction. And the newly-hired Parsons had "a burning thing for a contemporary take on country music". "His idea," said McGuinn, "was to blend the Beatles and country; to really do something revolutionary. Gram thought we could win over the country audience. He figured once they dig you, they never let go."

McGuinn was intellectually captivated by the concept. As such, he quite wholeheartedly bought into Parsons' persuasive logic and his concept of a 'new' country music. McGuinn's newfound devotion to country music reflected similar love affairs with jazz, Indian classical music and his first sweetheart, folk music. It was natural that McGuinn would buy into the idea of a country album. Since the Byrds craved new directions after such a substantial loss of personnel, McGuinn found Parsons' ideas challenging. As Johnny Rogan notes in *Timeless Flight*, McGuinn was desirous of a "greater challenge and an opportunity to show the world that the Byrds could once again compete with the Beatles and push back the boundaries of popular music."

After a fashion, McGuinn became a 'monster' in a sequined suit himself. He bought a Cadillac and listened to country radio all day. After the band's rehearsal time had been put in, the Byrds went out on the road again briefly to test some new songs and see what else could be extracted from country. After Byrds shows, Roger, Gram, Chris and Kevin would hit the country music clubs of Palmdale and Bakersfield or the more earthy City of Industry clubs.

While the concept album was vetoed, the record company still wanted a new album out of the Byrds, and pre-production work began. It was decided that it would be a radical departure for a bunch of California longhairs to record in the heart of country music's establishment, Nashville, and the decision was rightly hailed in industry magazines as a bold step.

Some claim that the idea of working in Nashville was Parsons' idea. Even so, this new direction was voted for democratically, as was part of the Byrds' methodology. Gary Usher, Hillman and Parsons all voted against McGuinn's electronic designs and voted to take a trip to the country of country. Further rehearsals and more songwriting sessions yielded two new original compositions courtesy of Parsons, and the band moved east to Nashville where CBS had booked a week of sessions beginning 9 March, 1968 at the CBS Studios on Sixteenth and Hawkins street (now known as Music Circle), near the Country Music Hall of Fame.

The calibre of session musicians that the band called upon was also of some interest to Nashville, since they were using the core of Music City's finest pickers. There was bass player Roy M. Huskey, who had worked for Lee Hazlewood, and there was Clarence White. Pedal steel players were the legendary Nashville steeler Lloyd Green and former Buck Owens Buckeroo Jay Dee Maness, a youthful steel sessioneer who had already worked with Parsons on *Safe At Home*. John Hartford, composer of country super-standard 'Gentle On My Mind', came on board as fiddler and banjoist, and Earl 'Pool' Ball submitted his CV as piano player extraordinaire. Also drifting into the mix was Jon Corneal, ex-Sub Band drummer, who the band felt had more of a presence as a drummer than the occasionally patchy Kelley, who would often drift out of time in a live context, although his drumming in the studio was nothing short of lovely.

Signing on as producer was Gary Usher, who had recently worked with the Beach Boys as well as producing the Byrds' *Younger Than Yesterday* and *Notorious*.... Engineers Roy Halee and Charlie Bragg were responsible for the technical side of things and Byrds roadie Jimmi Seiter arranged for the delivery of two eight-track desks and the attendant tape machines, which had to be synchronised carefully so that the new 16-track configuration would work properly. Bragg and Halee had the unenviable task of calming down the Nashville engineers, who were unused to artists showing up at two in the afternoon to begin work. As Seiter noted: "This was completely foreign to their attitude because they do six tracks a day, an album in two days. That's the way Nashville does things. We take three weeks, which is short for us but on *Sweetheart Of the Rodeo*, the Byrds were going for a feel anyway."

Many other local session players dropped casually into CBS to observe the longhairs at work and to see the two eight-track recording desks used in sync, a process that had not as yet found its place in Music City. Everyone in town dropped by that week, it seemed, all interested to see these interlopers at work in a pleasantly hostile recording environment.

The sessions were relaxed enough and the amount of pot smoke around the place was hardly a surprise for Nashville, given that most of the session players seemed pretty *au fait* with it. Then, they'd worked with the likes of Willie Nelson and Ray Price, both avowed smokers, and it can't have been that much of an oddity. It seemed that the haircuts were what amused them most. Parsons seemed to fit in on as many levels as are possible for a polite young Southern gentleman (albeit one with a longish fringe) finding himself back in the South again.

Columbia had been working on a suggestion by Parsons and McGuinn that they play on the Grand Ole Opry on the second day of their sessions in Nashville. Arrangements were made with Opry management, who reluctantly (but likely still intrigued by the idea) offered them a two-song spot in the half-hour show hosted by Tompall Glaser and the Glaser Brothers. The Grand Ole Opry was a conservative institution at a time of radical political change in the South, but the Byrds were always going to be nice and polite to the audience.

The Opry, which started as the Union Gospel Tabernacle in 1892, was renamed the Ryman Auditorium after famed steamboat captain William Ryman. It had been home to country music's most famous radio station since 1925 and it was an unapologetic Southern icon. Its 50,000-watt signal took it to 30 states and an average listening audience of about 20 million people at the time the Byrds played on the show.

Just as well for the Opry folks that The Byrds had mostly shied away from the kind of overt politicism some of their contemporaries espoused. McGuinn had warned David Crosby several times about making political stands in concert and in interviews. In addition to criticising the Warren Commission, Crosby used the concert platform to give LSD his public seal of approval and proclaiming Paul McCartney's endorsement of it. The rest of the Byrds all enjoyed drugs, except for Gene Clark, who preferred to drink. They had all used LSD at one point, but to encourage the young folks to use it? That wasn't on, according to McGuinn.

But there were no pro- or anti- anything announcements made on the Opry that night, at least not by The Byrds. It was a stiff show nonetheless and changes to the running order made the stage managers nervous and the regulars angry. Even Hank Williams and Johnny Cash, two of country music's greatest singers, had been fired from the Opry; the former for not showing up when he was supposed to and the latter for dragging his microphone stand along the front of the stage and smashing all the lightbulbs.

On the evening of March 10, The Byrds took to the stage of the Ryman Auditorium, after a longish introduction by Tompall. Gram elaborated: "The condition they let us do it on was that we were gonna do our single, 'You Ain't Goin Nowhere'. We were also gonna do a Merle Haggard song because they wanted me to do something that the audience could identify with, because they had these 'longhairs' on the Opry. Even though our hair was short at that period, we were considered longhairs. They knew what we were up to." Gram was dismissive of the Nashville hierarchy who held the dough and kept the artists in line. "They think they're being really big-hearted just because they patronise guys like Kristofferson, or one or two other guys with long hair. Or three. But they're really not very open-minded in Nashville. Some of the best musicians are still starving to death in Nashville."

Tompall mentioned that Gram's family was from Tennessee and that his grandparents were out in the audience. The Byrds were pretty down-home fellows and they were as country as it was possible for an LA rock band-in-town-to-make-an-album-of-country-ish-rock to be. They still looked like girls to the audience, who nonetheless gave them a generous Opry welcome, as Glaser suggested they would. There were the occasional catcalls, some "tweet-tweets" and more than one suggestion to "join the army" and "cut your hair". However, the audience was surprised to discover that The Byrds gave good country, proving to be sweet-harmonied and reasonably authentic-sounding, even to the palates of a conservative white audience.

"Now, you're gonna sing a Merle Haggard song, aren't you?" asked Glaser, proudly showing the direction these Byrds were flying so confidently in. "Actually, we're not going to do 'Sing Me Back Home'," said Gram sweetly, throwing a spanner into the works with a crooked smile. "Instead of doing that song, I'm gonna do a song now that I wrote for my grandmother, who used to listen to the 'Grand Ole Opry' with me when I was little, and it's called 'Hickory Wind'."

This was news to McGuinn, Hillman and Kelley. They grinned at each other, knowing that they were all a little stoned after a backstage blaze, but being confident showmen they held on and followed Gram's lead. Offstage, there was pandemonium. Roy Acuff, the gentleman of country music, was "having fits" and the Glaser brothers were getting more than a little "het up" about this change to the schedule. "The Glaser Brothers just flipped out, man," said Gram, finding the memory humorous. "They were yelling at us from offstage." But the gesture didn't go unappreciated by some members, in particular Skeeter Davis, who hotly defended the Byrds' inspired move. "Skeeter Davis ran up to us after it was all over and kissed us," said Gram. "She was so happy someone had blown those guys off."

Backstage after their appearance was a different story. Tompall collared Gram and accused him of making him "look a fool on the radio". But even Gram's aunt Pauline, who had accompanied her mother and other family members to the Opry, said that the crowd had loved The Byrds. Chris could see that Gram was just playing out a role – the new breed of country star. "He took the reins. He was right smack into that – 'Here I am on the Opry. I'm Hank Williams!' – so he went with it. He played the whole role out."

With that experience behind them, the group returned to the studio to cut more songs. The first day of the session, March 9, yielded takes of Parsons' 'Hickory Wind', which would become the song most representative of his dual songwriting motifs – the moral dilemma and acute nostalgia. Its meditation on the pitfalls and uncertainties of modern life, contrasted with the simple idylls and ideals of childhood, heralded the direction of Parsons' writing for the rest of his career.

The same day, the band turned to Dylan for material, as they had done many times before. This time, it was a tune unknown to the record-buying public, 'You Ain't Goin' Nowhere'. Later appearing on the cult Dylan and The Band collection, *The Basement Tapes*, the song's abstract layerings are given even more power by the Bakersfield swing, which make it pretty oblique for first-time listeners – what does the song really mean? Hillman and McGuinn had access to the Columbia tape libraries and had chosen the unreleased song, along with 'Nothing Was Delivered'. As with many Dylan songs, there are no absolutes and no reference points lyrically, but rather a series of purposefully abstract rural images redolent of Dylan's woodshedding in the Catskills after his 1966 'motorcycle accident'.

The Byrds stumbled through some takes of Gram's tune 'Lazy Days', with disappointing results. It could be that the song was too anaemic and inert to justify a serious attempt at recording it; perhaps only tried out of a desire to mollify Parsons' feelings about being the newest – yet most adventurous and influential – member of the group. The treatment is sickly Chuck Berry-style R&B, but it is executed mercifully in under 3.30, hinting at the possibility that it was being considered for a single. It's also possibly an exercise in damage control, lest the sessions became overburdened with choice cuts. Of course, they may merely have been having some fun with it.

The other Dylan tune was recorded at the end of the band's stay in Nashville, on March 15. The two Dylan songs would bookend the new album, giving a more contemporary feeling to a record, which was paying homage to country music as a broad church of styles, extending beyond the rural and the honky-tonk.

It was clear that McGuinn, Hillman and Parsons were attempting to place the accent on a respectful, traditional feel to all of the selected material. The musical environment of 1968 was charged and political, with many groups choosing to espouse anti-establishment viewpoints in song. By recording such an album, the band was moving against all the set trends and embarking on a musical movement that harked back to a different but no less troubled time in American history.

One artist who hadn't fallen into politicism was Dylan, who had always tried to avoid addressing the obvious in his music. After having been silent artistically for some time, Dylan's 1968 album *John Wesley Harding,* released in January, was a sombre, spiritual and reflective work tinged with his obvious personal quietude and domestic tranquillity. It was also moving more and more into the very personal realm at a time when rock music tended to address the public disquiet over Vietnam and the overbearing Johnson presidential administration. Dylan had turned towards the religious imagery of 'I Dreamed I Saw St Augustine' and, in general, a more compassionate view of a society he had once sought to admonish. The overwhelming perception of the album was that it was lacking in the hostility that had characterised *Highway 61 Revisited*.

Interestingly, Dylan had turned to a musical style that had confounded listeners everywhere. The obvious sparseness of sound, the reliance on melody, was effected by a basic group of Nashville session men, Kenny Buttrey, Charlie McCoy and Pete Drake. Dylan was no longer railing into the void; he was addressing problems in the modern world with a whisper, the musicians reinforcing the mood and sound that Dylan had previously captured either with his acoustic guitar or with the sweet metallic roar of the Band behind him.

In his Woodstock study, Bob was said to have kept a Bible open on a wooden stand. This, along with the collected works of Hank Williams, was to develop his sense of "moderation". Like William Blake, Dylan had found a palace of wisdom at the end of a road of excess. In his book, *No Direction Home*, author Robert Shelton noted that the works of 1965-66 had brought about "a new compassion, a sense of musical, physical, spiritual and religious calm". There was apparent in this new album "a very Judaic, even Christian sense of guilt and the need for atonement".

This sense of the need for redemption, if only as a concept aimed at bringing peace to a troubled society, was very apparent in the Byrd's new album. Songs like 'The Christian Life', a tune from the pen of country duo the Louvin Brothers, spoke of a religious conviction that may not have truthfully taken hold in the band in any way. Yet morality and a certain undeniable belief in rightness – if not righteousness – was part of the Byrds' very core. The Old Testament belief in the cycles of life had dictated (according to Pete Seeger anyway) the very ethos of the 1960s, a time to every purpose under heaven, a time for peace.

On March 12, the Byrds made a u-turn and cut Woody Guthrie's 'Pretty Boy Floyd'. The next day, electric guitars, drums and bass were abandoned for the recording of the bluegrass standard, 'I Am A Pilgrim'. "It was my idea to do 'I Am A Pilgrim'," claimed Hillman in an interview with Johnny Rogan for the excellent liner notes for the 1997 remastered re-release of *Sweetheart Of The Rodeo*. "I used to play that song with Clarence White during the bluegrass days."

The song made the grade as the second single to be taken from the album, "representing The Byrds' most serious foray into country music to date". The traditional bluegrass feel was as authentic as several versions released in recent years by the Kentucky Colonels, the hot bluegrass outfit that had first made Clarence White a studio name. White's hot bluegrass licks rolled with casual yet devastating power behind Hillman's fast and smooth mandolin work. McGuinn had picked up an electric banjo from Rickenbacker, who made the 12-string guitars brought to fame by both George Harrison and McGuinn. John Hartford added fiddle to the track, making it as authentic as any bluegrass track recorded at the time.

The Nashville sessions would eventually yield eight songs, five of which made it onto the final cut of the album. Of the unused takes from the Nashville sessions, only the droning blues version of Greenwich cult folkie Tim Hardin's '(You Got A) Reputation' is worthy of consideration. From the start, its hurdy-gurdy undertow and harmony-laden vocals are captivating, and the eventual exclusion of it from the finished product can only allow one to speculate as to how it might have affected the album. With its vaguely psychedelic air, it would sit equally as comfortably with any of the *Notorious* sessions of less than twelve months before.

Roger and Gram had also agreed that a more traditional folk tune would be in order, given the original conceptual vision the pair had for the album. The choice was 'Pretty Polly', a traditional murder ballad that McGuinn and Parsons were both familiar with from their respective folk singing careers. As it turned out, the song ran in counter motion to the rest of the songs and it was dropped from the draft track list quite early on.

At the end of their brief stay in Music City, the band packed up their instruments and their eight-track desks and moved out of Nashville, never to return. They embarked on a series of college shows around the East Coast. The Byrds, more energised than they'd been in some time, found the new line-up warmly received, particularly at MIT in Boston, where the band received standing ovations from the crowd. The audience profile was clearly changing, partly due to the audiences they were discovering on university campuses. They were now playing for a different and more discerning congregation of converts. Students, rather than the callow teens that had been the core of the Byrds' audience previously, were to provide the group with renewed credibility for the rest of their career.

They returned to LA in the first week of April for the West Coast debut of the new lineup and songs at the official farewell party for Derek Taylor, who was returning to London to work at Apple Records as the Beatles' publicist. The party was held at Ciro's, the club where, in 1965, the band had made its auspicious debut. This time Gene Clark remained in the audience, although he apparently attempted a brief comeback that evening, and David Crosby was nowhere nearby. The lineup was down to just two of the original members and came complete with a young man on pedal steel, to whom the band referred repeatedly as "J.D" or "good ol' J.D".

It was of course Jay Dee Maness, who until recently had been Tom Brumley's replacement in Buck Owens' Buckaroos group. *Rolling Stone* was on hand to comment on the new direction The Byrds were taking with their new band member, set in ink erroneously as 'Graham Parsons' by journalist Jerry Hopkins. "They appear secure in the country milieu," observed Hopkins sagely, complimenting Parsons on his talents. "Graham sings often and he sings well, sharing 'lead voice' with Roger."

McGuinn was his customary polite self, giving much credit for their new direction to Gram. "Graham's [sic] bag is country and we're going to let him do his thing and support him and work together on things," McGuinn enthused politely. The sentiments would shortly change. Back in the CBS studio in Los Angeles, on April 4 for a one-day session before a 10-day break, the band recorded the Merle Haggard song that earned a place on the album, 'Life in Prison'. Gram later claimed that the song's appearance on *Sweetheart was* purely accidental. He had arranged it as a 'warm-up number'. He went on to say that if he had had further input into the sequencing, it never would have made it on there at all. The fact that as many as 15 takes of the song were recorded indicates that it certainly had a better than average chance of being a contender.

On the 14th of April, the Byrds appeared on *Sam Riddle's 9th Street West* television show, miming to two songs unrelated either to the *Sweetheart* sessions or the renewed lineup – 'Eight Miles High' and 'So You Wanna Be A Rock 'n' Roll Star'. In between takes, Gram perched on the edge of the one of the risers the rest of the band were standing on, with his guitar in his lap, and mimed playing dobro. His presence in the band, like Kelley's, went unremarked upon by the host, who had no idea of the country music leanings the Byrds were soon to display.

Jay Dee had been unable to attend. Gram's continued insistence that Roger take the young steel guitarist on as a member of the Byrds had put Roger in the position of having to point blank refuse Gram's suggestion, something that he was unused to doing. Having failed to get Maness into the Byrds, Gram continued to talk about getting another steel player, Sneaky Pete Kleinow, on board.

Upon their return to the studio the next day, April 15th, the band went into overdrive to complete the album in order to meet touring obligations that fall. Spector and CBS were already in the process of organising a tour that would take in a good part of the western world, including Europe, Great Britain and South Africa. The band completed a version of the William Bell composition 'You Don't Miss Your Water', showcasing the influence of soul on the band, in particular that Southern phenomenon country-soul. Otis Redding had recorded a great version for his *Otis Blue* album in 1965, but the version the Byrds recorded adhered very closely to the 'blues-waltz rhythm' of Bill Bell's 1961 Stax original. By adding melodic country counterpoint to the song the arrangement actually transcends any specific genre, filling the space once occupied by horns with pedal steel, but keeping some of the R&B emoting that made the song attractive to Parsons and Hillman in the first place.

On April 17th, the George Jones drinking standard, 'You're Still On My Mind', was laid down. Penned by Luther McDaniel, this near-parody of alcoholic melancholy was treated to one of Parsons' best vocals of all time. It was doubly notable because it escaped the subsequent culling suffered by other Parsons vocal takes. 'One Hundred Years from Now' in particular was a beautifully paced track as sung by Parsons, with a driving feel augmented by some wonderful fills from Clarence White. The power of 'Hickory Wind' can't be underestimated either. Although a superior version can be heard on Parsons' later solo album *Grievous Angel*, the *Sweetheart Of The Rodeo* version had enough nostalgia and country canter to appeal to a wide range of listeners. Well, that was the hope of Columbia Records anyway.

But at the same time as the Byrds' lank haired, puppydog handsome newcomer was being feted by the press, who had been fed some great publicity angles by the record company, he was about to come up against a brick wall. One rather fearsome industry player whom he hadn't paid his proper respects to was about to make things very uncomfortable, and hasten his departure from the band he'd been a member of for only five months.

Gram has often been described as an 'official Byrd', but these days Hillman disagrees. He sees Gram as having been an interloper whose stay was short but effective. Of course, in his four-month tenure, he did rewire all the circuits, and broke the folk-rock mould so that they effectively became a country rock band for the rest of their flight. Gram claimed in later interviews that he had wanted to get the Byrds into playing country standards and writing some new material, rather than just "writing their own Dylan songs". He thought that McGuinn was content just to coast on past successes and "probably would have been happy just playing songs off the first two Byrds albums". He then added that he thought the originals were "a waste of time".

CHAPTER 5
CALIFORNIA STAR
Gram leaves the Byrds' nest

As the Byrds laboured over the mixing of *Sweetheart* back in Los Angeles, previous contractual agreements suddenly reared up to bite Parsons. News came from CBS's lawyers in New York that Lee Hazlewood of LHI Records had been in touch. He wanted to talk with the Byrds and their management about the small matter of a contract that Parsons still had with him. Hazlewood informed CBS that he owned the rights to Gram's vocal performances and would also try to assert a right to first refusal over any and all projects involving either Parsons' compositions or his instrumental works. The Hazlewood situation may have been exacerbated by the fact that Gram had casually announced to LHI that he was joining the Byrds. One apocryphal story has Gram walking into the offices of LHI and announcing to a stunned secretary, "I'm singing with the Byrds now, y'all. Goodbye."

This must have sounded like the worst turn of luck in the world for Gram. His star turn as vocalist on seven of the cuts and his general influence over the direction of the band was stripped away with the threat of a lawsuit. Once again, his boyhood dream of stardom became a slippery phantom, and it was the threat of action by Hazlewood that partially established a pattern in Gram's life.

As Gram put it, "Columbia, for some reason, thought they were going to get sued because my release from Lee Hazlewood looked kind of shaky. And so a few songs they overdubbed completely, things that shouldn't have been overdubbed and my voice was used way in the background, as a guide to go by. It didn't work. It gave too much of that old Byrds sound which we were fighting against at that time. Things really came out well until this thing about the suit and I don't know if everybody remembers it that way in the Byrds but I do and I think Chris [Hillman] does too. They were just about to scratch 'Hickory Wind' when somebody ran in with a piece of paper, that's the last one they had saved."

Indeed, Chris Hillman's very temperate overview of the situation bears some of Gram's claims out. "[Christian Life] should have been Gram's vocal but we had a contractual problem with Lee Hazlewood over Gram's vocals. Here's the story. Gram was signed to Lee Hazlewood and we had a problem letting him sing on a Columbia release. Lee Hazlewood International or whatever put out the Submarine album and we got Gram past on 'One Hundred Years From Now' but we didn't get him past on 'The Christian Life'. I don't know why... 'You Don't Miss Your Water' should have been Gram. Those two are the only ones that we didn't get by with and I don't know why."

When a journalist put it to Hillman that, "There have been stories that you guys went back and pulled his vocals because of his leaving the group," he vociferously denied it: "No, no. No way. His vocals were on and we really had to pull for them and that's the truth. We never would do that. Never would do that, never have done it. On *The Notorious Byrd Brothers*, David [Crosby] left in the middle of that and we did not pull his vocals off. We did not delete David's part at all. Nor would I ever do that or allow that to happen. So Gram had the vocals on those two songs and Lee Hazlewood was suing, so at the last minute Roger put his vocals on. We didn't want to, Roger didn't want to sing over them. They were Gram's songs."

No such lawsuit ever materialised, but the threat was enough to send a flurry of letters between solicitors acting for Hazlewood and CBS. After the phone call from Lee, Gram's vocals were mostly stripped away from the tracks they had once occupied. At the time, Gram was terribly hurt by the decision to remove his stamp from that part of the sound, although he gamely tried not to show it. He later lamented to *Rolling Stone* scribe Cameron Crowe that Roger "fucked it up". He was also heard to blame producer Gary Usher. Gram said in one interview that Usher had decided the album should be "Hollywood freaky and it wasn't the time for that. I thought it was the time for a *Nashville Skyline* or something like the album as I remember it, a serious country album. They just chopped up the album however they wanted to. I wasn't there when they chopped it. It was a great album that might as well have never been recorded. So there's another *Sweetheart Of The Rodeo* and, uh, I dig it."

Usher himself said before his death that Roger had been wary that Gram was "getting a little bit too much out of this thing.... He didn't want the album to turn into a Gram Parsons album. Yes, it is true that some of Parsons' leads were overdubbed because of legal problems, but those problems were resolved once we were down in Nashville, the attorneys back in Los Angeles were able to work that out. Whoever sang lead on the songs on *Sweetheart of the Rodeo* were there not because of what we could do legally but because that's how we wanted to slice the album up. We wanted to keep Gram's voice in there but we also wanted the recognition to come from Hillman and McGuinn, obviously. You just don't take a hit group and interject a new singer for no reason. There were legal problems but they were resolved and the album had just the exact amount of Gram Parsons that McGuinn, Hillman and I wanted."

These squabbles did nothing to prevent Gram working on the album or in fact remaining an active force within the band. It certainly gave McGuinn renewed interest in singing again, now that he had to cover up Gram's distinctive vocals with something more than his usual wistful singing. Enter one newfound Southern accent and some pretty interesting phrasing, particularly for a singer used to having three and sometimes four voices to back him up on record. Emmylou Harris noted that you could in fact hear a ghostly echo of Parsons if you listened to the album through a headset.

Terry Melcher, who would later attempt to produce an album with Gram, said that Gram bore a real grudge against McGuinn for what had occurred over the vocal tracks for *Sweetheart*. "Parsons got really mad because Roger told him CBS insisted on that, but [he] didn't believe it. He thought it was Roger's own idea. But Parsons had a lot of things in life distorted." Gram saw it as a power play, a grab for control of the reins again after the pretence of the previous four months of work as a 'democratic unit'. McGuinn and Hillman claim otherwise.

McGuinn says that when the problem was resolved Gram's vocals wound up back on some of the songs, but it was agreed that some of the tracks would retain the McGuinn vocals. It has been speculated that the removal of Gram's vocals from the second master of the album precipitated his leaving the Byrds. But, if McGuinn is to be believed, the timbre of the *Sweetheart* recording had, in fact, been an experiment. "I didn't view it as a permanent departure. I thought it was something we were doing for kicks, like kids dressing up for Halloween. And I got into it: it was a role-playing thing for me."

Perhaps more worrying was that in later interviews in the 1970s, McGuinn intimated that he suspected there was some sort of conspiracy underway on the part of Usher, Hillman and Parsons to get him out of the band. He later tempered this attack of paranoia by saying that he hadn't deliberately set Gram up for a tumble but that the cards had simply fallen where they had. "Gram was very ambitious and very charming. And he was a rich kid, which meant that he was already a star before he got to The Byrds – having money does that for people and they just have an attitude that they can do whatever they want. It was like *Mick Jagger* had joined The Byrds! And we just went along with it because he had a way of enticing you into doing things that he thought would be cool to do."

With the matter of vocals reaching a satisfactory resolution for both Lee Hazlewood and CBS, the album was in effect complete. CBS pressed up a single of 'You Ain't Goin' Nowhere' b/w 'Artificial Energy' to coincide with two upcoming tours, including destinations like England and Italy on the first leg then back to the United States. Two months later, gigs were planned for England, France and South Africa.

The choice of destinations didn't seem unusual, even though there may have been raised eyebrows over the inclusion of South Africa. The first show was in Rome, at the Piper Club on May 7th. Despite the language barrier, the group were very well received, even if the new sprinkling of country songs was confusing to an audience just coming to grips with *Notorious Byrd Brothers*. The Piper Club show was notable for three things. The first two were Gram's continued tuning problems onstage and the presence of Doug Dillard, adding his new-wave banjo playing to the Byrds hits of several years prior. The third is that a substantial and often-traded bootleg tape was made of the show, which is still available today. Roger McGuinn could be heard entreating the audience with the phrase, "Thank you, country music lovers" after every burst of applause.

Fortunately, the three UK shows in the second week of May, which took The Byrds to Middle Earth (May 11th) the enormously hip Covent Garden venue, were a vast improvement. Gram's keyboards and guitar were again augmented by banjoist Doug Dillard, and they played to large audiences that included Mick Jagger and Marianne Faithfull, who hosted the Byrds on that trip. Gram's role within the Byrds was being more clearly delineated by this brief UK tour, although it may not have been entirely to his liking. McGuinn was clearly happy to let Gram have as much creative freedom as he liked, while still asserting his authority as the senior Byrd. Gram might have dominated in the studio for the recording of *Sweetheart*, but 'showboating' was out of the question on tour.

It was on this lightning trip to London that Gram was to be introduced to Keith Richards and Mick Jagger, neither of whom had heard of or knew about this addition to the lineup. After the successful Middle Earth show, the two groups, with photographer Michael Cooper along for the ride, made the three-hour trip out to see Stonehenge, all piling into a Rolls Royce limousine one rainy night, with a few bottles of Johnnie Walker Red for warmth.

During the overnight excursion, McGuinn explained the forthcoming trip to South Africa and his personal reasons for doing it. As he explained, "We went down there as a political thing – to try and turn their heads around... I'd known Miriam Makeba since I'd worked with the Mitchell Trio back in the early 1960s. Miriam was from there and she'd managed to escape with the help of Harry Belafonte or somebody. She told me what a horrible place it was."

Both Jagger and Richards expressed their misgivings to McGuinn and Hillman about the trip to South Africa, but said no more. Not feeling that it was such an essential topic of discussion, Hillman and McGuinn were initially amused, then embarrassed, to observe Gram's reaction to hanging out with the Rolling Stones for the first time. They noted to each other wryly that the normally unflappable and mature Gram was, all of a sudden, seriously star-struck. His cool nearly went completely out the window. "Gram was just like a puppy dog with them," Hillman said later. "It was sort of embarrassing, like bringing your kid brother along on a date."

Back in London for breakfast with Mick and Keith, Gram was even more struck as Jagger sent the limousine driver out to fetch dry socks for the group, who were soaked to the skin after wandering in the Wiltshire countryside throughout the night, with only whiskey and acid for warmth. That night, sufficiently recovered from the Stonehenge trip with a few hours sleep and some clean clothes, the Byrds played London nightclub Blaises, the scene of their previous English triumph in 1965, when John Lennon and George Harrison had stood in the crowd and watched, sparking an intense period of creative rivalry and friendship between the two groups. The following evening, the Byrds played at London's Roundhouse club, where an excellent bootleg was taped.

The tape reveals how good this new version of the Byrds sounded as they stormed very convincingly through the first set, which was comprised of a thoughtful and wide-ranging selection of Byrds hits. After a short intermission, Roger took to the microphone and announced to the crowd: "Thank you, country music lovers. We're going to give you some country music now. I'd like to bring up Mr. Gram Parsons, who's over there with his guitar. He's going to sing a song called 'Hickory Wind'."

And so Gram wrapped up his part of the show with a tantalising look at this new direction for the group, which confounded music journalists and fans alike. But at a London press conference, McGuinn barely took time to explain this sound the Byrds had forged at the behest of Parsons, as he had so succinctly explained their diversion to raga rock to the cynical English press in 1965. Instead, one of the most widely reported comments of McGuinn's was to the effect that he had been the only member of the Byrds to actually play on their version of 'Mr. Tambourine Man'. All of this served only to bolster McGuinn's ego, as he must have felt some degree of control was slipping away with the presence of a driven and ambitious musician like Gram in his band. But even as the Byrds departed England, they were promising to return in July for another round of summer dates, before taking off on the mooted trip to South Africa.

Back in California, the Byrds began work on resequencing *Sweetheart*, which was now scheduled for release in late August, just a few weeks after the group was to return from South Africa. While the short UK tour was in progress, CBS's lawyers had resolved the issue with Lee Hazlewood fully and now there were no more tracks to be replaced.

As Gram's vocals could be retained on several of the tracks, the order was decided upon – 'You Ain't Going Nowhere', sung by McGuinn; 'I Am A Pilgrim', sung by Hillman; 'The Christian Life', one of Gram's original vocals that McGuinn overdubbed; 'You Don't Miss Your Water', again a Gram vocal overdubbed by McGuinn, and a song that Gram had already recorded a fine version of with Fred Neil; 'You're Still On My Mind', appearing complete with the original Parsons vocal; 'Pretty Boy Floyd', a McGuinn vocal; 'Hickory Wind', naturally a Parsons vocal original; 'One Hundred Years From Now', a Parsons composition with vocals by McGuinn and a somewhat submerged Parsons, and Hillman harmonies on the chorus; 'Blue Canadian Rockies', with a fetching lead sung by Chris Hillman; 'Life In Prison', performed with real feeling by Gram; and, to round out the album, 'Nothing Was Delivered', a McGuinn vocal lead.

So the final score, after all the paranoia and unspoken rancour about just who would get to sing what, was that McGuinn had six, Hillman two and Gram three vocal leads – not such a bad innings for his first album as a 'sideman' in a major American band. Still, Gram's feelings were mixed about this deal with the Byrds. It seemed that for the weekly salary, generous though it was, he was getting a lot of grief about his input, which he was under the impression had been initially welcomed by McGuinn. Even Chris agreed in principle with what McGuinn had said to Gram in a frank discussion about how the album would be divided up vocally – "You have to realise you can't have everything your own way, man." To be fair to the others, it wasn't too bad a deal for Gram, a relative unknown, to have such sway over the Byrds, not to mention having gotten two original songs onto the album.

Gram disagreed with Roger and, while he remained committed to the group, some of his demands became increasingly tiresome. He did get McGuinn to commit to hiring Peter Kleinow for certain shows in Los Angeles, but Roger soon refused to give any further quarter to Gram's requests, especially when Gram approached him and Larry Spector to talk about a salary increase and even asked at one point for 'individual billing' [as in 'the Byrds featuring Gram Parsons'].

Even Chris Hillman, a staunch supporter of Gram's contributions and ideas, was shocked by some of the demands. It soon appeared, even to those outside the group, that his ego was taking flight in the wake of a damaging blow to his self-perceived importance to the Byrds. Gram, whose ability and charisma had allowed him to simply walk in and take charge of different groups in the past, was finding the obdurate McGuinn much more of a challenge.

After a brief break from shows, McGuinn and Hillman approved a cover by Geller and Butler Advertising for the album, featuring an illustration by artist Jo Mora from a 1933 catalogue of clothing for rodeo riders, perhaps a subtle nod in the direction of Nudie Cohen. The rear cover was a somewhat different idea to the front, a coyote in silhouette howling at the moon. Whether this was some snide comment on the contents of the record has never been fully explained.

The Byrds were booked to appear on the bill for *Sounds '68*, a charity concert in aid of boys clubs, to be held in London's Albert Hall. Also on the bill that night were The Move, Australian rockers The Easybeats and English eccentrics The Bonzo Dog Doo Dah Band, a peculiarly English variant on the antics of Frank Zappa's Mothers Of Invention. This mixed bill might have seemed incongruous, but audiences of the time were used to such disparity in their rock concert-goings. July 7th was to be a prestigious concert for 'Grahm,' as his name was misspelled on the concert program. It was a momentous evening. Out in the audience sat Jimi Hendrix, Keith, Mick and Charlie, John Lennon and George Harrison, six people likely to instil either confidence or terrible fear in a performer. Knowing that his mind was already made up about his future in the Byrds perhaps gave him the confidence to step up to the microphone for his harmonies with Roger, who led the band confidently.

The Byrds hour-long set was a freight train, building steam from the opener, 'So You Wanna Be a Rock 'n' Roll Star', through to a stunning 'Eight Miles High'. Rapturous applause greeted McGuinn's introduction of Gram, who moved quickly yet powerfully into 'Sing Me Back Home', one of Gram's favourite Merle Haggard prison songs. Throughout the set, the audience grew increasingly frenzied. At the beginning of the second and final set of the show, during which the Move performed, the crowd called out for the Byrds to return for another set.

Later that week, a warm review of the show appeared in *New Musical Express*, whose Nick Logan noted that "a good section of the 4,000 audience was there to see them alone and they let them know it." After the show had finished, the band celebrated the successful show and drank with Hendrix, Keith and Mick and the large crowd of musicians backstage, before they retired to their hotel. Gram went to bed alone and spent the night agonising over the decision that he knew he had to make.

The next morning, as the group's bags were being loaded into a van to be taken to the airport, Gram took Roger and Chris aside and explained to them that he would not be accompanying them to South Africa. As usual, Roger was his impenetrably cool self and seemed to barely register the news, while Chris became very angry and had to storm away to avoid any uglier kind of scene. The news of Gram's departure quickly got back to the music press, who quoted Chris Hillman as saying candidly, "He thought he was more important than the Byrds. He was a drag personally, but a good musician. He knew we were going to South Africa long before England, why the sudden announcement?"

Gram issued his own statement to English music paper *Melody Maker*, saying "I first heard about the South African tour two months ago. I knew right away when I heard about it that I didn't want to go. I stood firmly on my conviction. The Byrds are a very professional group and they thought it very unprofessional of me not to do it. I thought it was short-sighted to say it was confirmed without finding out about the South African situation first. It was just two conflicting opinions. I knew very little about South Africa before the tour was mentioned. I knew there was an intense problem but I didn't know what it was based on. I began to talk to people who had been born there and I found out."

He then announced that he'd quit the Byrds over this dispute. Not so, says McGuinn. "He was let go because he didn't want to go to South Africa with us. He said he wouldn't play to segregated audiences. He refused to go to South Africa and his reasoning was sound from one point of view but he didn't understand, or he was unwilling to comprehend my point of view."

Chris Hillman was equally shocked at the statement, which he said was untrue. It was his opinion that Gram, never a confident flyer, was freaked out by the very lengthy flight to South Africa, which would take them via the Canary Islands. "Gram wanted to stay in England and hang out with Mick and Keith and he did not want to fly... he didn't like to fly. He was a very sensitive guy and very socially aware of the situation he grew up with in the South but the closest he came to black people was the servants he had in his home. So, the situation where he says, 'I'm not going to South Africa because of the apartheid' is garbage. He just didn't want to get on the aeroplane and he let us down."

The matter of South Africa had of course been discussed again with the Rolling Stones, even though it appeared none of them had tried to discourage either Hillman or McGuinn from going. The hand of the Rolling Stones cannot, though, be discounted in Gram's *volte-face* on the South Africa matter. It didn't seem to matter that the contracts for the SA tour had specified that the band would be playing to integrated audiences, surely a first for that country. Both Richards and Jagger assured Gram that it would not have been cool for him (or any person who cared about civil rights) to go there, and he evidently bought into at least part of their persuasive argument.

Keith Richards told *Mojo*'s Barney Hoskyns that Gram "didn't know much about the situation in South Africa, so Anita and I explained it to him in [art dealer] Robert Fraser's apartment. It was quite an intense way to meet a guy." Frank David Murphy insists Gram "agonised to the last minute about going" because of moral reasons. More cynical observers claimed the scarcity of high quality pharmaceuticals in South Africa played a larger part in dissuading Gram from going there.

Carlos Bernal, the Byrds' faithful and long-suffering roadie, was pressed into service as a guitarist. Bernal himself claimed that Gram dropped out because he couldn't have things how he wanted them. "He wanted a steel guitar to do a lot of his tunes. He wanted things that the band wasn't prepared to jump into overnight. So Gram didn't make it to the airport."

Gram was invited down to Keith and Anita's home, Redlands, where he spent several eventful weeks tutoring Keith in the subtleties of country music. "He started to show me the difference between, y'know, Nashville and Bakersfield," Keith told Barney Hoskyns. Keith was a willing and enthusiastic student and together they played songs that they had in common, Richards drawing on the well of '40s and '50s country songs that he had loved since he was a young boy. Gram was occasionally surprised by how much Keith already knew about American music. The lessons went both ways. Keith taught Gram about the blues, which had been his entrée into popular music. Of course, Gram already knew about and loved Chuck Berry and Ray Charles, but through Keith he learned about the hard-working black bluesmen who had cemented the foundations of much of modern popular music.

As Gram relaxed in the English midsummer of 1968, the Byrds went ahead with the South African leg of the tour, which, having already been sullied by the loss of one essential member, was shaping up to be wildly unsuccessful. Roger McGuinn became very ill, suffering 104-degree fevers for the two weeks they were there. Roadie Carlos Bernal stood in for Gram on guitar and the band managed shows in Johannesburg, Durban and Cape Town, all the while being heckled by white audiences.

They managed to attract some spectacularly bad press – it may be safe to say that the old adage to the effect that there is no such thing as 'bad publicity' does not apply in South Africa. One headline announced "Byrds say South Africa is Sick, Backwards and Rude". They even got death threats by telegram and received dozens of menacing phone calls in their Durban hotel rooms, despite requesting that no calls be put through to them. The final straw was the charges of drug possession laid against them by a hotel porter who was convinced he'd seen the band 'with drugs'.

To avoid arrest and a possible jail sentence, the Byrds got out of South Africa and into what was then Rhodesia in a friend's plane, and then returned to Britain where the Musicians Union threatened them with expulsion, until Roger produced some examples of the 'publicity' they had received. As another kick in the pants, the band was never paid for the tour, the promoters insisting that they'd have to come back and face trial on the drugs charges before being paid.

While the vilification and humiliation the Byrds had to suffer was painful, there was worse to come for McGuinn, who was left drained and angry at the end of what had been an extension of the post-Crosby and Clark wilderness experience for himself and the band. *Sweetheart of The Rodeo* was released on August 30, 1968, only a couple of weeks after Parsons quit the band. Gram had left the Byrds in a tattered mess, with an album of country music to promote to what would turn out to be a mostly disinterested rock audience.

The label was at a loss as to how to present this record. The radio ads show just how foreign the concept of country music was to the Columbia promotions department. On one radio ad, a young couple can be heard arguing about the new Byrds album. Clearly, the pair are meant to represent 'heads'. You can hear steel guitars and the denial – "That's not the Byrds". "Sure it is – they're doing Dylan!" You can imagine the Byrds blushing even today. The assertion at the end of the ad was "The Byrds take eleven trips to the country. Why not fly with 'em?"

An ad also appeared in music magazines, with a shot of the band, Parsons included, posing near a brick wall on which was chalked "This country's for the Byrds". The publicity machine for the Byrds moved up a few steps, but the frustrations of a dud tour and yet another fledgling Byrd out of the nest caught up with everybody in the record company. Meanwhile, the radio stations were saying "no" to invitations to get down in a country groove with the *Sweetheart of the Rodeo*, preferring to rehash their earlier material or ignore them altogether.

Underground FM stations found a niche for the new Byrds album, which made for some spirited debate in the music press for and against the country music milieu. There was a kind review in *Rolling Stone* from senior journalist Barry Gifford, but he, like many journalists of the time, misunderstood the direction that the Byrds had taken, confusing their country album with an attempt to offer 'straight C&W' or worse, 'easy listening'. This was not the case. The sound was obviously rock at its base, its derivation coming from soul and rock as much as from country.

The Gifford review sent Jon Landau, chief *RS* essayist, to the chair for the defence. He suggested that the Byrds in fact displayed a good deal of "fidelity to the rules of the style". He also added, kindly, that Byrds albums were always musically diverse, and representative enough of different styles that they were like "an audio magazine containing the things that interest us at the moment". This was sound logic, based on increasing audiences for roots and blues music. But as for the lack of both radio and rock listener support, that couldn't be explained away by editorials. As Ben Fong-Torres says, "if any music form represented the straight world, it was country – even if it was being played by dope smokers".

Country music was and would always remain anathema to most rock 'n' roll fans. It took the Eagles to insinuate country-ish beats and harmony singing into the contemporary format, but it was the spadework by the Byrds and later the Flying Burrito Brothers that set them up for success.

After the ignominy of South Africa and the slow sales, McGuinn was understandably down on the whole country music deal. There was also the matter of turmoil among the remaining members. Kevin Kelley stayed on board long enough to take care of post-tour publicity before disappearing shortly afterwards, his nerves shot and his confidence in tatters. He has not been seen or heard of by his cousin Chris Hillman to this day.

As if to add insult to the injurious tour they had slogged through, the new album stalled at 77 on the *Billboard* album charts. McGuinn even went as far as disowning the album. He didn't feel that way permanently, but for long enough to shepherd the new Byrds lineup into the studio to hastily record another album. *Sweetheart of the*

Rodeo would rightly become known as one of the most influential albums ever recorded by a rock band, and one that would change the direction of modern rock music forever. However, at the time it was as much of a disappointment as could be imagined.

Back in LA and trying hard to regroup, McGuinn put in a call to Clarence White, the veteran of *The Notorious Byrd Brothers* sessions, who'd allegedly been passed over for the spot that Parsons had nabbed, although Clarence was not one to hold a grudge. White was clearly ecstatic at the prospect and in August 1968 became a full-time Byrd, and ultimately one of the longest serving at that. White brought with him a new drummer for the band, Gene Parsons (no relation to Gram whatsoever).

Gene and Clarence had worked together briefly in Nashville West, probably the finest band never to record an album in a studio. Gene was an inventor with a ceaselessly turning mind. He and White had collaborated on the design of a device that mimicked the AB pedal bend of a steel guitar on a Telecaster. It raised the B string up a whole step, and the invention was to become known as a Parsons/White B-Bender. Best of all, this wizard device was installed in Clarence's beloved 1952 Telecaster and would be unveiled to the world on the new album.

The new lineup of White, Parsons, Hillman and McGuinn fulfilled several major engagements in mid-to-late 1968, not the least of which was the Newport Festival at the end of July. Chris remained with the Byrds until almost the end of September, happy that his old bluegrass pal Clarence was now in the band officially, but he had worries of his own. A meeting with business manager Larry Spector brought the unwelcome news that the band bank accounts had taken a severe beating in the wake of the SA tour.

There was only about $50,000 left in their separate accounts. Spector explained, somewhat unconvincingly, that the money to pay for the tour had to come from somewhere, since the South African promoter was refusing to pay the band for the tour unless they returned to face the drugs charges laid against them, even though the band had completed nearly all the shows under mostly unworkable circumstances. This was the bitter end for Hillman. His marriage had fallen apart while he had been overseas, his financial situation was dire and he had bills to pay. Hillman was so debilitated by the experience that he went into hiding for a brief period, just to get out from under what had been a rough trip over three months. "I was ready to murder Gram," he confessed. "The South African tour was a farce and he was right. We shouldn't have gone, but he shouldn't have let us down by copping out at the end."

It was not without some fervent soul-searching that he reached his decision. Chris unplugged his bass guitar after a show in New Mexico, threw it down, walked out, and quit the band. As for Gram, he had taken shelter in Sussex, hanging out with Keith and Anita, where he was momentarily immune to the blame that would inevitably be placed by management and by the music press. The master plan of winning the hearts and minds of rednecks, truck drivers, shitkickers and Middle America, had been thwarted.

CHAPTER 6
MODERN SOUNDS IN COUNTRY AND WESTERN
Burritos in Formation

Gazing at the cover of *The Gilded Palace of Sin,* one might imagine that this was the counterculture of the 1960s in its brightest, fullest flower; building a new kind of American music on the cornerstones of youth, sequins and revolutionary intent. But that isn't how it was perceived at the time. Certainly, the very name of the band seems to carry the imprimatur of psychedelia; it is no more ridiculous and no less 'trippy' than Moby Grape, Chocolate Watchband or Quicksilver Messenger Service, and it certainly made them sound like they had a sense of humour.

However, the point of it all is the music that was created, the purity of expression without the burden of traditionalism. Despite the fact that it was not just a pop record or just a country record, it still confounded listeners; it was seen as 'awkward' or unusual, even though it flowed with beautiful melodic ideas. It seems like it's taken a long time for people to appreciate it for what it is.

Peter Kleinow, whose contributions on pedal steel were pivotal to the style of the album, agrees: "Yeah, I wonder if they even appreciate it now as much as they – well, I won't say 'as they should' – but because it's so unique, the *Gilded Palace of Sin* was the seminal album that the group had and anything that came after that was not up to the standard of the uniqueness of it. To hell with the flaws in it, it was a wonderful album and it was driven by creativity. It was the album that introduced 'country-rock' to the scene. It's the one. Poco was something else –that was something different. It was honky-tonk country-rock that we introduced to the rock scene."

In a 1971 interview with Chuck Casell, Kleinow described *The Gilded Palace of Sin* as a true underground album, and his opinion remains steadfast: "It was. It really was. And nobody had ever seen people in the Whisky A-Go-Go wearing cowboy suits and rhinestones, all the appurtenances that brought with it."

It is this perfect distillation of a moment in history committed to vinyl that makes this album so powerful, sad and beautiful. Because of its reverberating impact, still being felt today, the first Flying Burrito Brothers album must surely take its place among the top 50 albums ever made. As with many of the great records, *The Gilded Palace of Sin* came about through a period of sustained creativity following personal hardship and pain, for both Chris Hillman and Gram Parsons.

"I hung out with Keith Richards for a while, for a couple of months in London," explained Gram to an interviewer in 1972, after he'd had more than enough time to process the circumstances and subsequent impact of his departure from the Byrds nearly five years before. "I'd met him several times before on an earlier Byrds tour in Europe and Keith and I had an affinity for country music. He really loved it and we started playing it and then finally he had to go to LA to mix *Beggar's Banquet.* And I was broke. They [the Byrds] had left me penniless there and Keith said, 'Well, that's OK – come on, I'll fly you over there.' And we came back to LA."

During the two months he'd spent in the south of England and in London, he'd had several long discussions over the phone with Chris Ethridge about starting a new group once he was feeling strong enough to make his way back to Los Angeles, where little was certain for him. In the wake of the unpleasantness of his departure from his previous band, he found Ethridge encouraging and supportive. As he told Chuck Casell: "Chris and I started going around, sitting in with various groups, like the Main Street Blues Band, which was like the beginning of the Delaney and Bonnie band and, uh, that was Jimmy Carstein and JJ Cale, Leon Russell, Jesse Davis – people like that. And finally Chris Hillman came around and said, 'Look, I'm sorry – I didn't want to go to South Africa either. It was the wrong thing to do and I think I'll quit the band and join you guys.' I said, 'Fine – two guys named Chris in the group.'"

Whatever stock one might put in Gram's version of events, Chris Hillman was in a precarious personal and musical situation, exacerbated by a deteriorating marriage and his financial problems. Gram's departure left the band in exactly the same position they had been in at the beginning of the year. As a result of this uncertainty, the Byrds would enter a new creative phase with their newest members, Clarence White and Gene Parsons. Chris remained with the group until September of that year.

The wrangling over money continued, even as the new lineup renewed their contract with CBS. Under the terms of the new contract McGuinn and Hillman would retain the rights to the Byrds name, with 'joint ownership'. Although money wasn't necessarily a big problem for Chris, it was the fact that Larry Spector had recently been named as the legal representative of the Byrds that peeved him, since Spector now had 'power of attorney over [the Byrds] financial affairs'.

Hillman took some time out and purchased some land in New Mexico. After quitting the Byrds and moving on from his marriage, he found it in himself to forgive Gram the ignominy he had suffered having to play South Africa as an under-par three-piece. Gram was naturally apologetic for his poor timing, but Chris could see that for both his refusal to play under apartheid and the more apparent desire to play up to the Rolling Stones, GP was a smart kid.

Hillman later admitted to *Spin* magazine that his split from the Byrds was acrimonious. But he was already thinking about the future. "Roger and I have always had a pretty close relationship, so maybe I was upset for one day. But I think Roger understood, and he felt the same way. He needed the stimuli as well as I did. And I just felt frustrated at that point – and what I really wanted to do, we sort of touched on in the Byrds' *Sweetheart of the Rodeo* album. I wanted to take it a step further, and Gram Parsons was the natural guy to do that with."

As Hillman's marriage break-up drew out toward divorce, he moved into a house with Gram on DeSoto Avenue, Reseda, in the northwest area of the San Fernando Valley, to the north of Hollywood. In the house, nicknamed Burrito Manor, the pair "smoked a lot of dope and sang a lot of country songs". With Chris Ethridge calling by just about every day, the pair or trio wrote a song a day, "according to daily circumstance".

Hillman describes this period as having been like working a normal day job, so regular were the hours they kept. "He was hard-working – a great guy. It was a good collaboration at that point, because we were leading fairly normal lifestyles and most of the songs were written in the daytime. One guy would get an idea and we'd work on it. For example, Gram got his draft notice, so we sat down and wrote 'My

Uncle'. I still look back at that as a very productive time working with him. The best vocal Gram ever did was 'Hot Burrito #1' and '[Hot Burrito] #2'. He put his heart into it. Cut the same night. I walked in, and he and Chris Ethridge had worked on those two and my mouth just fell open."

Gram was very keen to keep playing; fearing that he might lose some of the formidable keyboard chops he had worked up while with the Byrds. Using his brief experience with the band as a ticket, he got to sit in with some of the finest bands in town, usually at the hardcore rock and honky-tonk clubs out in San Fernando Valley, the City of Industry, and Orange County. He would arrive at a club reasonably early, and talk with members of bands like the Tulsa Rhythm Revue or Delaney and Bonnie, most of whom knew and liked him. He would be asked to sit in, although usually for some harmonies, organ, or piano. It was rare that he would be asked to sit in on guitar, for as he himself admitted, his guitar work was less than extraordinary.

Out in the non-'rock scene' clubs of the San Fernando Valley, Gram felt more at home, even though the regular patrons of the country music clubs were still suspicious of longhairs. But the blue-collar 'redneck' audiences were exactly those that Gram had always hoped to attract. He knew that once a country music audience found you and liked what you offered they were much more attentive and faithful than the younger pop audience, who tended to be extremely fickle. The two Chris's shared this view and besides, they liked hanging out in the San Fernando clubs too.

They regularly ventured as far out as Bakersfield where there were better clubs. These clubs were real honky-tonks, but they were cool – longhairs like them could go out and dig country without too much risk of being beaten to a pulp by California rednecks. "The clubs out in the Valley are really honky-tonks, and they're really funky and they're nicer than the honky-tonks in Nashville because people there are less liable to rap on you for having long hair – they see more of it – and you can go out there and boogie all you want," Gram laughed. "So that's real nice. That's the most positive thing I can think about LA, these places out in the Valley, like out of the Strip. The most negative thing I can think of is the Strip itself, with all the people addicted to carbon monoxide."

The influence of the country music they all listened to was tempered by other factors too, such as blues, gospel, and soul and to a lesser degree, rock. Gram didn't have a lot of time for commercial rock. The only contemporary groups he rated were the Stones and the Beatles; otherwise he never listened to anything except Jerry Lee Lewis, Bobby Bland and George Jones, preferring the solid roots of his Cosmic American Music to nebulous rock operas and pop hysteria.

The injection of country was what had given rock music melodicism and beauty in the first place; this would continue to be the reality. "Country music is going through its fad rapidly too," Gram said, trying to explain the difference between what he had started and what more commercial artists were inadvertently destroying. "I mean, it's been affected by the Nehru shirt scene. Glen Campbell, for instance, is a very, very good guitar player – one of the best, but he has been hyped, ruined – destroyed. So many of the country artists are just trying to pick up gimmicks. They always have but they're getting more and more into it...*Conway Twitty's* back. He's got the hottest new country band around, and he's out of sight. In his own right, he's better than all of us new country groups – 'cause he's paid more dues, he's older.

"As soon as young kids start digging old funky white artists like they dig funky old black artists...like they can listen to BB King but can they listen to George Jones?

They can listen to Albert King and Ike and Tina Turner and so on, but can they listen to Conway Twitty? You've got your Otis Redding, but you've also got your Merle Haggard. I suppose that we would correspond and parallel – we would be on the same level as the newest things that are happening in rhythm and blues, like down in Muscle Shoals. That's our scene more than Nashville, more than the studio scene. It's a bunch of young white people who are starting to play white music."

As always, he openly admired Bob Dylan and everything he did. In this regard, Parsons was certainly far from a purist. He usually preferred artists of a different era, mostly the late '50s. Bobby 'Blue' Bland was one of Gram's heroes and, if not an obvious influence vocally, was certainly one of the musicians that he had a good deal of respect for. Bland had cut a number of country sides during the '60s and openly admired singers like George Jones and Ernest Tubb; his permutation of 'Cosmic American Music' led him eventually to record several country-influenced albums in the early '70s.

Gram also liked to buy singles. His room was littered with 45s by Jerry Lee Lewis, George Jones, Percy Sledge and James Carr, as well as his favourite gospel sermons by the likes of Dorothy Love Coates and Sister Rosetta Tharpe. Gram would get them mail order from specialist record companies in Memphis and Nashville, ordering two or three at a time, then playing them for friends. He took great comfort in these recordings – it was never for camp value or novelty amusement. In fact, his listening habits were evangelical in themselves. Friends like Miss Mercy and Miss Pamela of the GTOs would come by Burrito Manor to hang out with Chris Hillman, whom the latter was seeing on and off. They would all sit down and talk, and Gram would attempt to educate Miss Mercy in the ways of country music, something she grew to enjoy after her initial knee-jerk reaction. He would play her the old Musicor 45s, inscribed with the legend

George Jones
The King of Broken Hearts

Miss Mercy was at first shocked to see a tear slip down Gram's cheek as he listened over and over to these records, surprised that hearing Jones sing 'Your Angel Steps Out of Heaven' could have touched someone so much. Soon enough, she was doing the same. "Imagine crying over some hillbilly with a crewcut," she said, shortly before her own conversion to country music was complete.

The tears that Gram shed over George might have been given some impetus by the breakdown of the relationship between him and Nancy, the mother of his daughter Polly. Late in 1968, Gram had left Nancy behind while he'd been in London, staying with Keith and Anita, and their relationship had been damaged by the lack of attention. While it would be unfair to speculate on the nature of the relationship at that time, Gram was prone to abandoning his girlfriend to go on tour. On his return, they had agreed to live in separate houses, although they continued to see each other, if only for the sake of little Polly. Soon, Nancy was living with Polly at Susan and Brandon De Wilde's Topanga home, which had become a refuge for a number of people, including Mickey Gauvin.

Gram paid a visit to Nancy at the De Wilde's place in November to propose marriage to her. Gram apparently spoke to her in a very courtly way, saying, "I'd like you to be my wife." Nancy searched his face to see if he was joking. She was fairly sure he was, since he had wasted no time in seeing other women after he had moved out of the Sweetzer Avenue house. Nonetheless, she accepted politely. "You've made me the happiest man alive," he replied. It sounded all too *Gone With the Wind*. A few minutes later, he had bailed Mickey up outside the house, accusing him of sleeping with Nancy behind his back. Mickey was naturally confused, since Gram had hardly been around to assert any kind of right to Nancy.

Nancy took Polly back to their house at Santa Barbara, where she awaited further developments. Gram had been talking about the idea of a real rock 'n' roll society wedding, something that might echo Hank Williams' marriage in New Orleans, where he had sold tickets to three separate marriage ceremonies on the one day, charging $1.50 a ticket. While the big ideas were being tossed around, Gram avoided setting a date or making out a guest list. All of this did little to allay Nancy's fears that Gram was all talk. Nudie Cohen offered to help Nancy with a wedding dress cut from the same material as Gram's suits. Finally a date was set: January 31st, 1970. That was the last mention of the wedding for a while, at least where Gram was concerned.

Involving himself with the day-to-day creativity back at Burrito Manor, Gram tried to forget his troubles. The regular listening diet at the Manor began to impact on Chris Hillman's songs, which had to some degree carried the stamp of bluegrass and country anyway. The quality of the songs, too, was improving in leaps and bounds. When in the Byrds, Chris had struggled against the obvious songwriting triumvirate of Crosby, Clark and McGuinn. The songs that Chris brought in were always country-inflected. It had been his idea to record 'Satisfied Mind', for example.

Working with Ethridge and Parsons firmed Hillman's belief in his own talent. As the elder songwriter in the band and the one with the most commercial success under his belt, he sought to create songs that were more elaborate. The new songs he was producing were full-blown country-pop-rock-soul confections, borne out of eclecticism and a desire to transcend dull rock cliché. Even by their own individual high standards, the three of them were ecstatic with the calibre of the songs they could produce together. They are easily the equal of songs by Lennon/McCartney.

Most of the original songs that appear on *Gilded Palace of Sin* were composed during that early fertile period at Burrito Manor, with the constant input of Ethridge, who had much more of a 'pop' sensibility. In particular, 'Sin City' was most indicative of the times in which Hillman and Parsons found themselves; "We predicted the rise of fundamentalism, militarism and earthquakes," Hillman claimed later. It was suggestive of a whole time and place, one that was going crazy but in a fun kind of way.

The religious content (and the stinging criticism for it) that had plagued the Byrds following *Sweetheart...* was more toned down, with passing references to a friend who "came around/tried to clean up this town/his ideas made some people mad". It also pointed the finger at Gram and Chris Hillman's ex-business manager Larry Spector, whose office on Brighton Way in Beverly Hills really did have a gold-plated door. In the wake of the controversy over misplaced Byrds money and some potentially hairy accusations, Spector, an heir to the Max Factor fortune, had given up on the music business for a reclusive life at Big Sur.

Gram and Chris presented demos of original songs to a number of A&R people from interested record companies, including Mo Ostin over at Reprise, Frank Sinatra's label. Ostin was prepared to invest in the Burritos, since he was aware of Hillman's reputation, and rumour had it that Keith Richards was to produce the album. He did not offer them a big advance, thinking that there was room for further development before laying out serious money, but he did not hesitate to offer them a deal.

With Ostin's keen endorsement in mind, Parsons, Hillman and Ethridge went to see Jerry Moss at A&M. They were following up on a tip from a guy named Tom Wilkes, who happened to be art director at A&M Records. Coincidentally, Wilkes was a neighbour to the lairds of Burrito Manor, and it was through Wilkes (who would later art-direct the covers for the first two Burrito Brothers albums) that word got back to Moss about the songs that were being generated there. Mo Ostin's offer was set aside in favour of A&M, who had nothing nearly so contemporary on their books. Perhaps it was A&M's lack of rock 'n' roll catalogue that made the Burrito Brothers (now so-named) seem appealing to the label. Via a recent distribution deal, A&M now acted as American label for British acts like Joe Cocker's Grease Band and Procol Harum. Other new signings for the company in 1969 included Merry-Go-Round and We Five. A brother and sister duet act, Karen and Richard Carpenter, signed their deal a week later.

However, if the Burritos were hoping that they could leverage the label's lack of acts to their financial advantage, they were out of luck. Gram claimed that the offer that A&M had made was too immediate and good to pass up, although in later interviews he recanted, saying the advance for the Burritos had been 'minuscule'. Chris Hillman agrees, remembering that it was no more than $1,500 for each member of the band.

In an interview for the magazine *Fusion*, on March 26, 1969, Gram and Chris Ethridge elaborated on the reason the band had signed to A&M: "When we got together, there were a lot of record companies eager to sign us – and anything we wanted they were willing to do – but we just happened to sign with A&M, mainly because of Mike Vosse, who came and got us. I mean, he was actually interested. He didn't set up appointments for us to come see him; he came and saw us. Tom Wilkes, in the graphics department, was a friend of Chris, you know. So we had a personal contact and they took a personal interest in us."

The next step was to find a pedal steel player to fit the tenor of the band. The word went out to a number of pedal steelers to see whether they might like to consider joining a new country rock band. The word went as far as Nashville but they had no joy finding someone. "About the only steel player in town at that moment who wasn't really strictly into working country bars and staying there, was Sneaky Pete," said Gram. "Good old Sneaky."

Sneaky Pete Kleinow came to California via Michigan in the mid-'50s. He was a stop-motion animator by trade who had worked on the 1960s kids' show *Gumby* (and in fact composed the theme song of the show). He spent his evenings playing pedal steel in various bands around the Los Angeles and San Diego areas where Chris Hillman had run into him over the years. He had done a few shows with the Byrds and since he was a few years older than both Gram and Chris and had a young family, he was universally regarded as a steady, mature guy.

He was known for the distinctive trebly sound of his 8-string pedal steel guitar and the fact that he had worked for local legend Smokey Rodgers' western swing band. Rodgers, who insisted that all members of his band have such nicknames (one of country music's most enduring practices), had given him the tag 'Sneaky Pete'. Kleinow had taken up working almost seven nights a week in Sin City itself, where he was playing in the clubs that Gram and Chris were frequenting at nights, letting off steam after being at home writing songs all day. These clubs were the earthy sort of place where you'd get threatened with a whupping for having long hair, but since Gram and Chris were laid-back enough, they'd get through the evenings unmolested by truckers accusing them of being 'faggots'.

The Palomino on Lankershim and the Lazy X further up the street were the sorts of places where the first incarnation of the Burrito Brothers (with Barry Tashian and Ian Dunlop) had powered through R&B and country sets to small but appreciative audiences. "At that time, I had a regular six-nights-a-week gig playing at the Lazy X and I played there with my pal Norm Raleigh, who was a good buddy of mine, and Johnny Meeks, and the drummer for the Ventures whose name I can't remember," said Peter Kleinow. "I was playing in this club all the time, just having the best time. Back then, we were backing up a lot of special acts during that time, like Ike and Tina Turner. We were kind of high profile there for a while because we were right down the street from the Palomino, just about a block away, and things were really hot around that neighbourhood at that time."

Gram and Chris approached Kleinow one evening at the Lazy X after a show and told him what they had in mind and would he be interested? He was. "Gram Parsons and Chris Hillman were looking for a steel player that was a little bit different, not the Nashville model," says Kleinow. "Gram had already done the Submarine Band thing, and I guess it was Chris Hillman who decided that they needed something unique, a different kind of approach. And they wanted me to put in lots of pedal steel guitar, in fact, to almost play everything and that was it. I was the whole backup band when I played. So that's why they came in there, they'd heard about me because several times they came in to see me play and they finally asked me if I wanted to join the band."

The idea of working with such young, hip guys was immediately appealing. They seemed to know what they wanted and his first impression was that it would be a lot of fun. Far from being fazed by the rockers with their longish hair, Sneaky Pete was intrigued: "I was never prejudiced against rock and roll at all. I didn't know them – I just thought they were a couple of North Hollywood guys trying to get something going. I never thought it was gonna be something big so I never gave up my day job or my regular playing. I played whenever I could. I still played about six or seven nights a week and I kept on doing that.

"I played other shows and then the first show I played with them – actually, I can't exactly remember what the first one was but we did several big shows that got us started, including the Whisky A-Go-Go and similar places. So we got together to cut the first album and we actually had no rehearsal, no nothing. I didn't know the material," he remembered later. Kleinow's introduction to the rest of Flying Burrito Brothers came "in the studio with Chris Ethridge on bass, whom I didn't know at the time until I came into the first session at Wally Heider's and we had [drummer] Chuck Blackwell, who sat in with us. We didn't really have a drummer."

Getting a drummer to complete the sessions was getting to be a hassle. The first choice had been session drummer Eddie Hoh, who had come on board and then vanished, taking his $1500 advance with him. "He just wanted the money and then he split," sneered Gram. Next on the list was Maurice Tarp, who had once played drums for Jerry Lee Lewis. That didn't come off either, and the band called on the services of three more drummers to complete the album. Sam Goldstein, a friend of Chris Ethridge, sat in for a couple of tracks, as did 'Popeye' Phillips. Finally, former International Submarine Band drummer Jon Corneal came down and stayed long enough to play on five songs.

Corneal was a fine and reliable musician, who had no untoward personal habits. He had proved himself a compatible drummer for the Byrds during his work on *Sweetheart of the Rodeo* in Nashville, and his drumming had the right amount of strength to run the Burrito rhythm section. He even appeared in early publicity shots of the band, but wasn't actually hired as a Burrito Brother, due to what some saw as being snobbery on Gram's part towards Jon. Despite their personal history, which dated back to the early '60s, and the fact that Jon had played drums on *Safe At Home*, there was a degree of continuing tension between the two. Jon resented Gram's attitude towards life and music, which he maintains was tainted by his personal wealth. Jon also felt that by agreeing to work with Gram, he was severely limiting the chances of pursuing his own musical career.

In *Hickory Wind*, Chris Hillman claimed that Gram looked down on Jon: "Here they were, both from Florida, but Jon was from the other side of the tracks. Someone who should be in the orange groves picking oranges: 'How dare you play in a band with me!'" As far as Corneal was concerned, the whole LA scene was a little too weird for his tastes anyway, and he was looking to get out of the Burrito Brothers circle. He found himself drafted into Gene Clark's group of musician friends, and he found their musical ideas and personal attitudes much more to his liking, playing on both *The Dillard & Clark Expedition* and *Through the Morning, Through the Night*.

Tracking for the first album began in November 1968 at A&M's Hollywood studio, the 'house of rock hits' at the time in West Hollywood. Larry Marks was chosen as the producer, a decision that Gram later reflected on as being a sensible one. "He was doing a real good job, giving us enough range on the first album to get the group started. We all had trouble getting anybody to believe that it could be done, because they'd hear connotations of "Okie this, Okie that" but they liked the Christian aspect and the gospel, Pentecostal feeling of joy."

Marks insisted that Kleinow do more than just embellish the songs with his steel guitar. He encouraged Sneaky to draw as many unusual sounds out of his instrument as possible. It soon became clear to Chris and Gram that the pedal steel was to play a dual role in the Burritos; drawing out the latent country music promise of certain songs, while adding a crazed rock tone on others.

Sneaky Pete, always ready for a challenge, pulled out all the stops. "I kinda knew what they wanted to do. They told me what they wanted – they wanted me to be the steel player and they wanted plenty of it. So I knew going into it what they wanted and I was kind of overjoyed but on the other hand, as I look back on it, I think there is too much steel guitar. But that's what made it unique. It was an attempt to dirty up the sound a little bit and I didn't really know what I was doing with it. It was a very primitive way of doing it and I was just expressing it and everybody encouraged me that I was on the right track. It really sounded great, just like Jimi Hendrix (laughs). Some of it I listen to and cringe when I hear some of the things that I played there, but that was how it was at the time and so that's what I did. I tried to find a different style from anybody else. I certainly didn't want to play any of that Nashville kind of stuff. I wanted it to have a twist."

The twist was the range of pedal steel sounds that Sneaky Pete conjured up during three full sessions of overdubs. The array of sounds that Kleinow produced at will – from floating, passing notes to symphonic string clusters and bombardments of hot chord groupings – was heavily featured on the entire album. As befits the talents of rock's first great pedal steel player, Kleinow is nearly as prominent in the mix as the vocals. Gram was similarly taken with Sneaky's ideas. As he laughingly explained to one interviewer, "There were times during the making of the first album that I wanted to quit because I just couldn't understand this guy doing like, eight steel guitar overdubs over himself... but I liked it."

Gram, age 13, gone fishing with Bob Parsons

Gram, aged 14

The Byrds
L-R: Kelley, Gram, McGuinn, Hillman
(Michael Ochs/ Redfern)

Gram with "Nudie" Cohen
(Raeanne Rubenstein/ Festival Records)

Flying Burrito Brothers onstage, March 1969
(Craig Folkes)

*Gram on stage during the Flying Burritos'
set at Altamont
((Robert Altman/Retna)*

Gram with Helix journalist Ed Leimbacher at the Seattle Pop Festival, 1969

(Retna)

(Retna)

Gram, Emmylou and the Fallen Angels onstage at Liberty Hall, Houston, Texas 1973
(John Lomax)

L-R: Phil Kaufman, Gram, Emmylou, Rocky Hill and Christine
(John Lomax)

Gram backstage at Liberty Hall, Houston, Texas 1973 (John Lomax)

Sailing with Gretchen, 1973

Gram's wedding... 1971, with sister Avis

Kleinow preferred not to use an amplifier in the studio, preferring to D.I. (direct inject) the pedal steel to the desk. "That's the only way I record. It does make a difference. Every other pedal steel player I know sets up their amp there and gets some microphones onto it. Well, that gives it a different sound. I'd use the two pickups without a phaser and that sound is very subtle. I have it so the signal is barely 'rotating' and that gives it an original sound too."

To create original, non-country sounds from within the structures of country songs was the creative brief. There had been no directives from the label to make it an 'underground album', although that's how it turned out. Perhaps it had to do with cloistering themselves in a studio, with only guitars and pot for company. "To do the album in L.A., we had to close ourselves off," Gram explained. "When the smog was heavy, we had to wear tanks of oxygen, and luckily, we were blessed with a fellow named Henry Lewy who can just cool out. He's an engineer unlike any engineer I've ever worked with, and projected an attitude of: 'We're not in L.A., boys, we're together.'"

The duo of producer Larry Marks and engineer/producer Henry Lewy was a relaxed one, a perfect cultural fit keeping in mind the mood of the sessions. "What do I remember about Larry?" asks Peter Kleinow. "Well, he was just one of the boys, fitting in with everyone. He always had a little grin on his face when he talked and he was just a real nice guy. Why, if someone was there smoking a joint, why Larry'd just fit right in."

Was there a fair bit of that going on in the studio?

Peter: "Yeeeeaaahh… some of us more than others, which I probably shouldn't go into. There were some people who did and some people who chose not to. Chris Hillman didn't do it a lot, well, he would do it once in a little while but mostly he didn't really… there was one member of the group who was quite enamoured with that kind of stuff but I won't mention any names."

In the studio, Parsons and Hillman decided to rearrange several different soul tunes for recording, and almost managed to upstage themselves in the process. By tackling Aretha Franklin's near-untouchable "Do Right Woman, Do Right Man", Gram laid it out with a different and striking perspective for all men.

They say that it's a man's world –
Well, you can't prove that by me
So as long as we're together baby,
You better show some respect for me

In Gram's hands, these lyrics sounded like the words of a man who has been stepped on, but one who has learned his lesson too. In the same complex, at another studio, David Crosby was working on another record. "He was walking around, so I grabbed him and got him to do that high harmony," said Chris Hillman. It's his voice that sweeps up to the high 'do' on 'Do Right Woman'.

The other soul classic they reinvented was 'Dark End of the Street', also by Dan Penn. While Penn has since gone on record as saying he didn't think much of Gram's version (or Linda Ronstadt's attempt for that matter), the Burritos took it apart, then reconstructed it with a white soul touch to the vocals. Of course, to begin with it was a very country-soul kind of a song, but even in the pedal steel guitar phrasing somehow echoes and rebuffs the soul influence – you can hear where the horn lines might have been in the curl and cry of Sneaky Pete's playing.

The two Dan Penn songs were given added vibrancy by Kleinow's approach. His mission to take the steel guitar parts elsewhere continued. He was trying to play them more like string or horn parts: "It was all unison note parts – octave above, octave below. I was trying to blend the sound in, rather than playing the note and quickly bringing the volume up. I experimented with that a lot, since I didn't have a clue as to how to get that to sound like real strings. That was something I did deliberately to get that effect... I don't know whether it worked or not, that's just what I did. I just did little things to make it all sound a little different. I tried to do things that nobody expected me to do. They didn't know what I was going to do. And to tell you the truth, I didn't know what I was going to do until I sat down to do it and that's the way everything went for me. You know, I always went into the studio with people, I'd listen to it once, run through the song once or if they had the basic track recorded, I'd try to get the idea of the song in my head as to what would fit. It was that loose."

By the same token, 'Christine's Tune (Devil in Disguise)' is the cautionary tale of a do-wrong woman, from those who should know. Miss Christine was one of the GTO's, and a longstanding fan of the Byrds and now the Burritos. A tall, beautiful frizzy-haired Southern girl (who starred on the cover of Frank Zappa's album, *Hot Rats*), she had been the cause of some friction between band members and girlfriends, because she always seemed to be around at shows, and then later backstage.

Part of the charm of the song, aside from its obvious musical debt to the Everly Brothers, is that this 'devil in disguise' is not necessarily at fault. She just is what she is. It says something about the weakness of a man's heart, knowing that while he's got a steady, her number is likely to fall out of his pocket at a bad (or possibly good) time. The woman in the song comes off worse than we might like her to; she's branded a 'dirty' liar, for example. But there is sympathy and tenderness extended too. 'Unhappiness has been her close companion/her world is full of jealousy and doubt", but she has her flaws. "It gets her off to see a person crying," say the singers, advising us that she's "just the kind that you can do without."

'Sin City' is the sum of the inheritance of 50s country music and its 60s update, Cold War paranoia having given way to an unpopular South-east Asian war, riots in the Sorbonne and the burning of Detroit. The song has its base almost solely in the country-gospel traditions of the Louvin Brothers, along the lines of their moderately scarifying Capitol album, *Satan Is Real*. 'Sin City' predicts all kinds of apocalyptic images that may apply equally today, just as they did in the era of Vietnam and the Manson Family. The song predicts earthquakes and the Lord's burning rain. Unlike the problems the Byrds had faced with being labelled 'Christian cowboys', the Burritos knew whereof they spoke and knew how to temper the flaming intonations of fundamentalism. Most satisfying is the way in which the imagery and the power of the song are complemented beautifully by the arrangement, a kind of sedate waltz tempo added to the gospel.

'Hot Burrito #2' just as quickly put out the fundamentalist flames, not that they were ever likely to set the Burritos alight completely with godly fervour. As Stanley Booth rightly points out, this song 'breaks the old 'honky-tonk-gospel taboo', like the same unwritten rule in black churches against playing the blues. It breaks this taboo (and a few others) by declaring

You better love me, Jesus Christ!

The song's complaint is why does she sell his clothes, yet claim to love him? Was there a girl who found a pawnshop that would gratefully accept Nudie suits for cash, no questions asked? Or was it a way of explaining the erratic fashion in which Gram had been known to conduct his relationships with women? It's a well known fact that Gram just slayed ladies all over the country with his soft, slow voice, his crooked smile and his chivalrous Southern demeanour. Most of them felt like they'd been hit by a slow-moving, loose-hipped Southern tornado. Parsons was a palatable mixture of Georgia cracker and effete, sensitive dandy. His Southern heritage ran through him, as Ian Dunlop described it, "as a wick through a candle." He was a young and mostly conventional man, but he knew how to turn on his conspicuous charms to get the desired results.

"Juanita" is a moving and chilling tale of a fall from grace and heaven. Somewhere in the darkness, there is contemplation of past wrongs, of the kind that make your head spin with guilt and pain. On the surface, it's the classic country tale of a broken heart told in waltz time. What's slightly unusual is how that heart is restored at the pale hands of a much younger girl, suggesting the restorative power of the muse. Gram may have been thinking of all the young women that drifted in and out of his life during that time. The house in Laurel Canyon was a focal point for interesting and available young women who found the duo of Chris and Gram irresistible. However you choose to envision the situation of the singer, the opening stanza is still a slap in the face, even for the empathic listener.

No affection were the words that stuck on my mind
When she walked out on me for the very last time

The song develops as a pseudo-religious awakening of the sexual kind, a conundrum that Marvin Gaye would have loved. Like Marvin Gaye, Gram may not have ever fully dealt with the problem of salvation. It is no surprise that in 'Juanita', the singer is imprisoned in a "cold dirty room", where the walls are constructed of opposite forces, terror and love, fear and validation, to create the most terrifying cell a human being can ever be imprisoned in. Like many before and since have found, the ever-present help in time of trouble is "a bottle of wine and some pills off the shelf". In close harmony, Gram and Chris explain the sweet shape that salvation suddenly takes in this predicament.

Then an angel appeared, she was just seventeen
In a dirty old gown with a conscience so clean

Each testifies, rather movingly, that 'she brought back the life that I once threw away'. Whether this is prescient of further drug problems or merely a projection of the kind of desperation that seemed suitable to the song is worthy of conjecture. In the time that the song was written, desperation seemed to fill the air. The world was a troubled place, with "wars and rumours of wars", and the attainment of peace, either internal or external, seemed an elusive ideal.

The dichotomous relationship between sexuality and spirituality that 'Juanita' addresses is something that eternally troubled the rock 'n' roll singers of that era, not to mention the many country and blues singers whose music had in many ways developed out of an interaction with the church as well. Gram wrestled with the concept of God the way that Jacob wrestled the angel, not out of fear or desperation but out of hope. Someone up there loved him, but his perception of God was riddled with doubt and anger. He despised injustice and inequality but he longed for spiritual satisfaction, which is more of a personal matter. His songs, inasmuch as they deal with his quest for love and therefore use the conventions of country, soul and blues music, are very much about a desire for peace and communality. His views on music were very much black and white – pigeonholing his music was pointless, but he, perhaps no more so than many other artists, got stuck with some unwanted genre labels.

He was at pains to point this out to interviewers who wanted his opinion on the "grand plan" he had for his music. "I think pure country includes rock and roll – I don't think you don't have to call it 'country-rock' anymore than you have to call something 'folk-rock'. It's either... you can call it rock and roll or you can call it country music. I just don't like the label 'country-rock'. I was brought up in the South and I never knew the difference between Negro gospel music and country music, it all was just music to me. I knew the difference in the sound and the difference in how to play it, but I was taught to play music by black people but I was never aware that was what was called 'gospel' or rhythm and blues or blues and rhythm as it used to be called. And the other was called 'country and western' – I never understood that. I've never been able to get into the label 'country-rock' – it just doesn't make sense to me. How can you define something like that? I just think it's music – either it's good or it's bad. You either like it or you don't."

Musically speaking, 'My Uncle' is more of a timeless concept –the hillbilly draft-dodgers anthem. This lament is the marriage of old hillbilly gospel and folk protest; the honeymoon couple climbing into bed with Country Joe and The Fish, only to face a baton charge from the National Guard. The song had its factual basis in the story of Gram going down to the letterbox to find a letter from the Selective Service regarding confirmation of his medical records. Of course, Gram did have his 4-F deferment from the draft board. Thanks for that were due to Bob Parsons who pulled the necessary strings, swearing that the communists would need to be at the back door of his home before Gram would ever have to face them with a gun in his hands.

It must have startled both Chris and Gram for them to write such a song; these Hollywood hillbilly objectors adding social comment to the medium in which they had chosen to work. Of course, Chris later pointed out in the liner notes to *Farther Along* that he was proud to have been the first to inject a little social commentary into country music. The exodus of young, draft-eligible men to foreign borders north and south was a cultural phenomenon of the late 60s – the conscience-stricken and those justifiably afraid of a valueless death on foreign soil made their way to Vancouver and Ontario, Mexico City and Sydney.

More along the lines of Gram and Chris Hillman's shared ideals was the hilarious and dead-on pastiche, 'Hippie Boy'. It was essentially a straight lift of a musical idea that people like Red Foley and Hank Williams (as Luke The Drifter) had been working with for years, the musical monologue. In this case, it was the tale of a dirty hippie boy encountered by a fellow from the country, complete with churchy Hammond, supplied by Gram, who liked the spirit they'd given the song.

"On 'Hippie Boy,' I mean, the album goes from Everly Brothers cuts to more modern, polished things," Parsons enthused. "But at the end of the album, there's like all of our friends there singing: the GTO's, Joel Scott Hill, Johnny Barbata, Henry Lewy, Larry Marks, Bobby McMann – we're all like singing together, 'There will be peace in the valley.' That song... well, we had that idea from the very beginning: we kept saying we got to do a song called 'Hippie Boy' about Chicago, and it's got to be a narrative song, and Chris Hillman has to do it. And he has to drink a fifth of scotch before he does it – just to really feel the whole thing. Not smoke an ounce of grass – but drink a fifth of scotch and do a narrative. And let's see somebody else do that – let's see McGuinn do that." The song equally amused Bob Dylan when he heard it for the first time: "Thinking about that poor hippie boy on his way to town," Dylan said, chuckling.

The Gilded Palace of Sin continued its musical sleight-of-hand, the legerdemain impressing everyone who would hear it. A reworking of a song from the Submarine Band's *Safe At Home* appeared on the new album, 'Do You Know How It Feels To Be Lonesome?' This querulous, heartrending beauty of a song, despite its propulsive bass line and somewhat jaunty honky-tonk piano, is at odds with the bitterness of its sentiment. It's a song of absolute wretchedness and despair, the heartcry of every sad-eyed, ragged-voiced musical hero from Gram to Kurt Cobain.

Arguably the album's finest moment, "Hot Burrito #1" – also known as "I'm Your Toy" – was perhaps the most striking contemporary love song of its day. It can be considered as a modern prayer to a lover, a statement of fidelity and desire. It is certainly the greatest song that Chris Ethridge and Gram ever wrote together, and they wrote at least a half-dozen wonderful songs for the first album. It certainly counts as one of the 60s' best and most moving songs, the more so since it operates outside of strict country stylings and embarks on a voyage through 50s pop, with changes that Johnny Mercer would have nodded approvingly at. It has all the elements of great visionary pop music, lush and sweeping with an arrangement that would satisfy Bacharach and David, yet it is sung so convincingly and with such passion, especially for a 22 year old. Simply put, he states

I'm your toy, I'm your old boy
And I don't want no one but you to love me
No, I wouldn't lie
You know I'm not that kind of guy

The pedal steel sweeps in behind this statement, playing a whole symphony line, a part redolent of strings and brass. The whole album is in fact, filled with such moments of blurry–eyed melancholy; there are moments when you doubt you could ever hear a voice like his again – never again hear songs sung with such conviction by someone so young. "We went through 'Hot Burrito#1' and '2' and we saw that we had the highly-polished musical thing by the nuts – we had it and we could do it" Gram explained shortly afterwards. "My piano playing and organ playing came back to where it was before the Byrds. I started getting funky again and everybody started getting funky again and it was time to end the album. And after we did it, it was time to beat it – time to get out of LA. We would love to have our next album called *Ray Of Hope*, you know. We'd like to find some place over in Europe where we're really happy and we could write about all the funky, nice farmers."

Work on the first album was completed quickly. Even by the working standards of the 1960s, a time when acts cut singles one day and released them the next, it was fast. Kleinow confirms that it was done in good time. "I can't say how long it took to finish the album… yeah, maybe two weeks, that's all. It was pretty intense, we kept after it every day. We certainly didn't take any days off when we were doing that album."

While the size of the advance had been problematic, the record label kindly sponsored a shopping spree for the band, led by Parsons. In early 1969, relations were good with the record company, although the normal healthy antagonism for bean counters shone through in Gram's conversation with *Fusion* magazine: "They have been real good. They've let us follow our concept, so to speak. I mean, they're in it for the money like every other record company, and if people start buying our records, they'll let us run with the ball. That's all I can say. I don't even know what will happen – otherwise, I don't even want to think about it. If I have to pay more dues, I'm willing to because I dig honky-tonk and rock and roll – and being on the street doesn't bug me at all. I don't need to have an image… so it doesn't matter, one record company or the other."

While Fusion reported that image may not have been all-important to Gram, he still brought his fellow band members to Nudie's Rodeo Tailor on Hollywood Boulevard, where they were outfitted for the kind of suits that usually only Hank Snow or Porter Wagoner would be seen dead in. Gram had his first jacket made by Nudie while he was still in the International Submarine Band, decorated with, naturally, a submarine.

Defending the sequins and rhinestones proved difficult. It seemed that this fashion preference vexed the underground press greatly; some considering that the band was making a statement aligning themselves with the rest of 'straight America'. "We are not a negative, put-down group," Gram said, hotly. "They're so uptight about our sequinned suits – I just can't believe it." Then his good grace returns and he calmly wedges his tongue in his cheek. "Just because we wear sequined suits doesn't mean that we think we're great, it means we think sequins are great. We think sequins are good taste. *Rolling Stone*, the *Free Press* – they think that we're a bunch of show-offs and we're trying to put everything down. We're merely reflecting everything, because real music is supposed to reflect reality. You can't build a reality in music, you have to reflect it.

"I'm using clothes because clothes are the most obvious thing you can point at... to see what a person is doing. And the other side uses clothes too. Richard Nixon and Governor Reagan see a bunch of little girls in pea jackets and wearing Onks and think they're the enemy of educational wisdom, you know. Maybe everyone would be a lot safer wearing sequins. We're wearing 'em because they're bulletproof."

The new outfits managed to cause some consternation over at A&M, although it was not because they were too outrageous or in league with Straight America – it was just that Jerry Moss had hit the roof when the invoice arrived from Nudie the Rodeo Tailor. Sneaky Pete remembers that the suits had cost around $1000 each back then. It seemed funny to the rest of the band, but that was just the start of the spending trend that would characterise that first honeymoon period with A&M. Never mind that first round of wild tailoring, the second act went something like this...

Starting the trip early one fall morning in 1968, art director Tom Wilkes and photographer Barry Feinstein put himself, an assistant and some camera equipment in the front of his Volkswagen and started driving out to the desert. Up front in a hired limousine rode the Flying Burrito Brothers, A&M's Michael Vosse, "resident freak" and assistant to vice-president Gil Friesen, with his ever-present Super 8 camera, and two models – one blonde, one brunette. The group took the limo on a three-hour journey out to Joshua Tree, with Michael Vosse recording portions of the predawn drive on his Super 8. The footage is now owned privately by a collector in Southern California, and I was privileged to view it on a trip to Los Angeles.

First stop was out near Cap Rock, the location suggested by Gram. The morning was freezing and windy. Vosse wandered around the site of the shoot with his camera, focusing rather too much on the attractive brunette model, who, aside from some askance looks at Vosse, pretended to be immune to the attraction of any camera lens. She tried to act bored, but she just looked cold, as they all did. The group huddled together, their arms around the girls. Gram stood slightly off to one side, smoking cigarettes as Hillman and Chris Ethridge, both yawning repeatedly, draped their arms good-naturedly over the models. Sneaky Pete looked on amusedly, as youthful as everyone else in the band on that occasion.

It was like Gram was being the perfect gentleman at the time, as he wasn't paying much attention to the girls. Soon Vosse was spending an inordinate amount of time trying to get as much footage of the brunette's behind as he possibly could. Ignoring the occasional violent gusts of wind and rain that flung sand and dead leaves around, the group then moved on to an area just off what would be considered the "main street" of Joshua Tree, where the session continued for another hour. Wilkes took photos of Hillman, Gram, Ethridge and Sneaky Pete posed grimly out by deserted shacks amid long grass, 30-year old beer cans strewn at their feet. With the two models, they struck shapes and poses, managing only to look serious and intense. Gram smiles a faint half-smile, hands on hips. It was freezing cold that day, and the guys buttoned up their shirts and suits against the slicing breeze that whipped past them, flicking their hair high.

While the band approved the album cover initially, Gram later expressed his dissatisfaction with the shot that was chosen. He liked Barry Feinstein as a photographer, but he couldn't understand why Tom Wilkes had chosen such a serious shot. "There were other better photographs from that shoot. The suits would always have photographed well." There was one shot that Gram much preferred. It featured the models and the Joshua Trees more prominently; importantly, the models were both draped over Gram and he had a mischievous smile on his face. The final cover showed the band looking pretty dour, like a bad-tempered bunch of rockers, rather than the fun-loving country musicians they actually were. It was the looks on their faces that had their friends wondering why they didn't choose a photo that better represented how they really were.

At the official launch of the album in April 1969, A&M decorated the old MGM studio lot where they were based with hay bales. Invitations had been sent out with handfuls of real hay attached to them. Reflective of the paranoia that existed on both sides of the establishment fence, the whole mail-out was held up while the US Post Office sent the invitations to a local government laboratory, who tested the dry, grassy substance. The tests revealed that it was not marijuana.

The launch could now go ahead, much to the relief of the label, who should have taken this interruption as being symbolic of the many misunderstandings that already existed about the band. With the addition of an old-time dance caller, and the curious falsetto performance of English singer/songwriter John Braden, the Flying Burrito Brothers got up and did it for the executives, the A&R people, their friends and journalists. It was all about letting them know that "Well, here we are", even if the overwhelming feeling of the time was that the musical prairie where the Burritos existed was nearly empty.

This wasn't exactly true. Gene Clark was doing country music at the time, as were groups like Commander Cody and the Lost Planet Airmen and the New Riders of the Purple Sage. Even Crosby, Stills, Nash & Young had a hit with a Graham Nash tune that was very straight country, with pedal steel played by a member of the Grateful Dead. Still, few of the too-hip music critics of the day were open-minded enough to cop the influence, because *country and western spelled establishment*.

Many of them missed the clear political point of the exercise, failing to note how effective it was to take conservative musical forms and subvert them so beautifully and to such good effect. 'Okie from Muskogee' might have seemed like pure hippie-bashing but hell, there was a common rumour around that Merle Haggard smoked pot too. Even Willie Nelson's tour bus smelled funny. Country music, no matter how you dressed it up with irony and abstraction, was fundamentalist and therefore suspect. It was up there with church, flag and tidy sideburns. How did heads like

Parsons and Hillman, two former Byrds, start playing country music?

As the *Gilded Palace* rolled onward in search of an audience, it transpired that some critics and reviewers really did understand. *Rolling Stone* published a fine review of the album penned by Southerner and one-time resident of Waycross, Georgia, Stanley Booth. The review was complimentary to Gram's talent and, in the tradition of the magazine, very knowing. Booth understood (possibly better than anyone) just how Gram felt being lost in the big city, adrift in its carnality and not "feeling at home" anywhere and called the new album "the statement of a young man who must feel at home nowhere, not in the big city or in Waycross, Georgia." Booth concluded: "Perhaps Parsons, coming from the country, feels more deeply than most the strangeness and hostility of the modern world, but he speaks to and for all of us. Gram Parsons is a good old boy."

A good review at last, from someone who clearly got the point, even about the Nudie suits adorned with pills, pot and naked ladies. Gram deeply appreciated it; he later confided to Booth that he seemed to have known exactly where Parsons was at when he recorded the album. Booth also had figured out for himself how being Southern nearly always made you the perennial outsider in any fast-moving West or East Coast city. He also knew that Southerners were known, in fact renowned, for making astute observations about the way everyone else behaved. He saw this in Gram's music and noted that Gram resisted the urges of sentimentality, but not nostalgia. Nostalgia is one of the South's great strengths – their very existence had been forever divided into antebellum and postbellum by the Civil War, or, as many liked to refer to it, "the late unpleasantness".

The rest of the Burrito Brothers were also excited about the review. Good press in *Rolling Stone* meant the likelihood of acceptance. In less than a year, the magazine – which in its initial review, had denounced *Sweetheart* as "ideologically-challenged" and worse, not very good – had picked up on what Parsons, Hillman, Kleinow and Ethridge were achieving. Still, among the members of the band, there was a suspicion – one that was fed by the hay, so to speak – that it wasn't just some critics who missed out on the idea. The record company had completely missed the point of what the Brothers were trying to do too. Gram later explained the modus operandi of the Burritos, that this is all supposed to be very simple. It was to "create goose bumps, make a little catharsis," he said, sadly. "But it was all too frantic. Everybody was trying too hard to prove to a lot of closed-minded people that we could compete with Merle Haggard."

Sneaky Pete's take on the wonderful eclecticism that fuelled the first album was that it was "a wild jumble of different ideas. The first album was certainly everybody's idea of an 'underground album' as far as I'm concerned. It was really different. As far as I know, the Burritos were the only ones who really did it exactly that way. There were other groups going in country directions with country ideas, but the Burritos were the only ones that were really doing actual true country music."

Kleinow also saw that the real inspiration was coming from rock bands doing a take on country, rather than from country artists themselves. While Gram's efforts with the Byrds and Dylan's *Nashville Skyline* and *John Wesley Harding* albums had moved to legitimise a country approach to rock music, bands like the Beatles and the Rolling Stones were also taking country to the kids, and they were everyone's favourites, not to mention being hip. "The Beatles, for instance, were doing things like 'I Don't Want To Spoil The Party' and all of their country-oriented things. As far as I'm concerned," said Kleinow, "everything good has come from the Beatles.

Dylan's been a great influence but the Beatles have been the greatest of them all as far as influencing the trends."

Gram would have agreed with that, although he wasn't about to buy into the myth that Dylan was now a country singer either. "After three years, somebody finally bought country music, somebody finally bought the International Submarine Band – and then they [Lee Hazlewood's company LHI] sold the name and everything. We paid more dues – but country music was being accepted and we didn't care. And now, everyone wants to get on the bandwagon; everybody wants to say they're country – including Bob Dylan, who I respect and dig, you know, but he is not as country as *Crawdaddy* seems to think he is." Chris Hillman interjects: "I don't think he himself is trying to project that image, but that it's imposed...."

"Oh, right, he's always been funky," Gram agreed. "People hated him when he started out. They said rotten things about him, but now they're trying to project the country scene onto him. And he isn't country. He's a poet."

Nineteen sixty-eight was a busy year, in which Gram's tenure with the Byrds had begun, then come to an end. In less than twelve months, Gram had been involved in the making of two classic albums that would eventually come to represent some of the true musical advances of the decade. The year had almost peaked six months early, as the Byrds released an album, then were effectively split down the middle. Some said it was a disaster, but, like honey from the (country) rock, from disaster came fulfilment.

Gram was brimming with concepts, questions, answers, and philosophies. Occasionally, he liked to baffle interviewers with his ideas. He crossed swords with Bud Scoppa in a friendly interview, where he dropped a laudably obscure snippet of Greek philosophy into the conversation, only to find that Scoppa was more than up for the task. He was full of bright ideas for the band, like relocation to Europe in order that they soak up some of the Rolling Stones' glory and create a movement in the UK that would be free of the misperceptions of American critics and audiences.

Some of the ideas stuck – like the Nudie suits. It was the central image that came to define the band more fully than the music they played ever would. To observers, they produced country music for heads and dressed that way to ridicule Hank Snow and his toupee. Of course, they were country singers first and foremost. Chris Hillman tired quickly of having to explain to journalists and critics that they had achieved that on their own terms. Hillman, Gram, Ethridge and Kleinow had been instrumental in producing what came to be hailed as an enduring album of its time, full of beauty, seriousness, and lighthearted joy. They had no idea that by placing themselves among the few who had experimented like this they were in for critical misapprehension, poor marketing ideas from the record company and, sadly, poor sales.

"Jerry Moss pinned it," said Gram. "He said, 'You're a second-album group, just don't expect that your first album is gonna be the greatest thing in the world.' He was probably thinking things like, 'Chris Ethridge isn't a country bass player but I can't tell this guy this because they're friends.' But he knew we were a country group and he knew what would make a country group – it's just that we didn't really have it together on the first album. He was hoping that we would on the second."

While the 'problem' of Ethridge's bass playing appears not to have surfaced again for a further six months, the rest of the band were very impressed with Chris's abilities. "Chris is a real bright guy and he had a very unique way of playing the bass," says Sneaky Pete. "He liked to hang out with anybody. He was one of the most gregarious people I ever met in my life. He'd just walk up to a stranger and start talking to them, like at the airport when we were getting off a flight, he'd walk up to somebody and start talkin'. He'd be like, 'We're the Flying Burrito Brothers and over here, this is Sneaky Pete.' People he'd never seen before. He's a funny guy. Again, he had a very personal way of playing the bass that didn't sound like anybody else. You can really tell Chris and you can recognise his playing on anything. He had a way of making himself heard; he would just stand right out. He'd get right on that one note and just go boom-boom-boom-boom-boom-boom-boom. He'd hang on the same note, play it like seven times or whatever, not go to another note. That was definitely a style."

Gram knew what Jerry Moss had suspected all along: It was a brave move to sign the Flying Burrito Brothers in the first place, and selling country rock to 17-year-old kids who found meaning and movement in psychedelia and acid rock was never going to be easy. Martin C. Strong, author of *The Great Rock Discography*, put it eloquently; "Clearly, playing the Grand Ole Opry as the Byrds had done before them, was out of the question, Parsons, no doubt past caring about the head-in-the-sand opinion of the country establishment."

While the establishment tut-tutted, and the album flummoxed its potential audience, the Flying Burrito Brothers decided that a tour of America was in order.

CHAPTER 7
THE TRAVELLING PALACE OF SIN
That Burrito Tour

In January 1969, after the recording and mixing of *The Gilded Palace of Sin*, A&M committed itself to sending their newly signed act out on the road to do an actual tour. All this attention conspired to get Gram off the hook where his wife-to-be was concerned. The wedding plans had slipped off the list of priorities Gram had set himself. Nancy was quietly heartbroken, since she had accepted long ago that Gram loved her but not as much as he once had. Even as he distanced himself emotionally from her, he insisted on spending time with her and Polly, which Nancy appreciated. But it produced problems of its own. The wedding dress, which cost about a thousand dollars, was displayed on a mannequin at Nudie's shop (where it would remain for many years), and Gram tried not to spend too much time there with his old buddy Nudie, lest the rhinestone-studded garment remind him of how poorly he'd handled the separation from his girlfriend. Worse still was the continuing matter of Gram's paternity of Polly, something that he was heard to drunkenly deny on occasion.

The Burritos were already spending a lot of time working as many gigs as they could possibly get, mostly at the Los Angeles and Hollywood clubs but also occasionally doing high school auditoriums. One high school student who got to see them both in a nightclub and at his high school graduation dance was California singer and songwriter Dennis Roger Reed. "In early 1969, I became aware of a band called the Flying Burrito Brothers. Their album *Gilded Palace of Sin* was released, and other than having to return it because I thought the tinny mix was a defect, I loved it better than my previous favourite recording, the Byrds' *Sweetheart of the Rodeo*. That record had made me a major Gram Parsons fan, and I'd also heard some of his International Submarine Band stuff as well.

"The Golden Bear [a Huntington Beach, California club] was apparently a legendary venue but to the Orange County suburban hippies, it was just a close venue for cool acts. I badgered a friend of mine to accompany me to see the Flying Burrito Brothers up close and personal, and we landed at the second or third row of seats, while our blonde girlfriends scarfed up spaghetti dinners we couldn't really afford. We sat through two full sets of country rock history. I was especially enamoured of Chris Ethridge's bass playing and I also loved the cover tunes that the boys did, from the Everlys to Merle Haggard.

"About two months later, I graduated from high school. The school district put on a 'grad night,' so that all us potentially drunk and loaded teens wouldn't end up dead behind the wheel of a Camaro. They had food and non-alcoholic drinks, games and live music. They booked the Spiral Staircase, Blues Image and the Peter Tork Band. I figured that the indoor miniature golf might be interesting, but the billing cards inside the event didn't mention the ex-Monkee, but instead said "the Flying

Burrito Brothers!" The other bands all took the stage before Parsons and crew. But eventually some of the skinniest guys (with some of the skinniest girls I'd ever seen) waltzed in wearing those famous Nudie suits.

"They took the stage to almost a complete lack of reaction – it was probably 2 or 3 am at that point and country music was not a hot high school item – they played about a one-hour set, mostly stuff from *Gilded Palace*. I climbed up on stage for a better vantage point, sitting under Gram's electric piano. About mid-set, he moved to the Rhodes to do 'Hot Burrito #2', and a roadie [probably Jimmi Seiter] shoved me off stage. But I was still only a foot away as he wailed "Jesus Christ" in the chorus. I may be having a hallucinatory memory, but I swear at one point in the set, Gram looked at Chris Hillman and said, 'Let's play another one for the little bastards.'"

As Jim Dickson and Eddie Tickner have both confirmed, the Burritos routinely played such high school shows. Occasionally, a complete lack of audience reaction would trouble the band. Chris Hillman didn't seem to mind so much. He liked to play, but this was starting to seem like reverse dues-paying. However you look at it, the fact that the Burritos had to play high school shows is almost absurd. All of the guys had done it before, but mostly while in their teens. Their audiences were mostly high school kids who didn't really dig the music, or couldn't understand why they looked rock and roll but sounded like shitkickers. From a financial point of view, the high school shows paid decent money and the band could pretty much play any song they wanted to, which meant it was going to be a rock and roll hoedown at least some of the time. It also gave the band the chance to brush up on new material, or run through a few chestnuts.

During this period, the lineup involving Jon Corneal changed. Jon had accepted the offer of a permanent drum chair in the Dillard & Clark Expedition, and their previous drummer – none other than ex-Byrd Michael Clarke – was invited to sit in with the Flying Burrito Brothers. Among other good factors, it meant that there were now more Byrds in the Burritos than there were in the Byrds. While Mike Clarke committed himself with vigour to both the Expedition and the Burritos, he had spent a lot of time painting in Hawaii after leaving the Byrds and it would be fair to say that he was not entirely convinced of the merits of being in a band.

Finally, it was suggested that it might be a good idea to do most of the projected tour by train, since airplanes were Gram's least favourite way to achieve great altitude. Gram's fear of flying was eating further into his mind, linking up with other paranoias and fears. There was no shame in being afraid of flying but it put a downer on being in a rock 'n' roll band, as Chris Hillman knew all too well. Gene Clark's own fear of flying had made life on the road very difficult for the Byrds, and Hillman no doubt groaned inwardly when he learned of Parsons' similar phobia. The rest of the band thought this was a novel way to cover some distance and have some fun at the same time. The band would ride the rails east in early February, bound for Chicago, and then drive to Detroit where the tour was to officially begin.

Brandon De Wilde and a large group of well-wishers were on hand to wave farewell to the group, and there was an awful lot of cocaine going around before the train pulled out. Along with the band for the ride was A&M's Michael Vosse. As the designated corporate hippie of the trip, Vosse had the 8mm movie camera and the corporate credit card to pay for everything. The band had already paid for the necessary amusements and diversions for the trip and there were a number of different narcotics on board. The band had great fun discovering where Michael Vosse had hidden his stash for the trip, and made short order of a bag of coke and some mescaline crystals.

Phil Kaufman was along as road manager, a capacity that was shortly reworded as "road mangler", a sobriquet that has stuck to him ever since. It was Kaufman who made all of the finer arrangements for the band. He could handle scrapes with the law, the need for grass or find someone a bed for the night at short notice. Most of all, he had previously offered himself as the "executive nanny" to the Stones and that made him doubly interesting to Gram, who hired him to watch out for the Brothers. He was the man who would always be around to take care of someone if and when such attention was required, which was not infrequently.

Phil called the musicians to order. "I said, 'Okay, look. We're going to go on this tour. First I want everybody's stash. I want all your drugs. If you want some, come and see me, but I don't want six bags of dope scattered around the train.'" There were some protests, but Phil warned them about the potential for disaster if they were busted with dope. "They didn't seem to realise that they could go to prison for that stuff," he said. "I did, and had."

As it turned out, the watchwords of this particular tour would be "poker" and 'coke', lots of both. Rarely without a hand of cards and a blast of Bolivia's finest, the band ran the camera and acted up, pulling frantic Beatle antics at the train station for the benefit of mostly unamused railway staff. The Super Chief's crew told the Burritos management, Steve Aldsberg and Rick Sutherland, that the band would be given their own dining car, so that if necessary, they could "run wild" without upsetting the other passengers. And run wild they did.

"It was like debauchery personified, going across America," remembered Phil. "The guys were gambling, fighting and being test pilots for new and wondrous drugs." The first extended break of the train trip was a two-hour layover in Albuquerque, New Mexico. Sadly for Phil, who was then still relatively new to the music industry, the guys had all ingested magic mushrooms and were wandering around the shops and stalls near the train station, buying Indian artefacts. "This was not the way I had pictured the music business to be," said Phil ruefully.

The Burritos arrived in Chicago a day and a half later, after many games of poker and not much in the way of sleep. They were all wasted from tiredness and they all were coming down with what Clarke thought was pneumonia, or at least a serious case of the flu. They checked into the Astor Towers hotel and continued playing poker late into the night. In the morning, they ordered a breakfast of lemon soufflés and coffee and kept the poker game rolling right along, until they all began keeling over with the flu. "Gram and Chris and I got a doctor who gave us a big shot of antibiotics and this cough medicine."

That night in Chicago, there was a meeting with the record company people. The band arrived in a parlous state. "We passed out in our food," said Clarke. "Chris was lying on a bench, Gram was out on his feet and I was dribbling." Despite the punishing schedule of physical abuse, the group apparently continued to cane themselves in the rental car on the way to Detroit. Gram drove as far as Detroit for the first show of the tour, while in the back seat Chris Hillman and the rest of the band, except Sneaky, played seven-card showdown. Gram, who was supposed to be looking at the road, was paying more attention to his hand, when Sneaky shouted, "There's the Detroit exit, Gram!" Gram grabbed the wheel hard and propelled the car across a lane indicator strip. No one dropped their cards or even broke the poker face, and the game continued all the way into town.

When the Flying Burrito Brothers arrived in Detroit, they were booked to play at a venue in a black neighbourhood that had been nearly destroyed by riots a few days before. Tanks had rumbled through the streets and the National Guard and the Army were on patrol. "We were cowboys, dressed in cowboy gear," said Phil. "It was very strange. We were playing with Procol Harum (how country can you get?). We played our shows and people stared at us. They had never seen a steel guitar before. Sneaky Pete was making all sorts of weird sounds and that was their introduction to country music."

Enlightened by the experience, the band headed back to Chicago for one show. They stayed at the Biltmore, where the hotel restaurant was Maxim's de Paris, one of the most reputable restaurants in the world. The band took in dinner there one night, arriving in their combination of Nudie suits, jeans and hats, catching the unimpressed eyes of the maître d' and the clientele. Sneaky Pete surprised everyone by ordering an expensive French wine in French. He then surprised everyone further by explaining to the wine waiter that the wine was undrinkable. The wine waiter suspected he was the victim of some rock and roll practical joke, until Sneaky insisted that he try a little of the wine. He quickly apologised for the wine and brought a fresh bottle, which was deemed more acceptable to the table.

Chris Ethridge and Gram were interviewed by radio celebrity and noted jazz fan Studs Terkel. They tried without success to explain to him what they were attempting to do musically. The next four shows were up in Gram's old stomping ground, Boston, where the Burritos were co-booked to appear at the Boston Tea Party with the Byrds on February 20-23. The Burritos took it like a challenge to work with some of their former team mates – Phil Kaufman hinted that the musicians may have even been close to being sober and straight for the shows.

However solid the Burritos may have been, the new Byrds lineup of McGuinn, Clarence White, John York and Gene Parsons was already a critical success, and many people considered them to be the best incarnation of the band in a live context. During the shows, McGuinn proved to be his usual slightly distant self but he was in a genial, generally good mood and the Burritos and The Byrds easily and naturally joined forces on stage for certain songs. Rather than the headbutting contest one might envision, there was an easy camaraderie between the two groups. At the end of the first show McGuinn officially extended the hand of friendship to Gram, inviting him to sing 'Hickory Wind' with them the following evening.

Each band's repertoire tended to cover very similar territory, as the Byrds were still using parts of *Sweetheart...* live and the Burritos included many of the same songs in their sets. They hooked up on stage during the Byrds' set to co-perform tunes like 'You Ain't Goin' Nowhere', 'Hickory Wind', 'Time Between', Pretty Boy Floyd' and 'The Christian Life'. The highlight of the evening, according to Johnny Rogan, was a surprising rendition of 'You Don't Miss Your Water'. It was generally agreed on by most of the bands' members that the two groups should keep playing more shows together, considering how well the audiences received them. The sound was gorgeous and the performances electrifying, according to Jon Landau of *Rolling Stone*, who was present for the shows. "Gram seemed to be entranced and in touch with his music in a way that he is not with the Burritos," was Landau's observation on that show.

Landau's comment came at a time when the Brothers were experiencing varying degrees of satisfaction from the tour experience. Even in the wake of an exciting and beautifully balanced first album, the writing was very much on the wall for the Burrito Brothers; each part weighed in the balance and a couple of them found wanting. Tempers were fraying from a blizzard of coke and a wave of trips of all kinds. Michael Vosse witnessed the problems firsthand: "Things were more difficult than anticipated. Shows weren't all that steady and here we were, just halfway through this thing and it was cold. And people started to snap. There was a lot of speaking through gritted teeth and screaming."

Conflict began to brew between the band and its management. Hillman, suspicious of managers, wasn't satisfied that they were doing their job properly, while the managers groused that the band was just getting stoned at every moment they possibly could. Gram took a brief respite from the heavy scenes and the crazed inhaling and spent a couple of days with his friend Jet Thomas at Harvard Yard, before an attempt to make the first of a series of shows at The Scene in New York. But the bad weather froze them into Boston, the airports were closed and the only way to get to New York was to drive.

Unfortunately, some of the band members got into town too late to make the show, disappointing a capacity crowd that was packed with celebrities, including Janis Joplin. This series of events was exacerbated by Gram then moving the band members *en masse* out of their booked hotel before check-in to the Gramercy Park, where rock cognoscenti like the Stones usually stayed when in town. It was known to be rock-star friendly, but the higher room rate bumped up the tour expenses considerably, something that annoyed Jerry Moss no end when Vosse rang him to fill him in on the change of accommodation. Next stop was Philadelphia, where Frank David Murphy caught their show at the Electric Factory, as they opened for Three Dog Night.

Murphy had been in a locked ward at the University of Pennsylvania Hospital and was possibly not in an ideal condition to be ushered into the arena of the chemically altered. "Somehow, I even convinced my psychiatrist it would be good for me to get a 24-hour pass to 'visit with an old friend who was briefly in town'; not mentioning the nature, locale or character of the visit or the friend. Another ex-Bolles friend signed me out and took 'responsibility' for me."

Backstage, Murphy could only look on as the tensions within the band played themselves out. "Gram was having a great time being the centre of attention while Chris, Sneaky Pete and Chris Ethridge were all trying to be serious, disciplined musicians. I realise that the burning question in everyone's mind is 'Gram = drugs?'. Here's what I know for a stone cold fact. Gram loved booze and downers. Booze was omnipresent since we were teenagers, grass was a sine-qua-non from certainly 1965 on and I suspect (though I had no knowledge from personal experience) before that. At the time when they played with Three Dog Night, Gram was playing with mescaline and psilocybin (the active compound in magic mushrooms) but had hard words to say about other drugs."

The drug intake must indeed have been varied, because Gram thought it would be a fine idea if the Nudie suits were paired with an attractive turban, each with a different-coloured jewel, that he'd bought for every band member. The turbans were a kind of R&B in-joke; black R&B groups would often wear turbans to suggest a more exotic East Indian background. Gram further refined his act to include falling off the organ stool at the end of the last song in the set for some light relief. All this seemed funny to most people, but it was just another indicator as to how off-beam things were in the Burrito camp.

The tour was, in hindsight, "stupid, really", according to Hillman. "We weren't very good on stage. We spent a fortune and didn't accomplish anything." Spent a fortune was right. There was a story going around in the late 1970s that the bills for that tour were still rolling in to the A&M offices. The final tally was around $80,000 on Vosse's credit card, an enormous amount of money, even by today's standards. Add to that the $25,000 for the first album and its promotion, and the picture that emerged placed the band in serious debt to the company.

The Burritos had worked up a new song while on tour, fittingly entitled 'The Train Song'. It was a definite winner of a song, reminiscent of a storming R&B track, but with the addition of some incredible fuzztone pedal steel courtesy of Sneaky Pete. It became a staple of their live shows and its sentiments seemed to make it popular with audiences, who greeted it with cheers.

Coming off the tour was something of a torture, but not in the same way that the tour had been torturous. The Burritos were still being asked to perform on the kinds of varied bills that were popular at that end of the '60s. It wasn't unusual for rock and jazz bands to play on the same bill, but it was still uncommon to hear a country group play with rock bands. The band were approached to contribute to a benefit bill at San Francisco's Avalon Ballroom on April 6th. Local bands Moby Grape and Quicksilver Messenger Service also played. A bootleg from that night reveals an over-refreshed Gram struggling to hit the right notes, as the band's live set lurches from bad to worse. The Burritos appear to hit their stride only on the medley of 'If You Can't Undo The Wrong' and 'Somebody's Back In Town'. They follow it up with a version of 'Sin City' and a fine version of Mel Tillis's 'Sweet Mental Revenge'.

They won the crowd over at that point, and started playing rock and roll like their lives depended on it. However, Gram's voice, ever under siege from coke and smoke, soon struggled to hold up for an hour-long set. He even shared the lead vocals with Hillman. These kinds of shows gave their critics ammunition, but for the fans proved that the Burritos didn't necessarily feel the need to be tight and well-rehearsed, a very rock and roll sentiment.

By the time *The Gilded Palace of Sin* was released in April 1969, the dynamic of the band was beginning to change. Their label was no longer so supportive, mainly because they were already in a hole over this deal and the likelihood of the band ever recouping A&M's investment diminished daily. Furthermore, with the kind of live reviews they were getting from the papers and the underground press, it sounded like critics resented their sloppiness live, as though they were expected to be superior to other rock and roll bands of the day.

The reviews for both the Burritos' record and live shows were a mixed bag. *Rolling Stone* defended them to the hilt, while magazines like *Crawdaddy* and the underground press in California could be damning, and damned cruel. Sneaky Pete leapt to the defence of the other brothers, saying the rough playing was deliberate because they were "outlaws" who operated outside the constraints of current modern rock music, some of which was equally rough. Eventually, the outlaw tag wore pretty thin, and seemed to become a byword for bands with lots of attitude and less talent. That wasn't the case with the Burritos at all, but it didn't seem to matter anymore.

The Flying Burrito Brothers continued to divide opinions, representing a troubling grey area to most music journalists. Many of them didn't understand what the Hell good a fusion of country and rock could have been for anyone. They could have been forgiven for thinking that it was a mutant from outer space, so 1950s was its drama and beauty. Satan might have been real, but Vietnam was now more real and more unpopular than ever. How had the era thrown up such musical diversity, when folk and rock should have gotten together to kick ass and make some statements?

Southeast Asia's most obvious contribution to the mainland USA was bodybags and opiates, neither of which recommended it to anybody. As the war effort and the number of troops committed to Vietnam doubled, so did the number of aluminium coffins and so did the smack. While heroin was no stranger to the US, there was now more of it around than there ever had been before, and enough of it to let folks dabble. Musicians were getting hung up on it quickly, and it had already taken its toll.

John Lennon was entering a harsh and introspective habit at the time, and many others found heroin's reductive, insulating properties satisfying. Some people got a kick out of spending that much time within themselves. Keith Richards had been into it for a while, but had refused to have it around too much in case he got hung up on it. This was one way for him to avoid admitting that he had a problem with it already, but at the time he actually preferred to drink enormous amounts and take acid. His real heroin problem was about to announce itself.

It seemed that, as egos inflated and drug habits grew, even some of the big concert draws became quite an unreliable prospect live. The likes of Janis Joplin and even Hendrix had been known to slip into sloppiness and self-indulgent jamming. It was almost the 70s, after all. Gram, for one, had already become convinced that the band's standards were a little lower than he would have liked, but he felt prepared at this stage of the game to press on. He had a thing about "paying dues" and felt that a certain level of vilification was bound to occur, but that it was all part of the dues-paying process.

To quote him: "We're treated great in one way and, on the other hand, we're completely misunderstood. Rock critics and country critics completely misunderstand; it would be the same with the R&B critics if they had the opportunity." But for Chris Hillman, this period of critical vilification was dispiriting. At four years Gram's senior, Chris was not used to critical slamming, at least not until Gram Parsons had come down the pike. At that point, the Byrds, having just sacked David Crosby, were suddenly open to all kinds of attacks, even though they had once been the critics' darlings, since they were the band musically closest in spirit to the Beatles. It didn't seem to matter that Chris, at close to 27, had already paid his dues with the Byrds, writing songs that displayed "country rock" tendencies while Gram was still in high school. As a musician, he had his pride and his reputation to protect, and he had to support his lifestyle too.

On the surface, it seemed that everyone caught up in the Burritos' lifestyle was having a good old time playing poker, getting dusted and screwing so many women that the doors of the new Burrito Manor on Beverly Glen were starting to come off their hinges. Poker became the entertainment regime, and the band would prevail on anyone they knew with money to join them. Their guests never realised they were being systematically fleeced of their dough. Chris once jokingly said that he made more money from poker than from being in the band; only later did he realise it was true.

The fun began in earnest when Gram began to split his time between Burrito Manor and his new pad, the Chateau Marmont. The Marmont was faded and hip, thus making it the perfect residence for a faded, jaded prince like Gram. When in early 1969 Gram moved into the bungalow kept by his friend filmmaker Tony Foutz, it still retained a sepia grip on the past, the hallways full of ghostly former movie stars, their faces drawn and thin. It was an appropriately delusional glamour. "At the time," said Kim Fowley, "It was a cross of the Fitzgerald and New York's Chelsea. Lauren Hutton and Faye Dunaway lived there alone at the time. It was a prestigious place to stay, in its own way."

There, on any given day of the week, you would find the likes of Kim Fowley, Faye Dunaway and Brandon De Wilde lounging by the pool and resting in the monied ambience of the Marmont. There, out by the secluded bungalows, it was cool and shaded, with a decent swimming pool and private bungalows that movie producers once used for casting sessions with blonde starlets, a place for them to smoke big cigars while the up-and-coming actresses splashed in the shallow end.

After the first wave of good times and the now-dead Summer of Love vibe had departed, the Strip was far less glitzy, the kids were all looking pretty vacant and you couldn't take five steps without encountering some acid or heroin casualty with a heavy tale of uncaring parents and no money. Behind the palm trees, set back off the Strip, the Marmont's room rates were a little cheaper and there was a good Japanese restaurant nearby with full bar service. It was perfect for a guy like Gram, whose disposable income allowed him to live just such a rootless lifestyle with a beautiful woman and a few bottles to hand of his favourite tequila, Sauza Conmemorativo.

The record company, beginning to sweat a little, could only look on as the album dribbled off the shelves of record stores in tiny numbers. Gram and Chris continued to push A&M to let them record 'The Train Song' as a single. The idea was that the song would be more "rock" and would then be more likely to pick up radio play. The single might include an album track on the b-side, and then A&M could see some return for their investment. Jerry Moss reluctantly gave in, and the label put up the money for it. It was a big production number and the band, at Chris and Gram's instigation, hired legendary R&B producers Johnny "Guitar" Watson and Larry Williams.

Williams, a native of Lawrence, Mississippi, was just 34 years old and already a respected producer and songwriter in R&B circles. Since 1966, he had worked with many different bands, not least of whom were the up-and-coming rock 'n' roll outfits who craved a certain hard R&B edge to their sound. Williams, a self-confessed Cadillac fanatic, was the man to give them just that dangerous sound they wanted so badly. After all, Williams lived a fast, dangerous life. He dressed like a bad pimp and was supposedly even involved in prostitution, although his sidemen and acquaintances nixed that claim later. Whatever – he drove a white Cadillac Eldorado with a gold Taurus symbol as hood ornament, a uniquely '60s play on the Caddy with steer horns.

Williams had written three big hits in the '50s, including "Bony Moronie" and "Short Fat Fannie". In later sessions the Burritos would cover the former, giving it an unusual hybrid treatment with Sneaky Pete playing the signature riff. Chris and Gram wanted the pair as producers for 'The Train Song' principally because they felt the R&B feel of the song would benefit from the input of two genuine R&B legends. Clarence White and Leon Russell were also involved in these sessions, which are reported to have been quite successful despite the massive amounts of cocaine going around.

For their part, Williams and Watson were intrigued by these honky boys and their freaky blend of country swing and R&B soul, but they were also captivated by the ever flowing cocaine and dope, and the fun the band were having in the studio. Gram kept passing a rolled-up $20 bill to the two of them, and soon the pair were thoroughly wired. Their involvement in the sessions eventually diminished to the oft-repeated mantra of Williams saying, "Watson, what'd you think about that there take?" To which Watson would reply enthusiastically, "Oh, I think it's great, man.

Say, give me another toot."

The single was issued in July but met with no kind of enthusiastic reaction whatsoever. Radio didn't go near it and Jerry Moss was seeing red. At this point, Michael Vosse's credit card bills had started arriving at the A&M accounts office and the eventual tally of somewhere near $85,000 was almost too traumatic for the suits.

As for Chris Hillman, just trying to get Gram to board a plane for a show was as much of a trauma. Hillman had seen Gene Clark behave similarly out of his terror of flying, although Clark had been in the unenviable position of having witnessed a horrific air accident while a young man in Ohio. Exactly what lay at the root of Gram's fear of flying is unclear, although some have suggested it was claustrophobia that caused it. Some have attested to seeing Gram calmly boarding flights while sober, using tickets he'd bought and paid for himself, but those flights had either been to England to take him to Keith's place, or to Florida to pick up his yearly stipend from the Snively trust fund. To be fair to Gram, he had avoided air travel as much as he possibly could in his short life.

Hillman could only watch as Gram medicated or drank himself into a stupor in order to gather the nerve to board a plane, just as Gene had done five years previously. Often, he could barely walk and would have to be assisted onto the plane. "He would completely turn into a wheelchair person," Chris confided to Ben Fong-Torres, "Breaking out into tears and we couldn't get him on the airplane." During one such incident, at the Seattle airport after a successful festival appearance there in 1969, airline staff were understandably concerned at his behaviour and appearance and refused to let him on the plane, such was his state of mind and body. "They'd see some guy slobbering in a chair, wearing these outlandish clothes and a top hat or something."

Either Jim Seiter or Phil Kaufman would then have to rent a car or a van, or put Gram on a bus to his destination. Most of the time, he was either incapacitated or recovering from a hangover so severe that he would drink more to feel less sick. Resentments grew as band members and roadies tired of making alternative travel arrangements and having to baby-sit Gram all the way to a gig, only to have him cop out and refuse to go onstage as he was feeling ill. Sometimes, he would be so wasted he could hardly be brought round to perform. Or if he did go onstage, he would nod off or fall over and make an ass of himself.

But not every show was a write-off. Sometimes, the group united to create something full of promise and wonder for the audiences, winning them over with wild outfits and great musicianship. Brian Day, a resident of San Francisco and long-time fan of the Flying Burrito Brothers, saw the band play numerous times. Here is his exclusive recollection as he sent it to me in the summer of 2000:

"We saw the Burritos play a few times here in SF", Day remembers, "And I saw them a few time in Los Angeles, twice at the Palomino, but oddly enough the one concert that stands head and shoulders above the rest (for strange reasons) is one the Burritos played in....Stanford, California, of all places.

"One fine Saturday afternoon in the spring of 1969, I think, I was cruising in my car on the Bayshore freeway listening to the local progressive rock station. Back in those days, 'progressive' meant that once in a while they'd play a cut longer than exactly 2:05. The dickhead jabberwocky bubblegum DJ came on and said 'Hey, listen to this one, haw haw haw.... the Flying Burrito Brothers are playing a free concert at Tressider Union at Stanford this afternoon! Haw, haw, haw, the Flyring Whooshit Breeders? Sounds like a third-rate circus act to me, but it's completely and absolutely free. If you've got nothing else at all to do, head on down and watch 'em do trapeze tricks...'

"My pulse shot up to triple-digit beats, and I resisted the urge to pull a 70-mph u-turn in the fast lane of the freeway. Instead, I calmly headed for the nearest exit and Stanford University. We got to Tressider, which is about a 400-seat amphitheater-type indoor venue, used mostly for poetry readings, overly serious folksingers with pretentious social messages and angry student leaders trying to whip up the bored rabble. But there, on stage, were the Burritos in all their Nudie-suited glory. There were amps and drums and a steel guitar all set up, and the band was going through that tuning-up thing that seems to take about three hours even if you're straight.

"I guess it was part of a small-club tour, or they were between 'real' gigs or needed gas money, or whatever, but there they were, it was free, and there I was and there was only one slight problem. In this reasonably spacious venue, I counted exactly 47 people at the appointed showtime hour. Maybe the Flying Burrito Brothers weren't as well known up 'Frisco way as they were at the Palamino? In retrospect, Stanford University was probably the worst place for them to play in the whole Bay area. During that time, it was the least radical college you could think of, and crawling with the spoiled children of rich, conservative, captain-of-industry establishment-types.

"Hardly the place to debut a cutting-edge musical art form based on wild all-nighters, Suth'n drawls, intense personal angst, drinking, drugging and womanising. But the band was present, if not wildly excited about playing to hundreds of empty seats. I saw a couple of tense on-stage conferences between Gram and Chris Hillman, Chris Ethridge and whoever was the manager. My guess is some Burritos wanted to pull the plug and go get high. They were clearly not a bunch of happy campers. It was the sort of thing that embarrasses both the performers and the audience.

"They were talking and gesturing and no music was forthcoming, and from the words I was hearing, it seemed they might just walk out and cut their losses. And then the most amazing thing happened: Gram suddenly shook his head angrily and said, quite loudly, 'Fuck it...' Then he turned towards the 'audience,' stepped up to his mike, pulled his acoustic guitar over his shoulder and hit the beginning chords of 'Sin City'. Singing all by himself, with the rest of the band just slouching in the background, Chris Hillman not even plugged in when he should have been singing harmony and Sneaky Pete all the way across the stage from his steel guitar. Gram sang the living shit out of the first verse, his voice cracking and full of pain and angst and the desire to make us all feel what he felt the only way he knew how. I can close my eyes right this very second and see him, eyes glittering like faceted sapphires in the stage lights, looking straight at each and every one of us as if to say 'I don't care if it's 47 or 47,000, we're gonna give y'all a show.'

"So give us a show they did. After everyone got settled down, the band ran through the entire first album, plus 'Cody, Cody' (first time I'd ever heard that one and it made me cry then as it makes me cry now), 'Hickory Wind', 'Close Up the Honky Tonks', 'Break My Mind', songs from the next album plus a whole big bunch of Parsons-tweaked C&W standards, plus who knows what else. If there were non-believers in any of those 47 occupied seats, they were stone-cold disciples by the end of the Burrito's wonderful set. We staggered out into the early evening twilight, ears ringing, big ole' shit-eating grins on our faces. The Burritos presumably stole away in search of even more excess.

"I saw the Burritos probably ten or twelve times total, at places like the old Fillmore, the Avalon Ballroom, Winterland, the Whiskey and Palamino. One of the best concerts I ever saw and heard was a gig they did out at the old Family Dog hall on the Great Highway here in San Francisco. The Family Dog was a huge old dance hall that was originally part of Playland at the Beach, a turn-of-the-century amusement park that had become run down and mostly abandoned. Some rides and amusements held on into the 60's, but the bulk of the buildings were boarded up by the time the San Francisco Sound started to emerge in 1965.

"It was a large rambling old place, later to become a slot car racetrack after the live San Francisco music scene faded away. It had good acoustics, a very high ceiling and was made of wood. It was a large venue, able to hold a couple thousand people so that promoters could book in larger acts and still make a bit of a profit. It was smack-dab across from the beach in what was then the middle of goddamned nowhere as far as most straight San Franciscans were concerned, surrounded by literally miles of free parking spaces. Best of all, there were no houses or apartments close-by, so the sound could be cranked waaaaaay up.

"It was probably 1970, and I was just about twenty. I can't tell you much about the opening act, but there sure were a lot of us eagerly awaiting the Burrito's set, you can bet your cowboy hat on that. Tension was so thick you could cut it with the proverbial knife, and I'm sure there were a few Buck knives in the crowd along with the prerequisite velvet floppy coats, Lennon glasses, patchouli oil perfume, bell bottoms and love beads, this being San Francisco and all. Country rock had actually started to sink in as a separate musical form by this time, the Byrd's *Sweetheart of the Rodeo* was accepted listening fare, and the next natural progression was *The Gilded Palace of Sin*, although it was a pretty far jump from 'Blue Canadian Rockies' to 'Wheels'.

"The Burritos took the stage a predictable forty-five minutes late and from the very beginning, you could tell they were pumped (or jacked up, hard to tell which without a Physician's Desk Reference). I was so close to the stage, I could almost touch Gram, and Chris Hillman with his innocent face and blonde curly Afro was just the other side of Gram on his own mike. Chris Ethridge stood there with his bass, intense and serious. I had a great clear view of Sneaky Pete on steel. Gram's hair was long and had those angelic pageboy flips just at the very ends. He was wearing one of his wilder Nudie suits, a red one I think, plus fancy-dan cowboy boots and a blue spangly scarf at his throat. He looked every bit the two-and-a-half-zillion dollar's worth of country-rock star, and all the girls in the audience lost their hearts to him the second he stepped up to the mike, shielded his eyes from the lights and asked us how we were all doin'.... Gram had a stage presence like you couldn't ever buy, he absolutely knew it and man, did he ever use it.

"They started out with a low-key tune, 'God's Own Singer', and then Gram sang 'Luxury Liner', a song I love, but the beginning of the set wasn't all that energetic. The band was in a great mood, relaxed, clearly glad to be pickin' and singin' for us. I recall an unusual amount of playfulness in the interaction as the songs reeled off, and a few special moments remain embedded forever in my brain. After a couple of slower numbers, they started in on 'Christine's Tune', one of the most recognizable songs from *Gilded Palace*, something the audience had been eagerly waiting for. The rhythm guitar riff that kicks the song off is so Pavlovian to me that I think I peed my pants when it came roaring like a steam locomotive out of the PA system, and Gram and Chris stepped up to their mikes. The bass kicked in, and then Sneaky Pete did his steel guitar black magic thing. Back then Pete was regarded as some kind of a mystical electronic pedal steel guitar god. I don't know if he had what they call 'technicians' but I never saw anyone but Pete himself fiddle around with the cables and such, so probably not. He had this button on the front panel of the steel guitar body facing his playing position, and it was the button that controlled the fuzztone.

"The band was just flat-out pounding 'Christine's Tune' for all it was worth, Chris Ethridge effortlessly holding down the bottom end with notes so deep and resonant they weren't heard so much as felt through the floor and rafters of the hall. The drums hit crisp and hard, the guitars nasty, ringing and Sneaky Pete's steel dancing and growling and leading everyone else around, all totally backwards from what you thought a country music sound should sound like. Chris Hillman and Gram were trading beautiful lead vocals and harmonies, and it was enough to make you see God I swear. Gram would sing a verse with Chris doing harmony. Then Chris would sing another verse with Gram on harmony, and they'd both sing the chorus.

"They were doing the harmonies just a tiny bit of a note off, so it created an eerie, floating, otherworldly dissonance in the hall. The whole band was trading glances and smiles, and when it came time for Sneaky Pete's trademark fuzztone riff, Gram would step back from his mike, turn towards Pete and grin like a Cheshire cat. Sneaky Pete would lean back in his chair and whack that button hard with his hand and launch into the riffs. No one in the audience knew if they were hearing a psychotic country musician on acid or some astonishing lead guitar rocker who really knew how to move the pedals on that weird-looking stringed box. It was awesome to see and hear.

"That evening the band played as hot and hard as I ever saw or heard them, ever, and they played the songs with feeling and sincerity so you alternately cried, laughed or simply stood there mouth gaping open, reeling under the onslaught of so much talent and concentrated emotion directed at you, and you alone, because that's the way Gram and the Burritos could make you feel when they really wanted to. The hall was hot, the air thick with dope smoke, the stage lighting haloed the musicians so it looked more like a messianic holy-roller snake-handling convention instead of a pop music concert. I think Gram would approve of this comparison. The Flying Burrito Brothers were preaching without judging, and we were hearing and being converted without having to lift one finger – all for the piddly price of admission.

"Later they sang 'Dark End of the Street', and Gram played a trick on Chris Hillman. Their mikes were just a few feet apart, and at the end of that song there's a section where they each sang 'You and me....' 'You and me....' 'You and me....' 'You and me....' a bunch of times. Gram would sing the words and then Chris would sing 'em, and so forth, normally. But on about the third go-round, Gram casually walks over to Chris's mike and sings Chris's words. So Chris walks over to Gram's mike and sings his words, and so they go back and forth, round and round in this loopy, funny, real-life game of musical chairs (or in this case, mikes). Gram would fake Chris out and lunge for his mike, then when Chris started to move towards Gram's mike, Gram would pull back, laughing, and so forth and so on. The whole thing was really hysterical because this was way before cordless guitar connections, so their guitar cords got tangled up and they had to stop and get things straight before ending the song. They probably strung out this genuinely playful ending to three, four minutes or so.

"I think some bands are unable to recreate the excitement and emotional intensity of their studio-recorded albums for various reasons. Then other bands do as good as what they can record, and maybe better. Sometimes, once in a real rare while, you'll get a bunch of musicians to whom the album is just a tight little flower bud, and their live performances are the full, fragrant, opulent blooms, far surpassing anything you could ever hope to hear or feel by just listening to the recordings. The Burritos could be all over the map. Sometimes they were too weirded out by the tense interpersonal relationships, especially when Gram got so caught up in getting high that his music became sloppy. At other times they could, almost literally, walk on water. The sheer force of Gram's vision, the collective talent and beyond-cutting-edge musicianship, the spare but spine-tingling arrangements made them special to those of us who were touched by the music in our hearts and souls. But the Flying Burrito Brothers were, what, 20 years ahead of their time? Being pioneers, someone once said, gets you shot in the back with arrows and buried in a shallow grave."

✻ ✻ ✻ ✻ ✻ ✻

Gram was now living full time at the Marmont, sharing a bungalow with filmmaker Tony Foutz, although Gram's current girlfriend Linda Lawrence, an ex-girlfriend of Brian Jones, would also stay with him. Soon, they rented a separate bungalow. Foutz was supposed to have worked with director Stanley Kubrick on *2001: A Space Odyssey*, and he was in the process of making his own film, which was being shot on weekends out in the Joshua Tree Desert. The film, which was called either *Saturation 70* or *Ecology 70*, was about flying saucers and aliens, a subject close to Gram's heart. Testament to the "loony" creativity of Foutz, no one involved in the filming can remember what the plot was, if there was actually any narrative at all. Michelle Phillips, Gram, Linda Lawrence and her son Julian were all put in front of the camera at various times. Ben Fong-Torres' *Hickory Wind* cites Andee Cohen as saying that the film was about "four cosmic kittens who are banished from outer space and came here to clean up the planet".

By August, Gram was spending most of his spare time with Linda and Julian, working on Tony's film out in the desert and playing the occasional series of club dates with the Burritos. The work was there for the band most of the time, although there were plenty of weekends that Gram spent out in the desert staring at the dark, empty sky. Gram and whoever else was along for the ride would just hang out, drop acid and wait for visitations from UFOs, something that Gram claimed he saw a lot of.

After one such long weekend spent shooting random scenes with improvised dialogue, the producer behind the film decided that he wasn't getting anything for his investment, so he withdrew his finance and the film withered away. No one seemed badly upset by this development – it had all been good fun. Gram went away to perform a series of shows with the Burritos in mid-August, and to do it, according to Phil Kaufman, he had turned down an offer to appear at a music festival in upstate New York, near the town of Woodstock.

It later transpired that the Rolling Stones and the Byrds had both done the same thing. In their respective cases, both bands had grown tired of badly organised festival appearances where they would be trapped at the concert site by the massive crush of the crowd, the playing times were frequently ridiculous and in many cases, acts would not even get paid if they *did* show up to play. Of course, they wouldn't know until after it had happened what a momentous festival it had been.

CHAPTER 8
WINESTAINED COWBOYS
Burritos begin to fray at the seams

Such was Gram's diminishing interest in the band he had conceived so controversially in 1968 that, consciously or unconsciously, he began to dismantle his involvement and investment in the Flying Burrito Brothers. The rest of the Brothers did not take kindly to what Gram was doing, since none of them had the luxury of a wealthy family or a trust fund to fall back on when it all got too hard. Hillman could empathise with the difficulties Gram had in dealing with his past – he too had lost his father in similarly shocking circumstances. But, as hard-working musicians, Gram's bandmates interpreted his attitude as part of an overall inability to comprehend how life could be less than comfortable for those without a safety net of any kind. He probably was not deliberately trying to break up the band, but the influence of drugs and a subsequently diminished work ethic were among the factors that prevented him from appreciating the necessity for hard work.

At 23 years old, he had experienced some of the bleakest realities of this life, including death and addiction. Perversely, it was the tainted family money that was cursing the band, withering all their best efforts. The effects of increased drug use (a habit again facilitated by that family money) showed themselves as Gram began to slacken away from the desire to make his mark on the world by sheer hard work alone. The talent burned within him, and for him to succeed on his own merits would not have been difficult. His songwriting was getting stronger, and two or three more albums might see his natural ability develop fully.

Once again, the Burritos were writing songs and being creative; there was talk of another album in the works. The album was to be called *Things*, and would traverse similar territory to the inaugural Burritos record. This time, there would be more originals and only occasional recourse to cover versions, which would include a Dylan tune called 'Tomorrow Is a Long Time'. The band arrived back at A&M's Hollywood studios to begin recording. Present at the sessions was a young musician named George Bullfrog, who was a confirmed Burritos fan.

"I don't recall the exact date of the session, but I believe it was September or October '69. I believe I was invited by Gram, when I delivered the edited Palomino tape to him, backstage at the Aquarius Theatre on Sunset Blvd in Hollywood, where they were doing an A&M showcase with the group Bread. This was the only time I saw them in a concert setting. Most of their LA area gigs were in bars. They played first and things went from bad to worse. It was a rock and roll crowd, and the place was full (of mostly Bread fans, I suspect). Gram was a beautiful man, I don't know how else to put it, and that combined with his attire, which included a silk scarf, a spangly shirt, and cowboy boots with rhinestone heels, probably appeared to some folks there as somewhat effeminate."

Opening the set with 'Christine's Tune', it appeared that they'd won the crowd over and Gram started singing some slower songs. Contrary to what one might expect, the crowd grew restive. A few songs later, some boos and hisses were heard. The final stone through the stained glass was some guys down the front who began shouting, "Faggot!" at Gram. "I don't think people today realize how tough it was for them, knocking down the barriers," says George Bullfrog. "It all ended with Gram dropping his Tele to the stage and walking off."

Looking at each other horrified, the band gamely kept on playing through to the end of the song, not knowing what else to do. Finally, they walked off themselves to a chorus of boos. "When I went backstage, Gram was visibly shaken, with a tear in his eye," remembers Bullfrog. "The rest of the band was pissed. When I handed him the tape a few minutes later, he was very gracious – as he always was – but I knew that what had happened earlier had really affected him."

When Bullfrog asked the band what they were planning to do after this show, Gram and Chris were soon telling him about a planned recording session the following week. George found himself invited to observe at A&M's West Hollywood studio. He arrived at the session early and seated himself unobtrusively in the corner of the control room, where he observed all the comings and goings as the group prepared to record.

Mike Clarke, recently involved in a motorcycle accident, was hobbling around on crutches, his broken left leg in plaster up to the knee. Jimmi Seiter had to assemble his drum kit for him. Once they were set up, the band began running through the songs they would be recording. Engineer Henry Lewy, overseeing production too, set the levels and hit 'record' while they ran through the songs. With A&M's meter ticking over in the studio, the pressure to produce a "better" Burrito Brothers album was on. Jim Dickson was unrestrained in encouraging the band to give the record company a more commercial album, since he had a vested interest in seeing the group have a hit record. Parsons did bring one initially intriguing number to the party, the striking and new '$1000 Wedding'.

'$1000 Wedding' was a tune Gram had written in the difficult period of 1968 when he had left Nancy for good, although not quite at the altar, as the song might suggest. Amid the recriminations and slanging matches about whose child Polly was, '$1000 Wedding' took shape, albeit with a thundercloud over its head. The title of the song refers to the wedding dress that Gram had commissioned his friend Nudie the rodeo tailor to make. It was a Nudie one-off, studded with rhinestones and beautiful in a strange way. After the cancellation of the wedding, the dress was never picked up.

The Burritos initially took to the song with some interest, but soon, even they thought it was too long, and any potential it had was lost on Dickson, who hated it. "It was an overwhelming listening experience," confirms George of the slow-burning ballad, which despite the best efforts of the band, refused to catch flame. "The session lasted about seven hours as I recall – most of it spent getting '$1000 Wedding' right. It was a complex song, and [the chord structure of] it was literally burned into my brain."

The band concentrated hard on Gram's new tune, but the right feel seemed to elude them and each take dragged out past nine minutes, sometimes going up to ten. Dickson must have been horrified to hear this latest opus – a mournful ballad about a wedding and a funeral. In that incarnation, it was a real dirge, too long to be of much use to anyone. So Gram folded his cards. He would successfully play that ace in the hole later on in his career. He and Chris once again collaborated on some songs, but the spark was no longer there. There was no more Burrito Manor, and no more productive pot-fuelled song-writing sessions.

If '$1000 Wedding' meant anything it spelled a new direction, but one that the rest of the band may have been unwilling to pursue beyond this session. It was agreed that they would attempt a new song that Gram and Hillman had written, entitled 'Two Hearts'. That ran a little smoother and the band settled into it easily after the several hours spent working on '…Wedding'. Bob Dylan got a nod with 'Tomorrow Is a Long Time'. After another break, the band went back into the live room and cut 19 takes of the Dylan tune, the results of which the band seemed mostly happy with.

Towards the end of the session, Leon Russell arrived at the studio. He greeted the group warmly and they discussed the possibility of using him on future sessions. "After everyone listened to the night's playback in the control booth," George recalls, "Someone – maybe Eddie Tickner – approached Gram and told him that another artist, who was way more famous than the FBB, wanted to cover 'Hot Burrito #1'. This artist wanted permission to change the name of the song to 'I'm Your Toy'. Gram was opposed to the idea. [Eddie's] powers of persuasion went into overdrive, pleading and explaining how good this would be for them to have this artist record the song. Gram wouldn't budge, and finally in his calm southern drawl, he said, 'You know I'm not that kind of guy.' Gram was incredibly charismatic for someone so young, and he carried himself with grace and confidence."

In the control booth, George was confronted by the unusual playback system. Because the sessions were recorded on an 8-track machine, there were not the standard two studio monitors but rather there were eight, one per track. "I was taken by the recording process, which was quite different from the way things were done just a few years later. They played live in the studio with headphones, and there was not much in the way of isolation between instruments. Chris and Gram sang into different sides of the same mike, and the drum kit was right out there in the room."

George was awed by what he had seen that evening, having been privileged to see the band working so closely together in the studio with the original line-up, which was soon to change. He'd also witnessed them arranging and recording three great songs, which have been nearly forgotten about. George's recollections of this session serve to confirm that, far from being a band in trouble with their record company and lurching around in the creative doldrums, the Flying Burrito Brothers were in fact still moving right ahead. Nevertheless, the songs they recorded that evening at A&M have not been heard since.

Having listened to the fruits of that session, Jerry Moss told Michael Vosse that it was unacceptable for the band to produce something like '$1000 Wedding'. It was uncommercial, and given that the band was heavily in debt to the label, they should try to get something else in the can. Even the Dylan song was a downer.

The September 20th edition of *Rolling Stone* magazine announced in its Random Notes that Chris Ethridge had departed the band, without going into exactly why. Following his general disillusionment over the recent sessions, Ethridge had tendered his resignation from the group. He hadn't been happy for a while and, according to Phil Kaufman, had picked up on other people's bad habits and felt the need to get away from it all. The band was no longer holding his interest. His departure was supposedly related to Gram's opinion that Chris "wasn't really a country bass player but he realised it before anybody."

He would later work with Willie Nelson, but his abilities as a bassist were never in doubt, as a country player or otherwise. What had been more noticeable was that Chris was growing bored with the Burritos, and had even fallen asleep onstage one night. Gram might have later cast doubt on his abilities to play in a country style, but the excesses involved in being a member of LA's premier rock 'n' roll country group no doubt took their toll too.

Once Chris had quit, the band started to change. The sniping got worse and the pressure was again on from the record company. Of course, the new album that Moss was expecting had to come soon. Among so many dubious little pleasures, it soon became apparent that some days Gram could hardly care one way or the other about the band. This bothered Jim Dickson, who began to anticipate a problematic studio session with the group.

One reason why it was unlikely that Gram would ever achieve more than he already had with the Burritos was the presence of Keith Richards in Los Angeles that summer. The word went through the hills and valleys of California like an earthquake along a fault line. The Rolling Stones were back in town, this time to put the finishing touches to their new album *Let It Bleed*. They were also preparing for an upcoming American tour. Those weeks before the touring would begin were times when Gram would just hang out with Keith, play the piano and sing country songs together. Gram and Keith liked to talk and sing together and they did it often. Singing was the shorthand that existed between them, and not even Mick Jagger could break that.

There was appreciable harmony between the two artists. Gram was a young Southern gentleman, the kind of man who instinctively stood up when a woman entered the room. Not only was he old-fashioned in that sense, he was also a thoroughly modern man of the world, with all the right, not to say fashionable, habits. Another bond between them was the consumption of things pharmaceutical. Richards was vocal in his approval of Gram's appreciation of quality – good booze and the best cocaine, the latter purchased from Gram's dealer, a Black Panther dentist in Watts. Gram's penchant for getting fucked up on only the best available stimulants and narcotics ran parallel to Richards's predilections.

Despite their small but noticeable age difference, Gram and Keith tended to think alike. They analysed situations and gave their opinion, they monitored the behaviour of others and dissected it; in short, they took more in than anyone gave them credit for. Behind the blissful, slightly smeared veneers lurked enquiring minds. But mostly, they liked to get wasted and sing, since that required little or no effort at all.

There was no mistaking their lust for life. With Phil Kaufman at the wheel of the car, Gram took Anita and Keith out to the Joshua Tree for a weekend out of the city, bringing Marianne Faithfull along for the ride. The night they spent at Cap Rock was not unlike the evening over a year before, when Gram had taken a limousine ride down to Salisbury Plain with the Rolling Stones. Anita, Keith, Phil, Marianne and Gram took psychedelics and spotted UFOs in the night sky. Gram was always fascinated by the night sky. He would happily crane his neck for hours, scouting out shooting stars and unidentified flying objects, a phenomenon in which he was a big believer.

As Chris Hillman points out, part of the attraction of Richards for Gram was that he liked to seek (and would usually get) Keith's approval on various matters. Gram always sought reassurance for Keith on matters of band politics, for example. After all, who knew better about dealing with the relationships that exist in a band than one half of the Glimmer Twins? Gram also wanted something concrete from Keith about the possibility of making a record with him, but was too polite to ever make an issue of it.

In the background, there had lingered, for some time, a vague promise to produce a Flying Burrito Brothers album that Keith had made one drunken evening. That's not to imply that Richards would not have fulfilled such a promise, but he was a busy man and the odds of a Richards-produced album coming to pass in the near future were very slim. This was the prize on which Gram kept his eyes, but typically, though he did not ever press the matter with the Stones' guitarist, it didn't stop him putting the word around that it would happen. Keith indulged Gram in this, even encouraging him to use his name if it would help grease the wheels. However, he was not to know that the other members of Gram's band were suffering from the lack of attention.

As far as Chris and Sneaky Pete were concerned, Gram's interests lay only in hanging out with Keith at mixing sessions at Sunset Sound Studios, riding his Harley into the desert or just getting wasted and missing out on rehearsals, and occasionally live dates. The Burritos were already booked to play a number of club dates during September, including the Corral Club in Topanga Canyon, the Palomino and the Golden Bear in Huntington Beach. Now that Ethridge was gone, the band had turned to a number of different pickers for support, including Clarence White, who despite his recent commitment to the Byrds was more than happy to lend a hand whenever he was able. The Burritos were asked to play at Atascadero State Prison, a maximum-security establishment down the California coast from LA. They did the show as a four-piece, winning over the inmates and the warden. It was hard work, and draining on the band, but the gig put them all in a good mood.

Chris Hillman put in a call to Bernie Leadon to provide some fresh ideas. For a while, it appeared that Gram too was energised by the strength of Leadon's musical input, which included new and well-written songs. His appearance onstage also strengthened the sound, and musically Chris and Bernie gelled well. They were of similar temperament, and that helped. Leadon, a quick-witted and intuitive young man who had worked previously with Dillard & Clark on the Larry Marks-produced *Through The Morning, Through The Night* album, came via a recommendation from Sneaky Pete. Kleinow was impressed by Leadon's abilities with his newly acquired Telecaster, fitted with a Parsons/White B-Bender. His reputation was solid enough already and it clinched him the lead guitar spot, which meant Hillman was now back to playing the bass as he had done in the Byrds.

What he did mind was that while the Stones were around, they could forget about Gram showing up at rehearsals. Some nights, he couldn't even be relied upon to arrive on time for gigs. No one was under any illusions about the incidence of no-shows – Hillman for one felt there was something unpleasant about the way GP was always drawn to the Stones' flame like a moth. "We had a working group," Leadon explained to Ben Fong-Torres. "But – bad news for us for three months. Gram was over at Keith's house all the goddamn time and wouldn't show up for rehearsals. He just wanted to be with Keith. The music, the chicks, the drugs."

As Gram caroused with Keith, Hillman was getting very pissed off about the missed club dates and the way Gram seemed to be dismantling all the things he'd once told Chris were important to him, like being in a great band and singing good country and rock music. The nights that he did show up to play would suffer as a result, and if he wasn't nodding off, he was maniacally jumping around on stage, doing Mick Jagger impersonations. Still, people like Stanley Booth who were around and saw the band play swear that the interaction with Parsons and the Stones made the Burritos a better band. Besides, in his estimation Parsons was a glittering star already, holding his own quite apart from the Rolling Stones.

It seemed that all of Gram's desires were being fulfilled through a vicarious association with the Stones. Roger McGuinn later accused the Stones of "romancing Gram" and "ripping off" his knowledge of country music for their own gain, and perhaps this is true. Equally, Gram was borrowing all kinds of stuff from the Stones, including 90% of Jagger's stage mannerisms and moves, and he was perfecting his own version of Keith's wasted cool, which seemed a little pointless for anyone who wanted to be a coherent lead singer.

The Stones, who were beginning rehearsals for the upcoming tour, would often come along. Stanley Booth was in LA with them, covering them for a book he was writing. Like so many who found themselves within the Stones' circle, Booth could only back out of it once everything precious to him had been lost. At the house on Oriole Drive in Laurel Canyon, Gram and Keith sat at the piano, "Mick on the couch, leaning over the back, the three of them singing unintelligible hillbilly songs", while Stanley and Charlie Watts looked on. Afterwards, he was telling Stanley about his sore throat and tried to explain the 'Parsons Health Plan' – "It's the drugs, they keep you healthy. That's what I tell all my health food friends."

A few nights later, the Stones and their entourage packed into three limousines and headed down to the Corral in Topanga Canyon, to see the Flying Burrito Brothers play. "…It was on the left, a little roadhouse, capacity about two hundred, tables and a small dance floor, crowded with rednecks and members of Los Angeles rock and roll society. Bruce Johnston of the Beach Boys was present, and so were the young ladies Miss Christine and Miss Mercy, members of the Bizarre Records act called the G.T.O.'s, meaning Girls Together Outrageously or Orally or anything else starting with O.

"Miss Mercy was dark and heavy, a fortune-teller with kohl-rimmed eyes, many bracelets, rings and scarves. Miss Christine, willowy and blond, in a long red dress with virginal lace at the bosom, was a California-bred magnolia blossom. Dancing together, they glided before us like one person, red, yellow and blue jukebox lights washing over the room as Gram sang "I made her the image of me". We sat at a long table, the Stones Gang and their friends and women, drinking pitchers and pitchers of beer, whooping and hollering while the Burritos played 'Lucille' and old Boudleaux Bryant songs, a real rock and roll hoedown."

After the train tour, aborted studio dates and a disparity in expectation between band and label, resources had been drained. While the Burritos struggled on and covered for him, Gram was hard at work getting the group onto the bill of the free concert that the Rolling Stones were planning. It was part of his plan one day to share a stage with the Stones, and it was looking pretty likely. The band was keen to be a part of this planned concert, as it would provide them with much-needed exposure. Rumour had it that the Maysles brothers, who were currently filming the Stones US tour, would wrap up their document of the tour with footage of the concert, something along the lines of the *Woodstock* movie. As Bernie Leadon noted, "We'd be crazy if we weren't involved."

The Stones literally had to be forced into holding a free show, as criticism came from several quarters over the high price of their concert tickets. The most vocal of these was renowned jazz critic Ralph J. Gleason. In one of his regular opinion columns for *Rolling Stone*, Gleason – in years past a fervent supporter of the English group– had accused the band of ripping off their audience. As they crossed America playing shows, journalists regularly asked them the same question – why were they charging up to $12.50 for a ticket when the biggest American band of the day, the Doors, were only charging $6.50 tops?

Mick Jagger pleaded ignorance on the topic but began hinting at the free concert idea, mostly for the benefit of the press. Then the idea became a germ and grew and now it appeared that the Stones really were trying to organise a venue for a free concert that would challenge Woodstock for size. Appearing at a hastily organised press conference at the Rainbow Grill, a hip eatery atop the Rockefeller Center in New York on November 28, Jagger announced that there would indeed be a concert for the kids. It was just a matter of finding the right place to hold it and making it completely free.

Attorney Melvin Belli was in charge of ironing out the attendant legal problems of the concert, smoothing over zoning issues and negotiating the necessary contracts for the artists, who would be paid out of the Stones' pocket. The Grateful Dead, who had helped in the organisation of the concert, were on the bill, along with Jefferson Airplane, the Flying Burrito Brothers, Crosby, Stills, Nash & Young and Santana. None of the assembled press believed this was in any way altruistic, but it was given much coverage in both the straight and underground press. It would be a one-day concert as opposed to three and the Stones, who had been roundly attacked for not appearing at Woodstock, intended to make up for any perceived slight on America's youth by making the day unforgettable. It turned out to be vividly remembered by all those who attended, but not in the way the Stones had intended.

By early December, the Rolling Stones tour of the US had come to an official end. It had been nearly uneventful and a massive generator of revenue for the band. Chip Monck, who had done the ground work for the Monterey Pop Festival and Woodstock, was called upon to act as a consultant and supervise the building of a stage for the free show. Due to a lack of notice, the organisation of the concert was poor, with the venue changed only a day before it was to begin. Pressed for time, Monck still managed to obtain a very large PA and lighting system for the event, and finally, just twenty hours before the show was to happen, a suitable venue was decided upon.

The concert would go ahead in the grounds of the Altamont Speedway in Livermore, an 80-acre property fifty miles east of San Francisco that usually featured demolition derbies and stock car races. In a rush to get the stage itself set up, a frantic crew of mostly coke and amphetamine-fuelled riggers and roadies assembled the PA and lights and a stage in the middle of the night.

The morning of December 12, 1969 was chilly but fine and Frisbees sailed through the air, just like at Woodstock. As many as half a million young people arrived on foot through lines of cars, abandoned by their owners when they saw that there was no more road to cover. Past the hundreds of tents and small fires, sprawled sleeping bags and wandering dogs and children, a phalanx of motorcycles made their way through the crowd, down to the front of the stage, their engines blasting loudly.

It was the Hell's Angels, who were attached as 'security' for the event, a sure-fire way of keeping the police out. The Grateful Dead had used them for security at their free concerts many times, all without incident. It was, as Rock Scully, the Grateful Dead's manager had noted, "a natural, not to say, *organic* choice". But today the crowd were confused by the aggression of the Angels, as they parted to let the dozens of motorbikes through. Pretty soon, the Angels were patrolling the edge of the stage, weighted pool cues, knives and old motorcycle chains in hand, warning the crowd away from the artists' area and bashing anyone who looked at them the wrong way. Into the bargain, the acid chemist Augustus Stanley Owsley III whipped up a batch of his most potent LSD, which he laid on free for all performers, the Angels and anyone else who could grab a glass of the spiked fruit juice.

The hastily erected stage somehow ended up only being four feet off the ground, hardly a great barrier between the stars and the swarms of young people standing around. The Angels took it upon themselves to discourage any stage invaders by massing their motorbikes in a cordon around the front of the stage, whipping anybody who got too close either to them, the stage or their beloved motorcycles.

The day began pretty peacefully, but the descent into chaos began as Jefferson Airplane took to the stage. There were incidents between the band and the Hell's Angels after Marty Balin had tried to protest the treatment being meted out to the crowd by the 'security' – in particular, a black man had been badly beaten by the Angels directly in front of the stage. For his trouble, Balin was knocked unconscious by one of the Angels, an incident caught on film by one of the Maysles brothers' roaming cameramen. Even more frightening was that when Paul Kantner said into his microphone, "Oh wow, the Hell's Angels have just knocked out our lead singer," a group of them began to threaten him. Some of the crowd, already tripping early in the day, began to freak out. Marty Balin eventually recovered consciousness and the band gamely finished their set.

The Flying Burrito Brothers flew in to San Francisco that morning and hired a van for the trip out to Livermore, some 54 miles away from the city. Sneaky Pete was at the wheel when they encountered the huge traffic jam signalling the start of where most people were just getting out of their cars and walking to the festival site. "There's a lot of things in the last 35 years I don't remember at all, but I can recall this so well. We drove up to the site bumper-to-bumper. And then somebody sideswiped us and put our van in a ditch. The traffic all stopped and Gram flagged down a motorcycle rider – I don't know if this was a Hell's Angel or not – and climbed on the back and went off and left us."

The event already augured ill so far as Hillman was concerned. He maintains that the day was "dark and depressing. There was definitely an unpleasant atmosphere about it all." Gram had disappeared on the back of a motorcycle, promising to get someone to come back and help them out of their predicament, though the band held out little hope of this actually happening. Eventually, passers-by helped them get the van full of gear out of the ditch and back on track for the festival site. The traffic was too thick for them to get any closer than about half a mile, so the band unpacked their guitars and hoisted as much of the gear as they could down to the backstage area. With their instruments held high, they wrestled their way through the squash of bodies milling around everywhere. There was no security to speak of, the Angels seeming interested only in beating up those they didn't like, or whose behaviour broke one of their codes.

Arriving just as Jefferson Airplane finished their set, Chris could see the Burritos' roadies already waiting down by the stage, having arrived much earlier in the day with the amps and the drum kit. The atmosphere of violence staggered Chris as he watched a naked Hispanic boy being beaten and kicked by Angels. Ordering the roadies into the melee, they gamely retrieved the naked guy and threw him in the back of their van, out of harm's way. All this happened as Crosby, Stills, Nash &

Young took to the stage. The mood had noticeably darkened and the Angels began skirmishing with the audience. Michelle Phillips of the Mamas and Papas came backstage with her friend Ann Marshall bearing tales of mayhem, that the "security people" were "bouncing full cans of beer off people's heads".

Gram sat with Stanley Booth in the backstage tent, singing old country songs while outside Bernie Leadon and Chris Hillman stood behind the stage, watching the roadies assembling the amps to be taken onto the stage. CSN&Y looked ill at ease and their music seemed lost on this violent crowd of thugs with weighted pool cues. As Crosby came off-stage, Chris saw him and waved him over. "I remember saying to him, 'It's an interesting day.' He just looked at me and said, 'Oh, boy...' and he fled."

As the Flying Burrito Brothers took the stage, the vibe of the day seemed to change. Unlike most of the bands present that day, the Brothers had no political or revolutionary statement to make, nor did they seem to be reaching out to some "darker power". Their only agenda was to play good-time music for people to cool out to. Happily, that was what happened. The Angels looked on, some of them digging the steel guitar sound and the R&B feel of the tunes. "We got a gentler mood going," says Chris. "I guess because we played a different kind of music." The band had not dressed up for the event, preferring jeans and shirts, although Gram modelled a Nudie-tailored rhinestone shirt and suede pants. The tiny stage was barely big enough for the group. Stanley Booth remembered "moving along, heading down toward the stage, we heard the Burritos playing in the distance, 'Lucille' and 'To Love Somebody' driven to us on steel-guitar beams".

Rolling Stone noted: "The simple verities of their countrified electric music soothed the warriors. There were no fights. As luck would have it, Mick Jagger and Keith Richards chose to emerge from the backstage trailer where they'd been holed up to have a look at the stage and the audience during this period of calm. They strolled about (and) wound up on stage, smiling, for a bit." Having the personal blessing of the Stones seemed to mean something on this occasion. The band plugged away through their set, Chris Hillman all the while monitoring the Angels out of the corner of his eye. He could see Angels all around him, lurking on the scaffolding and the risers at the side of the stage, looking like vultures waiting for more violence to begin. "They were just looking for trouble," he said.

The band finished their 30-minute set on a high note, while at the edge of the stage Mick and Keith smilingly signed autographs. Their part of the show had been sunny and uneventful; some said it was the only highlight of that strange, violent day. Furthermore, their version of 'Six Days On The Road' made it briefly into the *Gimme Shelter* film, which recorded everything that seemed frightening about the Stones and those who encountered them. As soon as their set was over, Chris, Bernie and Sneaky Pete threw their instruments into their cases and made good their escape. "We left as fast as we could after our set. Gram stayed, of course. The Stones had a trailer and Gram was hanging out with them."

Sunset came and the Grateful Dead disappeared, leaving the Stones to close the show. Finally, the sky darkened. Night came and the Stones still had not appeared on stage, because Bill Wyman was stranded in San Francisco, awaiting a helicopter out to the festival site. Nothing, not even music could bring relief to the terrified audience who could only look on as the Angels, now acting like berserker warriors on cheap speed, red wine and acid, attacked defenceless kids trying to get closer to the stage. Lit up by the red spotlights on the stage, the whole eerie scene made the

Angels appear to be drenched in blood. They stomped women and young kids alike, unable to feel anything except the urge to commit violence.

Violent tremors ran through the crowd at the front, while those further back could only watch, numbed by the plummeting temperatures and cheap booze and drugs. Finally the Stones came out; their massive banks of amplifiers humming and crackling as Keith, Mick Taylor and Bill Wyman plugged in their instruments and began to tune – a loud and clamorous sound.

A few hundred feet away from the stage, four Highway Patrol cruisers sat, sirens blinking noiselessly, ready to spirit the band away from this madness the moment they stepped off stage. The band had already refused to ride with the cops, and so the only real police presence for miles stood back and observed the madness. Plainclothes detectives moved around backstage among the milling Hell's Angels as Maximum Leader Sonny Barger took a microphone and ordered everyone, including his own men, off the stage and the band struck up 'Jumping Jack Flash'.

They made it through a version of 'Oh, Carol' and were about halfway through 'Sympathy For The Devil' when someone's motorcycle blew up near the front of the stage. The band ground to a halt, and for the first time could see the whirling shapes of Angels going after the audience with pool cues, bashing and kicking. The band ran through part of a Jimmy Reed shuffle, then 'Stray Cat Blues'. Finally, Keith unleashed the opening bars of 'Under My Thumb' and there was another explosion of violence as a young black man named Meredith Hunter tried to fight off a group of Angels who took exception to his having a blonde girlfriend.

Irrationally, the eighteen-year-old high school student pulled out a nickel-plated revolver and started waving it around, while his girlfriend looked on mutely. Almost immediately, he was stabbed in the back by one Angel, while many more descended on him, mutilating him with their knives and bashing him with garbage cans. The Rolling Stones saw none of this, only that the crowd was quaking with fear. 'Under My Thumb' ground to a halt until the band could regain their bearings and begin the song again. They started into 'Brown Sugar' and the Hell's Angels took the stacks of red and yellow roses that were stacked at the side of the stage and began throwing them into the audience, a surreal scene. The Stones followed that with 'Midnight Rambler', all about death and mayhem, and rolled it out over the crowd like a bloodied carpet.

The Stones ended their set with 'Street Fighting Man' and, with Gram and Michelle Phillips along for the ride, made a run for the helicopter that waited to take them back to Livermore airport, where a fifteen-seater aircraft would take them to San Francisco airport. Gram was coming onto Michelle, kissing her. She endured his attentions for the duration of the flight to San Francisco and the limousine ride to the Huntington hotel, where they regrouped and listened to the news reports of the killing at the concert. Gram returned to LA with Michelle the next day. He went to stay with his new girlfriend, actress Gretchen Burrell, to whom he had been introduced to at the Stones' mountain hideaway only three weeks before. Michelle went back to Dennis Hopper, and the Stones returned to England.

After a break for Christmas and most of the first month of the New Year, the band began talks with A&M about getting the album that was already in the can released. Interestingly, Gram had obtained permission from both Mick Jagger and Keith Richards to record a version of the Stones' tune 'Wild Horses', a song about which all kinds of legend has sprung up. It was written for and about Anita/Marlon by Keith; Mick wrote it about Marianne Faithfull; it was a song for Gram by Keith and given to GP as a gift; it was written by Mick for and about Gram.

The truth is that Gram certainly did nothing to set anyone straight about the story behind it, since the mythology about the song's origins was far more interesting than the truth. "I have a phrase that fits what I'm playin'," Keith explained to Jim Dickinson and Stanley Booth at Muscle Shoals Studios in Alabama, while they were recording the song. "Like 'Satisfaction' – I had that phrase and Mick did the rest. I wrote ["Wild Horses"] because I was doin' good at home with my old lady, and I wrote it like a love song. I just had this 'Wild horses couldn't drag me away' and I gave it to Mick, and Marianne had just run off with this guy [Italian film director Mario Schifano] and he changed it all around, but it's still beautiful."

Gram had heard a cut of the new song the day after the Altamont experience. "We were just shaking from the whole experience and they [the Stones] were leaving the next day – or at least Mick was, to take his suitcase of money to Switzerland (laughs). Mick said, 'Look, I want you to hear this song because I think it's something that you might be interested in.' And he played me 'Wild Horses' and 'Brown Sugar'. They'd recorded them down at Muscle Shoals about a week or two before and I dug it."

Gram was quite taken with the song, for the primary reason that Jagger had implied – that it was, in a musical sense, a tribute to Gram's approach to writing and singing, which had benefited them. Even more exciting was the opportunity to work on the track as producer. "It was a couple of months later, I got a call from [Mick Jagger] and he said, 'If I send you the master, will you put a steel guitar on it?' I said, 'Sure I will.' He sent me the master and I got Denny Cordell to produce it, and we went into the Record Plant and we got Leon Russell and somebody came in with some sort of strange dust and things just went haywire. The engineer forgot where he was, things like that. So they didn't use that. And I asked Mick if we could put it on our next album and he thought about it and said 'All right.' And I think they didn't release it until almost a year after that – I don't know why, it's a beautiful song."

Gram had to promise Jagger that the Burritos would only release it as an album track and not a single. Having permission to record 'Wild Horses' made the rest of the Burritos happy. Gram had been able to capitalise on the Stones connection without abusing it too much. It was a good moment in the studio for them, despite the problems with drugs and general mayhem going on in their personal lives.

Hillman said of this period, "After that brief initial burst, Gram and I just couldn't seem to hook up again. *Burrito Deluxe* was written and recorded without any of the feeling or intensity of the first album, and it seemed that we were walking on different roads. He was getting into a lot of drugs and – well, you know the story.... He just went headlong in the direction of physical abuse and it was an area where I just couldn't help him at all. There was nothing that any of us could do. I think his major failing, as far as being a member of the group was concerned, was that he lacked the sense of professionalism, discipline, reliability and responsibility which you must have if you work with others."

Added to that, there was the feeling that 'Wild Horses' was shaping up as the true peak of the album, rather than spurring the principal songwriters to come up with originals that could hold their heads up alongside it. Leon Russell was asked to play piano on it, which he gladly did, providing several takes of a distinctive piano solo that truly enhances the Burritos' version. In the end, they chose the take that had one wrong note but a great deal of beauty.

Just four out of the ten songs that appear on the finished album reach the listener's expectation level. 'Cody, Cody' is the kind of immaculate Byrds pastiche that not even Byrds fans could find fault with. Its plaintive refrain and jangling twelve-string not only strongly hint at the previous careers of three of the Burritos, but also pre-empt the ill-fated Byrds reunion of 1973. The song also drafted the blueprints for American power pop in the next decade, influencing Tom Petty, Big Star, REM, Let's Active and even Scottish pop group Teenage Fanclub.

To prove the point, the Fanclub recorded a sprightly version of the Parsons/Hillman tune 'Older Guys'. The original is a pleasant and somewhat amusing boogie, further highlighted by a very funny early music video that showed some embarrassed Brothers on board a motorboat, miming along to it. Gram dances around the deck like Mick Jagger, posing, strutting and flicking his hands effeminately at the camera, while Chris Hillman pops up, red-faced, out of a hatch on the boat to hit his high harmony on the chorus.

Gram waves his cap and points at the camera, while the wind whips his fine silk scarf into his face, delivering his lines with a certain camp bemusement. Bernie Leadon appears barely unable to contain his mirth at this somewhat farcical sailor scenario but delivers the pealing licks of the solo convincingly, while his guitar strap slips off his shoulders. Sneaky Pete is resplendent in a Hawaiian shirt as he stands, rather than sits, behind his steel guitar. Michael Clarke is barefoot and looks right at home on the back of a boat with a full drum kit in tow, although his face appears to be similarly red.

'Farther Along' is a busy arrangement of an old public domain country standard that illustrated Hillman's vocal talents. He was clearly giving the song his all, there standing in front of the studio vocal microphone, back to the console as he found himself casting his mind back to the times he had sung this very song with groups like The Hillmen, the Greengrass Group and the Scottsville Squirrel Barkers.

They dug again into Dylan's back catalogue and chose 'If You Gotta Go', a tune that had already been recorded a number of times. If 'Farther Along' was at least elegant, the swift and rowdy punch-up that 'If You Gotta Go' is treated to seems positively amphetamine-fuelled – an irony that Bob might have appreciated, although the fact that it is one of his most-covered works seems a miracle, given its unadorned suggestiveness.

Gram treated the Harlan Howard song 'I Made Her the Image of Me' with more indifference than he ever had treated a great country song, considering the passion with which he had occasionally delivered the song in a live format. He appeared to be holding something back; rather than a measured, emotional break or real tears, it was almost certainly a yawn. His voice seemed occasionally precarious, but less out of emotion than that disagreeably wispy cocaine-affected vocal sound common in the early '70s.

The band also cut one of the songs that had been left unrecorded from *The Gilded Palace of Sin*, 'High Fashion Queen'. Depending on your worldview, this was either about a young girl who can't seem to get into bars or a transvestite. Either way, it was an unremarkable track. The song's latent promise finally surfaced some years later when Chris Hillman re-recorded the song as a hard-hitting honky-tonk duet with Steve Earle for the Gram Parsons tribute album *Return of the Grievous Angel*.

One of the album's better and most straight C&W songs came from the pen of Bernie Leadon. In a roundabout sense, the song became associated with Gram through its use as the epitaph on Gram's grave marker – 'God's Own Singer'. The song is both traditional and respectful, equal parts genuflection and meditation, not to mention being a handshake with another generation of country singers and honky tonk heroes. The song could not even accidentally be viewed as some sort of tribute to Gram; it's about an aging singer whose voice no longer cuts it but who is loved and respected by the regulars at the dirty bar he frequents. On odd occasions, the old man sings his songs when his voice feels strong enough, and graciously accepts the praise of his friends as they stop to listen to him.

'Lazy Days', Gram's staple fallback in times of musical adversity, was once again pulled out of the drawer. Finally it made it to vinyl; having already been recorded once by the International Submarine Band for the soundtrack of *The Trip* and never released, it had been foisted on the Byrds, who gave it an agreeable treatment during the *Sweetheart* sessions. It didn't get released then either, and perhaps Gram should have taken it as a sign.

When A&M had initially agreed to the album, it was with major reservations. They kept a tight leash on expenses and monitored progress very closely. They were in the hole for up to $100,000 with this renegade bunch of longhairs, and the going wasn't smooth. In fact, Jerry Moss and Michael Vosse made a pact to keep the album on budget and get it out on the racks as soon as possible, ideally with some radio-friendly singles into the bargain. The label was pinning its hopes on 'If You Gotta Go' as a potential single, as the song had already charted with treatments from groups as diverse as Lyme & Cybelle, Manfred Mann and Fairport Convention. However, when Jim Dickson and A&M management heard the results of the initial sessions, they were horrified, realising that they had invested good money in a project in which one of the principal players had lost all interest before it even started.

The record company, aware that having forced the group's hand they had what appeared to be a dud on their hands, made the decision to withhold *Burrito Deluxe* from release. Jerry Moss and the label management put into action their contingency plan, which consisted of coercing the Burritos to return to the studio post-haste and at least deliver an album of country standards. The idea was that if an album's worth of material could be quickly produced and released that summer, then A&M might possibly recoup some of the financial losses they were already experiencing. Jim Dickson gathered the bemused Burritos and sent them straight to the Sound Factory, a newly opened studio located in the heart of Hollywood, to attempt something more along the lines of straight-ahead country.

Jeffrey Gold's liner notes to *Farther Along* hint that the songs are "either the Burritos... trying out a new studio or an early attempt to make a pure, honest country album". Chris Hillman doesn't remember much about the session, except to say that he thought the tracks that were recorded were rehearsal takes and nothing more. The haphazard nature of the arrangements would seem to indicate this, except for the fact that the tracks do actually sound well-balanced and mixed and the instruments properly miked; possibly they were final mixes, but those who were there have some difficulty remembering what actually occurred. However, the tracks credited to the Sound Factory sessions are listed as having been "produced by Gram Parsons for Tickner/Dickson Productions", which suggested someone had some kind of control over them.

The tracks that they recorded over a couple of days were eventually released all over the world under different names. Ariola, the Dutch/Belgian affiliate of A&M, released *Honky Tonk Heaven*, which showcased all the tracks that were recorded in that time, plus some extra out-takes from the Rick Roberts-led Burrito album that followed Gram's departure. The songs were mostly country standards like 'Your

Angel Steps Out of Heaven', 'Close Up The Honky Tonks', 'Sing Me Back Home', 'Tonight the Bottle Let Me Down', 'Dim Lights', 'Crazy Arms' and the Buck Owens' weeper 'Together Again'.

At Gram's insistence, the band tackled R&B tunes like 'Bony Moronie' and some of the more recently released country-flavoured rock material, like 'Honky Tonk Women' (issued only a matter of weeks before), 'Lodi' and a song by 'Tobacco Road' songwriter John D. Loudermilk, called 'Break My Mind'. Interestingly, they also cut the Bee Gees' 'To Love Somebody' and Dylan's 'I Shall Be Released', a scrap of which appeared in the runout grooves of A&M compilation *Farther Along*.

It appears that there was a minor band mutiny, as the Burritos checked out of the Factory as quickly as they had arrived, though possibly the visit had only been experimental. Ostensibly, they were to hit the road for further touring. Dickson was peeved that the band hadn't bothered to add harmonies to the songs, or any kind of overdub in fact. The songs were, as far as the band was concerned, unfinished and most likely would stay that way. But, as the band readied for another lengthy and potentially demoralising tour of the US, Gram's problem with travelling by plane had again surfaced. The rest of the band began to lose patience with him, complaining to Dickson that Gram just didn't care enough to even make the effort to tour.

It didn't matter much to Gram at the time; he was disinterested in life itself and suffering depression, which he buried with the effects of tequila and downers like Tuinal, a depressant that indirectly and directly aided the suicide and death of many people. Gram had begun to follow the path of Elvis Presley into pharmaceutical addiction, in league with his abuse of cocaine, heroin, speed and marijuana. The combinations were varied and nearly lethal – some felt and even voiced their opinion that Gram would not be long for this world if he continued.

Fearful of the reaction of record buyers and annoyed at being handed a set of unreleasable rehearsal tapes by the group, the label were somewhat reluctant to release the album, but since they had been sitting on it for nearly six months, they had to do something. Gram and Chris' former neighbour, A&M art director Tom Wilkes was given the job of arranging a photo shoot for the cover, albeit with a minimal budget. Exasperated with the label and short on money for the artwork, Phil Kaufman rounded up five pairs of white surgical coveralls from Tony Foutz's collection of props for his UFO movie *Saturation 70*. So, for no real reason at all, the Burritos were photographed by Jim McCrary wearing the coveralls, scarves knotted around their throats, clear plastic gloves and surgical boots, their hands all pressed together in what appeared to be a traditional Indian, or perhaps Buddhist, greeting.

In order to elaborate on the title the band had arrived at – *Burrito Deluxe* – costumier Nudie was pressed into service. He thoughtfully provided two 'hot burritos', one attractively dressed with rhinestones. Despite the steam that rose off the burritos on the cover, there was nothing particularly hot about the contents of the album. Nor was much publicity given to it, since that would cost money that A&M weren't prepared to cough up.

Although some magazines found worth in the album, it stiffed almost immediately, having little impact beyond the lowliest reaches of the charts. It was estimated to have sold less than 25,000 copies, and those who did buy the album, mostly fans of the Byrds interested in seeing what their heroes were up to, were confused by it. The Stones cover was much lauded and talked about for years and 'Cody, Cody' was a fine little tune, if somewhat of a 'Byrds-by-numbers' composition. As for the rest of the album, it was deemed "half-assed boogie," full of "lazy country clichés". Gram was mostly disinterested in the whole affair, and Chris Hillman would later admit "We strayed from our roots."

Gram was embarking on a new wave of no-shows, when he wasn't offering underdone vocal performances at the gigs he did make it to. Promoters still wanted to book the Burritos, since their collective reputations preceded them. But there was no telling what kind of an impact they could hope to have with a lead singer who was clearly uninterested in being onstage with them most of the time. Gram's excuses and disappearances became more frequent and annoying. Worse still were the dramas that ensued when the rest of the band attempted to transport him to and from shows. Promoters were booking them all over the country and they were playing high school auditoriums for little or no money, gigging in prisons and occasionally being added to small rock festival bills with big name acts they had little in common with, musically or otherwise.

Gram's personal downturn ended abruptly in May 1970, not long after he had shown up at the studio where the Byrds were recording with Terry Melcher. Gram's contribution was noted in Byrds publicist Derek Taylor's liner notes for the album and Terry Melcher stated for the record that Gram had indeed been at the studio that evening. "I'd have loved to have seen Gram back in the Byrds," Melcher admitted to Johnny Rogan. "I think I was drunk that night and he came in and asked to do the harmony."

For some time, Gram's fascination with the *Easy Rider* lifestyle had been causing his friends no end of concern. His first bike had been a little BSA, an easy ride indeed for someone of Gram's less than solid physique. But the desire to carry some kind of Peter Fonda cool led him to buy a Harley Davidson chopper that had been customised by Tony Foutz, which he had decorated with a buckskin seat and fringes everywhere and the *pièce de résistance*, a coffin-shaped fuel tank. But the fact remained that the bike was too big and powerful for Gram to handle. Chris Hillman had penned the lament 'Wheels' after Gram made some comment to him about 'not being afraid to ride and not being afraid of dying'. The words became a cautionary tale. "He wasn't strong enough to hold it all the time. I knew he would eat it on that bike," Hillman recollected. John Phillips, Gram's motorcycle buddy and friend from the Greenwich Village days, felt the same way but didn't know how to tactfully impart any suggestion to Gram that he should think about learning to ride the bike properly.

Gram wasn't much good at maintaining the Harley either, and when the front forks loosened, he made a rough attempt to tighten them, then fixed the loose front wheel with a bent coat hanger. One May morning, Gram, a female friend of Gram's named Maggie, John Phillips and his actress girlfriend Genevieve Waite all took a ride out of Bel Air, where Phillips lived. Maggie was wearing Gram's helmet, while Gram rode with only his hair covering his head.

Just outside Brentwood, the jerry-rigged front wheel wore through its coat hanger repair job and the front forks of the bike snapped clean off, taking the handlebars with them. As the engine struck the tarmac, Gram was propelled headfirst into the kerbstone at about 40 mph. He bounced back into the middle of the road, which was where he lay as Phillips and Genevieve returned after noticing he was no longer behind them. Maggie lay winded and concussed on a grass verge, breathless and partly conscious but otherwise unharmed. Blood roiled out of Gram's ears, nose and mouth and onto the road as he lay unmoving on the baking asphalt.

The driver of a passing car had already begun to pull a blanket over Gram as Phillips pulled up, ran over and knelt beside his friend. Phillips was convinced that Gram was dead. He called his friend's name – "Gram, Gram, Gram." But there was life in him yet and he moved slightly. "John," he said dramatically and true to form, "Take me for a long white ride." He was alive after all. Friends were quickly notified and they all marvelled at his seemingly limitless ability to take the punishment he routinely handed out to himself. He was taken to St. Joseph's Hospital in Burbank and stitched back together.

Doctors expressed fears that his brain was under pressure from the severe oedema following his head injuries. There was quite possibly mild brain damage and his face, which had borne the brunt of the impact, was fractured and swollen black and blue. Pamela Des Barres paid him a visit and was stunned by the parlous physical state that Gram was in. For many of his friends, there was a certain relief that Gram's self-destructive spiral had been halted, if only temporarily. Three weeks in hospital and many painkillers later, Gram was discharged. Mangler presented Gram with a trophy made from the foot peg of the deceased chopper, inscribed with the words "Dumb Bike Rider of the Year". Gram was tickled and appreciative of Kaufman's morbid little memento.

He returned to the Chateau Marmont to recuperate, and within two weeks felt fit enough to rejoin the band on the road. During his stay in hospital, he had mulled over a number of decisions about his career, and arrived at a point where the music he was currently involved in making no longer interested him. He decided that his time with the Flying Burrito Brothers would shortly come to an end, but for the time being was content to return to the fold until something else came up.

The Burritos shepherded Gram to San Antonio, Texas in early June for a series of dates at the Jam Factory. While the band was very well received, Gram had already made his decision to quit, and not even the sound of applause could change his mind. But it wasn't until a club date in late June, back in LA at the San Fernando Valley's Brass Ring, that Gram commenced some rather petulant displays of sabotage. With influential and famous friends like the Bramletts and Leon Russell watching on, Chris would count into a song and start singing and Gram would start off a different song, in a wildly different tempo and key. Some suspected it was indicative of the damage he had suffered in the accident, and tried to empathise.

But Chris and Michael Clarke had both understandably tired of these sort of antics, as he'd pulled similar stunts before the accident, and it soon transpired that Gram was not about to leave the band in an honest manner. In fact, he was going out of his way to make them fire him. Backstage at the club that night, Chris lost his temper with Gram and sacked him from the band. To drive the point home, he picked up Gram's beloved new Gibson J-200 acoustic guitar and smashed it against the wall of the dressing room, breaking it into pieces. He instantly felt terrible about breaking the expensive instrument, but preferred doing that to hitting Gram with it. "He wanted it all," said Hillman sadly. "But he didn't work at it. And that's what I finally realised – he didn't put his time in. Discipline was not a word in his vocabulary."

Gram tearfully picked up the pieces of his instrument, placed them in the guitar case and left the club with a friend, who drove him home. He immediately tried to put a brave face on things with the band, as he imparted to *Rolling Stone* writer Judith Sims in early 1973: "I got bored with the Burritos, and that's a terrible thing to do. You bore other people when you play to them. Somehow, I got off the track and I needed some time to think about it." Gram also intimated the same idea to writer Chuck Casell the same year. "It didn't get me off, it didn't have the spirit that involves everybody, it puts me to sleep and I need excitement. I like going to hear somebody and getting surprised and thinking the music's good even if I don't think it's so polished."

While no one had ever accused the Burritos of being a polished live act, the insinuations that they promised much more on their first record than they had ever delivered live hurt Chris and Gram. Prior to Gram's departure, they had been attempting to hone their live sound and become less ragged. Things had improved with Chris stepping back on bass and Bernie Leadon coming in on guitar, and future Eagle Glenn Frey could be seen down the front at just about every Burrito Brothers show, watching and learning.

After his spectacular dismissal, Gram thought about doing it all over again, getting another band together and working out his ya-yas with country music, always reaching for that 'deluxe number'. By 1970, record and TV producer Terry Melcher had established himself as one of the most creative, if not one of the most troubled, industry scene-makers. As the son of Hollywood legend Doris Day, Melcher had been initially scorned over perceived nepotism, but his fearlessness and his work with the Beach Boys and the Byrds had cemented his reputation as one of the best record producers in Hollywood.

It was his production work that could be heard on 'Turn, Turn, Turn' and 'Mr. Tambourine Man'. He had later produced urban blues man Taj Mahal and soloist Ry Cooder for the Columbia label, then gone to work for a time as an independent producer for the Beatles' Apple Records. Melcher was wealthy, mercurial and restless. His youth and talent earned him a great deal of respect in an era when the concept of the producer as star was coming to pass. His only rivals were Phil Spector and Gary Usher, who had also worked for the Byrds. But, despite his wealth and self-confidence, the golden-haired boy wonder of the 1960s was running scared in 1970. Not someone who ordinarily had a lot to fear, he found himself in a unique and terrifying position. Through the contacts he had made during his short but eventful career in the music industry, he had come across Charles Manson.

If Beach Boy Dennis Wilson had in the end been absolutely black and white in his dealings with Manson, producer Terry Melcher had made the mistake of being iffy. Manson sought his help because Melcher had been involved with the Beatles and the Apple record label. Charlie had been utterly captivated by their 1968 release *The Beatles*, better known as *The White Album,* and felt that it contained messages personally meant for him, messages that were of an apocalyptic nature. The song 'Rocky Raccoon' had great resonance for him. He believed it to be about a civil war that would take place in America, a war between white and black. It was Melcher's disinterest that angered Charlie. Initially, Terry had been happy to talk to Charlie but found him strange and overbearing. Rather than openly snub Charlie, Terry talked about giving him his help, gave him an audition (as he regularly did with aspiring singers), handed him $50 and told him he'd call, then did nothing about it.

At the horrific end of Manson's tether, seven bodies were cold and the police took some time to close in on the Family. Meanwhile, everyone who'd ever met Manson and the girls quaked in their boots, particularly Melcher, who had once lived in the house in 10035 Cielo Drive with his ex-girlfriend Candice Bergen. He knew who had done it and why. He suspected it was a message to him. He was only moderately relieved after the arrests to discover that the police had recovered a telescope belonging to Melcher, which had been stolen from his Malibu hideout.

The Family knew where he had been hiding from them and they hadn't come down there to kill him. Maybe he wasn't on their death list anymore.

Melcher was only partially relieved from the stress he had been suffering, but eventually he started going out to see live bands again. Ann Marshall, a mutual friend, had introduced Gram to Terry one night out at the Corral in Topanga Canyon in 1969, when the Burritos had played. Stanley Booth was there that night, along with the Rolling Stones and members of the Beach Boys.

It was a glittering night: Gram's blonde highlights shone in the spotlight and he was a star in his Nudie suit, a new Elvis astride the globe perhaps, except that to Melcher he was coming on like the white Jimi Hendrix. Terry and Gram hit it off nicely, talking about music and getting to know each other. Soon, the friendship extended to talk of doing an album. This talk inevitably took place over a mound of blow from the huge stash that Melcher kept hidden in his Benedict Canyon house, where Gram was spending most of his free time in the wake of the motorcycle accident and the Burritos rift. Melcher valued the friendship highly, recovering as he was from a time of horrific paranoia that he had sought to calm with guns, coke, booze and lady friends by the handful. For the first time since the Manson business, Terry was keen to get to work on some music, and it was to be the new Gram Parsons solo album which would reignite not one, but two careers that had been momentarily set back.

In the summer of 1970, Gram was personally at a loose end. The threads were beginning to unravel in his life, and many of his friends continued to fear for his health, physically and mentally. Friends like Delaney and Bonnie Bramlett were beginning work on the album that would become *Motel Shot* for the Atco label (a spin-off from Atlantic Records). Gram arrived in the studio, blind drunk and coked out of his head, a combination that made him rather annoying to be around as the booze puffed him up and the coke kept him on enough of an even keel to keep walking. He wandered into the live room of the studio. "He was off his face" Delaney recalled in 1996, "And staggering around while we were playing, going, 'Goddamn, this a pretty song – you ought to be recording this', and we're going, 'we are recording this, Gram. We are!'"

Terry fronted Jerry Moss at A&M as Gram's producer and started talking about a solo album. Jerry took Melcher very seriously and had faith in his talent-spotting abilities. Against his better judgement, he agreed to front up the use of studio time and some advance monies for this new album. Never mind Parsons' spotty reputation where Moss was concerned, Terry was reasonably reliable. Or he had been. Jim Dickson, who had worked with Gram on the two Burrito Brothers albums, warned Moss that there could be trouble with these two. After all their bad experiences and alcoholism and cocaine use, both Parsons and Melcher were in trouble with their health and with their reputations. Gram blustered on coke, bragging to everyone about the songs and how great the album was going to be. Terry believed him and, after some jamming, they were ready to tackle the songs with the help of some influential friends they had hired.

Musicians like Ry Cooder, Clarence White, Earl Ball and Spooner Oldham were seconded to A&M studios in Burbank for tracking. The sessions went ahead and were, in fact, mostly successful to begin with. Ten songs were recorded, in varying states of completion. In a startling precursor of the *Byrdmaniax* fiasco, where Melcher would bury a number of songs under inappropriate strings and choral singing without the knowledge or consent of the Byrds, Melcher invited singer

Merry Clayton along to the studio, where she wailed soulfully along behind a version of Merle Haggard's 'White Line Fever'. Gram was too wasted to provide a decent final vocal on the track, and producer and artist agreed to lay it aside to work closely on an early, and by some accounts morbid, version of 'Brass Buttons', and on the Roy Orbison song, 'Dream Baby'.

Also recorded were versions of 'Sleepless Nights', a Boudleaux Bryant song offered to Gram by Ann Marshall that he would later record to better effect with Emmylou Harris, George Jones' 'She Thinks I Still Care' and another pass at Dan Penn's 'Do Right Woman'. All of them seemed like logical choices for an album, yet the alarm bells were already ringing at A&M's creative department. If they were to do anything with this project, which they had not yet committed themselves to, then it was clear that Gram would need to provide something more than just versions of other people's songs.

Gram wasn't Elvis Presley; he didn't have access to an unlimited number of great songs written purposely for him. And, although unlike his boyhood hero Presley Gram had the ability to write very convincing and beautiful songs, he certainly hadn't bothered to write any for this project. Gram and Terry liked nothing more than to get loaded and sit around the piano singing old songs, much in the same fashion that Gram and Keith did. But the creative process was coming undone – Gram's muse had a deviated septum from all the coke that was going around. An album of covers wasn't really the best way for a singer known for all-too-brief flirtations with other bands to kick-start himself a career.

The sessions weren't a total write-off. As Terry later pointed out, Gram was no more out of it than anyone else recording in Hollywood that year. Gram knew what he wanted to hear, and always had. He knew that the musicians they had hired were the best, and his career was at stake. But at some point, a kind of fatalism crept in to the sessions.

John Beland, the former Swampwater guitarist, remembers attending one of the sessions at Sunset Sound with Clarence White. "One day Clarence calls me and asks if I would like to hang with him while he plays on this guy's session at Sunset Sound. 'Sure', I say, and later that night I'm cruising down the Strip with Clarence, who drove like a madman. We get to the studio and all the lights are low – booze and drugs and groupies are everywhere. And in walks Gram Parsons, flanked by two tall lean biker chicks. The session was for a solo post-Burritos project for Gram. Anyway, I sat in the booth quietly and watched as the session proceeded well into the wee hours. After it was over and the musicians were packing up. Clarence brings me over to meet Gram, who by now is completely wiped out. 'Gram', says Clarence, 'I want you to meet Linda's guitar player John Beland.'

"Gram gives me a long stare, smiles and throws his arms around me and says in that unforgettable Georgia drawl. 'Hey John...you picked your goddamned ass off tonight.' As he's squeezing me, I look behind him, and see Clarence with his eyes rolled in the air chuckling. I just said 'Thanks, man,' even though I hadn't played a lick all night, but was only a spectator in the booth!"

Gram knew that he wasn't producing the goods. His talent, big though it was, could not be fed through a straw or controlled with a diet of coke and downers. The A&M Gram Parsons solo album died a natural death. It was given a proper burial about the time that Gram threw up in the concert Yamaha grand piano in the A&M studio. It cost hundreds of dollars to have it cleaned after that. Terry fell asleep at the desk and Gram tried to sing lying down *à la* John Lennon, although only after falling off his stool. No one seemed to be offering direction, but that was likely precluded by Melcher's fierce and demanding nature and Gram's jaded behaviour.

Even Terry saw the fault lines opening up. "Gram saw himself as a victim, starting with his family and extending to the music business. He thought he was too much an artist to be understood by the industry. He was such a romantic character. He was one of these people who thought it was great to die young." Fairly or not, Gram partly blamed Melcher for the whole sorry experience, and their friendship petered out. "I didn't know what to do with him," said Melcher, ruefully. "I knew he was going to die here or somewhere else."

After one of his regular long-distance phone calls to Keith Richards one morning, Gram listened as Keith explained to him about the record label the band was setting up, Rolling Stone Records – a project for which the group were negotiating with Jerry Wexler of Atlantic Records. As the conversation meandered along, they tossed about the idea of doing an album of country songs together, possibly as the first release on the label.

That same evening, Gram ran into Bernie Leadon at a club where the Burritos were playing and tried to sweet-talk him out of the band with promises of a possibly lucrative Keith Richards-produced solo album. "Why don't you leave these fuckers and come with me? I talked with Keith this morning and he wants you and me to come over and record with him." Bernie, already wary of Gram's tactics, refused the bait. Leadon was characteristically blunt with him. "I'm gonna stay in town. I don't have any money. You've got your trust fund and you can run all over the fucking world if you want to."

Gram didn't make it over to see Keith that year. Instead, he was kept busy in various minor scrapes with the law. Being sufficiently paranoid, he usually kept his sizeable stash on his person when he would leave the house to go to Schwab's Drugstore on Sunset, less than a hundred yards from the Marmont. One day, while running an errand, he was busted for jaywalking and the cop who arrested him found drugs on him. Kaufman found it hilarious – "He must be the only guy that ever got busted for felony jaywalking." Kaufman had introduced Gram to Bruce Wolfe, a good attorney who had assisted Phil in getting out of jail. Due to Gram's carelessness, Wolfe was on call to get him out of various busts and arrests, as was personal bail bondsman Harry Fradkin. Gram would call Phil to come get him out of the caboose and Phil would always oblige, organising the lawyer and bail. It was all part of the "executive nanny" service.

Besides, true to form, Gram lost interest in the possibility of furthering his own career. With the actual headaches that came from the accident, he also had the headaches of trying to drum up other musicians to work with. But the LA scene wasn't huge and Gram's reputation preceded him, so whenever he approached other musicians they were wary of getting involved with him. Then came the invitation he had been waiting for, to go and hang out with Keith in the UK as the Stones prepared for another tour and a recording session. Gram decided that a holiday in England would be the perfect cure for his Pan-American blues.

CHAPTER 9
"MY DELUXE NUMBER..."

Just a kid acting smart
I went and broke my darling's heart
I guess I was too young to know
They took me off the Georgia main
Locked me to a ball and chain
I heard that long, lonesome whistle blow
I Heard That Lonesome Whistle Blow, Hank Williams

Keith Richards has been gracious in admitting Gram's heavy influence on the Rolling Stones' sound in certain directions. Parsons' influence was notable on *Let It Bleed* and more overt on *Sticky Fingers*. By *Exile On Main Street* there was criticism being levelled at Jagger and Richards for "ripping him off". Gram never saw it that way. "They've certainly done some more country-sounding things since I've gotten to know them," he said, considerably downplaying his own awareness of just how much influence he had on the Stones.

However, in the intervening years, Richards himself has, in various interviews, sought to play down any conjecture about Gram having physically contributed anything to the Stones' albums, and in particular 1972's *Exile On Main Street*. For one thing, Keith explained, Gram was always too polite and too much of a gentleman to insinuate his way onto a Stones record. Mick Jagger may not have approved of the idea either. But the fact remains that of all the records the Stones have produced since their association with Gram have had at least one country-styled song.

Gram was able to work his friendship with the band to his own advantage, with their express permission of course. Being a friend of Keith Richards gave a person *carte blanche* in certain circles, and the Rolling Stone's name had been dropped into conversations with A&R people. He had learned to keep it to a minimum around other musicians, since their resentment, or more often disbelief, was a little hard to take. Keith's name had already opened doors with the Burritos – their appearance at Altamont was much to do with Gram politely working the entire Stones infrastructure in order to get on the bill. There was also the matter of 'Wild Horses', which probably demonstrates the respect that both Mick and Keith had for him. His politesse was legendary, and if Gram wanted something out of someone there was a better-than-average chance that he would get his way in the end.

Gram and Gretchen arrived in London in March 1971, Gram in particular feeling fragmented by his recent experiences in Los Angeles. It was good to have a break from America and Gram was ready to get down to work on the A&M album. Before leaving town in March, Gram had visited the Hollywood offices of A&M,

exchanged some pleasantries with the receptionist and went into the tape library to retrieve the masters of the Melcher-produced solo album. Having checked them out of A&M, he had been thinking that the project should be completed in London, if for no other reason than that he wanted Keith to hear it. There apparently had also been talk that Rolling Stone Records might release Gram's solo record, with Richards overseeing the last few overdub sessions as producer.

Gram had always enjoyed coming to Great Britain, the place where he had forged his friendship with Keith. Now he was back in London, just over three years after leaving the Byrds, and he was glad to be back. The musicians he fell in with in England were unpretentious, and many were sympathetic to his idea of 'Cosmic American Music'. Gram talked about starting a band there. "I've always had a dream about doing stuff in England," he said, his words melting on his tongue. "Starting a country band in England, because England is so unjaded that way, they're so open-minded about it really, maybe it's just a dream but it seems like a perfect place to start a country music scene."

Their first evening together, Gram and Keith dipped into some tequila and jammed until late, renewing their friendship over 'unintelligible' hillbilly songs. Here, the musical shorthand between him and Keith was as stimulating as ever. Keith was simply glad to see him. They talked briefly about the country album Gram wanted to make for Rolling Stone Records. He had hardly spoken of it with Keith previously, not wanting to badger him about it, but he would mention it to anyone else who would listen. The story of the Richards-produced Parsons solo album on Rolling Stone Records had gained momentum since 1969, and had even been reported in the underground press, but as far as Keith was concerned any recording sessions would happen when there was neither a Stones album nor Stones tour on the cards, and at present both were impending.

Still, he generously insisted that Gram use their connection to its fullest advantage, whether it be for recording time, A&R meetings or Keith's English and US connections for everything from clothes and coke to custom-made guitars. Keith even agreed that Gram should use his name to underwrite a record deal for himself. It was all in the timing, Keith suggested sagely, and said no more about it. Either Gram was unprepared for it, or Keith had sensed that Gram was not as yet ready to push himself quite that hard. He had completed no new songs, and the originals he had kicking around in his head were relatively lightweight.

The second evening of Gram and Gretchen's stay perhaps illustrates exactly why the Rolling Stones were planning to leave England *en masse*. Besides the tax problems that afflicted different members of the group, there was the almost-constant harassment by police and by the media. This had been a semi-regular occurrence since 1966, but originally it had been Brian Jones who had suffered most. Now that he was no longer around, Richards had become their target. Keith and Anita took Gram and Gretchen out for the evening to a restaurant. Getting into the chauffeur-driven Bentley, they had only travelled a few metres down the street when they were stopped and searched by the police.

"They were definitely trying to find something on Keith, but couldn't," Gretchen said. Keith was purely frustrated and angry by this kind of harassment. Anita was just annoyed. Gram however, was amazed that someone of Keith's stature in England could be so vilified by the police. Gram was *très* sympathetic – after all, he'd had regular run-ins with the police himself and already had a sizeable arrest record, though mostly for minor infractions.

There were other incidents involving police on the 'Goodbye Britain' tour. Travelling with a group that comprised Keith, Anita and Marlon, Boogie the dog, 'Spanish' Tony (Keith's valet), Gram and Gretchen and any number of assorted hangers-on, meant that there were regular scenes in hotel rooms, bars and even on aeroplanes, when Keith would try to smuggle the dog on. There was one incident in Glasgow when Keith called the police himself after trying to get Boogie onto a midnight flight back to London. The police arrived and Keith talked the airline officials down, despite the fact that he was in possession of enough illegal substances to have him put away for a long time.

When the inevitable buzz that surrounded Keith and his friends subsided, there were always one or more willing participants who would strum old songs with him. The jamming between Gram and Keith in particular was constant. On tour, Gram was always in the corner of the room, with an acoustic guitar in hand. Since their enviable musical fun nearly always excluded Mick Jagger, there was tension with the lead singer's camp. But the rest of the band loved having Gram around. Charlie Watts thought Gram was "really a very nice young guy. A girl comes into a room and he just stands up naturally, without thinking about it."

The ten-show tour of the UK took in Glasgow, Edinburgh, Leeds, Newcastle, Manchester and Liverpool, with a concluding show in London. A Stones tour in the early '70s could be a rather dour affair, as several members of their entourage were in the grip of patterns of drug abuse that would balloon into full-blown addiction within several years. Generally, too, the band suffered from boredom on the road, and having Gram's politeness and surreal sense of humour to lighten the mood buoyed them up. He cheered them up in miserly dressing rooms when they sat hungering for drugs of some description, by opening the door and jokingly calling out for 'drug dealers'. Everyone laughed, and the early afternoon wakeups would be more bearable for having him around.

While Jagger liked Gram, he didn't really feel the need to go out of his way to welcome him into their camp. That didn't make much difference where Keith and Gram were concerned – they did their own thing independently of the rest of the group. By the end of the 'Goodbye Britain' tour, Gram was still hanging around Keith in London, while the Stones prepared for the big move to the South of France. Keith had truly enjoyed having Gram with him on tour and at home in London, although the same couldn't be said for Anita Pallenberg and Gretchen Burrell, as they could barely stand each other. While Anita had had enough of the flock of hangers-on that usually accompanied her husband, Gretchen claims that she herself had had enough of the whole Stones scene.

As for Keith, he was suffering under the weight of excess. Unsure about whether there would be sufficient and reliable connections in France, he thought he should kick the smack and promptly booked himself in for nurse Smitty's apomorphine cure, which had been taken by many a high-profile user, including William S. Burroughs. Michael Cooper, the Stones' ever-present photographer, had also done the cure and, despite the fact that he was fairly well hooked on heroin again, recommended it to Gram. After Keith's first cure, which took place at Redlands, he returned to the Cheyne Walk house and promptly went back on the drug. The party continued, and Gram, Anita and Keith kept after the hard stuff. There was another sustained period of such madness and finally, the three of them did a detoxification program together.

"Me, Keith and Gram, with two nurses that William S. Burroughs had recommended," says Anita Pallenberg. "I have crazy memories of Gram always running away and hiding, never being there when they were looking for him." The piano in the Cheyne Walk house became the bulwark against which they leaned, taking the cure and taking no calls. Arguing like an old married couple over the changes and lyrics for Ernest Tubb's 'Filipino Baby' got them through their trauma, and their friendship was cemented. Then it was time for Keith to leave to go into tax exile in the south of France. Gram and Gretchen loved London and decided to stay on there for the time being, taking up residence in what photographer Perry Richardson – then Michael Cooper's assistant – referred to as "a terrible little flat". Cooper kindly found the couple a much nicer home in Kensington's Abingdon Villas.

On arriving in France in April to begin their self-imposed exile, Keith and Mick almost fell out over Jagger's impending marriage to Nicaraguan model and socialite Bianca Perez de Macias (whom everyone in the band affectionately referred to as 'Bianca the wanker'). Keith was the only Stone invited to Jagger's May wedding in Saint-Tropez.

Things continued to go well for Gram in London. He went to Olympic Studios in Barnes to audition the unfinished A&M tapes for Trevor Churchill of Rolling Stones Records. Churchill was very encouraging about the tapes, but did not have the authority to say 'yes' to releasing an album. The feedback on the unfinished tapes was valuable to Gram, and he booked time at Olympic, paying for it himself in the absence of a record deal. Perry Richardson, who came along to the studio to hang out, remembers Gram playing '$1000 Wedding' on the studio piano, as well as "doing a little overdubbing… This went on for a few days."

Gram and Gretchen enjoyed a quiet, romantic summer in London, as the cold weather finally slipped away. Even so, the promise of being able to stay in the Richards' family mansion in Villefranche-Sur-Mer was too tempting, and the couple left England in late July. Arriving in the south of France they walked into Nellcote, the stage upon which myriad dramas were being played out every day. A houseful of junkie guests was too much for Anita, who was trying to cope with her own heroin addiction. While at Nellcote, she attempted to kick it using cocaine and immediately started having terrible seizures.

There were a lot of drugs about the house, since it took only a week for the word about the crazy English musicians at Nellcote to start attracting Marseilles gangster types and hard-up students returning to England via Morocco with pounds of hashish in their bags. Trouble of every variety kept turning up, all of them with stuff for Keith, and he rarely, if ever, knocked them back. Worried that undercover cops were likely to start arriving without warning, Anita and Keith came up with an escape plan should there be a bust. Enter Gram and Gretchen, she not even 20 years old, thrust into the madness that filled the house Keith was renting for $10,000 a month.

Gram was a welcome guest, "a pleasure to have around," according to Richards, but there were others making themselves at home around the place who were not at all welcome, and Anita, for one, had given up on trying to tell the difference. Left mostly to her own devices when Keith and Gram got together – often for the best part of the day – Gretchen tried gamely to make friends with Anita, who had taken to throwing knives, usually at anybody walking through the house. "This knife would go whistling through the hall and stick in the door," said Anita. "Just to give 'em a feeling of, 'don't fuck with us.' But then they still did."

Gretchen said the tension at Nellcote was "relentless". Anita grew to dislike her even more as the sessions wound on late into the evenings. Anita would either be incredibly civil and sweet to Gretchen or, if all the coke had been snorted, she might have a screaming fit. Sometimes, she would just fall asleep elegantly holding a cigarette. The house became filthy, with empty beer bottles littering the tables and mantelpieces, endless cigarette butts, dogs and children all over the floor. Sometimes, she would fix her gaze on Gretchen and pass some devastating comment on her. In her less charitable moods, she considered this houseguest to be an intrusive whiner: "I was very aloof from all these California girls" Anita reflected. "Gretchen was a bit moany, always reproaching Gram for being who he was. That was the vibe I got."

Aware of the ill feeling between her and Anita, Gretchen tried to keep out of her way, attempting to maintain a level head. But her youthfulness, coupled with the rarefied atmosphere of the Richards house, made things tenser. As a result, she and Gram would argue, often violently. As the full heat of summer came on, Gram and Keith moved the piano out to the balcony, where they would sit shirtless all day, hammering out songs and arguing over lyrics. Still, Keith tried to keep the atmosphere light and insisted that the musicians bring their kids with them when they came to record. Jimmy Miller was frantically organising the Rolling Stones mobile recording unit for the "Tropical Disease" sessions, only to find out that the local electricity supply was unreliable and cantankerous, to say the least. The solution was to illegally tap into the railway grid for power. Soon enough, the trailer was parked around the side of Nellcote, and hundreds of miles of leads and power cables ran through the house, up and down stairways, and through the kitchen.

Any recording that took place at the house was entirely subject to the whims of Keith, who would spend hours putting the kids to bed before coming downstairs to the fetid basement room where the rest of the band and hangers-on were gathered. Not even electric fans could shift the fuggy air, and everyone was getting around in shorts and t-shirts. As author John Perry points out in his book on the making of *Exile...* the new album was very much Keith's baby, with only five tracks featuring the actual line-up of the Rolling Stones.

Sometimes, Jagger would disappear for a few days to the Monte Carlo casinos with Bianca, leaving the band to bash away in the basement in his absence. Even mild-mannered Charlie Watts got the shits with the endless waiting around and would take a week off with wife Shirley and daughter Serafina to look for his own property. As for the elusive Bill Wyman, Anita Pallenberg doesn't even remember him being present for the sessions, which mostly he wasn't. The rest of the time, it was the Nellcote regulars, Jimmy Miller, Bobby Keys, Mick Taylor and Keith who did the basic tracks for the album.

The recording would often shift to the kitchen, where the acoustics were better and it was a little cooler in the evenings. Gram also felt more comfortable about being around when they were recording in other parts of the house, as Jagger, when he was around, had made it clear that the basement was off-limits to everyone except the musicians. "We did a lot of recording in the kitchen. Gram was there nearly all the time," said engineer Andy Johns, who considered Gram to be set apart from the rest of the houseguests, whom he reckoned were "fucking wankers". "He was a very nice, pleasant, true fellow. Very out of it though. I remember one time he was sitting on a Vox amplifier with a foot pedal up to his ear, thinking it was a pair of earphones going, 'Yeah, Tuuuuuuuuuuumbl-ing De-ice.' It was really terrible, man. Poor fellow."

As for the basement studio, "I don't think Gram even went down there," says Anita Pallenberg. One thing is for certain, Gram's presence at Nellcote impacted on the song writing for the sessions more than anything else. Even though he avoided going anywhere near Jagger, his musical partnership with Keith made Mick angry sometimes. Since Richards didn't make a point of being in the studio every day, Gram would often be the focal point of arguments between the Glimmer Twins. "[Gram] was the other side of the coin," says Anita. "There's always that other stuff going on – whoever is the one that they're all always going on about. Boys will be boys, I guess. So Gram was on that end of [the aggression between Keith and Mick], you know, and Mick Taylor was on the other end of it."

Still, as many musicians will be aware, tension can keep the songs coming, and the tunes were pouring out of Keith and Mick in that period, despite the relationship dramas. The sessions could run for a day or more non-stop, and strong and rootsy music came through the floorboards. Gram may not have ventured into the basement often, but his influence was ever-present in that hot funky room in the form of Keith's singing. He had started to stretch his phrasing on the backing vocals, which pleased Jagger, who, despite mixed feelings about Gram's presence, enjoyed his singing and even borrowed a few little tricks from him when it came to writing songs. "Mick likes to write… and Keith is all about sound," says Anita. "He plays what he hears and knocks up a song when it comes. So a lot of that was going on, and Gram was always a bit like pig in the middle."

It only took a month before Gram's behaviour, while nowhere as outrageous as some of Bobby Keys' antics, got him into trouble. Gram had been staying up for two to three days at a time with Keith, bashing out songs, doing line after line of cocaine, and fighting exhaustion. The songs they tried out acted as a release valve for Keith, and as an antidote for Gram's own depression. The music was working to calm the situation at Nellcote down, but in time, Gram began to go downhill from the stress of too many chemicals and too little sleep. He began passing out at odd moments, causing everyone much concern.

Keith, in the middle of one giant bender with Gram, became so worried about his friend's welfare that he rang Gram's ex-girlfriend Linda Lawrence, by now married to Donovan and living the quiet life on an island in the north of Ireland. "Could you please take Gram? He's out of his head and he needs to be with somebody." Linda readily agreed to the idea, as she remained equally worried for him. But she never heard anything more about it. Gram's conspicuous consumption, despite his willingness to always pay his way, was his downfall. While Bobby Keys was hitting the smack just as hard, he at least had something to contribute to the album. Gram and his girlfriend were mostly benefiting from Richards' largesse just by being able to stay there in the first place, particularly since Keith was spending a huge sum of money on his guests every week.

Finally, Keith had to confront the situation, but true to form, he could not tell his friend to get out. Rather than cut him adrift, Keith offered him some advice – "Just lay low, man." But Gram either could not or would not lay low. It was not exactly in his nature to take it easy, not when there was "cotton candy" to be had. Everyone at Nellcote had formed an attachment to the potent, pink, uncut smack that Keith and Anita had gotten from one of their Marseilles connections.

Meanwhile, Jo Bergman, the Stones' ever-patient personal manager, used to having to deal rather severely with the parasites who sponged off the Stones, received orders from someone in the Stones firmament to put Gretchen and Gram on the next plane back to London. It was a rather unpleasant end to the Parsons' stay in Nellcote. As they were getting ready to leave, everyone was doing their best to be sympathetic to the young couple; even helping them pack their bags. Keith asked Gram to move something, and Gram's back stiffened; "I don't know if I can do that," he replied very deliberately.

"It was very easy to get caught up in the vortex that surrounded the Stones," says Perry Richardson. "Gram got caught up in it. The thing people forgot so easily was that Keith always had his own life and his own problems. And I know that Gretchen was very young to be in that situation and found it very difficult to deal with. At that time, I guess a pattern had been set whereby Gram would take whatever was around, probably more than anyone."

Gram went to Michael Cooper before they left Nellcote, and asked him if he and Gretchen could stay at his Holland Park home until they got themselves another place to stay in London. Cooper agreed, at least to Gram's face, but was uncomfortable with the idea. He rang Perry Richardson, saying that Gram would be calling him soon to ask about picking up the keys for the flat – would he tell them that he'd lost the keys, or didn't have them with him? Perry, although mortified, agreed. Gram called only an hour later but Perry could not find it in his heart to tell a lie to his American friends. He explained the situation, and while Gram was gracious about it he was internally wounded by all this drama. So Gram and Gretchen returned to London with a shadow hanging over them, Gram in particular hurt that Keith hadn't told him why they had to leave to his face.

Gretchen claimed that Gram was so upset about this development that he tried to overdose on the toilet one afternoon. "There's a history of people getting pulled into that vortex," Perry Richardson elaborated. "And then, for whatever reason, they feel they've been rejected from the inner circle. It's all such bullshit, but we forget how young everyone was." Once through the worst of that experience, the couple were faced with either renting their own place or getting a hotel. In the meantime, they decided it would be better to catch up with some friends, and so they telephoned Ian Dunlop.

He had already extended an invitation to them to visit him and wife Valerie on their organic farm, near the tiny fishing village of Tregidden in Cornwall. Since 1968, after the first line-up of the International Submarine Band had split up, Dunlop and his wife Valerie had lived the simple life in a fourteenth-century stone farmhouse, where Ian worked his farm, picking vegetables and making butter and wine. Ian certainly preferred the rural life and had willingly gone as far from smog-bound Los Angeles as he could go, which was back to art school in London, and then on to the pastoral scenes of Tregidden. As Gram and Gretchen discovered, the agrarian life had its benefits.

Ian hadn't given up on music; he had just given up on trying to make a living out of it. He was still writing songs and making up names for bands, along the similarly nonsequiturial bent of the Flying Burrito Brothers. He told Gram about his current project, Harvey and the Sequins. "Jesus," said Gram. "Who are the Sequins?" "I dunno – we were always looking for another member," replied Ian, which cracked Gram up.

Gram and Gretchen stayed for several months, and Gram, unable to score in pastoral southern England, managed to again kick his heroin habit. Together, he and Gretchen patched up their strained relationship and investigated the rural life together. In the evenings, the two couples would venture to the local pub and sample beer and apple wine. It was all good, clean fun and the toxic after-effects of a summer spent indulging in French excess were shaken off. In the late English summer Gram limited his drug intake to pot and alcohol, and his demeanour and health seemed to improve.

Gram took the opportunity to call up his old friend Rick Grech, the former bass player of Family and later Blind Faith, whom he'd met poolside at the Chateau Marmont in 1969. Grech and his wife Jenny lived in Sussex, and they invited Gram and Gretchen to stay with them in their farmhouse. It was a match made in country music heaven. Grech was – like Gram – something of an outlaw. He was also a rich kid who was spiritually adrift, although in the English countryside, which was less troubled by temptation than Los Angeles was.

Together, Gram and Rick tried to exorcise their various demons. They ended up feeding off one another musically and the friendship grew. Taking downers and smoking pot, they would tape themselves doing long country music jams on the prairies of Sussex, Gram playing guitar and Rick picking up the fiddle. Out of the union of Grech's own urbane musical sensibilities and Gram's white-soul came some beautiful co-writes. Some of Gram's strange attempts at humour were also showcased. Out of a long list of song titles and album titles Gram drafted in his journal came these gems: 'White Punks On Dope', 'These Blues Have Made a Nigger Out Of Me' and 'Ain't No Beatle, Ain't No Rolling Stone'.

Together, they planned to make an album. Gram started talking about the solo project that was never far from his mind. He still wanted to do it, but had been waylaid several times, usually by his own failures. Rick understood how it was. He even made the offer to produce Gram's solo album. This was the first such concrete offer that Gram had actually received from a musician he truly respected, outside of Keith's vague offer to work on an album for Rolling Stone Records. The bond between them was intensified as Gram and Rick built their friendship on respect, common musical interests and getting stoned. They passed the days drinking at local pubs and playing old country tunes. Eventually, the pair began to collaborate on actual songs.

Gram's distance from the American music industry during his stay was turning out to be a healthy decision. In nearly five months away from the US, after the lost weeks in France and England, it was the simplicity of hanging out with Rick and Jenny in the Sussex countryside that made Gram consider his options more seriously. He came to his decision; he would return to the United States, marry Gretchen and try to make an all-or-nothing push for a solo career.

Gram returned to London for a while, staying at a house in Holland Park. He sought out medical assistance for a minor ailment, having been directed by Grech to the home of Dr. Sam Hutt. More to the point, Hutt's office was in a flat shared by Roger Chapman, the lead singer of Family, and also by legendary groupie Jenny Fabian, who penned one of the more eye-opening and frank books on the topic of female fandom. When Gram entered the flat that day the lounge-cum-waiting room turntable offered up a Fred Neil record to anyone who cared to listen. Hutt had only recently discovered Neil, and was rapidly becoming a fan of such songwriters. As far as Gram was concerned, the doctor was in. "Hey, that's Freddy Neil," commented Gram as he took a seat. Hutt, unaware that anyone else might have heard of Neil, was astonished. "How do you know Fred Neil?" asked Dr. Hutt.

"Know him? I played with him." Gram introduced himself to Dr. Sam. At the sight of this character dressed in jeans and boots and the pigskin Nudie jacket he'd worn at Altamont, Hutt was incredulous – he looked more like a rock 'n' roller. Grech had rung him beforehand to let him know that this friend of his would be coming in to see him. Somehow, he'd imagined a 'squat country and western singer.' Instead, here was this angelic young guy with a wispy moustache, and his cute blonde girlfriend.

Hutt was a fan of the Byrds, and had seen the show at Middle Earth, but he preferred the folk-rock stuff to the pedal steel and banjo textures of *Sweetheart*. Swayed by an in-office performance of 'You're Still On My Mind', the doctor and Gram started a friendship, another such relationship based on Gram being teacher to a willing pupil. With twice-daily applications of George Jones and Merle Haggard, Dr. Hutt was fully cured of any lingering dislike of country music. Later on, he became a country singer himself, outside of the surgery anyway.

Despite their initial friendly rapport, Hutt could see that Gram had been using heroin. Whether he was an addict or whether it was just a general availability – or through his innate ability to make connections – Gram and Gretchen went through some testing times during their short stay in London. Their relationship came close to failure many times. Smack, easily obtained in a country where addicts were once registered and received pharmaceutical grade heroin, exerted its inexorable pull on the pair. Gretchen was repulsed by it. Theirs was not the only friendship it tested. As a regular visitor to the Parsons household, Sam Hutt had several times encountered the unpleasant sight of Gram, slumped unconscious on the toilet with a needle still trapped in his arm. "He'd almost be over the edge. I thought of him as someone who'd know how much people loved him by pushing himself further and further and seeing if they'd pull him back."

Frank David Murphy concurred. "Gram was always doing stuff like that. One time he was telling me how he was studying karate. So I was like, 'okay'. Then his fist came flying towards me over the table, stopping just an inch or two away from my face. It was a case of 'See how much control *I do* have.' He was always that way. But I always sensed that he might go too far with it one day."

Back in LA, people had started wondering where Gram had gotten to. There was a rumour going around that he'd shaved his head and gone to Mexico to join the priesthood. Another story went that he'd disappeared into Europe, true enough as it turned out. Some people thought he was living down in New Orleans, trying to get off drugs. Frank David Murphy would periodically try to call him up. Avis told him that as far as she knew he was still living in London, but that he was sending postcards once in a while, threatening to come back home.

That was the plan, as Gram had worked it out. In spite of the relationship problems they were experiencing, Gram and Gretchen were going to get married. London's summer was winding down, and it was wet and cold. The two of them longed to get home to the US, back to better weather and friends and family. Gram called Jet Thomas from London and asked him if he would officiate at their wedding ceremony. Taken aback, Jet agreed to do it.

Jet had been living in California, doing graduate work in theology, and he was pleased to hear from Gram, although he was initially puzzled by the idea of Gram getting married in New Orleans, especially at Bob and Bonnie Parsons' house. He wondered whether it was Gram's way of extending some kind of olive branch to his stepfather, now his only link to Waycross and the pain of childhood. Anyone who knew Gram knew that he didn't trust his stepfather as far he could throw him.

Gretchen hadn't met the "family" before, and she was shocked. "Here was this bop-a-doo California girl finding herself in something like *Suddenly, Last Summer*," said Eve Babitz. Gretchen thought Bob was a creep with fast hands and pinkie rings, but she could see that Gram was attracted to at least part of the man's emotional make-up. In his own way, Bob was something of the socialite showman, one who cared about appearances, and one who lived a double life even when Gram's mother was still alive. For sleeping with Bonnie, the babysitter the family had hired to take care of Bob and Avis' daughter Diane, he earned the contempt not only of the Snivelys but also of most of the people who knew him. Marrying Bonnie after the death of Big Avis, further alienated him from most people except his personal social circle in New Orleans.

Gram still kept in contact with him for the sake of Little Avis, Gram's sad-eyed sister who was still in his custody. Little Avis had gotten pregnant during this time and Bob, never one to miss the opportunity to cast doubt on the sanity of someone else for his own gain, had had her committed to the DePaul Hospital, just across Audubon Park, down the road from Parsons' home. Gram resented this but, for whatever reason, still commissioned Bob to put on the wedding. Avis supposed it was because Gram trusted Bob to throw a decent party. "I suppose it was just one of those things where he felt like it'd be done the way he wanted it. He felt as though Bob would do it right."

The couple flew home to New Orleans in September 1971, to a hurriedly arranged wedding ceremony. Jet knew no one else at the ceremony except Avis. None of Gram's musician friends were invited to the nuptials, an oversight that Gram hadn't necessarily tried to correct. Bob Parsons, true to form, threw a memorable wedding for the couple, a big, boozy affair with many guests. Some members of the Snively and Connor families were present but they felt like interlopers, two lovers being wed in front of strangers, all friends of Bob and Bonnie. It was like a movie set without the cameras. Jet performed the ceremony, delivering a simple and quick service that seemed unlike Gram. No doubt he recalled Gram's big plans for a flash wedding and a $1000 wedding dress. There was none of that, just a hollow feeling. The couple left New Orleans for LA and honeymooned at Disneyland. After that, they drove back from the fun park to the Chateau Marmont, unprepared for the roller coaster ride ahead.

❖❖ ❖❖ ❖❖

Four hours flying time from LA, Emmylou Harris was just about to give music up as a bad joke, or at least, she was tired of making her way through life when there was so much she had to push against. At just 24, she was, by her own admission, jaded and cynical from all the struggling. A talented, pretty single mother of one, she was a veteran of the wrong end of the music industry, the end where talented souls struggle to ignite, occasionally catch fire, but burn out while the audience's backs are turned. Add to this heartbreak one short-lived marriage and you have the stereotypical life of a country singer, except that Harris had only a passing interest in country music.

She was, as Gram himself had been, a folk singer – in this case, Emmylou's one album, *Gliding Bird*, had gone by unnoticed except by critics, local musicians and a few fans. While Emmylou wrestled with the never-ending problem of finding a regular babysitter for her tiny baby daughter, she also had to book gigs for herself and an assortment of auxiliary guitarists in pick-up joints and singles bars, where music played second fiddle to mating rituals. For this, she might earn $10 or $20 a night, a dispiriting development for a one-time beauty queen with such an eerily erotic voice.

Emmylou Harris had not yet seen through the bar mirror to the other side of this life. From childhood, she moved around year-to-year, having been born into a military family in Birmingham, Alabama. Her father, Walter Harris, was the scion of a Howard

County, Maryland farming clan of some generations' standing. Walter's father worked for the Tidewater Oil Company and the family had moved around with the work, through the 1920s and into the Great Depression. Walter went on to University to study chemistry and was called up to serve the nation in wartime as a Marine pilot, like Gram's father. Following his wartime service, Harris chose to remain in the Marines. It was this dashing war hero who, shortly after the end of the war, met, courted and married the beautiful Eugenia Murchison of Clanton, Alabama.

The couple's first child, Emmylou, was born in 1948, just as Walter was accepting what would be the first of many different postings across the United States. By 1949, the United States had been plunged into the first of two troublesome Asian wars, the Korean conflict. Walter felt that it was appropriate for him to sign on for active duty in the conflict, and in 1950 he was shot down over North Korea and spent the duration as a prisoner of war. "I was actually standing next to my mother when she got the telephone call" Emmylou recalled. "I was five. We were at my grandparents' house. I knew something terrible had happened and she said, 'Your daddy's missing in action.' Of course, I didn't know exactly what that meant, but I remember the terror of it – that I might never see him again."

For the 18 months he was in captivity the family could only pray for his safety, as occasional heavily censored letters from Walter arrived via the Government, allaying their fears for a time. All this took place while Emmylou was still very young, but the years without her father's influence had taken their toll on her, and she began to very much value her father's presence in her life. Once again off active duty, Walter continued his military service for what would be a 30-year career.

Emmylou's regimented upbringing on various bases was offset by the fact that Walter was not an inflexible Marine officer to the letter; rather, he was a kind and understanding parent who was only too well aware of the problems that children can face when the family moves around a lot. Emmylou built many friendships as a child, only to be faced with the prospect of yet another base, many miles from the last, with more new faces and new names to learn.

It was dispiriting for Emmylou, who remained shy, if naturally friendly to her schoolmates. Upheavals and house-moves were one thing, but as Emmylou matured into a strikingly beautiful young lady it was obvious that her academic ability had not been affected in any way. In fact, her study had been one of the few activities that she devoted her time to. She was a straight-A student throughout grade school, eventually making class valedictorian. Naturally musically inclined, she took up the clarinet in 10th grade, although without complete enthusiasm. As a result, the very shy, self-effacing girl whom most considered rather withdrawn soon became more outwardly confident.

As a beautiful but somewhat awkward teenager, she learned to play the alto saxophone and joined a marching band. It was the twin influences of Bob Dylan and peer acceptance that saw her taking up the folk guitar and even entering a beauty pageant, which she easily won over seven other contestants. She was never part of the in-crowd, but a desire for acceptance blossomed and she had started to come out of her shell by the time she graduated from high school. But it was to music, one of her greatest loves, that she would always remain faithful.

She enrolled at the University of North Carolina in 1965, ostensibly to study the dramatic arts. But the release of *Another Side of Bob Dylan* the previous year had taken hold of her, as it did many artists during this period. Dylan's departure from what the critics called "protest music" was a huge shock for the folk community, but it cemented his reputation as an artist unafraid to take chances or make unprecedented leaps into this new and personal area of music. The album was hugely inspirational to her and she picked up the guitar and began to concentrate on folk music. Her studies began to suffer as she elected to spend her time at a local folk club, the Red Door, rather than attend lectures.

Finally, she rebelled completely and withdrew from university and headed out to New York City to sing folk music. Emmylou, now obligated only to her talent, found herself in Greenwich Village, living out of the YWCA and playing in Village clubs, singing folk and even a little country music, which had in some small way been embraced by some of the Village folkies she knew, like Jerry Jeff Walker and David Bromberg. There was something defiant about the genre that attracted her. For all its conservatism, it was as much a "folk music" as anything Woody Guthrie or Pete Seeger wrote, and Emmylou picked up on Loretta Lynn and Kitty Wells' brand of proto-feminist country songs, answering back with wry smiles and flinty metaphors about the growing divide between the sexes.

By early 1969 Emmylou had moved down to Nashville, where she spent time working in clubs, singing a mixture of country and folk music. Her singing attracted attention from record companies, although the one that offered to pay for her to record and release an album was based not in Music City, USA but across the state line, in Virginia. Jubilee Records, based in Norfolk, paid for a day of studio time in Nashville, where Emmylou cut *Gliding Bird*. It was rich in folk music tradition; the songs were mostly covers and the singing as sharp and pure as grain alcohol. But it didn't take.

It was in late 1969 that Emmylou met and married her first husband. As the record sank, and with it her hopes, she found out that she was pregnant. The album had done a little business, but not nearly enough to rescue her from financial dire straits. As money was tight for her and her husband, she wore loose fitting clothing and got a job in a Polynesian-themed restaurant as a cocktail waitress, until her girth began to alarm her boss, who had to let her go. Sadly, her marriage was breaking up by the time her daughter Hallie was born. Eugenia and Walter encouraged her to come back home so they could help her raise the baby.

By mid-1970, she was back living with her parents in Maryland, working full-time as a real estate agent during the day and in the evenings making tentative moves towards the stage. Her desire to sing never departed, and soon she was singing folk once more in the Washington DC area. Together with her new bass player boyfriend, Tom Guidera, she formed a folk group that included local hotshot guitarist Gerry Mule, a classically trained folkie who would later, for one luminous show, be the guitarist for Gram Parsons and the Fallen Angels. The group, who would at various times include members of local folk-rockers Sageworth & Drums, was soon working six nights a week in clubs around the DC area, including Clyde's, a singles bar in Georgetown.

Yet, despite this frequent work and the occasional review, the period of dues paying that followed seemed unnecessarily harsh, particularly for Emmylou, who had moved from the security of her parents' home to live in a house that literally verged on a highway. The house was little more than a shack, which she and Hallie shared with a couple and their small child. Soon, the regular shows dried up and she was once more forced to subsist on infrequent and poorly-paid gigs with the help of food stamps and what little welfare assistance a single mother could expect. But, despite the sometimes vicious poverty she found herself in, she was being heard and getting noticed around town.

Like any folk singer in the 1970s, Emmylou was influenced by Joni Mitchell's confessional, dark folk music and would often dig into her back catalogue, along with hushed, sweet versions of Beatles numbers and forays into country music, something she had become appreciated for locally. The bar manager at Clyde's liked her singing and kept her on there, even if it wasn't so financially viable for him. It was at Clyde's one late fall evening in 1971 that banjo player Kenny Wurtz and Rick Roberts, the young man who had replaced Gram Parsons in the Flying Burrito Brothers, first caught sight of Emmylou Harris onstage.

Roberts was amazed at her singing and introduced himself to her at the end of the evening. As he explained who he was, Harris was nonplussed – the name Flying Burrito Brothers meant little to her, but even so she listened politely to Roberts' praise. He found out that she was playing the same venue the following night, so Rick made sure to drag Chris Hillman along with him, regaling him with tales of how great this chick was. Hillman, initially sceptical, nearly didn't go to Clyde's, as the Burritos had just played one of their final shows in DC, and he was tired of the grind of it all. But Roberts was insistent and talked Chris around to coming out for a few drinks.

"What the hell?" thought Hillman, who on hearing her was equally enthused and just as knocked out by her talent. Earlier that evening he had taken a phone call at his hotel from Parsons, who was back from the south of France at last, finished with sucking up to the Stones. He was down in New Orleans but was heading north to visit friends. Hillman, more or less over the previous years' heartache at having to kick him out of the band, invited Gram to come visit the Burritos on tour, and maybe sit in for a few songs. Gram had been telling Chris about his latest project, a duets album to be produced by Keith Richards that would be like a "head" version of George and Tammy. 'Yeah, yeah – great idea,' thought Chris. 'It'll probably never happen.'

But now, this Emmylou girl had him thinking less dismissively about things. His mind began to tick over. He had talked often about getting a duet partner and now… maybe Emmylou could be the girl. After all, she was as good-looking and innocent as Parsons was, in her own way of course, and a Southerner too. Pretty sexy and talented, actually. In later years, there would be talk that Hillman considered asking (or actually *did* ask) Harris to join the group. That may not have been the case but it is a likely (and intriguing) scenario.

According to this alternative version of events, Linda Ronstadt was whom Chris had in mind previously, but in the meantime, here was Emmylou Harris. She was stunning to look at, tall and willowy, with a kind face and talented beyond belief, with a high and pure voice unlike any he'd heard. Maybe it was time to think about going co-ed. The Burritos were playing in Baltimore the next night and Chris almost certainly invited her to come down, but Harris had a prior gig commitment and couldn't go. The story of Emmylou perhaps joining the Flying Burrito Brothers in their final hours throws up innumerable "what-ifs". After all, the fortunes of the Burrito Brothers had turned for the worse long ago, even before Gram had been pushed out, and here they were playing their last few shows together as a band. Chris was, unbeknown to all, taking up an offer from Stephen Stills to join his new group, Manassas.

But who should arrive back from Europe at that exact moment in time but Gram Parsons. He'd put on a little weight, didn't seem to be drugging too hard, and through the band's manager Eddie Tickner he and Chris had, in the course of a phone call, repaired their relationship to the point of civility. At the show in Baltimore, Gram and Gretchen arrived backstage after sound check to do a little catching-up. Everyone was friendly, and Gram was in a good humour and looked clean and sober. Chris immediately began to tell Gram about this amazing singer he and Rick had caught down in DC. "Man, you gotta check this girl out. She is something else. You and her oughtta get together."

As Parsons himself liked to play the scene, it was that: "I was just very lucky – I was in Baltimore – the Burritos had two more gigs to play as 'The Flying Burrito Brothers' with Chris Hillman and everything – one was in Charlotte [Indiana] and one was in Baltimore and they called me and asked me if I'd like to come up and play the last couple of gigs with them. I said 'Sure – why not', 'cos Byron Berline was there and a bunch of guys that played bluegrass [Country Gazette] and stuff and I thought it'd be fun. Chris happened to mention to me while I was there, he said, 'Y'know we happened to be in Washington a while back and I heard this chick singer.' He said, 'She's nothin' but a folk singer but she could probably be developed into a really good country singer.'

Chris Hillman is known industry-wide as a pragmatic guy, not at all given to exaggeration, and Gram picked up from the level of Hillman's enthusiasm just how good Emmylou obviously was. But he had no idea how to get in touch with her. Rick didn't have her number either, although it had crossed his mind to ask her for it. Then a girl sitting backstage with the group, a local fan of the band, put up her hand. "By luck," explains Emmylou, "it turned out that the girl who babysat for my two-year old daughter was there at the gig – she went to every show within a 100-mile radius and had the ability to get backstage every time. She said she had my phone number. So, yes, it was all down to Tina the babysitter."

While Gretchen looked on askance, Gram took down the number. "I'll call her for sure. This little girl sounds like she can sing." And call her he did, the very next day. He introduced himself as the former lead singer of the Flying Burrito Brothers and practically kin to those same enthusiastic rockers she'd met earlier that week. Emmylou was touched by Parsons' obvious sincerity and his courtly Southern ways, but she'd never heard of him.

"I was a jaded 25-year-old single mother struggling to raise her daughter and playing clubs six nights a week, three or four shows a night and I was lucky to make 100 dollars a week. He said, 'Why don't you come up to Baltimore?' I said, 'You got to be crazy!'" It transpired that Gram had no idea how far it was, especially when Emmylou had only a Ford Pinto car that had been damaged in a recent accident and she was somewhat unwilling to drive 30 miles for this Graham character, no matter how famous he thought he was. "Oh, is it that far?" he asked sheepishly.

"I suggested he take the train down to me and I would meet him at the station. That's what he did and he came to my gig." So Gram, acting on a tip from Hillman whom he knew he could trust, journeyed down to DC on the train from Baltimore that afternoon, with Gretchen and a guitar alongside him. As legend would have it, their vocal blend was luminous and beautiful from the get-go. Not so, according to Emmylou. She mentioned to the headwaiter that this guy might be showing up who was a singer. The headwaiter had heard of this guy and with a piece of cardboard and a felt marker whipped up a sign reading:

TONIGHT
Special Guest
Gram Parsons
Appearing here

There was no discernable upswing in business that evening, in fact it was raining and the crowd was a little thinner than usual. Rather than exploring this newfound vocal blend, Gram and Gretchen sat in the audience drinking through Emmylou's first two sets of the night. During the set break, Gram and Emmylou disappeared into the basement of the club and, perched on some beer kegs, worked up some songs that they could sing together. "People ask me what songs we sang and I can't remember," Emmylou confessed. "Isn't that awful?"

Ben Fong-Torres claims that one of the songs was Hank Williams' "I Saw The Light". There may have been several more. Gretchen sat and watched, a little suspicious of the flaxen-haired folkie with whom her husband had evidently become enchanted. After the set, Gretchen told Emmylou that she liked what she had heard. Emmylou didn't know what to make of the child bride Mrs. Gram Parsons, but was impressed with his singing. "It sounded good and we went back to a friend's house afterwards and played a bit more," says Emmylou. "But I admit that I didn't really hear the uniqueness in Gram's voice until later. I was still a folksinger who dabbled a little bit in country and I did it almost tongue-in-cheek. I didn't quite get it." The friend's house where they played together again was in Georgetown, and served as the homestead for Sageworth & Drums.

Gram's version of that first meeting is not exactly the same. "Chris didn't know she was from Birmingham, Alabama and she knew more about country music, probably, than both of us. It took a little bit of getting together but I called her up and she said, 'Come on down.' I met her at the train station, she took me over to her house and we sat in her kitchen and I knew, at the first duet – I was saying to myself, 'OK, let's see if she can cut it or not' so I thought up one of the hardest country duets I could think of to do, which was 'That's All It Took'. And she just sang like a bird, you know? I said, 'Well, that's it.' We sang them the rest of the night and she just kept getting better and better the more I looked at her. She's got fantastic eye-contact – she can sing anything that you're doing in perfect harmony as long as you look at her and if you raise your eyebrows if you're going up on a note, she goes right up on it with you in perfect pitch. It was beautiful."

However the scene was played out, Emmylou evidently came up with the goods on that night and Gram was sold on her ability. After the evening was over, Emmylou generously drove Gram and Gretchen back to Baltimore in her dinged Ford Pinto. Gram told her that she had a job with him in his band, whatever that was. As they got out of the car at their hotel, Gram leaned back in the passenger side door and said, "I'll call you and let you know what's happening." He took down her telephone number in his ever-present journal. Of course, he neglected to mention that the band didn't yet exist yet, except in his imagination, but sometimes that was all it took, just the germ of an idea for Gram to run with it he lost his enthusiasm for the project. That had happened several times before, but, as friends noted, he was pretty enthusiastic about Emmylou and the whole cosmic duet shebang.

"I've been looking for someone with a high enough voice to sing with for a long time", Gram explained. "It's hard to do duets with someone who's sitting in back of you where you can't see him. So he does great harmony work but you need somebody who's there playing guitar with you, that you can look at and it's especially great with a girl because you can do love songs and things like that. Doing a love song with some guy with a high voice gets a little bit weird sometimes, y'know? Most of the guys with real high voices who do that kind of thing are a bit strange..."

Gram and Gretchen returned to LA, registering for a bungalow at the Marmont where they could enjoy some privacy after the goldfish bowl experience at Nellcote.

Gram got up to speed with some bad habits once back in his familiar environs and Gretchen gave up trying to monitor his intake and instead stayed home, as she was still too young to go to nightclubs and bars with her husband. She was there to mother him and to pick him up in her car when he was too loaded to pilot his Harley safely home. She often received phone calls from his friends, club owners or the highway patrol to come and fetch him in the instances where the services of his lawyer Bruce Wolfe and bail bondsmen weren't required. Like Hank Williams before him, Gram grew familiar with the inside of jail cells.

CHAPTER 10
PARSONS FLYING SOLO

Newly married and feeling the strain of their long stay away from the US, Mr. and Mrs Parsons returned 'home' to the Chateau Marmont, ostensibly to face the music. Gram was still unprepared for a solo album and once again immersed himself in partying and drinking. He had put on close to 30 pounds in weight, and his drinking was increasingly out of control. His friends, like writer Eve Babitz, hardly recognised him. He appeared blown out of shape, his good looks buried under a layer of fat, bearing an increasing resemblance to Elvis Presley, who was himself becoming the victim of the same junk food and prescription pills that had killed his mother Gladys. Gram's alcohol dependency was at its worst. His drinking problem had him shaking like a leaf until he'd had his third morning glass of tequila. With the dissipation came the notion, according to Babitz, that he had really "let go of everything", that he was just this "white punk on dope".

The vision of Gram as an overweight alcoholic, old before his time, was shocking to everyone around him. Friends had romanticised this gifted kid who found such joy in the mythology of country music; this kid who wanted to be the new Hank Williams was instead finding a new love affair. With his casual acquaintance with the needle – a relationship that works only in ever-decreasing circles – and his on-going taste for self-corruption, Gram seemed to be displaying signs of a deep depression. Gretchen Carpenter claims that her young husband made no attempt to sober up: "His mental health became very precarious. He was ill, and you can only beg someone so many times, Please don't bring these people over, please don't give him anything, water down the drinks. There would always be somebody going 'Hey, Gram, lemme buy you a drink... hey, look what I got for ya... I couldn't fight it."

Chris Hillman was equally saddened by his young friend's downturn. "His pants and shirt wouldn't button. It was almost like Elvis at the end, when he couldn't get into his suit. Here was this good-looking kid who turned into this monster three years later, this overweight, loud, stupid person." There was talk around town that one of the reasons for Gram's obvious ill health and discomfort was that he suffered from some kind of heart problem. Whether this was as a result of substance abuse has never been proved. One other scenario that has been put forward is that Gram's 'heart problem' was hereditary. But whether he in fact did have such a serious health problem has never even been properly established. Gretchen Carpenter maintains she never saw Gram go to a doctor, claiming that he would not go to see a physician for any reason – obviously ignoring the fact that Gram had consulted Dr. Sam Hutt about an unknown condition while they were in London.

For the remaining months of 1971, Gram "mentally prepared" himself to record his first solo album proper. Whether or not he was having problems getting material together, the fact was that he had made himself look foolish to A&M and other record companies over the debacle with Terry Melcher and the so-called "cocaine album". Word of this sort of paranoid activity didn't surprise anyone who knew Melcher, but rumours about Gram tended to get through to the other labels as well. Still, the 1970s were an era of all kinds of excess and Gram's behaviour wasn't out of character with the time, nor did it make him look completely unappealing to everybody.

The story goes that Gram was flipping through his address book and had come across the name Eddie Tickner. Tickner was the original business manager of the Byrds, before the Larry Spector days. He had a reputation as being a solid, trustworthy fellow, well connected and with a history that stretched back to the heyday of New York folk music. He had been involved with the Flying Burrito Brothers in the months leading up to Gram's departure, and under his direction the band had remained liquid enough to keep the interest up at A&M. Although Gram didn't know him that well, Eddie quickly proved to be a real find. "Gram gave me a call about a year later," said Tickner to Phil Kaufman. "After he had left the Flying Burrito Brothers. He acted to me like I was his long lost brother. He said, "Would you help me finalise a thing with Rolling Stone Records? They want to sign me as the first artist outside of the Rolling Stones'.""

The two met for a drink and Gram mentioned that Keith Richards was going to produce this solo album for the Rolling Stones' own record label. This was not entirely true. It only took Eddie a couple of calls to London to find out the truth of the matter – that while Gram and Keith were good friends and a solo album had indeed been discussed, things were too busy in the Stones camp just at the moment. But on talking to Gram again, the sad tale came out about how the Burritos had turned their backs on Reprise, just when a deal was being offered.

Tickner immediately took Gram to see Mo Ostin, the chairman of Reprise at the Burbank offices of Warner Bros. Ostin, a keen-eyed talent scout himself, put Gram through the usual audition process, to see whether he had the songs and the goods for a solo album. Warners had just assembled its first country division that year and A&R man Andy Wickham was put in charge of overseeing the auditions for new acts. The "audition" ended up being held in Gram's bungalow at the Chateau over a few tequilas. Gram took out his guitar, played some song fragments, mentioned the Rolling Stones a few times and the deal was set.

Next on the agenda was to find a producer. Gram had a shortlist already but, Keith Richards notwithstanding, first on his *other* list was country music legend Merle Haggard. Merle was one of Gram's big heroes, a hard-drinking, no-nonsense Okie who was, coincidentally or not, represented by Gram's attorney Bruce Wolfe. Gram milked this connection for all it was worth, having heard through the grapevine that Haggard was looking for his first opportunity to produce somebody else. Gram was invited down to Haggard's home studio in Bakersfield, California, where the two drank, played with Merle's train set and talked about music.

Gram watched Merle working in the studio alongside his long-serving engineer, Hugh Davies. Haggard's band operated in a pointedly different manner from the wastrel notions of rock musicians in the studio. Rock bands had, since the mid-60s, spent more and more time in creating a mood or vibration in the studio, while old-school country bands spent more time in clubs and on the road and got to work on arrangements that way. They would go into the studio as a tight, hot-picking outfit and it was not unusual or difficult for a band of this calibre to record and mix three or four songs in a day, if the timing was good.

Haggard was a perfectionist in the studio but he left band-leading duties to pedal steel player Norm Hamlet, who directed the band extremely well. Another thing Gram discovered was that Merle was not actually a hippy-hater – despite the right-wing sentiments of "Okie from Muskogee" and "The Fighting Side of Me"; he was more of a hippy-baiter. He smoked grass himself at the time, and constantly found himself having to try to justify his position to journalists. His last word on 'Okie…' was that "people in Muskogee smoke grass, hell, they probably smoke more pot there than anywhere else." Furthermore, Haggard thought Gram was a nice kid who mentioned the right influences and sang nicely, so he agreed in principle to working with him.

Then, the day before recording was due to start, Eddie Tickner called with bad news. Merle had split up with his wife, Bonnie Owens, the previous day and was now holed up in the Holiday Inn, drinking heavily and refusing to answer his phone or leave his room. Gram was staying down the road at the Roosevelt, where Eddie and Phil had put him under hourly watch in order to dry him out before the sessions started. Gram was devastated. He took Hag's marital problem as being both a sign and a personal rejection, and began to hit the bottle hard. Once again, that elusive glimpse of fame was dissipating as quickly as smoke. "I think Merle not producing the album was probably one of the greatest disappointments in Gram's life. Merle was very nice, very sweet," said Gretchen, who accompanied Gram to visit Haggard. "But he had his own enemies, and his own demons."

Gram called Emmylou with the news. While she was disappointed, Gram assured her that the sessions were only temporarily called off and would go ahead later in the year. Faced with this setback, Gram tried to take stock of his situation. Rick Grech called in May with news that he was planning to do a country record with Dr. Sam Hutt, and would he like to join them? Gram was overjoyed at this development, and in June Gram and Gretchen left LA to return again to London. Staying briefly at Rick's farm in Sussex, the pair listened to the latest George Jones and Tammy Wynette album, *We Go Together*, and the plans for the Hutt-Grech album were discussed further.

Gram related his meeting with this "new chick singer", as well as the sad tale of how Merle Haggard had almost come to produce his solo album. As always, Rick lent a sympathetic ear. He could see that Gram was upset by one more in a long line of almost-dids and could-haves. Rick could further see that Gram wasn't just being indulgently self-piteous about it. He reassured Gram that Merle's involvement, however great it might have been, was not fundamental to the album. Thus encouraged, Gram and Rick talked about the solo album again, just as they had done 12 months previously. Rick reiterated his earlier promise to produce the album, and Gram decided that Rick would indeed be the one.

Upon returning to London to prepare for the album he was to record with Rick and Dr. Sam, Gram, with Gretchen, rented a little mews house in Belgravia. Perry Richardson was again a frequent visitor to their home. Their stay in London was not lengthy, but it was full of surprises and interesting dinner invitations, including William S. Burroughs and Brion Gysin at their home in St. James. Another pivotal moment in London was the day that Gram received his first royalty cheque. It was the songwriting royalties from Joan Baez's cover of "Drug Store Truck Drivin' Man", which had appeared in the hugely successful *Woodstock* film and the attendant soundtrack record. While not an enormous sum of money, Gram was "hopping all round the room", saying, "This is the first money I ever made for myself!"

Gram played Perry some of the songs he had selected for his solo album. Even with their basic arrangements, songs like 'Streets of Baltimore' sounded great. Perry remembered that Gram "had a beautiful humour toward that song" in particular. Even with all the good news, there was something bothering Gram during his time in London – the growing commercial success of the Eagles. It peeved him that, while he was met with frustration at every turn, 'Take It Easy' and 'Witchy Woman' had ascended the charts both in England and just about everywhere else. Tempering his jealousy about the pretenders ascending a throne that was rightfully his was the realisation that he was "doing the real thing" as opposed to the "country-rock" tag that both he and the Eagles had been tarred with, according to Perry. Still, the commercial considerations did not escape him. "I think Gram wanted a wider audience," said Richardson. "He'd have liked to have been as big as the Stones."

Whether it was absolute fame or simple recognition that Gram craved, he certainly wanted to get back into doing the album. But other things had to be done first. Gram brought some smack along to a London meeting with Rick and Sam, and geezed up in full view of the doctor. Sam didn't join in the fun, and it soon became obvious to him that neither Gram nor Rick had the drive to do the album. Impervious to anything else that was going on around him, Gram packed up his tent and headed back to Los Angeles, taking with him tapes of some songs that he and Rick had worked on together.

Next, Gram contacted Eddie Tickner and asked him if he would begin negotiating with Elvis Presley's band to have them appear on the album. Gram was aware that getting the King's touring band to play on his album would be a real coup, giving him the credibility that this first album would need if it were to succeed. Then it was time to contact Emmylou, who had been waiting nearly a year for that promised phone call and round-trip plane ticket. It was all arranged within days, and Emmylou packed her bags and sublet her house in Washington, arriving in town later that week for the pre-session rehearsals.

Having contacted Glen D. Hardin, Eddie was pleased to report that the band would indeed be available for the sessions. Furthermore, Glen invited a large group of the people involved in the album to come to Las Vegas to see an Elvis show at the Hilton. Gram and Gretchen, Rick and Jenny (who had only just arrived in America) and Eddie and Barry Tashian attended the show. "Yeah, I got to go see Elvis," says Barry Tashian, relishing the thought 28 years later. "It was great just getting to play those songs, but it was great that I got to play with James Burton and those guys."

After the Hilton show, Hardin took Gram and Rick out gambling in the casino. Gram, an experienced gambler, was humorously put out by the antics of Rick and Glen, who were acting like a couple of high rollers. They ended up being asked to leave the casino. As casino security men escorted them to the door, Glen D. Hardin was telling them off. "Let me apologise on behalf of the United States for the way these assholes are treating you!" he said to Rick. Gram just shook his head in mild disgust, and left them to it, returning to his hotel room, where he sat down and began writing the words to a song that musically very much echoed the experience of seeing and hearing one of his great idols play, while contextually touching on the allure of the 'crystal city'. "Ooh, Las Vegas," he wrote, "Ain't no place for a poor boy like me." On returning to LA, he picked up a guitar and started writing a tune to go with it. Barry Tashian was staying with Gram at the Chateau that week, and together they worked on the song. Barry contributed a verse to it and the song was nearly complete.

After booking in to her room at the Bel Air Sands hotel, Emmylou dropped by the Chateau to learn some songs, and Gram played her 'Ooh, Las Vegas'. Emmylou listened politely and suggested that he change a line from "this funky hotel" to "the Holiday Inn", because "that's the reality of the situation, isn't it?" Gram agreed and changed the line.

That night, Gram took Emmylou and Barry into the lobby of the Marmont and sat them around the grand piano, while he played them some of the songs he'd been arranging. Barry sat on the sienna-tiled floor, leaning against the wall as Gram sang them '$1000 Wedding'. "It just raised the hair on the back of my neck," says Tashian. "It was just so... heavy, just so *noir*, so beautiful. Emmy and I just looked at each other, like 'Wow. Oh, my god.' It made me think that somehow, his songs are sacred, you know? When you hear something like that, it touches you. They have this sacred quality to them, that it's like he tapped into some other... cosmic place. He drew those songs out of a deep, deep well."

Sleeping on the couch of the Chateau bungalow suite, Barry was concerned for Gram's well-being, even as he explains that he never felt like he knew Gram so well. Gram, Rick and Barry had many late nights at the Chateau, listening to Bobby Bland and Holy Roller meetings on tape. Even though Gram enjoyed listening to the sermons and singing, Barry detected that there was a great deal of spiritual emptiness there. "I knew he was in trouble at the Chateau Marmont, but you know, I had this thing where I thought I could save him. I remember leaving him this message at the Marmont room, saying, 'This [album] could be a turning point for you.' I mean, we had some fun in that suite, you know? There was lots of room and we would just play all night, until we couldn't keep our eyes open.

"Anyway, I remember that he was reading this book, called *Hank Williams – Sing A Sad Song*. And I kinda looked at the book and thought, 'Hank Williams... Gram Parsons.' That gave me chills. I didn't know anything of Gram's background, all of the madness and the suicide, and how this affected his behaviour at the time. It seemed that that was what was gonna happen. Even at that time, the whole world of addiction, the concept of addiction as a disease, it wasn't understood. Maybe I'm reading too much into it in hindsight, but these are my fantasies, you know?"

Soon, the songs were taking a more complete shape. As she and Gram rehearsed 'That's All It Took', all Gram had to do was raise his eyebrows and Emmylou would ride up to the high notes. The shorthand was coming together. "His singing was so extraordinary, and I was learning so much from him that I just became a total country-music convert. I had been a bit of a purist folk-music person, and I looked down my nose at country music, and then when I did listen to it, I didn't hear it with my heart. Gram never told me what to do, he more suggested things. He'd say, 'You can go up and sing that high note, but maybe it's more effective if you actually go down and lower the harmony.' And one of the things that I learned subliminally from working with Gram is that there's a an economy of emotion in the music, a restraint, that is essential to the country style of music."

A tape of rehearsals recorded the week before the band was booked into the studio showcased the arrangements as they stood at that point. Without the input of Glen D. Hardin, most of the songs are completely recognisable, although the demo version of 'How Much I've Lied' is in a different key (G) to the album (F) and is missing one of the minor chord resolutions that Hardin added when he was asked to tackle the song. It also has a standard Jimmie Rodgers introduction.

It's not that the demo version is lacking in any way, more that the song in its unadorned state is much more a straight-ahead, chugging bluesy country number than the sweet confession it would later become. Gram gave Emmylou a tape of Carl and Pearl Butler singing, 'We'll Sweep Out The Ashes In the Morning'. The tape also contained some Louvin Brothers songs. "I had never heard the Louvin Brothers before," says Emmylou, "and that really melted my butter." In one of those wonderful twists of fate, the tapes of Gram teaching Emmylou to sing that very song are still in existence.

Just prior to the sessions, Gram and Gretchen had decided that they should leave the Chateau because it was getting to be a drain on finances. They went looking at houses and finally settled on a place on Laurel Canyon Boulevard, near Mulholland Drive. The stability of actually having a home to go to, rather than an expensive hotel bungalow at the Marmont, must have worked wonders for Gram's sense of responsibility.

However, if Rick Grech had thought he was going to be intimately involved in the making of his friend's album, he was wrong. Barry Tashian thinks it happened on either the first morning of sessions or the morning before sessions were due to begin. The two of them were having breakfast at a coffee shop across the street from the Marmont. "Aretha was on the jukebox, it was that song 'Ain't No Way' and Rick was in the middle of his scrambled eggs. He just suddenly doubled over, going, 'Owww!' He feels this sharp pain. We went back to the room and called an ambulance. We got in the car and followed them to UCLA hospital emergency room and spent the afternoon there, worried about him." It turned out Rick had a kidney stone. It had to be removed, and the operation was on the first morning of recording. He stayed in hospital for the duration of the recording, nearly three weeks. The hospital bills were enormous, and his unfortunate absence put the responsibility for production entirely in the hands of Gram and Hugh Davies. Both men covered the task admirably well and, for the most part, Davies found Parsons very knowledgeable about the studio process for someone so young.

Without Rick in the studio to act as counterweight, Gram had initially gotten nervously drunk, and made a spectacle of himself in his excitement to be working with such a fine studio band. He was in bad shape, "falling down drunk" according to one of the musicians. He had set himself on a stool with his acoustic guitar and dropped his pick on striking the first chord. He slithered off the stool to fetch it and found himself scrambling for it drunkenly. There were no repeat performances of this nature. Tashian had drawn up chord charts, xeroxed them and passed them around, instructing the players about the tempo and feel. While Phil took Gram to a nearby coffee shop to sober up, Hardin took the opportunity to write up "onion skins", basically the arrangements of the songs written on transparent paper, so that amendments could easily be made. As for Gram, he remained sober for the rest of the sessions. Tashian had noticed that Gram's behaviour was still erratic and his hands were shaking badly just about the whole time, which Barry thought was the effects of long-term drug abuse.

On the whole, the sessions went smoothly. There was a little nerves problem for Emmylou initially, but she became a good luck charm in the studio and her presence was calming, according to the other musicians. She would sit and crochet in the corner, but paid close attention to the vocal takes in particular and would good-naturedly point out any problems that she thought could use some ironing out. "You know the funny thing was that I didn't really know who these people were. I was really isolated musically. I'd done a little bit of country music, but I didn't really understand it. And I really didn't know what was happening in pop music at that point. I'd been isolated for a few years.

"So it was like I was coming from the hills or something. I was just trying to figure out what I was doing as far as singing with Gram, and doing whatever it was that he wanted. I was more concerned with coming up with the goods, [and] I wasn't really clear what that was. It seemed very disorganized. Gram hadn't been in the studio for a while. I didn't see the method in his madness until later. It was really the beginning of a phenomenal musical education for me, and looking back at it now I don't know how I handled it. I think it was my naïveté that got me through."

Pedal steel was, as always, an important component of the album, so Gram called upon the services of ex-Shiloh multi-instrumentalist Al Perkins. Perkins was a genuine country music rebel whose steel playing was about second to none in LA. Perkins and Burton set to work in their hotel rooms to prepare parts for the session, with Gram's request that the two try to emulate the interplay of steel wizard Speedy West and Jimmy Bryant that had enlivened many country albums in the 40s and 50s.

Hugh Davies was actually excited to be working alongside someone like Gram, since he had that unpredictability that Davies enjoyed being around. More to the point, as a producer Hugh obviously had tapped into the feel that Gram was going for: "I really liked the music. I could enjoy myself. It was sort of funky country. Not quite rock, but beyond traditional country. I really looked forward to each session and working with Gram," Davies remembers. "He was interested in getting it recorded with the flavour and style that *he* wanted." Al Perkins concurred: "Gram had a real vivid impression of certain people like Elvis, Merle and others and he tried to follow in their footsteps, right down to the musicians. In particular, that meant requesting certain things of the musicians, such as getting James Burton and Al Perkins to play twin parts, "like were heard on country records of the '50s and '60s, and that were just no longer done," said Perkins.

James Burton, Elvis's lead guitarist, had played on some of the classic '50s rock 'n' roll tracks like 'Suzie Q', and was the man responsible for that great stuttering solo on Rick Nelson's 'Hello, Mary Lou', a solo that millions of aspiring guitarists had sweated over. Glen D. Hardin, the King's pianist, and Emory Gordy, the bass player, also came on board. Hardin had worked with the Crickets in the early 60s, and later worked with James Burton and Delaney Bramlett in the *Shindig* TV show band the Shindogs. By 1969, he was working for Elvis Presley, and was much in demand as a studio arranger. Ronnie Tutt, the TCB band's drummer, was hired to play on some of the tracks, although drumming duties would also fall to session players like Sam Goldstein and John Guerin.

The first song recorded was 'Still Feeling Blue', an up-tempo shuffle that went so smoothly, everyone felt it gave real confidence and groove to the project. It was one of six songs that Gram had either written or co-written for the album, and the others were all equally strong and melodic. Tapes of vocal run-throughs show all three vocalists, Gram, Emmylou and Tashian, singing live together. Gram's phrasing doesn't vary most of the way through, as though he had it set in his mind how each song would be sung.

'The New Soft Shoe' in particular was very pretty. It displayed extraordinary sensitivity and a lyrical turn of phrase that Dylan would have been proud of. The song, Gram said, was about people using other people and also about discovering who you really are and what you are finally capable of. The old-time huckster who peddles from a shoeshine stand attracts a crowd to preach and to teach but what he could possibly be selling is unclear, there seems almost to be no purpose to the allusion. The final verse of the song is a series of question marks, each a self-fulfilling prophecy. The first verse is a meditation on Erratt Lobban Cord, builder of Cord automobiles.

Erratt Cord had built and lost three fortunes before his 21st birthday, but he was an again-wealthy young man of 33 when he commissioned the line of automobiles that bore his name. Born into a poor family in 1896, Cord, through his highly developed sense of salesmanship, had built his own transport dynasty, a modern American empire that included Lycoming, Columbia Axle, Checker Cabs, New York Shipping, Duesenberg (who built the Auburn Roadster) and Century Airlines (now known as American Airlines).

Perhaps some of Cord's uniquely American entrepreneurial achievements were part of the fascination for Gram. More likely, it was Cord's working of unexpected, unthinkable or radically new ideas into an existing form that was inspirational to him. It was precisely what Gram would do with his contemporaneous take on an established American musical form, but, as with Cord, widespread recognition of these achievements would not arrive in full within his lifetime.

'She', a song co-written with Chris Ethridge during the days of the Flying Burrito Brothers, is nostalgic and slow, with a vamping piano intro. The lyrics take on the cast of a Carson McCullers story; a woman of uncertain age and plain looks who comes from the "land of the cotton". Whether that land is *"nearly forgotten by everyone"* is debatable, since it seems to have regularly appeared as part of American literature and song. In fact, the working of the cotton, its processing and its movements up and down the Mississippi to northern cities has been celebrated as typifying the rural experience – there can be few jobs so down-home and so near to the soil as picking cotton.

White and black music have celebrated cotton picking as a metaphor for backbreaking labour, representing what was once an aspiration – to play music rather than pick cotton. BB King picked cotton, so did Charlie Rich. When Creedence Clearwater Revival recorded 'Cottonfields' it was a projection of the urban experience, since no one in the band had even been that far south at the time they recorded it. Merle Haggard wrote 'California Cottonfields', a sad and beautiful tribute to the mass westward migrations of Oklahomans triggered by the Great Depression. Gram took this song and put it in the repertoire of the band he would lead around America to tour the new album. The experiences of poverty and disenfranchisement were not foreign to him; although he came from a wealthy family, he had seen his family destroyed by tragedy.

The story of 'She' brings to mind the biblical story of Ruth and Boaz (Ruth 1:1-10), where a Moabitess woman, Ruth, enters the fields of a wealthy man in order to find food. She picks up discarded grain, probably rye or wheat, to feed herself and her relative Naomi. The people of Israel were commanded, in Deuteronomy 24:10, not to "look back over a field [after harvest] but leave it for aliens (foreigners) or those in need". Boaz observed Ruth in the field where the harvesters had been, picking up discarded grain, and his heart was moved to kindness. He took her into his home and invited her to eat with him. She did so and her heart, initially distrusting of an Israelite, was turned towards Boaz. This plain country girl finds love and salvation through song, and fulfilment of promises broken.

'A Song For You' was more abstract and philosophical. It reveals itself as a search for true meaning in God, using some Biblical parallels. Parsons sounds almost ill at ease here, unwilling or unable to openly embrace "religion", yet freely using its metaphors to suggest his true feelings, which are of ambivalence as it turns out. There is talk of Jesus building a ship, and while nothing of this is especially Biblical (although Jesus once preached from a boat) the metaphor sits well. The last line of the stanza comes out like a prayer of intercession –

"Some of my friends don't know who they belong to
Some can't get a single thing to work inside."

The covers on the album were well weighted. Gram chose songs that he felt Emmylou had blended particularly well with him on. These were 'That's All It Took', a George Jones song, and a Joyce Allsup composition 'We'll Sweep Out The Ashes In the Morning'. 'Cry One More Time', a nod to Boston rockers the J. Geils Band, came out sounding very 50s R&B, with Barry Tashian, who had brought the song along to the session, singing it on the album. Some subtle and impressive arrangements updated the chosen covers beautifully, allowing them room to move within the more contemporary parameters of the originals.

Tompall Glaser's 'Streets Of Baltimore' is on the surface a fairly unexceptional tune, utilising just three chords. Within the framework of a simple melody the tale builds of a man who willingly sells everything he owns in Tennessee, just to take his woman to a place far out of his frame of reference, to Baltimore, that 'resort town on the east coast'. She is captivated by an ideal, a better life in a city where the lights seem brighter than she's used to. He settles into a routine working an uninspiring factory job, simply happy to be providing a cottage in a quiet suburb and allowing a new kind of life for his sweetheart in a new city.

But with his willingness to provide for her comes her dissatisfaction. It seems she wants more than she can get from what he provides, and whether he would ever provide more willingly is unclear – she wants new friends, dim lights and thick smoke. The song ends with the crestfallen protagonist returning resignedly to the South, while she remains behind in the thrall of the bright lights. It's a sad, sweet song and Glaser's ear for a turn of phrase and a simple and effective melody is impressive.

'Kiss The Children' is a fine tune from the pen of Rick Grech, and is a song that could easily vie for the title of "most perfect country song ever written". It is sentimental and moving, yet deliberately menacing and earthy. Grech later recorded the song himself, after Gram's death, but went on record saying that the first recorded version was perfect.

Its images can be divided into three parts, outside of verse/chorus/bridge/verse/ chorus. Firstly, the statement of intent. The set-up is a classic country metaphor of hard times,

"It's been said my life has been so free and easy
But I'll tell you now the story isn't so."

Both Grech and Parsons were rich kids, both had enjoyed the pleasures of life, but both had been touched by tragedy. The opening lines demonstrate their riposte to those who assume that their wealth acted as a buffer against hurt – although, as Gram's life showed, it was possible to keep a certain amount of hurt at bay with chemical protection. Rehearsal tapes of Grech and Parsons working on the song reveal different, more intense lyrics to round out the song.

"And don't you play this crazy game with me no longer
Cause I won't be able to resist my rage
And the gun that's hanging on the kitchen wall, dear
Will be the final witness to it all
And the gun that used to hang upon the wall, dear

Will be smoking when they find the rest of me."

Gram's vocal performance hinted that he had tasted hot tears of regret over many things in his life – his father's death, his mother's death, his sister so troubled that she had been committed several times to mental institutions, and more recently the death of Brandon De Wilde in a car accident. He had achieved a lot but there was much more to prove. He had removed himself from the Byrds with a vain hope of finding his way into the Stones' inner circle. Then he had lost his way in the Burritos, through too many drugs and too much booze.

Now, at 25 going on 26, he was no longer a kid. His hair was longer, he was starting to put on weight and his finely stitched Nudie suits no longer fitted him the way they once did. People commented. Buttons stretched open on shirts, his pants grew tight and his hands shook terribly in the morning without some kind of chemical assistance – usually three or four water glasses of tequilas would calm him down, a few more would make him gregarious. After that, he evolved into the original white punk on dope. It was a big step away from the doe-eyed Magic Christian of 1969. A look would creep across his face, suffused by a personality that wasn't his – that of the bad Southern cop.

He dreamed of losing some weight, and assured his friends that he would look great again soon. But eventually he lost interest in his expensive tailored clothes. Gram had quit wearing his Nudie suits; he gave some of them to Phil Kaufman who stored them in a trunk. Gram instead found solace in old denims and boots, not quite caring about his looks or the way he dressed. Whether he knew it or not, he had begun to resemble a longhaired Elvis, another artist who had vanished inside his own dreams, who had begun not to care, in the wake of a devastating divorce. The dream of being a flamboyant new country singer had evaded him, another dream of gold turning slowly to shit.

Gram still had a lot to prove to disbelieving friends and music industry players; he had to show that he had a solo career in him, the kind that would allow him to shake off his erratic reputation and establish him as a key songwriter. All around him, artists got their careers going or got them restarted. Chris Hillman was in Manassas with Steve Stills now, making money out of touring and releasing albums. Steve Young was gigging compulsively and getting interested in Buddhism. Even Jesse Ed Davis, who knew the value of getting high, had a solo album out. His friends Delaney and Bonnie parlayed their working musician ethic into a successful, continuing road show that on any given night could include George Harrison and Eric Clapton. And the Eagles – those pricks had picked up every one of his ideas and had turned them into gold records.

Everyone had gotten out of his or her slumps in 1972, and it seemed that they were all travelling down the middle of the fast lane. But Gram had been discouraged by his motorcycle accident and had perhaps sustained mild brain damage, not to mention internal injuries compounded by drug abuse. A recent fight with Gretchen had left him with a perforated eardrum after she belted him with a coat hanger across the ears, which caused his singing to suffer as he struggled to hear a note in the clamour of a band. "I don't know about Gretchen," says Barry Tashian. "At least, she's a very pretty girl but I always felt that their relationship was strange. I don't think there was much of a spiritual connection there. They weren't real compatible. There was a lot of ego trips going on there and she was concerned about him, rightly so. But it wasn't a very tranquil domestic *scene*."

Once the album was completed, Gram, Emmylou, Barry and Rick – by now mostly recovered from his surgery – accompanied Hugh Davies to Capitol Records for mixing and some vocal readjustments. After initial guide vocal takes at Wally Heider's, the Capitol sessions reveal that Gram and Emmylou had been working hard on their duets, and the new vocal tracks were sterling. Everyone was ecstatic at how great it sounded when the two of them blended that way, and it made the album stand out from everything that was going on at the time.

Of the two stellar tracks on the album that really caught people's attention, 'That's All It Took' and 'We'll Sweep Out The Ashes', it was the latter that really allowed Gram and Emmylou to take the duet idiom into a whole other dimension. In an interview with Holly George-Warren, Harris said that the harmonies she performed with Parsons came about through "osmosis": "Just by singing with him," she said, "I learned that you plough it under and let the melody and the words carry you. Rather than this emoting thing, it will happen on its own. As you experience life and know more, then it's gonna come out almost unconsciously as you sing. You have to have restraint in how you approach a song. On 'That's All It Took', I was still into it being very dramatic and that I must go up very high. And Gram said, "You know what? On this last tag, let's just voice it down." That's one of the few things I remember him telling me to do specifically."

Now that the album sessions were finally finished, it was time for mixing and mastering. The musicians went back to gainful employment in the service of the King, while Gram relaxed a little with Rick and Jenny. The completion of the album, now titled *GP*, was a significant milestone in Gram's life. He had never before been completely and creatively in charge of making an album, and he liked the feeling.

GP fills the senses so completely with its morality and beauty that one has to turn to the relatively sedate George and Tammy for some sort of relief. Either that or keep playing it until the grooves wear off. Bud Scoppa, in reviewing the album for *Rolling Stone*, noted that while the duet vocals on a surface level worked as well as those of George and Tammy and Conway and Loretta, they had the "added principle of moral uncertainty". This astute observation portrays how the innuendo inherent in most similar country songs (which most duet acts would only occasionally downplay) worked so compellingly with the exciting tarnish of West Coast excess. Most country duets worked well on a somewhat different level. Love and lust are different enough, but the words of 'We'll Sweep Out the Ashes' were given a new resonance. These two people, caught up in the cauterising heat of desire, would know an end to this affair soon enough, but in the meantime there was a fire burning out of control.

CHAPTER 11
SIX WEEKS ON THE ROAD

Putting together a successful road band is never an easy task, particularly when that group differs substantially from the musicians who played on your album, as Gram was discovering. He had the basic elements of a band agreed upon, with Jon Corneal deputising on drums in early rehearsals until the arrival from Ohio of former Remains drummer Neil Smart (also known as ND Smart II).

Phil Kaufman stepped in to organise a pedal steel guitarist for the road band, now that Warners had tentatively approved the idea of a tour to promote the Reprise album. Eddie Tickner had approached Warners with the idea for two media showcase gigs, one on each coast. All the hip rock critics and underground press gangs were to be invited, giving the record company a chance to get Gram some more exposure with little or no risk. However, the decision was made by the record company to send Gram on the road with a band, giving them more coverage for their investment.

Tickner started making telephone calls to as many clubs and promoters as he could, although he knew of one place where Gram and the band could play, a club in a Boulder, Colorado shopping centre called the Edison Electric Company. That proved to be the first booking. Now that the tour was happening, Tickner and Kaufman thought it prudent to organise the band formally. In conversations with musicians they knew the word had gotten out about the Parsons gig, and while most were keen to participate, they were mostly also aware of Gram's tendency to quickly lose interest in such projects. Barry Tashian, who had tried to instigate a Gram Parsons band earlier in 1972, decided not to go on the road with the group. Steel player Ed Black also backed out, choosing to tour with Linda Ronstadt instead.

Mangler got the number of Bobbee Seymour, a Nashville-based session musician. Seymour was playing mostly studio dates, which were well paid and too regular to consider giving up on, even for a month on the road. But he recommended a friend and fellow steel player Neil Flanz for the task. Flanz, a Canadian born in Montreal, worked for a band called The Kelly Rodgers Breed who worked five nights a week at the Broadway Barn in Nashville. He was a little perplexed at first, but was delighted by the offer of $250 a week for a month on the road. "I had no idea who Gram Parsons was – I mentioned his name to the group I was working with, and they said, 'Are you crazy? You gotta go! Don't even think twice about leaving the group.'"

Flanz caught a flight out to Los Angeles the next day. It was raining hard. "Phil picked me up at LAX and then we went over to Gram's place, then we went over to a friend of Gram's place, his name was Sidney Kaiser. The first thing I noticed when we got to Sidney's house was that there was a large dish of Peruvian marching powder and quite a bit of grass over there, so we all got drunk and high and that was how I first met Gram."

Jon Corneal was in L.A., just hanging out. He'd missed out on a tour to Europe with the Everly Brothers band because of a serious snowstorm in Nashville. He arrived in Los Angeles with his trailer full of equipment. He stayed with Warren Zevon for a few days, before Phil heard he was in town and rang to invite him over for some rehearsals that Gram was doing. "He said, 'come on out here to my place in Van Nuys.' So I did, and I slept on the floor for a few days between two Great Danes named Alice and Big Head – and they snored, among other things. As it turned out, it was the same floor where Gram would be having rehearsals for the pre-GP tour. So they used my P.A. and my drums. The drumming job had already been delegated to N.D. Smart."

Informal rehearsals began the next day. A limo would be dispatched to pick up the musicians from their various hotels in the North Hollywood and Van Nuys areas and deliver them to Kaufman's house on Chandler Boulevard, where Gram was now living full-time. Kyle Tullis was also present. Jon Corneal was still acting as stand-in for Neil Smart, while Gerry Mule arrived from Washington DC with Emmylou. He was a quiet sort of guy, without much to say. Opinion in the band was divided on Gerry's abilities as a country guitarist, since his background was more in folk and classical music, but he was a nice guy, a prerequisite for joining the band. On working with Emmylou again, Gram became much more animated and alive. Everyone noticed how well they worked with each other and how their voices played off one another, Emmylou's strengths compensating for Gram's occasional weaknesses.

Flanz joined in these frequently unfocused rehearsals, which were a social occasion for Gram, mostly a chance for the five musicians to smoke a little pot, drink beer, play George Jones songs and get to know one another. They all developed an admiration for each other's musical strengths, but the original idea was to get some air into the songs from the Reprise album. But while the camaraderie grew, the band wasn't necessarily getting tighter.

ND Smart II arrived from Ohio the next day, bringing with him a sarcastic sense of humour, which he was going to need for the tour. With Smart keeping time, the band's rhythm section became a little firmer. "We were supposed to be involved in serious rehearsing, learning all this stuff from the *GP* album, but it never got that serious," says Neil Flanz. "We had more fun, we had too much fun. Around six o'clock, Gram would say, 'OK – rehearsal's over' and he'd just break out into a whole bunch of George Jones songs. So we rehearsed for about two weeks, if you can call it rehearsal."

The musicians worked on songs for a week, and were certainly getting on well together. For example, they could jam beautifully on 'She Thinks I Still Care', even if Gram's originals weren't faring too well. Harris was still in the buzz of being involved in a real tour and did not second-guess Gram's questionable rehearsal techniques. "Rehearsal for Gram was just playing lots of songs that he liked," says Emmylou, "but we'd never worked out getting an end or a middle and I just thought there was some mysterious process where it was all going to fall together. It started out pretty grim before we went out, but Gram was not a very disciplined person. He loved to just sit and play, and we'd just play a lot of songs with no beginnings or ends or arrangements. I'd never gone on the road before, so I just thought, 'this is the way it's done.' I just thought some magical thing happens when you walk out onstage."

A set list had been drafted up that reflected how Gram felt about most of the originals on the album. Of the *GP* tracks, he included 'Cry One More Time', 'The New Soft Shoe', 'Streets Of Baltimore', 'That's All It Took', 'Still Feeling Blue' and 'A Song For You'. They worked some of their rehearsal jams into the set with the Buck Owens theme instrumental 'Buckaroo', Merle Haggard's 'California Cottonfields' and more R&B-flavoured material like, 'If You Don't Love Him', 'Hang On, Sloopy', 'Baby, What You Want Me To Do', 'Bony Moronie', 'Forty Days' and 'Almost Grown'. At Gram's suggestion, Neil worked up a version of 'Flint Hill Special', which would serve as an opening instrumental, that, because of the key it was played in, would allow the other members to tune their instruments to it.

At various points during the rehearsals, the question of a suitable name for the band came up. Gram's suggestion, 'the Wild Turkeys', was greeted with disbelief. Even Emmylou said that she hated it. Gram, ever democratic, backed down when the band named themselves the Fallen Angels. Gram thought it was a good name too, and everyone who heard it agreed. It suited the nature of what they were doing, longhairs doing country music, and doing it properly. For their impudence, they would have been cast out of Nashville, just as the angel Lucifer and his cohorts were expelled from heaven.

As Eddie Tickner and Phil Kaufman continued with the bookings and arrangements, they also managed to get themselves a bus for the tour – an old Greyhound. Someone painted up a vinyl banner for the back with the legend 'On Tour – Gram Parsons' on it, and the image of the new country rock 'n' roller was nearly complete. A former US Marine named 'Leadfoot' Lance was engaged as driver. The reason no one can or will reminisce about Lance is that he was what the liner notes of *Sleepless Nights* call 'a fugitive from…justice'. Suffice to say, he was reliable. There was enough room to load up all the gear and give the band plenty of room to sleep. At least, that was the idea.

Phil held a party to give the band a send-off, hiring a group called The Oily Scarf (or Skarf) Wino Band, who came along and played the send-off. Friends and neighbours came by to wish them luck on the tour, and stayed for the free beer and food. Mangler had whipped up some of his *menudo*, a Mexican stew made mostly from tripe, and fed the hordes. Among the guests at the party that night was Dale McElroy, a friend of Phil's who would soon figure heavily in the life of Gram. She had arrived back in town, having been doing the 'expat thing' in India. While travelling there, she had met an Australian guy in Goa, name of Michael Martin. Michael had, according to various stories, lived as a junkie beggar on the streets of Bombay and had managed only recently to get out of India by the skin of his teeth. Now back in the US, Dale wanted her friend to see the country, but the two of them were broke and looking for work.

On the day the bus was due to pull out, Michael asked Dale if he could go on the road with the band. Dale, no fan of Gram's personally, thought it would be a good way for him to get a look at the US, and Gram agreed. He thought it might be handy to have his own streetwise 'Spanish Tony' – some sort of Keith Richards-style conceit. Michael was hired as his 'valet'. Martin dug the idea and got to carry Gram's stash and anything else he might not want to be caught carrying by the cops. On board the Greyhound when it pulled out the next morning were Phil and his girlfriend Janet, Lance, Gram and Gretchen, Emmylou, Neil, Kyle Tullis, ND

Smart II and Gerry Mule.

After torrential LA rain, the bus got bogged up to its axles. Phil's yard got churned up when they tried to drive off. The guys all climbed out and put boards under the wheels so it could be driven off Phil's front lawn. The band finally left LA, bound for Boulder, Colorado, a full day's drive away. While Gram was happy to be out on the road with a band again after nearly three years, taking his own music and his own vision to whoever might be glad to receive it, there were those on the bus who were unsure about the band's state of readiness for this first gig.

Despite two weeks of rehearsals in LA, there was apprehension by the time they reached Boulder. Gerry Mule, for one, felt pangs of fear, especially in being so musically unprepared. Arriving at the Edison Electric Company club, the band was in for the first of a series of unpleasant scenes. "Right next door to the club was this motel, which was constantly bitching about how loud the bands were that had played at the club," says Neil Flanz. The club had in fact, been closed down by the police two days previously, because of noise complaints involving jazz-fusion group Weather Report. Fortunately the club, which was located in a shopping centre, had been able to reopen for business after appealing the police closure. Gram and the Fallen Angels were able to go ahead and play the first two of what was supposed to be six shows at the club.

Richie Furay, Gram's old folk music buddy from Greenwich Village, was in town with Poco, who had been rehearsing upstairs. Furay hadn't been in regular contact with Gram, even though they lived not that far from each other in LA. Richie's career with the Buffalo Springfield had had as many ups and downs and disappointments as Gram's career with the Byrds, but he took it all in his stride and his band was about to really take off. Poco seemed like the logical extension of the Burritos – they had taken that renegade rock and country mix and tightened it up, giving it a certain amount of gloss with the fine musicians they had in the band. Furay was aware of Gram's tendency toward excess, and admitted to him when they met in Boulder that he was interested in hearing this new band play.

On the eve of the first show, nerves were high and confidence was generally low among the band members. During the rehearsal, there were a lot of mistakes, big and small, being made. "We had had our first rehearsal over in Boulder, and Poco came out to see us," says Neil. "They were in the audience that night and I really believe they were embarrassed about how unrehearsed and unprepared we were." Reports on just how bad that night was vary. Richie Furay to this day remains embarrassed for Gram and the band about that show – "Gram looked about 50 pounds heavier; he was just big, fat, dumpy. His band was atrocious. The only good thing was when he and Emmylou sang together. I felt embarrassed for him."

Others, like club regular Stephen Ferron, still a Boulder resident today, thought the band sounded a little rough but put it down to first-night jitters. The audience were pretty generous at first, but soon enough there was an air of disbelief as guitar lines meandered, solos stopped and started too soon, vocal parts strained and then missed their resolutions, and drum fills occasionally fluttered out of time. The high point for the audience were the rock songs that Gram had chosen to pepper the set with, mostly standards that didn't need to be rehearsed so closely, like 'Hang On, Sloopy' and a Chuck Berry medley. At the end of the show, Furay went backstage to speak with his old friend and found him in the process of getting high. He couldn't honestly hold back his opinion of the show.

"Our first gig in Boulder was just a train wreck," said Emmylou. Everyone else was inclined to agree. Guitarist Gerry Mule in particular seemed upset about the show, and it was clear to the rest of the band that they were still under-rehearsed. Gerry told Gram that he didn't think he could continue with the rest of the tour, as he felt unprepared for playing under these sort of rough rock and roll conditions. Gram understood how he felt and paid him out for the tour. The rest of the band was somewhat demoralised and they congregated in Gram's hotel room that night, talking about how they might solve their problems. There wasn't going to be a mutiny, but morale was low. Gram, aware that they had some time to find another guitarist between this gig and the next in Austin, Texas, decided to keep going. He was characteristically confident: "We'll put the word out that we're looking for the best picker in town – we'll hire him."

The next morning, Tickner got a phone call from Warners. The word had gotten back to them via publicist Sherry Reed that the gig had been a complete failure and that the band was sloppy and under-rehearsed. Warners were talking about removing their support. For a record company, keeping a band on the road can be very expensive, even though it is believed that Gram was partially funding this exercise himself. "I was concerned about him keeping up his commitments," said Reed. "In fact, I called Mo Ostin about it. Mo got on the phone to Eddie and Eddie ended up flying into Boulder to make sure that Gram was okay."

Having talked the record company people down, Tickner then assured them the problem could be solved by hiring the Austin nightclub they were to perform at in advance and setting the band up there to rehearse for a couple of days. It wouldn't be too expensive and the record company would see a lot more for their money with just a little investment. On his arrival in Boulder, Tickner told Gram that he would pull the plug on the tour right there and then unless Gram could promise to lay off the refreshments, at the very least until after the show. He remonstrated with Gram, trying to make him see the importance of getting more rehearsal time in when they arrived in Austin.

Meanwhile Gram was continuing his search for a guitar player. He had been talking to local musicians, and the name Jock Bartley came up. Jock was something of a local hero, who had played in Zephyr, a Boulder band who had enjoyed some notoriety. Jock wasn't a country player by any means; he was a rock player, but one capable of subtlety, and he was keen. In Jock's opinion Gerry didn't cut it anyway, and he thought Emmylou was the most beautiful woman he'd ever seen.

The Edison club-owners, bothered by the reports of drug taking that had gone on backstage, asked the band not to play any more of their scheduled dates. Gram was unfazed. "We were meant to be there for six nights or so," said Emmylou. "But they'd decided to fire us for some reason." Eddie was naturally furious, but to make up for it the Fallen Angels were invited to play at the Pioneer Inn in the town of Nederland, some twenty miles or so up the road.

The band made the occasionally hair-raising trip up into the mountains to the Inn. Jock was already there at the modest concrete-floored club, sitting in with the first band on the bill. Gram took the opportunity to ask him if he wanted to get up and do something with them. "We set up and played, and Jock sat in with us," said Neil Flanz. "Well, he didn't really play country – he was a rock and roller. And I was very disappointed. I can remember going back to our motel with him after the gig. He and Gram were sitting in the hotel room next door talking, and I was in a room with ND Smart and Kyle Tullis. I mentioned to Kyle and ND that I didn't think Jock played country worth a shit, to tell you the truth."

ND, for whatever reason, wasted no time in deciding to talk with Gram about this matter – Gram was right next door and he and Jock were sitting on one of the beds. ND opened the door, barged into the room and said, "Hey Gram, Neil says that Jock can't play country music worth a shit." Neil was mortified at the disclosure of his remark, as he hadn't really planned on confronting Jock on his country music picking, or lack thereof, since the decision was ultimately Gram's. "Now I guarantee you that if there was a high enough bed in the room, I would have crawled under it in the blink of an eye," says Neil. "I was so embarrassed."

Gram was entirely gracious on Jock's behalf, since he looked pretty embarrassed himself. "Gram said, 'I like Jock, he's got nice hands.' I never said another word again, except that I of course apologised to Jock, and spent as much time with him as possible," says Neil. "And we became friends."

Despite this early humiliation, Jock was now officially a Fallen Angel, perhaps the most rock 'n' roll longhair in the bunch, blessed with blues licks (and few country chops) in a group comprised mostly of hippies playing a hybrid form of country music and R&B. It seemed like delicious irony, and musically speaking there was a wonderful juxtaposition of styles at work. Now, juxtaposition was all well and good but it was time to get in the bus and head for Austin, to begin some more formal rehearsals. Gram had to work the new guitarist into the band, get some more solos going and then deliver the show that the crowds in Texas would no doubt be expecting.

After the drive to Texas the band was exhausted, but they set up in the empty Armadillo World Headquarters and began practising as though their lives depended upon it. "Man, we really got down to some serious rehearsal in those couple of days," said Neil Flanz. "Endings, solos, turnarounds – who was playing what when. And I taught Jock as much as I possibly could about country guitar. I thought he did a good job. We needed some more rhythm to hold up the bottom end of it. That's why on the CD [*Gram Parsons and the Fallen Angels – Live 1973*] you'll hear an awful lot of steel and a lot of him playing rhythm guitar."

Before the shows, Gram and Emmylou went down to legendary Austin radio station KOKE to talk country music with local celebrity DJ Rusty Bell, who considered himself an expert on the subject. "He asked us what we thought about progressive country," commented Emmylou during the taped WLIR concert. "We told him we played 'regressive' country." Gram was displeased with Bell's efforts to pigeonhole him for the satisfaction of his audience and refused to cooperate, to the point of merely shaking his head or nodding when the DJ asked him a question. As he told the crowd at a radio show two weeks later, "We had this DJ the other night... and we ripped his EBS box out, which tells us all if the third world war is coming or not. His EBS box kept humming and jumping up and down while we were doing the interview and he said, 'Hey, man – do you know how to disconnect that thing?' I was sitting right behind it, so I said, 'Sure, man – I do. Watch this.' And I took it apart." The crowd cackled, hip to the whole joke.

As for Bell, he ended the segment with the derisive comment "Thanks for the worst interview of my life." Gram shrugged, and he and Emmylou walked out of the studio and back onto the waiting bus. The band had been sitting in the bus, drinking beer and listening to the radio show. They thought it was hilarious. Gram opened his jacket and with a wry grin showed everyone a plaque he'd prised off the wall of the station as they were leaving.

Two nights later, following intensive rehearsals in which a sober and thoughtful Gram took songs apart piece by piece and rearranged them properly, the Fallen Angels and their leader were ready to play. Fittingly, it was a great show; the kind the band knew they had in them. What Neil wasn't prepared for though was the kind of mania with which the Texas hippies greeted them. In his assessment – "We literally blew the roof off the place. It was a place for longhairs, y'know? There was about two thousand of 'em that came rushing towards the stage, trying to touch us – I've never experienced anything quite like it, certainly not at the Opry."

It was a success, all right. As the huge crowd gathered respectfully and loudly at his feet, Gram was in fine vocal form and Emmylou won the crowd over with her sweet, almost shy, stage patter and her palm-bruising tambourine playing. The longhairs were in love with the whole band and refused to let them leave. "We ran out of encores and had to do the same songs over and over again," Neil reminisced. It seemed not to matter to the crowd.

The next four dates, at Liberty Hall in Houston, were similarly well-attended and a group of future country singers were down in the audience, including Steve Earle, who had hitched into town from San Antonio specifically to see Parsons' latest incarnation. "Gram's first solo record was an 'event' in my little circle of musicians," says Earle. "When I heard that Gram and co. were coming to Texas, I was off like a prom dress, down I-10 to the big city. It was loose but it was tough. Gram's hair was frosted and his fingernails were painted red. He sang through his nose with eyes closed while the band played catch-up for most of the night. I saw and heard Emmylou Harris for the first time that night. I left a little bit in love and absolutely certain of what I was going to be when I grew up."

During several of the eight Liberty Hall shows, a small production company brought in video cameras to tape the show for a local channel broadcast. According to John Delgatto, the broadcast was shot on Sony EIAJ reel-to-reel tape, which was already fast on its way to becoming outmoded. By the time the original footage had made its way to Sierra Records, Delgatto says he was only able to salvage about twenty-five minutes of it, as the tape was already unstable: "It played once and it never played again."

Appearing onstage at the Sunday night show were Neil Young and Linda Ronstadt, who were appearing at the Sam Houston Coliseum in town that week. Young, a fan of Gram's work, got up to jam with the band at one point, and Ronstadt helped Gram and Emmylou work up a version of 'Sin City' for the growing group of young Austin guys in the audience calling themselves the Sin City Boys. The group had heard the song some years before, and periodically turned up to Manassas concerts to shout the words "Sin City!" at a bemused Chris Hillman. The song was much appreciated by the whole crowd, including Led Zeppelin's Robert Plant and Jimmy Page, who were also there that night.

After the show, Neil Young sent a limousine to pick up the Fallen Angels and bring them back to his hotel room for a party. The band brought some guitars with them and Young and Gram traded songs all night. Young surprised everyone by playing steel guitar beautifully. Partied out, they went back to their hotel and slept, before setting off for a two-day road journey across Mississippi and Arkansas to Chicago for the next couple of shows. The first stop along the way was Blytheville, Arkansas. The bus pulled into this tiny Southern town late in the evening and they checked into the Holiday Inn. Everyone was feeling tired and they all headed for their rooms after booking in, except Gram who decided to go and sit at the piano in the lounge bar and play for the few remaining drinkers.

After a couple of hours, Gretchen came down to get Gram and there was a scene. The motel manager asked them to leave the bar, which they did. They went back to their room and continued their argument, too loudly for the satisfaction of one guest, who called the police. The police arrived and hammered on the door, demanding to be let in. When they barged in, Gram pulled a karate pose for the benefit of the cops. They promptly maced him and he was then beaten to the floor with nightsticks. With Gretchen screaming at the officers, they dragged Gram out of the hotel with a nightstick under his jaw.

Phil Kaufman's girlfriend Kaphy tied his long hair into a bun and put a cowboy hat on his head so he could go down to the police station and bail Gram out. As he stood at the desk, filling out the various forms for bail, he could hear two sounds – Gram mouthing off at the cops, and Gram being belted with a nightstick. Mentally willing GP to keep his mouth shut long enough to get bailed out while still able to function for the rest of the tour, Phil signed the forms and produced the bail money. Gram was handed over, bruised and bleeding, with a traumatised throat. He could barely talk, let alone sing, after being maced, and he had a shiner to beat the band.

It was a subdued Gram that left Blytheville, Arkansas that morning. Wearing a floppy hat, some of Gretchen's makeup and a big pair of sunglasses to hide the bruises, he told the rest of the band what had happened. The band were shocked by this development, but the mood had sufficiently improved by midday that the bus stopped to pick up liquor and fireworks for the trip. The partying continued all the way to Chicago, and soon Gram and Emmylou were singing together again. There were what Emmylou calls 'bus songs', tunes that never made it into the live set but which the two of them enjoyed singing together. Gram was always teaching Emmylou new songs, like 'Widowmaker', 'Love Hurts' and 'Don't Let Her Know'.

'Love Hurts', the Felice and Boudleaux Bryant tune the Everly Brothers had had a hit with, sounded exquisite backed with the diesel engine and the other musicians sitting around listening, so Gram decided to add it to the set, starting with the Chicago shows. After all, the rest of the band remembered enough of the song to play it without rehearsing. It was a timely addition to the set, because more than anything it showed just how strong the duets were getting. Emmylou has voiced her opinion that 'Love Hurts' and 'The Angels Rejoiced' (the Louvin Brothers song that appears on A&M's *Sleepless Nights* compilation) are two of the best examples of their singing, and one would be hard pressed to disagree. The band was on a collective high following the warm reception from Texas crowds, but north of the Mason-Dixon line audiences were a little different.

The band arrived in Chicago, booking in at the "LSD", the name given by musicians to the Lake Shore Drive Hyatt. The hi-jinks continued. Following Gram's giggling lead, the band indulged in a little "rock star" tomfoolery. Soon, various Fallen Angels and friends were flinging their dinner plates out the windows. Neil Flanz wasn't particularly impressed by this level of maturity and could only watch aghast as Gram, with the help of someone else, pushed a loaded room service trolley out of the 12th storey window, to watch it crash to the parking lot below.

Despite this sort of behaviour, the band was now at a new level of harmony. Neil and Jock sat in their hotel room to work on the rhythm guitar aspect of the songs, and soon Neil was encouraging Jock to take some more solos. Mostly, Jock had to play electric rhythm to counteract Gram's at-times only average strumming. Bartley's confidence was growing, and Gram was impressed, mostly because it seemed like the band was succeeding *in spite* of him, at times. His band-leading skills with the Fallen Angels were below par for several reasons, mostly to do with the two-year layoff. Moreover, he was still a little shaky from his alcohol problem, and when the shaking had stopped he was often too relaxed to remember some of the hand signals the group had worked out with him. While Gram's intake might have caused some of the musicians concern, none of the live tapes recorded during this period show any weakness whatsoever in Gram's performances. His singing is in fine shape and there is no evidence that he was unable to complete shows or was too wasted to even start.

The Chicago shows, at the popular Quiet Knight club, were mostly well attended, and the Chicago *Tribune* offered a kind assessment of the charms of Parsons' music, praising in particular Neil Flanz and Emmylou Harris, "the newest member of the group". Chicago had proved to be most amenable to this new kind of country music.

The next stop was Cleveland, where the Fallen Angels played a bar called the Smiling Dog, which Emmylou remembered as looking like "the original setting for [Robert Altman film] *McCabe and Mrs. Miller*. But I loved it." Flanz thought the place was a little rough, but was surprised to hear that Emmylou was afraid they were going to get "shot or knifed." "It was a pretty rowdy place and I heard later that most of the band members were pretty scared about it." During the set, the band saw guns being pulled and watched bemused as two women fought it out down on the floor, pulling each other's hair.

They could only walk away from it and laugh. The next stop was New York City, a hard place to find country music at the best of times, but in the cold winter of 1973, country music still seemed like an anomaly. The weather was better than they had been expecting, though. Chicago had been particularly cool, although the snow had melted off the streets. New York seemed balmy by comparison. There were three shows at Max's Kansas City, home to the Velvet Underground, the Factory crowd and similar NYC rockers. Those same folks came out to see the band, because even some of the heavy New York critics, like Dave Marsh, dug Gram.

Emmylou says there wasn't much of a crowd that first night, while Flanz remembers long queues down the three flights of stairs to the street, just to get into the club. There were people sitting on the backs of the booths and crowded onto the floor, eager to see the band. Dave Mason from English rock band Traffic, got up to jam at the second show, and Gram channelled his inner rocker for the night. "We got to boogie for a little bit," Gram said, which pleased the late-night crowds no end. "I thought that show was a blast," says Neil. "We were there two, maybe three nights. I don't think I have any recordings from those gigs but I thought we sounded pretty good by then."

The next stop on the itinerary was a good one – a live-to-air broadcast on WLIR, an FM radio station in Hempstead, Long Island. The station would supply a tape of the broadcast for the band and Gram liked that idea a lot – a live album. When the bus rolled up to the Ultrasonic Recording Studios, from where the show was being broadcast, the band felt right at ease. It wasn't an actual radio station, but a recording studio with plenty of good microphones and monitoring equipment.

The band set up their gear, did a sound check and then headed across the street to a nearby Chinese restaurant. The group ate their fill and then remained relaxing in the restaurant, drinking beer and talking for about two hours. When they all strolled back across the street into the station, one of the studio employees stuck his head around the door and said that the broadcast was already starting, and would they kindly get onstage? Neil started out with his opening instrumental, 'Flint Hill Special', and the band tuned up as quickly as they could while he played, noticing that a respectably-sized audience of young people had gathered in the studio. The station ran a few announcements, then host Ken Kohl stepped up to the microphone: "Welcome to Ultrasonic Recording Studios for one in a series of live radio broadcasts. Our guest this evening has been making a lot of music for a lot of years. You may be familiar with his work with the Flying Burrito Brothers and the Byrds. Would you please welcome Mr. Gram Parsons?"

The Fallen Angels started with 'We'll Sweep Out the Ashes', a version that made this cheatin' song transcendently gorgeous. Gram and Emmylou singing together like one voice, without the artifice of the studio atmosphere, made shivers run up spines. The audience were clearly taken aback by the intensity of the duet singing, trying to compare whatever experience they'd had with country music with the piercing clarity and rock attitude of the playing. Jock peeled off a clean-sweeping solo, not country at all but perfectly at home within the song. Neil Flanz bent into a fine pedal steel solo that captured the "soul with pedal steel vibe" that Gram was always aiming for.

As the flames of the song died down, the tiny audience was delighted with what they'd just heard. "Thank yuh very much." Then Emmylou took a bashful yet confident swing through the bluegrassy 'Country Baptizing', a Kentucky Colonels tune. Her voice was piercing and beautiful. This song accentuated the balance of pedal steel and choppy, percussive gospel/rock fills that Neil and Jock had worked out so carefully. Kyle Tullis performed a great bass-led breakdown, with accents from ND and Jock. The audience applauded strongly.

'Drug Store Truck Driving Man' came up next, one of the songs that had been suggested by the band, rather than by Gram. Although he co-authored the song with Roger McGuinn, he hadn't thought about playing it. He and Neil arranged a reverent two-step version of the Byrds' song, which Gram delivered with all the solemnity of a Methodist hymn. "This is an old song that I did with the Byrds," announced Gram, his voice breaking. "When I was in fear of getting my life taken away from me. Sometimes, all you can do is sing gospel music."

Its highlight, though, was a very moving pedal steel solo by Neil. Despite the occasionally surreal lyrics, the song is treated with far more dignity than it was in the Byrds' 1968 version from *Dr. Byrds and Mr. Hyde*. His approach to this song highlighted Parsons' genuine commitment to country music tradition, and remained unadorned by any kind of contemporary stylistic moves, except the lyrics. As he delivered the line "*I'm an all-night musician in a rock and roll band/ and why he don't like me I can't understand*", his voice reached a moment of true heartbreak, as though he was questioning his own life up to that point.

ND Smart delivered the introduction to 'Big Mouth Blues' with a sly grin – "this song's about New York, or at least, that's got a lot to do with it". The opening guitar salvo, the steel guitar and Les Paul intertwined in a near-perfect synthesis of rock, country and R&B, was played much more convincingly than on the album *GP*. Jock's guitar held down a fine choppy rhythm and peeled off a great 70s rock solo. Neil played his steel guitar like a slide, turning out licks with a wonderful bluesy exuberance nearly devoid of any trace of country influence. Jock followed this with another fine solo, outdoing his first. The applause started during the song's closing moments. "We're finally in New York, aren't we?" said Gram. "I dunno, we were just heading out of New York City, it didn't matter which way."

"This is off the album on Reprise – it's called 'the New Soft Shoe'." Neil's pedal steel and ND's drums set the perfect feel to 'New Soft Shoe', with some finely strummed vibrato guitar from Jock. The pedal steel echoed the melody line of the refrain and added a beautiful hook to the song, that again is not heard on the album. There were three-part harmonies – Gram, Emmylou and ND adding strength to the melodic curl of the lyrics. Neil's steel was utterly restrained, with a strong bar vibrato. Then, in the third verse, the steel guitar is distorted and more distant than the clean sound, bringing out the purposeful intensity of the song. 'Cry One More Time' also possesses blues-rock inflections that extend to the lyrics. Although Barry Tashian sings this on the record, Gram was in fine voice. "*I've really got it baaaaaaad....*" Neil was absolutely untouchable on the steel as the audience applauded during his solo.

'Streets of Baltimore' was moderately more upbeat, again there were more three-part harmonies. Gram's phrasing was impeccable and his voice as strong as can be. There is no evidence of any slurring in his speaking voice, and he does not appear to be out of it in any way. ND introduced 'That's All It Took': "Country music prominently consists of this one beat that we call 'the Shuffle' – 2/4 beat and we're gonna play a song now that just almost purely typifies [Gram yawns audibly] the word 'country shuffle', as it were. Anyway, it's called 'That's All It Took.' I guess that's all it did take." Emmylou's solo verse in this version was wonderfully rendered, pushing the bluesier reaches of her voice. She did not miss one of Gram's cues, nor ever audibly hit a wrong note. The song ended beautifully, the two voices blending down together like honey flowing from a rock. 'Love Hurts' was delivered with total conviction. Gram and Emmylou brought this version alive – it is arguably superior to the version that would later appear on *Grievous Angel*. The pedal steel solo that Neil delivered also defied superlatives – the crowd seemed momentarily stunned.

Earlier in the evening, several audience members had called out for a Merle Haggard song, so Gram put one in the set that they had happened to rehearse. It was one of Gram's favourites. "Y'all wanted a Merle Haggard song – here comes a Merle Haggard song." It was 'California Cottonfields,' not one of his best-known songs, but one of his best; a tale of Okie hardship and longing for the promised land of California, as set out by "pretty girls in magazines". It was nearly time to leave the stage, the broadcast having only a few more minutes to go. "We're gonna leave you now with a song," said Gram. "I know, we were leaving anyway – 'Six Days On The Road.'" To add to the feeling of excitement in the studio over what the audience had witnessed, Emmylou added: "And we're gonna make it to Philadelphia tonight."

CHAPTER 12
TRUCKERS, KICKERS, COWBOY ANGELS

The Grievous Angel's ascent to the firmament began in early February 1973, when a young Boston-based poet named Tom Brown read in a local paper that singer/ songwriter Gram Parsons, formerly of the Byrds and Flying Burrito Brothers, was on his way to town. According to the article, Parsons and his band the Fallen Angels would be in Boston for several shows, as part of a month-long promotional tour on the back of the singer's first album for Frank Sinatra's label Reprise.

'Return of the Grievous Angel' was a lyrical love poem that found its place among the stars and constellations, composed not by Gram but almost entirely by Brown. In this work, written at a desk in his small apartment on Beacon Street "in about 20 minutes", Tom attempted to encapsulate his feelings about the courtship of his first wife, the "sweet Annie Rich" of the song's introductory stanza. Aware of Gram's history with Boston, knowing that he had once attended Harvard, Tom instinctively wrote in a manner that partly heralded Parsons' return to the city, as well as looking at the already tangled mythology that surrounded him. The lyrical poem spoke of the depth of devotion that led him to "follow a calico bonnet", although he says it was not from Cheyenne to Tennessee, as that was a change made by Gram. "Gram changed a word here and there ('roughnecks' to 'kickers')", says Brown. "And he added the bridge lyrics, "The man on the radio..." I wrote the rest especially for Gram, out of love and admiration for what he was doing."

Gram and the Fallen Angels rolled into town early, after a few successful shows at the Bijou Café in Philadelphia, where one gentleman, a young lawyer, filmed them with his Super-8 camera. The shows were getting better and better, and Frank David Murphy showed up at Gram's hotel after work one evening. Murphy was decked out in his suit and tie, and was uncomfortably aware that Gram was staring him down in a way he was not familiar with. Finally, Gram cracked up with laughter and started rolling on the carpet. "I get it, man," he told a somewhat bewildered Murphy. "That's your corporate disguise!"

Murphy invited Gram and Emmylou back to his home on a day off from shows, and took them driving in the countryside in his brand new 1973 Dodge Charger (the model popularised by the TV show *Dukes of Hazzard*). Gram and Emmylou entertained their hosts with beautiful harmonies from the back seat.

On arriving in Boston, the group checked in at the Fenway Boylston Motor Hotel, located across the street from the Red Sox home ground. During the week that they were in Boston, Eastern Burrito Brothers Barry Tashian and John Nuese stopped by to lend some vocals to the live show. Gram narrowly escaped another brush with the constabulary after he and Phil chose the hotel car park as the perfect spot to set off all the roman candles and rockets they had purchased legally in Arkansas (then illegally transported out of state), just after the last incident involving police.

Both the fire department and the cops were soon banging on Gram's door, as the hotel manager immediately suspected the longhairs of being involved in the explosions. No charges were laid, but as soon as the police and fire trucks drove off, members of the band were again flinging dinner plates out of their hotel room windows onto the street below. The band created noise wherever they went, and Gretchen was certainly a part of it. One evening, feeling that Gram was avoiding her in preference to Emmylou, she went into the room of another musician. When he courteously but firmly led her out of his room, she began running up and down the hallway on her floor, weeping loudly and kicking hotel room doors as hard as she could. After the hotel management threatened to have them removed from the building, a crisis meeting was held and the members of the Fallen Angels all encouraged Gretchen to leave them in Boston and return home to LA because they were finding her presence stressful. The previous evening, Gretchen had gone to the front of the low stage at Oliver's and started dancing and singing along, trying to attract Gram's attention away from Emmylou and back to her. The rest of the band was cringing but they kept playing. Gram ignored her presence and she eventually got the hint and took her seat.

While his relationship with Gretchen troubled him, some say it was at this point that he had begun to think more about Emmylou. She had in a short while become one of his closest friends. There had been no romantic overtures made by either of them but his friends thought it was patently obvious that there was a romance in the making. Of course, Emmylou had a steady boyfriend, and she had a child too. There was, on Gretchen's part, a constant suspicion that there was something going on between them, but the reality was that Emmylou had a great respect, admiration and a lot of platonic love for Gram. The feeling was clearly mutual. Jet Thomas agrees: "They had a special kind of relationship and if there was any kind of romantic relationship, it came after the music and not before. I think the music was the most important thing to them."

There was little time on the road or in the studio for the kind of shenanigans Gretchen was convinced were taking place. Still, the vocal blend was suggestive and the way the microphones were placed on stage seemed significant in the manner in which they lay entwined across each other. Like George and Tammy, Gram and Emmylou worked well together. But the First Couple of country music had felt the flame while each was still married to other people, so there was the power of mutual attraction. Then they got married, they shared their secrets and the intimacy was conducive to a further vocal blending. They thought alike musically and phrased similarly. Conway Twitty and Loretta Lynn may not have been married to each other but there too was the hint (even if it was untrue) that they shared more than just compatible vocal styles.

It was clear also that Emmylou idolised Gram in some ways, with his knowledge of music, his worldliness and other-worldliness. His combination of native shyness and star quality made him approachable and his fondness for getting wasted meant he could be difficult to be around sometimes. But at the same time, there can be no doubt that Emmylou's true feelings for her mentor were beginning to take shape. "We were moving in that direction," Emmylou told one interviewer. "But I got cautious. I think I was so aware of something quite beautiful happening between us as musical partners. And he was married at the time – though, let's face it, none of those rules applied to my generation. I just didn't want to go there, I guess."

The evening that Tom chose to attend the Fallen Angels' live show was notable for both the beauty of the music and the obvious difficulties Gram was having. Brown was a fan of all kinds of music, but he had bought a copy of *GP*, and found it moving in its musical simplicity and lyrical complexity. He was in the audience one night during the group's weeklong residency at Oliver's. He stood alone by the bar, watching the band play. He was enraptured by Gram's performance, not to mention being amazed by his star quality. He leaned back against the bar and drank beer by himself, watching as Gram's songs unfolded. Brown took the papers out of his pocket and gathered the nerve to approach Gram.

"Between sets, I asked a member of Gram's entourage if I could meet Gram and give him a poem I wrote," remembers Tom. But Gram and Gretchen were arguing down the back of the club, so Tom naturally hung back from the loud discussion that was going on. "Barry Tashian said he thinks it was Michael Martin who cheerfully led me to Gram. As we approached, there was a big scene being made by Gram's wife, Gretchen. I naturally hung back and got 'stuck' talking with Emmylou Harris. In the end, I had to just turn the poem over after saying 'hello'. I think I added that I would be at the bar, but that was it. When I saw Emmylou years later, she walked up to me and said, 'It's been a long time...'"

Gram was immediately taken with the work and the ambiguities and contradictions contained within it. He resolved to use the poem as the basis for a song, which he began composing almost right away on his return to California. Brown's intuitive knowledge and insight into how Parsons dealt in mythologies about himself would lead later fans and critics to erroneously conclude Parsons had written it himself. That situation wasn't helped when Brown's name was initially left off the credits of early pressings of *Grievous Angel*.

Anyone who knew of Parsons' love for Elvis Presley found it easy to believe that the stanza, "*The news I could bring I met up with the King / On his head an amphetamine crown*" referred to Elvis (as the King of rock 'n' roll). But Brown denies this, insisting that the King with the amphetamine crown is not Presley but Gram, the new king of country-rock, articulating the pain of the broken-hearted and those who have grieved. In a modern context, Parsons sings of himself from the perspective of someone who is attuned to his troubles. "Strange to say, but I felt an absolute certainty that Gram, a big hero of mine, would like the poem and make it a song," says Brown, some 28 years after the event. "The title derived from the fact that I thought GP had a sad and angelic-looking face. At the time, I was very active with the American Poets' Workshop in Cambridge, so dashing off a poem or lyric was nothing unusual for me. It's also true that I was shy when it came to standing around talking between sets, but I did have the happiness of meeting Emmylou, who remains an all-time favourite [of mine]."

Gram was now the "king" of country-rock in the same way that Kerouac was crowned "king of the beats', though the title was mostly unwarranted and certainly undesirable. Like Kerouac, Gram was no doubt unwilling to wear that crown (or any other), and was no more willing to take responsibility for supposedly fathering the country-rock movement. Like the Beat poets that worked independently of Kerouac, there are others who can rightfully claim equal importance in the lineage. Since Poco, the Grateful Dead and the Byrds also had input into the development of this musical form, Gram was right not to try to stake any claim to the invention of "country-rock", since that was not his vision alone. Anyway, the very conjoining of the words together made Gram retch.

After the five Boston shows, Gram and co. were invited to appear on a television show where pop bands routinely mimed. The band talked about the TV appearance; since ND Smart hadn't played on the album, he suggested that he would pretend to play piano on the television show. Phil Kaufman became the fiddle player, stringing up a $5 pawnshop violin (which belonged to Emmylou) with bailing twine; he rosined up a drumstick and fiddled. Leadfoot Lance became the drummer. Gram and Emmylou stood out front, playing it sincerely, all the while looking like a hippy George and Tammy. The rest of the 'band' yucked it up behind them, acting comical as the singers glided together. They did two takes of the song. As the musicians loaded their equipment into the luggage bays of the old Greyhound, it suddenly hit them – this was the end of the tour.

They had been away from home for more than a month and all of them were feeling the strain of the eight cities they had visited. Eddie Tickner wasn't very complimentary about the results of the tour, calling it "silly", which in part it had been. It had all the elements of a tragi-comedy, complete with one musician MIA, police brutality, a television appearance and mixed reviews. "And that was the tour pretty well," says Neil Flanz. "Warner Brothers offered to give us a plane ticket anywhere in the United States we wanted to go. Gram tried to talk me into going back to LA, saying that I'd have all the session work that I wanted. But I kinda missed Nashville so I chose to go back there."

The band left for New York the next morning, carried home on a wave of mixed feelings and high emotion. Gram smoked pot and relaxed on the way back to NY, singing country songs with Emmylou part of the way. The rest of the band, along with Phil and Michael Martin, drank and played poker. Gram would occasionally join in, but for the most part it would be a quiet and direct trip back to Los Angeles. Gram and Gretchen flew home after Gram had sedated himself nicely. Six miles high over the Grand Canyon, within two hours of home, Gram began to think about a new album and another tour. This time, he would produce his own album. He wrote down some ideas for songs; again lacking the drive to produce new, complete material, he dug deep into his old repertoire. But it would be good, he promised himself.

He decided then to hire Elvis's band again, seeing as how they had done such a good job for him last time. While the Fallen Angels had rallied well together after their live shows, they were not in contention as part of a studio line-up. Gram was also thinking of asking Clarence White to get involved again. There was even talk of resuscitating tracks from the Melcher sessions. But Gram listened to the tracks again and wasn't pleased with what he heard. He had grown beyond the influence of cocaine in the studio and found the Melcher recordings to be very suggestive of the time in his life that they were recorded. He even spoke to different friends about cleaning up his act in readiness for a new tour late in the year. All the signs were there for further renewal of his career.

The unhappy couple hadn't been back in LA very long when they received a phone call Bob Parsons. He and Bonnie were planning to take Bob's sailboat on a trip to the West Indies. Knowing how rocky their relationship had been, Gram and Gretchen thought it might be a good idea to go and try to work on the marriage. But once on the boat, Gram followed the lead of his stepfather and started hitting the bottle hard.

One night on the boat, in the first week of the trip, Bob had a lot to drink and began speaking very honestly and directly with Gram about Big Avis. Gram never really discussed his mother with anyone and to hear Bob refer to her upset him. As Gram tried to hold back tears, it became obvious that Bob himself was carrying a heavy load over her premature death. After several more drinks, Bob confessed that he had directly contributed to her death of alcoholic malnutrition that day in 1965. He told the shocked couple that while Avis had been in hospital, with her stomach lining destroyed and her liver burning out, he had brought her little airline bottles of vodka in order to make her what would turn out to be her final martini. Gram was absolutely devastated by this revelation, and he and Gretchen put ashore at the next major island and flew back home immediately.

"That's when his seizures started," claimed Gretchen Carpenter. "He just wasn't there mentally anymore. He would just t-a-a-lk like thi-is… it scared the shit out of me." His body was beginning to manifest its inner troubles. His seizures became more frightening. His brain would slow down, and then collapse. A slurred voice and shaking made people think he was just plain wasted, but the convulsions seemed to occur more frequently when he tried to clean up his act. Gretchen was terribly upset by the convulsions, especially as Gram would come to as paramedics were strapping him to a stretcher or trying to keep him from swallowing his tongue and choking to death. "Who are these people?" he would ask her, gently befuddled by the attentions of people who were trying to keep him alive. Soon the questions became accusatory: "What are you trying to do to me here?" he would ask Gretchen, angrily.

After a brief stay in St. Joseph's Hospital in Burbank, where in 1970 he had recuperated from his motorcycle crash, Gram had improved with the help of some medication and rehabilitation. By June 1973, there had been talk at Warners/Reprise about a 'country rock road show'. The confirmed line-up would feature the reformed Kentucky Colonels, Gene Parsons, now a solo artist in his own right for Warner Bros, and Country Gazette, the remnants of the final line-up of the Flying Burrito Brothers, including Kenny Wertz (who had been the first to spot Emmylou) and Byron Berline.

Emmylou returned to LA from Maryland with her boyfriend Tom Guidera. It was Eddie Tickner's idea to bring Tom along, in the hope that this would straighten out Gretchen's perception of the Gram/Emmylou situation. The couple stayed down at the Sportsmen's Lodge Hotel in North Hollywood. Gram and Emmylou were together again, rehearsing. Gretchen was not even nearby – she was holidaying in Hawaii with her parents. Still, she managed to call Gram up to five times a day, either at home or at Emmylou's hotel. Gram found the constant calls annoying, even as he realised that Gretchen's unfounded suspicions were at a new height.

Gram and Emmylou rehearsed for the "country-rock" roadshow, which was to be a trial run – a travelling show that would give each act the opportunity to headline as well as to be a part of the other acts' performances. Gram was no more together than he ever was, but the shows were by all accounts excellent, and the audience reaction as generous as ever. The only real trouble occurred when Gram hopped onstage during Clarence White's solo set and started motioning for the band to turn their instruments down. No one was quite sure what was going on, but the crowd seemed to find it amusing. Gram grabbed the drumsticks out of Gene Parsons' hands and he was left patting the snare with his hands. White, momentarily stunned, stopped playing his guitar. Just as quickly, Gram handed the sticks back to Gene and disappeared backstage. White, who never lost his temper, rolled his eyes, shrugged, and calmly resumed playing. The set ended with much applause.

Backstage, White laid his guitar in its case and turned to Gram, telling him off for the unwelcome addition to the show. There was no display of aggression, no shouting or abuse, but the normally mild-mannered White was obviously annoyed by that bizarre stage invasion, which he saw as unprofessional. If he was awfully pissed off by Gram's antics he did not let loose on Gram, either verbally or physically, as has been claimed. White tended to be non-confrontational at the best of times, and when Gram realised what he'd done he was mortified, and immediately began to apologise profusely to Clarence for offending him. "I don't know where my manners went," he said.

Any offence was dismissed and Gram's stage invasion was forgotten. White and Gram were already in the process of becoming good friends, and after that incident, their friendship became stronger. Gram started to spend time hanging out with White, getting to know his young family and his wife, Suzie. The country road show travelled through the Eastern Seaboard for two more dates and wound up at the Tower Theatre in Philadelphia on June 5th. It was to be the last live show that Gram would ever perform. Returning to LA with Emmylou and his guitar, Gram thought it was time to start planning another album. The many hours he'd spent with Emmylou rehearsing songs for the showcase had reinforced the strength of his feelings about her, both as his duet partner and as a woman. He announced that he intended to bill the next album equally, as 'Gram Parsons and Emmylou Harris', rather than the somewhat reduced billing she had received on *GP*.

His relationship with Gretchen was already at breaking point. Emmylou's return to Los Angeles brought out the jealousies Gretchen felt at being abandoned in LA, while her husband toured with another very beautiful young woman. Gram was unsure about it all; Emmylou was his equal in every way, and Gram didn't know if it could work out. Truth be told, Gram wanted someone that he could dominate, although it seems that Gretchen did not want to be dominated by her husband at all. Emmylou was much more on Gram's level, and her intellect allowed her to spar verbally with Gram.

It became clear to all that the two of them were sparking off one another, and that if they hadn't done so already, they most likely would be bonded by more than just music. A photograph taken at that period says as much as anyone might wish it to – Gram, flanked by Phil Kaufman, has a very protective arm around Emmylou's shoulders. They both look completely at ease, signifying for an onlooker that they are both comfortable with each other. For all the world, they look like boyfriend and girlfriend. Nonetheless, he was still married, and felt that he owed it to Gretchen to break the news about the divorce he had planned, even though there may have been any number of reasons why he might institute a dissolving of the union.

However bad he felt personally, nothing would prepare him for the call he received on the morning of July 15th, 1973. It was Chris Hillman with the news that Clarence White had been run down by a drunken motorist the previous evening, as he and his brother Roland were loading their instruments into his car. Gram was devastated, as he always was by death. But as he struggled with death, he had learned now to accept it as part of the fragility of life. Members of his family had died tragically, his dealer and good friend Sid Kaiser had passed away only weeks before, and Brandon De Wilde had died in an automobile accident in Denver, Colorado in the summer of 1972.

Far from pushing death away, he decided that he would embrace it, knowing that was the only way to deal with the fears it held. Whether it was bravado or pretension, Gram planned to attend the funeral and tried to accept the fact that Clarence was dead with good grace. But by July 19th, the day of the funeral, Gram was in a poor state, following a three-day bender on tequila and pills. He wisely remained outside the church where the funeral was held, St. Mary's Catholic Church in Palmdale, California. The service was a high Catholic requiem mass, very long and very traditional, the Whites being from French-Canadian stock.

There was no music during the mass, but later on at the graveside, where his family and friends felt more comfortable expressing their grief, Gram, standing with his arm around Hillman and Bernie Leadon, began to sing 'Farther Along', which had also been the title of the final Byrds album. Soon, the assembled family and friends were singing along and tears were flowing freely. After the graveside service was over, Roland White came up to Bernie and hugged him with his good arm, to express his appreciation for the spontaneous musical tribute. Roland's other arm was in a sling; he had dislocated his shoulder trying to pull Clarence out of the path of the oncoming car.

As the priest said the final blessing and sprinkled the coffin with holy water, Gram turned to Phil and looked at him. "Phil, if this happens to me, I don't want them doing this to me. You can take me to the desert and burn me. I want to go out in a cloud of smoke." "We had told Gram we wouldn't let him have one of those long family-and-friends funerals," Kaufman remembers. "Gram and I had gotten very drunk and made a pact whereby the survivor would take the other guy's body out to the Joshua Tree, have a few drinks and burn it. The burning was the bottom line." Other friends can remember Gram saying similar things to them; that an emotional funeral was too stiff, he wanted to be remembered but not in such a morbid fashion, if that was possible. Somehow, he had come upon the very Pentecostal idea of the joyous funeral, that the person had gone on to a better place and there was no point in being too grief-stricken. But he held Kaufman to the pact and reminded him of it on several occasions afterwards.

Some people felt that Clarence's death had a sobering effect on them and caused them to re-evaluate their behaviour, and in some cases regulate their excess. Sudden death was an ever-present risk in the music industry during the early 1970s, but for someone as sober and professional as Clarence to have been lost to his friends seemed harsh. Gram chose to be reflective about death, as he had seen enough of it up close. "Death is a warm cloak," he was quoted as saying. "An old friend. I regard death as something that comes up on a roulette wheel every once in a while. It's sad to lose a close friend. I've lost a lot of people close to me. It makes you a little bit stronger each time. They wouldn't want me to grieve. They would want me to go out and get drunk and have one on them."

It was only a matter of days later that Gram was almost prematurely immolated. Having briefly returned to his Laurel Canyon home and Gretchen, with whom he was attempting another reconciliation, Gram was in bed smoking a cigarette. He went to sleep and woke up to find the carpet and curtains ablaze. His cigarette had landed on the deep pile carpeting in his bedroom and set the place on fire. He roused Gretchen, who ran into another room and threw a telephone through a plate glass window and leapt through it. Gram grabbed as many of his personal possessions as he could, notebooks with lyrics, books, records, jewellery, and a guitar.

Most of his stage outfits, a couple of Nudie shirts, expensive jackets, and pants and boots were destroyed. Also destroyed in the blaze were the master tapes of the incomplete Melcher sessions. This "album" has been missing for close to 30 years, yet Parsons fans continue to ask after the tapes, offering large sums of money to anyone who might have a half-remembered idea as to what happened to them. Others mysteriously imply that Gram actually destroyed the masters himself, saying that he had good reason for not ever releasing it. It has become one of the great lost albums of the era.

One of the popular stories about the fire at the time had Gram so out of it that he ran into a closet under the impression it was an exit. Firefighters supposedly found him asleep under a pile of his own clothing. The house was nearly completely destroyed by the time the firefighters arrived. Gretchen's father Larry Burrell collected them from the hospital, where they were treated for smoke inhalation, and brought them back to his own home, where they stayed for several weeks. Gram soon tired of living with his father-in-law, who readily liked and accepted Gram but whose views were "somewhere to the right of Attila the Hun".

Gram left Gretchen for the last time, although he didn't know it then. Amid growing record company confidence in his talents and their encouragement to produce another album for them, Gram had once again started to descend into a black hole of depression. Gretchen stayed with her parents and Gram moved into the "back house", a little cottage behind Kaufman's Chandler Boulevard home in Van Nuys. They continued to see each other regularly, although Gram dated plenty of other women. He spent a lot of money doing strange things with his spare time. He would order tanks of pure oxygen, which he swore by as a hangover cure. The pharmaceutical company that delivered the tanks would also bring with them boxes of goodies that Gram always seemed to have a prescription for. It didn't seem to matter that Kaufman would raid his little cottage while he was out and steal his stash and either use it or flush it. He would steal needles and horse from Gram, who would only scratch his head, puzzled and say, "I was really loaded last night and I must have done it all. I better go get some more."

Phil could only look on as dope dealers and hangers on called by to visit Gram with hundreds of dollars worth of drugs. "Occasionally, I'd see the dealers coming in my house. I'd catch them at the gate and say, "Oh yeah, let me have that. Gram said to give it to me." I'd take it and either cut it in half or not give it to him at all, accusing the dealer of stealing his money. Everyone knows drug dealers are less than 100% honest. Gram believed my stories and never suspected I was rationing his drugs."

Gram tried his hand at writing some new songs for the album, which by now he had a title for – *Sleepless Nights*. The album cover was to be a photograph Ginny Winn had taken of Gram and Emmylou, sitting on Gram's new, well-maintained Harley in Mangler's back yard. Gram was feeling inspired again, although some of the inspiration came from the pain of a failing marriage and an awareness of his drug problem. His frequent boozing and drugging, coupled with the effects of head injuries from the motorcycle accident three years earlier, were taking their toll on his body.

According to Kaufman, Gram's little problem got out of control and his always-erratic behaviour became downright obnoxious. One night at the Palomino Club, Gram dipped into some coke with the head waitress and got a little obstreperous. He got in someone's face that night; it turned out to be a plainclothes cop, and once again Gram was in the slammer. However, Harry Fradkin was not available to throw bail and so Phil called Nudie Cohen, who said, "Ole Gram's in jail again? Let's go get him." The two arrived in Nudie's Cadillac, which was decorated with steer-horns, Winchester rifles, silver dollars and pistols for door handles, much to the amusement of the police force. "Gram spent a lot of time in jail," reckons Kaufman. "He was the only guy who had a cell with swinging doors."

Mangler's efforts at regulating Gram's drug intake had succeeded in proving that his only obstacle to the writing and composing process of music was his prodigious usage of downers and booze. In a reasonable state of sobriety, Gram was more than capable of writing intensely moving songs like '$1000 Wedding', but that had been back in 1969. Of course, when it came to actually composing new material, Gram suffered from the problem that many songwriters face – developing a song that he could be fully satisfied with, lyrically and musically. Songs did not necessarily flow out of him. In some cases, his best material had only come from the input of other writers. In fact, the strongest songs he had come up with for the Burritos had been in the early days when he and Hillman wrote together. Each would act as a sensitive critical voice for the other, making suggestions and adding lyrics and turnarounds, middle eights and other devices that allowed the song to develop fully.

Without the input of another partner, Gram felt his muse slipping away. He had in this time managed to pen just one song, which was arranged on the piano with help from Emmylou, who added harmonies from its inception. Gram gave her a half-credit on the song as a result. 'In My Hour of Darkness' articulated the sorrow he felt at the death of three of his closest friends in the previous twelve months. The song became a soaring hymnal that had strong gospel music flavouring, not least with its prayerful chorus. With the lyrics, he did ample justice to the memory of his late friend Brandon De Wilde, who was the "young man [that] went driving through the night", only to lose his life "on a deadly Denver bend". Clarence White's most touching eulogy came as the "young man [who] safely strummed his silver stringed guitar". His dear friend Sid Kaiser was the older man who read Gram "like a book". Indeed, Sid was an insightful and loving man in his 40s who had acted paradoxically as dealer and mentor to a number of rock musicians, including George Harrison, who thanked Sid in the liner notes of his monumental *All Things Must Pass* album.

Of course, any problems he might have had in producing songs of his own did not extend to his ability to rework his own older material, particularly 'Brass Buttons', a song which had its genesis in the death of his mother. He had written it during his time at Harvard in 1965 and had debuted it in a Boston club soon after. This meant the song was effectively eight years old, but it had aged remarkably well and its allusive poetic style gave it a romantic, almost Gothic feel, similar to what Mickey Newbury had achieved with his 1969 album *San Francisco Mabel Joy*.

Gram also gave his personal standard 'Hickory Wind' a makeover, changing the key from G, in which the Byrds had recorded it, to a more reflective, studied feel in A. It suited his slightly modified register better, and now sounded much more convincing. He resuscitated a song that he, Barry Tashian and Rick Grech had written for *GP* called 'Ooh, Las Vegas', which picked up on the cautionary theme of Presley's 'Viva Las Vegas' but with a more worldly tone than that of the hopeful neon-struck protagonist of the Presley song. As songs about gambling and losing go, it's one of the best ever written.

Finally, he turned to the cardboard box of lyric sheets and tapes that had been salvaged from the Laurel Canyon home during the fire. There, he picked up the lyrics of 'Return of the Grievous Angel'. Almost immediately, Gram was overcome by its poetic and cultural references, from the "waves of grain" to the "billboards and truck stops passed by the Grievous Angel". It brought up an almighty rush of inspiration, and over a period of days the melody and changes unfolded, as were did minor additions to the lyrics. The idea of "unbuckling that old Bible belt" articulates the desire of a southern man to leave behind his associations with the old-fashioned South and learn to deal with the problems associated with living in "the complex modern world". It is moral uncertainty, matters of personal belief coupled with a nearly contradictory desire to get back to his roots, which inform and drive the song, along with its very potent imagery. The lines "*And the man on the radio won't leave me alone / He wants to take my money for something that I've never been shown*" echoes the Rolling Stones' 'Satisfaction'.

It elaborates on the pressure of stardom, not that Gram had too much of that. Stardom foists new pressures on the unsure; suddenly, everyone is a huckster, a shyster pushing something new onto you, wanting your arms, legs, and heart. But Gram has his redress in the country, in the mythology of the Old West, with its images of calico bonnets, crossing prairies, a switchman waving his lantern at passing cars in the night. Gram often looked back; musically he was looking over his shoulder because, unlike facing the future, he knew what he would find there.

Emotionally, it wasn't necessarily a feeling of warmth; there were no real connections to the past for him anymore. His parents were gone; his sister Avis was living in Tennessee with her Uncle Tom Connor, trying to raise her child. Gram's child was out of reach, partly because he rejected any paternal role, and his wife Gretchen no longer held any interest for him. There was only confusion. His stepfather was manipulative and scheming, and he had no one to turn to that he could absolutely trust or rely on. As surely as he had felt alone in his first weeks at Harvard, or after having ditched the Byrds mid-stride in England and finding himself friendless in London, Gram was alone again. His only comfort was his friendship with Emmylou.

While Gram woodshedded at Phil's place, he began to adapt other people's songs to suit his vocal range. He was very adept at arranging previously published material by other writers and artists to suit him. For example, as he assembled songs for his second solo album, he arranged no fewer than six cover versions, namely Tom T. Hall's 'I Can't Dance', the Louvin Brothers' 'Cash On The Barrelhead', Boudleaux Bryant's magnificent 'Love Hurts', 'Sleepless Nights' and 'Brand New Heartache', and one song by Emmylou's boyfriend Tom Guidera.

Guidera's song, 'Hearts on Fire', was originally a rather sarcastic country music send-up about heartburn, but within the parody lay a rather lyrical and stunning song. Its sentiments worked well with or without the benefit of irony, and Gram had been tickled by its straightforward musicality when Tom had played him the song while watching Gram and Emmylou rehearse at the Sportsmen's Lodge one day. "The first album was not as planned out as the second one," Harris recalls. "I was still learning a lot. We worked stuff out – while we were on the road, we worked up a couple of things, like 'Love Hurts'.

The work of Nashville husband and wife song writing team Felice and Boudleaux Bryant had been greatly inspirational to Gram, in terms of furthering his range as a singer. The Everly Brothers first brought their songs to prominence, thanks to a minor hit with 'Love Hurts', which was featured on their second Warners album, *A Date With The Everly Brothers*, in 1961. Following *Grievous Angel's* belated January 1974 release, Glaswegian rockers Nazareth took 'Love Hurts' into the American Top 10, while Jim Capaldi knocked out a slightly better version, which hit the number 4 spot on the UK charts in October of 1974. Was it inspired by Gram's resplendent version? Most likely so. Gram and Emmylou's version of the song would belatedly be nominated for a Grammy in 1982. While it would not win, it would bring Gram's talents back to the attention of the public.

'Brand New Heartache' was an older tune, having appeared on the 1958 album *The Everly Brothers*. Gram and Emmylou had devised a sombre adaptation of the song on the bus during the Fallen Angels tour and worked it into the set almost immediately; such was its obvious power and appeal. 'Sleepless Nights' was more of a pop tune in its intricate way, but Gram and Emmylou wrestled it into the duet format and the Bryants looked set to enjoy reasonable royalties as a result.

While his choice of songs was nicely described as 'a hotchpotch of old and new, borrowed and blue' by author Martin C. Strong, *Grievous Angel* was a substantial addition to Gram's oeuvre. In hindsight, the album is near perfect and as mature an album as any released by similar singer/songwriters at any time during the 1970s. Purloining such choice material from other writers seemed to be the best bet when personal songwriting inspiration was lacking.

Eddie Tickner once again called upon Elvis's Vegas show band to provide the basic arrangements and flourishes that had so enlivened *GP*. Working with Gram was a task that the hardworking band took to with relish, as it gave them a chance to play straight country with a more contemporary edge, something that all of them enjoyed, particularly James Burton. As Glen D. Hardin recollected of that time, "Phil and Gram used to come over to my house at night and we'd work on the material. We'd sit around, drink, have a good time and get some work done. Gram was a great guy. I always enjoyed his company, loved working with him." Also joining in were Bernie Leadon, who had admired the *GP* album, ex-Shiloh multi-instrumentalist Al Perkins and fiddle player Byron Berline, another of Gram's good friends and admirers. The sessions took place at Wally Heider 4 in Los Angeles, with some overdubbing work at Capitol Studios in Hollywood.

The studio environment was more relaxed than it had been for the *GP* sessions, as the musicians were now well acquainted with each other, and Gram's sobriety and self-discipline during the tracking reinforced the sense of camaraderie. There was now no threat of unexpected visits from Gretchen, so Emmylou felt a little more comfortable in the studio, and her presence again made the band feel calmer. Almost immediately, the group began whipping the somewhat flabby and drawn-out '$1000 Wedding' into shape.

It was duly transformed from its previously funereal pace to a more elegant, svelte song with a mid-tempo arrangement borrowed partly from George Jones and Tammy Wynette's 'We Go Together', which, while celebrating their real life marriage, manages to incorporate some devastating heartbreak songs into the bargain. Without resorting to such overt heartstring yanking, there is an appealing serenity to the song. The song is played in C#, not a very traditional country key, but one which allows for moderate pacing, offset with its stirring resolution to a G# – D# bridge. It is this effective device that dominates the song right to its conclusion, allowing Gram to deliver the hard punches of the lyric, which in part were to do with the breakdown of his relationship with Nancy Ross. It also openly displayed that the deep well of feeling behind the song had not been dimmed by its long gestation.

'Hearts On Fire' was given a four-star treatment by a band comprising ND Smart II on drums and Bernie Leadon on lead guitar. This song is indicative of how a road band might have sounded, given that Smart was part of the Fallen Angels and Leadon was a former Burrito, now enjoying success with The Eagles. It is equally interesting to note that at the time, the Eagles were flying high, and record companies were seeing country-inflected rock music as a viable commercial vehicle. It says a lot about Gram's feelings about the Eagles as a concept that he stayed away from allowing rock and roll guitars onto the album, or even pursuing some sort of 'outlaw' stance, as the Eagles had done with their recent and hugely successful *Desperado* album for David Geffen's new Asylum label. Instead, Gram's moderate approach and delicate songwriting was almost a world away.

Linda Ronstadt was another Eagles friend who was experiencing renewed commercial success, as well as working from a similar vantage point to Gram, in that her interpretations of other people's songs brought her attention. She was a fine and marketable singer; it was the combination of her sweet, clear voice and her dark good looks (courtesy of a Mexican/German heritage) that made her so attractive to David Geffen in the first place. Ronstadt had known Gram from around the scene and, while initially sceptical about the manner in which he occasionally conducted himself, she soon came to admire his talent.

By mid-1973, she was even seen at a party with Gram, although the straight-talking singer was less than impressed at having to wait all night for him for come to at the end of one of these parties so she could get a ride home on his motorcycle. It was a timely cover of Monkee Mike Nesmith's 'Different Drum' that had propelled her band The Stone Poneys into the charts in 1967, but it was her first Capitol solo album, *Hand Sewn – Home Grown* (released in April 1969) that showed her to be cut from the same cloth as the Flying Burrito Brothers.

Ronstadt had been digging deeper and deeper into traditional country and 50s rock for her inspiration, in the same way Gram had years earlier. She even had the foresight to record John D. Loudermilk's 'Break My Mind' and the Burritos' version, cut later the same year, is a near-identical arrangement, right down to the rocking tempo. She had also delved into the work of folk hermit Fred Neil, recording 'Dolphins' for *Hand Sewn*. By the time her second solo LP *Silk Purse* was on the shelves in late 1970, it appeared that the LA country and rock scene was making money for the same songwriters. She delivered a stinging version of 'Sweet Mental Revenge', which the Burritos had been working into their live sets for some time. She also had some success in revitalising songs by acts as diverse as Fontella Bass, The Supremes and Hank Williams. In 1972, she pulled together a band comprising Randy Meisner (ex-Rick Nelson, Poco), Bernie Leadon, Glen Frey and drummer Don Henley, who had previously played alongside Al Perkins in Shiloh, to help her record her album *Linda Ronstadt*. Having fulfilled their duties as backing band, the group became the Eagles.

Gram had asked Ronstadt to come in and add another layer of harmonies to 'In My Hour Of Darkness'. Far from feeling threatened by this, Emmylou became firm friends with Ronstadt, a friendship that has continued to this day. The two women had met in Austin, Texas earlier in the year when Ronstadt and Neil Young, who were touring together, had arrived at the Armadillo World Headquarters to check out the new band. The pair had ended up onstage, adding harmonies to the show that had 'raised the roof'.

Tracking for the album took three weeks, with further vocal overdubs at Capitol Studios. The sessions produced twelve songs in all – 'Return of the Grievous Angel,' 'Sleepless Nights', 'Brand New Heartache', 'I Can't Dance', 'Cash On The Barrelhead', 'Love Hurts', 'In My Hour Of Darkness', 'The Angels Rejoiced', '$1000 Wedding', 'Hearts On Fire', 'Las Vegas' and 'Brass Buttons'. If the new album was to be released with all these tracks, or if Gram had planned a provisional track listing, it was never mentioned to anyone. It's likely that all of the songs would have been released together at the same time, although the possibility remains that he may have chosen to leave off one or more of the multiple songwriter covers.

If so, then at least one of the Bryant-penned numbers would probably have been culled, though only for reasons of variety, since all of the songs were of equal quality. Only one, the Ira and Charlie Louvin song 'The Angels Rejoiced', was more dramatically traditional than the others, since it was steadfastly '50s in its styling, without drums and possessing heartrending pedal steel and mandolin flourishes. It was strikingly modern, yet old-timey; Gram and Emmylou's voices soared together with a previously unrealised power, scaling emotional highs and lows in order to press the listener into an understanding of the scope of the tune's sentiment. It is this one song, which was released on the A&M album *Sleepless Nights* in 1976, more so than even the masterpieces littering *GP*, that presented these two immense talents working together as never before, contemporising a time-honoured country music tradition. Emmylou Harris was soon to become a *bona fide* country singer, a career that perhaps she had never imagined for herself before her introduction to Gram. She considered her tenure with Parsons to be an education in music that money could not have bought, that no institution of learning could ever have provided her with.

Such was the all-encompassing nature of Gram's unique vision that her own vision had expanded a hundredfold – she now had a greater idea of what she could accomplish for herself. The chemistry they now had after almost a year of working and singing together hinted at a goldmine of future possibilities. She had learned to anticipate every possible change in phrasing, and could cope with a change in octave with only the subtlest of visual cues to work from. Gram very much enjoyed playing with phrasing – it had been part of his vocal style for a long time. It had come quite naturally to him, arising partly out of his earlier interests in rhythm and blues, jazz and soul, but also as a nod to the way in which George Jones, Frank Sinatra, Elvis Presley, Conway Twitty and Willie Nelson (all of whom Gram much admired) also toyed with phrasing. By elongating certain words, drawing out phrases and repositioning them over the melody, a song was given character and subtlety.

The album had a mock-up cover ready, a photograph by Ginny Winn of Gram and Emmylou on his Harley, her arms resting casually on his shoulders. Draped over the foot peg was the 'Sin City' jacket presented to him by fans on the Fallen Angels tour. The new album cover would make them appear as the hippy answer to Conway Twitty and Loretta Lynn. This new style of duet singing exemplified Bud Scoppa's comment about the vocal blend on *GP*, having the 'added principle of moral uncertainty.'

As soon as the sessions were finished and mixes were completed, Gram began to ring his friends and family. He sounded enthusiastic and relieved, elated and confident. He called sister Avis in Tennessee to tell her about how successful the sessions had been. "This new album is a lot more like what I wanted to accomplish," he told her. Avis was thrilled. She had long been concerned about the broad path of self-destruction that her big brother had embarked on. Avis had become involved in a religious group, which followed the teachings of Oklahoma seer Edgar Cayce. She felt that her life had more purpose now. She could tell that Gram, despite his elevated mood, was suffering under a terrible weight of personal stress, some of it self-inflicted, some of it not. He told Avis and a few other friends that he was getting a divorce. In reality, the papers hadn't yet been drawn up, although the matter was in the hands of Bruce Wolfe, the attorney who had extricated him from several moderately serious drugs charges.

Warners had gotten back to Eddie Tickner with plans for another US tour, to be followed up by a small European tour, to capitalise on the popularity Gram already enjoyed in places like Holland, France and England. His work was beginning to get out there among the people, where he had long wanted it to be. It was a feeling like no other, knowing that fame was merely months away. The new album would serve notice of both his and Emmylou's talent. More than ever, Emmylou, who shared his microphone for nearly every song, was becoming part of his identity as a singer, as much as he was part of her identity.

For those who had the chance to hear the mixes, it was a revelation. Gram was clearly on solid ground again as an artist. There was no hint of the meandering spirit, the soul that searched for the truth or the man with a broken heart. Instead, there was new sight and sound; it was like Gram finally had the eyes and the voice to match up with the vision of Cosmic American Music. It sounded like a pipe dream to some people, while to others it was the distillation of the Spiritual Americas. As *Grievous Angel* shows, under the superficial use of traditional country music there was real heartfelt emotion, and truth that could not be pushed aside. It destroyed the notions of those who felt the music was "redneck" or "shitkicker" and forced those who felt ideologically opposed to C&W to admit its surface embracing of traditional ideals now extended to compassion, humility and passion. If country music was "racist", was there now proof that a musical style could rise above this conservatism? This was all the evidence that anyone ever needed to see musical beauty in new places. As artists like Mickey Newbury, Steve Young and John Prine realised at the same time, there was room for exploration in these discovered countries. You just had to be open-minded about what it was you would unearth for yourself.

This time, there would be no half-hearted attempts to create a buzz about his music. Gram had begun to believe in the strength of his talent, and that he had enough of it to take his music far beyond the United States. As he had once dreamed of moving the Flying Burrito Brothers en masse to Europe, Parsons began to make those hard decisions that would forever change the course of his life. He had his attorney draw up divorce papers to serve on Gretchen. During a series of telephone conversations with John Nuese and Barry Tashian, Gram discussed putting together a hot backing group, and organising a lengthy tour to promote the album.

It would all begin in October. Elated by all he had accomplished, and edgy about initiating what could be a messy and painful divorce, Parsons decided that his only course of action now would be to take a vacation at one of his favourite spots: Joshua Tree.

CHAPTER 13
ASCENT OF THE GRIEVOUS ANGEL

I always thought Gram was a complicated Christian, an artist who bore within him the magic seeds of one of the best and worst of our generation. He was in the tradition, the classic tradition of the fucked up young lord zigzagging his way from purity to debauchery and singing songs about orange blossoms in the Chateau Marmont to someone who was watching him with unashamed mental note-taking because people like Gram don't last, they'd rather light their candles at both ends, then sweep out the ashes in the morning.

Eve Babitz, Rolling Stone, *November 8th, 1973.*

If you have the chance to visit the grave of Gram Parsons in New Orleans, just off the highway near the airport, you will find that there is no elaborate marble or granite tombstone to be seen. In fact, for years after his death, there was only a wooden marker on the spot. It read, 'Gram Parsons, Singer'. The Snivelys in Florida seemed to neither know nor care where he laid, and the Connor family, back in Tennessee, did not know where he rested either. During the early '80s, with less than 10 years left to live herself, Little Avis, the last in the line of Coon Dog's children, had a small bronze plaque made to mark her beloved big brother's grave. All it says is "God's Own Singer" and "Gram Parsons". And at that, perhaps it says enough.

While Gram Parsons' official death date was September 19th 1973, it was on the 18th, in the high desert town of Joshua Tree, that his story really ended. A mystical name for a tiny desert town, Joshua Tree was given its name by weary westward travellers to California, who in the 1840s had been struck by this stony desert and the almost-humanoid trees that the settlers thought resembled Joshua reaching toward Heaven. Gram, likewise, had always reached for Heaven in his personal way, wherever that Heaven might be. Occasionally, sweet and beautiful angels reached down for him in his time of need, like something out of an old country song, or even from a song he might have sung.

Heaven for him now was a place he had discovered in 1967, not long after arriving in California. Lost in his own internal dry place, he looked for a physical place that could hold him. Joshua Tree, a place of vast, unblinking sky, rocks and sand was just such a place. Mostly it was a Mecca for devoted UFO-watchers, in whose number Gram counted himself. Joshua Tree, home to sand hermits living in clapboard shacks blasted clean of paint by sand and wind, was his kind of town. A town where his drinking went unremarked upon, where he could consume mescaline or LSD and watch the soundless expanse of galaxy rolling across the blue-black night.

Its solitude drew him there for extended weekend breaks and vacations time and again. Most of his friends had accompanied him there several times. Tony Foutz had filmed much of *Saturation 70* out there, and Keith Richards had watched the skies with him on several occasions. When he was in town, Gram preferred to stay at a small cinder block motel called the Joshua Tree Inn, out on 29 Palms Highway. It was private and low-key and, charmingly, desert wildlife had been known to venture into your room if you left your door ajar.

Furthermore, the Inn was only a short distance from the town centre and its bars, most of which were little more than weather-beaten shacks. Gram would take his guitar and a bottle of tequila with him to Room 8, and stay there all day singing and drinking. If he got bored singing in his room, he'd head out to one of the local hole-in-the-wall joints and drink and sing there. "Everyone out here liked Gram," said Alan Barbary, the owner of the Inn. "He got into fights in bars sometimes – Gram liked to play, and if they didn't want him to play, he'd play anyway and they'd throw him out. Most of the time they wouldn't throw him out because he was good. When he went into a bar, it got crowded, and there were lots of happy people." Gram liked to drink at the Hi Ho Lounge, where he would play pool with the locals and sing for them. Two of the regulars remember him well. One, a retired warrant officer named Sarge thought highly of his hippy drinking-buddy. "I remember Gram. Used to come in here weekends and sing. That boy could really shoot pool."

Occasionally, he would venture out to the nearby airport to drink at its slightly more salubrious bar, which had pool tables and a jukebox. "He was always anxious to get there," Eddie Tickner told *Rolling Stone* shortly after his death. "I visited him there once. It was nothing exciting... but he knew every bar and saloon in the area." Phil Kaufman didn't think much of the area either, but as Gram's friend and road manager he often took the two-hour trip with him. The motel's owners at the time, Frank and Margaret Barbary, got to know Gram as a regular patron but they knew Phil better, because he was the one who usually took care of the bill for the rooms. Gram arrived at the Joshua Tree Inn on the afternoon of Monday, September 17th for a week's stay. He was preoccupied with thoughts about the upcoming tour, which would take him to Europe, including England, the Netherlands, France and Germany. With him that day were Michael Martin, Dale McElroy and Margaret Fisher. Fisher was an old Florida acquaintance he had known since the early 1960s, while still a student at the Bolles School. He had invited her up from Florida to stay with him in LA, sent her a plane ticket then asked her if she felt like taking a brief stay in the desert. She readily agreed and joined the party. They left Los Angeles in the early afternoon, travelling in Gram's late-model Jaguar. Dale McElroy, then living in San Francisco, came along with her boyfriend Michael Martin even though she was suffering from the effects of hepatitis.

Monday night was spent drinking in town and relaxing, the only tension seemingly coming from McElroy, who could not drink and was subsequently not enjoying the pleasures this desert town had to offer the inquisitive individual. Someone was having a good time, though, because by Tuesday morning the four of them had smoked most of the marijuana they had brought with them. Michael Martin, although an unlicensed driver, volunteered to go back to Los Angeles at midday to pick up more grass to cover the rest of their planned week's stay. In Martin's absence, Gram happily escorted Dale and Margaret to the area's bars and saloons. By lunchtime, they were out at the airport. Dale begged off any further bar-hopping, since the idea of watching Gram and Margaret fall further into a drunken stupor held little appeal for her. She went back to her room at the Inn and napped for the rest of the afternoon. At some point during the day Gram and Margaret came back to the Inn, supposedly after scoring from a Hollywood connection in town on business. Gram took his seizure medication, and lay down for a nap, soon falling into a deep and dangerous repose.

What he did not know was that his body had reached its limit. His breathing became laboured as his medication interacted with the large amount of alcohol he had consumed that afternoon. While his brain began to shut down, his breathing became ragged as the muscles that support the lungs began to slacken.

Stretched on her bed, half-asleep, reading a magazine, Margaret was surprised to hear a terrible gurgling snore. At first, she thought Gram was vomiting in his sleep, and choking on it. As she examined him, she noticed straight away that his colour did not seem normal. Margaret ran to awaken Dale. On entering Room 8, Dale, in a brief moment of panic, thought that Gram must have overdosed. Margaret pulled a tray of ice cubes out of the freezer, fumbling them onto the carpet, as her mind fell back on that old junkie standby of inserting ice cubes into the rectum, which drives the internal organs into mild shock, and can have the paradoxical effect of waking an overdose victim up. She did so, and sat back, having done what she could.

Gram slowly came to. The girls were overjoyed – they thought they'd lost him for a minute there. He was still woozy from the medication, but slowly he became more alert and was now aware that his jeans were partly off. He joked with the girls about what they were doing with him and they relaxed. Margaret got Gram standing and walking around, and told him to move around some more until he was fully awake – then they could get him to a doctor. Margaret went out to get some food and drinks, but asked Dale to remain with Gram and keep him alert at all costs. Food would help him, she reasoned. Dale agreed, and they returned to Room 8, where she sat with Gram for a while, talking with him. He seemed all right, just disconnected and vague. Soon, he began to show signs of extreme tiredness, and he stretched out on the bed again, laughing softly at Dale's insistence that he not go back to sleep. "I'll be OK," he assured her. "I just need to rest."

Margaret seemed to have been gone for hours. Dale sat with Gram for a long time, finally slumping on the floor beside the bed and watching him sleep. Soon enough, his breathing returned to its earlier laboured state, and Dale heard for herself the rattling, ratchetty breathing. Dale had little, if any, experience with overdose victims, and she could only look on as Gram struggled in his sleep, wondering what the hell she should do. If only Michael or Phil were here, they'd know.

She did not call for help at any time, since as far as she was aware there was no one else at the motel – in this, she was mistaken. She attempted to resuscitate Gram by climbing onto his chest and pummelling him, beating on him and trying to find a pulse – all without success. Margaret returned soon afterwards with food, and together the girls realised their friend was in life-threatening difficulty, and there was nothing that they could do to help him. Margaret ran to fetch the owners of the motel and returned with their ex-serviceman son, Alan Barbary. He claimed that there was nothing that could be done for Gram, because he had "morphine poisoning'. An ambulance was called, and arrived within minutes.

Although there were some signs of life visible, including a thready pulse, the medics did not attempt resuscitation on the spot. They instead chose to get him to the nearest hospital in Yucca Valley, a twenty-minute drive away. By the time the ambulance arrived at the hospital, Gram was displaying no further signs of life. He was declared legally dead at 12:30AM on the morning of Wednesday, September 19th, 1973, following numerous attempts to restart his heart. Routine blood tests revealed a high blood/alcohol reading – 0.21% – enough to stop a man from thinking clearly or driving, but not enough on its own to kill. Despite Barbary's claims of morphine poisoning, no opiates of any kind were present in the blood, although there were emergent traces in liver tissue and urine. This clearly refutes the oft-cited "death by heroin overdose" scenario put forward by others. If Parsons had died either of a heroin or morphine overdose, as has been claimed by several different parties, opiates would have been found in his blood. Since they were not, it is safe to say that Gram was not a victim of the drug that he had casually and incautiously abused since the 1960s. The urine tests showed up traces of alkaloids common to cocaine users, as well as more powerful evidence of barbiturate abuse. Barbiturates exhibit similar symptoms to alcohol, and when combined with large amounts of alcohol, are often fatal. Gram had been prescribed an epilepsy medication called Phenobarbital, for controlling the seizures that he had been experiencing as a result of his 1970 motorcycle accident. This drug is notable for its serious side-effects, including hypotension (low blood pressure), and for its danger to those with any kind of cardiovascular sensitivity, including heart murmurs, which some believe Gram suffered from. It was also most often injected, which may sometimes have led people to believe that Gram was shooting up something far more dangerous. All in all, it is safe to conclude that Parsons was a victim of his alcohol problem, rather than his drug problem. While tragic and avoidable, his is in fact one of the most common accidental deaths.

Back at the Inn, the police interviewed the girls. They had had the presence of mind to hide Gram's stash before the cops arrived. The police were treating the matter as an accidental overdose, actually a common occurrence in the area, a haven for dope dealers and other escapees from city heat. From the phone in the lobby, Margaret tearfully called Phil, explaining what had happened. Phil instructed the girls to stay where they were and he would be out to collect them as soon as he could. The sun came up and the girls hadn't slept a wink all night. They were both burning out from lack of sleep and grief at what had taken place only hours before.

There were many questions that begged for answers. How had it ended there? How was it possible that after his new personal victories, after the recent triumphs over his past, that death had nailed him? His most recent work had been committed to tape and was now forever entombed within those tapes. His body, which had struggled against many wounds – some self-inflicted, some not – had given up the ghost, although not without a fight. The doctors who examined him were perhaps a little shocked to see someone so young lying there before them. Soon, as they sampled and weighed, there would have emerged a detail of this still life. Analysis revealed the presence of different kinds of narcotics, perhaps enough to have contributed to his death. "Multiple drug toxicity," wrote one. "Drug toxicity, days, due to multiple drug use, weeks."

In Los Angeles, Phil Kaufman, who had not slept since he'd heard, was notifying Gram's friends of his death. Phil propped up his road managerial veneer of imperturbability with vodka, trying grimly to make out that he wasn't as grief-stricken as he was. Kaufman didn't know the full story yet, or that there was soon to be another chapter in the Gram Parsons saga, in which the Road Mangler would play a starring role. As such, Phil Kaufman's job was always going to be a fairly unenviable one, as good it might sound on paper. As "executive nanny" to Gram Parsons on a full-time basis, they had a friendship and an understanding.

It was his job to find and hide the drugs that Gram regularly taped to the underside of the toilet seat or in his shoes. Keeping Gram on the straight and narrow was hard enough – it further fell to him to field the regular phone calls from Gretchen, wanting to speak to Gram about this rumoured divorce that he kept denying was happening. Phil knew full well that Gram had already asked Bruce Wolfe to draft divorce papers so he could finally extricate himself from his marriage. When Gram got busted for bizarre offences like his one-off felony jaywalking charge, it was Phil who took the call and arranged bail. Such were his duties – no matter where he might have been at the time, he could be relied upon. After a while, he developed a kind of second sight for his charge. There is no doubt that Gram and Phil loved each other deeply, nor is there any doubt that Gram trusted Phil with his life. But when the phone calls started coming from Phil, some people would get upset, usually because Gram was in jail again or too drunk to drive home safely.

Throughout the day of Thursday, September 20th, Kaufman rang people, spoke to some and left messages for others who he knew would be upset. "I was at work in Philadelphia and for some reason that I don't now recall, my wife was home that day," recalled Frank David Murphy, who had spoken to Gram five days before. "Phil had called during the day and told her that Gram was dead – I believe had just died that day – giving only the simplest explanation and said to have me call. This, as near as I can piece together, must have been very shortly after Phil himself knew about it... it certainly hadn't hit the news yet, and it did get into the papers pretty quickly. I had no sense that Phil was denying anything, I asked him about drugs and he said, 'No, he might have gotten a little bit dusted but otherwise, he was fine.' I talked to Phil once or twice in the succeeding days and his story didn't really change... although he never mentioned Margaret Fisher (maybe he didn't know that I knew her). I believe that he did mention that things were getting ugly between Bob and Gretchen about the disposition of the body and that was when he told me that the divorce from Gretchen wasn't complete and she was trying to claim everything."

As word began to spread of Gram's accidental death, his friends recoiled in horror. Keith found out about it backstage at a Rolling Stones show in Birmingham. He hadn't seen much of Gram that year – the Stones were in Australia and Asia during the Fallen Angels tour and then they'd toured the US again. Gram had been around for parts of the Stones' US tour that year, but he was mostly preoccupied during that time, his thoughts centring on Emmylou, the divorce from Gretchen and the new solo album. Backstage, both Keith and Bobby Keys learned the news and they stood there, shocked. Nick Kent, who was present on that tour, said that Keys and Keith were "deeply, deeply shocked" and that the grim set of their jaws made them look like a couple of grizzled cowboys, lamenting the death of a friend.

It was a confusing story, full of contradictions and half-truths. No one, not even Phil Kaufman, knew what had really happened. The first story that leaked out was that Gram had OD'd out there in the desert, shooting up with the often-fatal combination of alcohol and morphine while staying in some motel in the town of Joshua Tree. That story was the first to get fed to the media, who delighted in its sordidness. Even more unfairly, singer Jim Croce was killed in a plane crash the same week, another sad event that overshadowed Gram's passing. Croce was on the cusp of major stardom, having had a hit with a country-ish rock song called "Bad Bad Leroy Brown". Croce was what some people liked to call country-rock, although Jim would probably have denied it as vehemently as Gram always did. No matter, because Gram's star, which might have ascended somewhat higher into the desert night sky with just a little more publicity, seemed only to dim.

The underground press duly reported that there were two young women with Parsons at the time – some named the pair, most did not care for the specifics. The most ignoble details were seized upon enthusiastically – it was reported in one magazine that one of the girls was supposedly on her knees, jerking him off and saying, "I love you". That certainly never happened. Alan Barbary, son of the then-owners of the motel, further confused the issue, saying that when he had come into Room 8, he went to give Gram mouth-to-mouth resuscitation but claimed that if he had, he would have been "poisoned by morphine". He then went on to say that Parsons' body was giving off the "odour" of morphine. Since morphine is essentially odourless, this is highly unlikely. Furthermore, the only way morphine would likely be present in the mouth is if a person has ingested it orally, which Gram did not do.

The ice cubes anecdote was true, an old junkie remedy for heroin overdose victims. The sudden cold, moving through the highly absorbent mucous membranes, drives internal organs into shock, causing the brain to react by increasing blood flow to the heart and lungs. Judging by the story Dale McElroy told of Gram's breathing becoming laboured, it is likely that he was in respiratory distress, not because of vomit blocking his airway as is often thought, but rather a grim prefiguring of heart failure. It is also possible that Gram had fluid in his lungs, often a symptom of heart trouble.

Gram may even have known that it was life-threatening, particularly since he had sought medical help in 1972, while in England. Following his stay at Nellcote with Richards, Gram had returned to the UK, where he spent some time recovering from the excesses his body had been subjected to. His heroin problem (which cannot, in the interests of factuality, be called full-blown addiction) had possibly caused him some respiratory difficulties or other related health issues, for which he had paid a visit to Doctor Sam Hutt. Hutt knew about Gram's various dabblings in drugs, and recalled several near-overdoses that he had personally witnessed. He and others believed that Gram's time on earth was likely to be short if he continued to abuse himself in this manner, whether with heroin or other substances. The inevitability of his death, as a logical outworking of the life he led, is still a concept that seems foreign to those who knew him and those who know his music.

Others, including Emmylou Harris, don't buy into the "only-the-good-die-young" myth. "No, no, I didn't [expect his death to happen]. In fact, it was totally the opposite with me because he was so important to me and I was so enthusiastic at learning from him and working with him. And he did seem to be getting stronger the longer I knew him. The music seemed to be really healing for him, and having the work meant that he was spending more time singing, less time drinking.

"He wasn't drinking so much. He really seemed to be, I thought, maybe in hindsight there were signs that I didn't see but I was very shocked. It shocked everybody. There were people who said, 'Well, I could have seen it,' but I don't know about that. Gram had lived dangerously but I think we were still in that early period of rock 'n' rolling where we thought people could survive that sort of thing. And because he was not actively involved in certain things, you assume somebody is out of the woods but you don't realize how much you can weaken yourself. I mean, literally weaken yourself."

Chris Hillman was aghast at the news, but felt frustrated that any help he could have offered to Gram would have been ignored. He had seen this coming for at least three years, between the last few months of Parsons' tenure with the Flying Burrito

Brothers and then his two-year layaway, in which time he pursued cocaine and alcohol with all the insouciance of the country music playboy. "It had gotten to the point then when he was working with Emmylou, where I just wanted to grab him, shake him and say, 'Wake up, you're wasting all this wonderful, God-given talent'. And I couldn't do that and he wasn't gonna listen anyway. He was on a one-way road to a bad ending."

Despite sounding so final about the passing of a young man with whom he had created such fine music, Chris admitted: "I did have contact with Gram while he was making the solo albums. When Emmylou and Gram got together and started to do the two albums, I was in contact with him off and on. I felt pretty much overboard at that point – he was drinking a lot and it was hard to...let me put it this way – here was a raw talent. A very, very talented, bright kid who didn't have any discipline."

Bob Parsons was entitled to a share of Avis's money as Gram and Little Avis's sole living guardian and adoptive parent. He now suddenly found himself in a position to inherit the whole lot. He had already had Little Avis committed to an institution in New Orleans, but she'd gotten out of that and was living with her birth father's brother in Tennessee. As a result of Gram's unexpected passing, the details of which were sketchy at best, all Bob had to do to come into some big money was prove that Gram had at some point been a resident of the state. It would not be hard to do – Gram had not made out any will with conditions to the contrary, and had listed his stepfather's address as a forwarding address for mail while he was abroad in 1971 and '72.

In order that he might further a claim of residency in New Orleans, Bob Parsons arranged to have Gram's body shipped to Louisiana by air, which would only take a day or two from California. Once buried in New Orleans at a hastily-procured plot at the Garden of Memories cemetery, the claim of residency would be complete and would likely be successful, since Avis Parsons, the only other living heir to the trust fund, having once been committed to an institution might be deemed unfit to oppose his claims. Bob flew out to California to oversee the return of his stepson's body, but he had neglected to factor in one Philip Clark Kaufman, who was hatching a plan of his own.

As for Avis, the last time she saw her adored big brother was in court. She and Gram took Bob Parsons to a Florida court in June 1973 in order to iron out the inequities of their trust fund affairs. With members of the Snively family having occasionally taken out large loans against the fund, and their stepfather having the final say over their financial matters, they both felt that their inheritance could be better protected in their favour. The court agreed and the judgement put them on an equal footing with Bob. This consequently gave Gram and Avis more power as a unit to decide how their money could be spent and how much was available to them at any one time. "We're never going to let Bob Parsons have his way again," he told Avis. She believed him. After all, her brother was the only true family left to her. "I was his number one fan," she said. "Gram had such a deep religious side to him, but he was like, schizophrenic. One day, he'd be so pious, the next day he'd be shooting up smack in the back room."

After the death, the police in Joshua Tree and Yucca Valley had still not been in contact with Phil, who had spirited Dale and Margaret away from the Inn without presenting them for an interview with the coroner. In the meantime, Phil was beating himself up over the fact that he had not been present at Gram's death. Now the Mangler got wind of Bob Parsons' cynical attempt to transport Gram away from his only friends. Phil and Michael Martin, Gram's Australian 'valet', hatched a plan that could only have come from minds beset by grief, alcohol and other forces. They would snatch the body from the local airport, where it was to be deposited the following day for Parsons to identify and take with him back to New Orleans. It would be unjust and wrong to let Bob Parsons make off with Gram back to a city that he had little connection with, either in life or death. Moreover, there was the matter of the infamous Pact – the words that Gram had uttered to Phil and others in the weeks after Clarence White's death came back to him. It only took a call to the Hi-Desert Hospital and a funeral parlour in Yucca Valley to learn that the body was in the process of being transferred to Los Angeles International Airport and would arrive at 8 o'clock that evening. From there, the casket would be placed on board a Continental flight to New Orleans. Phil called Dale McElroy, to ask her if he could borrow her hearse, which she had bought to go camping. She agreed and Martin and Kaufman, both attired in the same clothing in which they had toured the US with Gram, decamped to the Continental Air Mortuary Services hangar at LAX.

Despite their outlandish dress, and the fact that the hearse was unregistered and the driver was at the tail end of a three-day drunk, Kaufman and Martin made a very convincing case to the staff at Continental. Even as they did so, a police car arrived at the hangar and boxed the hearse in. Phil, trying to keep levelheaded, started to panic. After a while, it became obvious that the cop had nowhere else to be and wasn't looking for either of these desperadoes waiting for a coffin. The paperwork was completed and Continental duly signed over the coffin, which was placed in the back of the hearse, complete with the accompaniment of clinking bottles. Then Phil asked the cop to move his car, which he did. Michael was driving and as he eased the hearse out of the hangar, managed to ram the car against the wall. They jumped out of the car, saying, "This is it – we're fucked!" The cop looked on, amused. "Yeah," he agreed. "I wouldn't want to be in your shoes now."

Phil and Michael drove out of the airport and headed east onto the San Bernardino Freeway that night, driving as fast as they could under the circumstances. They stopped at a petrol station for a can of gasoline with which to perform the deed, and then they continued driving. It was early in the morning when they arrived at their destination. The hearse drove off the sealed road and onto rough metal road, where they skidded around in search of a favourable location. Kaufman says now that the spot they chose, beneath the silent gaze of Cap Rock, had no significance whatsoever, it was just the first spot they came to. He may well not remember, but it was at this exact spot four years before that Phil, Gram, Anita and Keith had stood looking for UFOs. What's more, there are photographs, taken by Michael Cooper of all of them standing at that very spot.

Manhandling the coffin out of the hearse seemed like a great effort. Their hearts were leaping out of their chests as they opened the coffin lid. Kaufman poked Gram in the chest, then flicked his fingers in his face, an old routine they'd pulled on each other a million times. There was no response. Phil shook his head sadly, and made a comment about the size of Gram's penis. It seemed somehow appropriate at the time. Smoking cigarettes and drinking warm beer out of the back of the hearse, Phil and Michael repeatedly toasted their good friend and employer. Finally, the time had come for Phil to make good on the promise he had made to Gram less than four months ago at Clarence White's funeral.

Taking the can of high-test [high octane] gasoline out of the car, Phil fumbled for matches. He emptied the can into the coffin and struck a light. In the brief glare of phosphorus, Phil caught sight of Gram for the last time. He threw the match into the coffin. The flames sucked the oxygen out of the night air, and within minutes the coffin was a vessel of fire. The ashes "were going into the desert," Kaufman recollected in his book *Road Mangler Deluxe*. "We looked down. He was very dead and very burned. There wasn't much left to recognise."

The two body snatchers got back into the hearse and left Joshua Tree the back way, across the mountains. Outside the town of Big Bear, they pulled over, exhausted and paranoid that they would be arrested any minute. Too drunk to continue on to LA, they slept in the back of the hearse. The next morning, a little more sober, they realised the hearse was bogged in sand and worse, wouldn't even start. Michael Martin went and hired a tow-truck on foot, returning within several hours. The hearse was repaired, and Martin and Kaufman bought more beer for the trip home.

It was in this drunken and remorseful state that Phil and Michael hit the usual daily build-up of traffic on the outskirts of LA. Slowing down near a traffic pile-up where several cop cars were parked, lights swivelling, Phil didn't apply the brakes exactly as he might have and the bumper of the hearse kissed the fender of the car ahead of them. A cop heard the minor impact and came over. The patrolman opened the hearse door and empty beer bottles fell to the ground. "Alright, you two," he said, "Step out of the car." Having handcuffed the pair together, the officer was distracted and did not ask for their licences. Michael, who had spent months evading the police on the streets of Bombay, slipped his hand out of the handcuffs. They climbed back into the hearse and reversed off the off-ramp. They made it back to Phil's Van Nuys house, cut the handcuffs off Phil and hid the hearse in a friend's garage.

Over in New England, friends and fellow musicians gathered together to mourn Gram's passing. Emmylou Harris was invited up to Barry and Holly Tashian's home in Connecticut. John Nuese and Bill Keith arrived, and together they sat down to listen to a tape of the final mixes of the new album. They sat silently, stunned at the beauty of it all. "I guess that's the last time we get to hear that beautiful voice," said John, and it was at that moment that the enormity of Gram's death hit Emmylou. Soon, she was weeping strongly. The others knew not to make any attempt to soothe her; but just let her know that they understood why she wept. Her future, which was starting to look so complete, was now tattered.

Gram left many hearts broken and many loose ends to be tied. While the wrangles over the inheritance money continued, Gram's remains were shipped back to Bob Parsons. He had his stepson's mortal remains interred after a small ceremony, with only a few members of the Connor and Snively families in attendance. Finally, Gram was at rest under the shade of oak trees at the Metairie cemetery, in an area called the Garden of Memories. It did Bob Parsons no good. He died in 1975 of cirrhosis of the liver, a victim of his hard-drinking lifestyle. He never made a cent out of his stepson. The inheritance went mostly to Little Avis, but was also partially divided between Gretchen, Nancy and Polly, the daughter he had so infrequently acknowledged.

The next day, the Los Angeles newspapers gave some space to the story of the body jacking and speculation on the "ritualistic nature" of the burning. Phil decided to turn himself in. When the police arrived to arrest him, Phil's home was being used as a set for the Arthur Penn-directed Gene Hackman thriller, *Night Moves*. When the story unfolded and Phil was handcuffed as he got into the police cruiser,

Penn uttered the immortal words: "I think we're filming the wrong movie."

Harry Fradkin and Bruce Wolfe were already at the Venice police station to meet Phil, who was fingerprinted, photographed and released on bail. There was little for the police to charge him with except the destruction of the coffin, which cost $708. At the bail hearing, Phil and Michael were arraigned to appear in court to face charges on November 5th, 1973. The charges were dropped and the two men walked out of court, to face the press photographers who had gathered. Their shots captured the uncertain smiles of victory on Michael and Phil's faces. Those half-smiles are no doubt tempered by the knowledge that their friend Gram would have been 27 that day.

Notes on quotes and sources
for God's Own Singer

Chapter 1

1. "I was ready to start thumbing..." Gram Parsons interview 1972, with Chuck Casell
2. Waycross, Georgia as the 'asshole of the world': Stanley Booth, *Rhythm Oil*, page 107 Vintage Books
3. "culture exists there only in the anthropological sense': Stanley Booth, *Rhythm Oil*, page 107, Vintage Books
4. "Waycross hasn't really grown a whole lot...": Author interview with Billy Ray Herrin, July 2000
5. "At that time, the country was in the grip of...": Author interview with Stanley Booth, December 17, 2000
6. "What can I tell you about Gram?" Author interview with Barbara Walker Winge, May 2000
7. *ibid*
8. *ibid*
9. "Waycross was the only time...": Author interview with Billy Ray Herrin, July 2000
10. 'Coon Dog' was not the itinerant country singer Gram claimed: 'Ex-Byrd Gram Parsons Solo: He's no longer in a hurry' – interview with Judith Sims, *Rolling Stone* magazine, March 1, 1973
11. He took his son and brother and father out hunting regularly: From author interview with Billy Ray Herrin, July 2000
12. "I've spoken with a lot of guys that worked...": *ibid*
13. "I believe that's why he was so emotional...": *ibid*
14. "Hello there, you're Elvis Presley...": Gram Parsons, interview with Jan Donkers 1972
15. As allegations of mismanagement of the family company came up: Author interviews with various people have referred back to Coon Dog Connor's suicide as being related to possible mishandling of Snively money. It is not reported as an established fact, but as conjecture.
16. The last time Gram saw his father alive was...: Author interview with Billy Ray Herrin July 2000
17. "I think that was without doubt the most influential event...": *ibid*
18. "He was a real war hero...": Author interview with Stanley Booth, December 2000
19. Somewhere along the way, Avis stopped referring to her son as Cecil: Author interviews, various sources
20. "He was just intrinsically hip": Author interview with Jim Carlton, 17 Jul 1997
21. "When I met him...": *ibid*

Chapter 2

1. "Carl, Gerald Chambers and I...": Author interview with Jon Corneal, October 2000
2. "He was grooming himself for stardom...": 'Jim Stafford: Swamps & Spiders & Snakes' *Rolling Stone*, March 28th 1974
3. "We played a zillion teen centers,": Author interview with Jim Carlton, July 1997
4. "We'd place one of its 10" speakers...": *ibid*
5. "He loved the image of being the guitarist/ lead singer": *ibid*
6. "We played a lot of really nice gigs in '62/'63": Author interview with Jon Corneal, October 2000
7. "Gram was NOT into country music at all...": Author interview with Jim Carlton, July 1997
8. "I said to him, "you got country roots...": 'Jim Stafford: Swamps & Spiders & Snakes' *Rolling Stone*, March 28th 1974
9. "In every interview I do about him": Jim Carlton, July 1997
10. Back at the Bolles School: Author interview with Frank David Murphy, 1996
11. He once turned in Bob Dylan's *Mr. Tambourine Man* as a college assignment: *ibid*
12. 'Prereminescence': composed by Gram Parsons, appearing in the Bolles School Literary Magazine, Spring 1965. Reprinted with permission.

13. "The first group that I joined was the Shilos": Author interview with Paul Surratt, 25 August 2000

14 "Folk was very big at the time and it was commercial": *ibid*

15. "No, we were not political at all": *ibid*

16. "This guy was singing that night": *ibid*

17. "Gram was also into the Journeymen": *ibid*

18. He was also a great liar: Author interview with Frank David Murphy, 1996

19. "We got together the next day, made contact": Author interview with Paul Surratt, 25 August 2000

20. "When Gram met us": *ibid*

21. "We won the talent show": *ibid*

22. "Gram had complete control": From Paul Surratt interview with Sid Griffin 1980, printed in *Gram Parsons: A Musical Biography*. Used with permission.

23. "He helped us quite a bit": Author interview with Paul Surratt, 25 August 2000

24. "He's a very gentle person": *ibid*

25. "Gram was very well-groomed": *ibid*

26. While Freeman made all the right moves: from interview with Paul Surratt

27. "He was like a brother figure to me": *ibid*

28. "We did have that": *ibid*

29. "We eventually rejected the idea": *ibid*

30. "George had a good voice": *ibid*

31. "At the time, he was not a great guitar player": *ibid*

32. "We'd do a concert": *ibid*

33. Gram's grandmother Haney Snively: gleaned from accounts in Ben Fong-Torres' *Hickory Wind* and Sid Griffin's *Gram Parsons*.

34. Finally, Joe snapped: gleaned from an interview with Paul Surratt

35. "Gram had been to Greenwich Village before": *ibid*

36. While the rest of the gang found themselves: from liner notes to *Warm Evenings, Pale Mornings, Bottled Blues* by Glenn A. Baker.

37. His friends in the Shilos all sent their condolences: interview with Paul Surratt

38. "George had gone to college too": *ibid*

Chapter 3

1. "He was a good kid": Chris Hillman, in an interview with Barney Hoskyns, 'The Good Ol' Boy': *MOJO* July 1997. Used with permission

2. His father became Coon Dog Connor, itinerant country singer: various sources, published during Gram's lifetime, reiterated this story.

3. Another story Gram told: This tall tale about the Snively family supposedly owning Tara was told to Eve Babitz by Gram, in 1968.

4. "I guess they had enough class presidents": 'Ex-Byrd Gram Parsons Solos: He's no longer in a hurry': Judith Sims, *Rolling Stone* March 1, 1973

5. "At Harvard, you don't major": from Warner/ Reprise Publicity Dept. bio of Gram Parsons, December 1972. Used with permission.

6. From a letter to his sister Avis in 1965.

7. 'Havenite Brings Go-Go to Staid': taken from Ben Fong-Torres' *Hickory Wind*

8. "Gram was...a moderate piano player": Author interview with Ian Dunlop, December 1997

9. "You have to remember these were serious young musicians": *ibid*

10. "It wasn't going all that well": *ibid*

11. "Several of us came out of completely different backgrounds": *ibid*

12. "He was a really funky drummer": Barry Tashian to Sid Griffin

13. "We approached songs that were like set lessons": Author interview with Ian Dunlop, December 1997

14. "He would refer to us as his backing group": *ibid*

15. At Christmas, Bob sent for Gram: as told to the author by Frank David Murphy, 1997

16. "The idea was...": Author interview with Ian Dunlop, December 1997

17. "In early 1997, I had been working": Author interview with Ron Maharg, 1999

18. "Several pints later, I discovered": *ibid*

19. "We spent several months going back and forth": Author interview with Ian Dunlop, December 1997

20. "We found that we had become like a computer card": John Nuese to Sid Griffin in *Gram Parsons*.

21. "It came to the point that...": Author interview with Ian Dunlop, December 1997

22. Taken from *Don't Tell Dad* by Peter Fonda 1998

23. "We were quite ambitious": Author interview with Ian Dunlop, December 1997

24. "A definite mouthful of R&B grit": quote from the Byrdwatcher site – www.ebni.com/byrdwatcher

25. "The music got a little too diversified": Barry Tashian to Sid Griffin

26. "There was quite a bar band-type scene": Author interview with Jason Odd, September 2000

27. "We got involved with a bunch of people...": Author interview with Ian Dunlop, December 1997

28. "The Sub Band split was...": Barry Tashian to Sid Griffin in *Gram Parsons*

29. "I had to go to Hazlewood...": Gram Parsons to Chuck Casell, 1972

30. "We had a basic style...": John Nuese to Sid Griffin in *Gram Parsons*

31. "I had also worked for Kitty Wells...": Author interview with Jon Corneal, October 2000

32. "There were hours and hours of rehearsals...": Suzi Jane Hokom to Barney Hoskyns, 'The Good Ol' Boy' *MOJO* July 1997

33. "She and I disagreed on how to do things": John Nuese to Sid Griffin

34. Gram and Jon Corneal began clashing: Jon Corneal to the author

35. "I was thinking about it the other night": Gram Parsons to Chuck Casell 1972

36. "The Glen Campbells and others I knew": Suzi Jane Hokom to Barney Hoskyns, 'The Good Ol' Boy' *MOJO* July 1997

37. "Suzi was a nice person...": Author interview with Jon Corneal, October 2000

38. "In the early days in LA...": *ibid*

Chapter 4

1. "I'm coming down off amphetamine": 'Artificial Energy' lyric by Chris Hillman/ R. McGuinn/ M.Clarke

2. "We were playing these little gigs and it was terrible": Roger McGuinn to Johnny Rogan

3. "A horrible, watered-down Disneyland kind of bluegrass": Roger McGuinn to Vincent Flanders

4. "This was heaven. I'd found an ally, and quite possibly, my future": Chris Hillman in the liner notes to *Farther Along: the Best of the Flying Burrito Brothers* A&M 1988

5. "Gram was the first person": Chris Hillman to Sid Griffin

6. "John Nuese and I had the opportunity to go on the train": Author interview with Jon Corneal September 2000

7. Lyric from 'Hickory Wind' by Gram Parsons and Bob Buchanan, Wait and See Music BMI

8. Lyric from 'Do You Know How It Feels' by Gram Parsons and Barry Goldberg, Guitar Music BMI

9. "A chronological album starting out with old-time music": Roger McGuinn to Johnny Rogan, from the liner notes to the CD re-issue of *Sweetheart of the Rodeo*

10. "His idea was to blend the Beatles and country": Roger McGuinn to Johnny Rogan, *Timeless Flight Revisited: The Sequel*

11. "A greater challenge and an opportunity to show the world": Johnny Rogan in his book *Timeless Flight Revisited: The Sequel*

12. "This was completely foreign to their attitude": Jimmi Seiter to Sid Griffin

13. "Tompall Glaser and the Glaser Brothers were hosting the Opry": Gram Parsons to Chuck Casell 1972

14. "They think they're being really big-hearted": *ibid*

15. "The Glaser brothers just flipped out": *ibid*

16. "He took the reins.": Chris Hillman to Sid Griffin

17. "They appear secure in the country milieu": Jerry Hopkins, *Rolling Stone* magazine May 1968

18. "Graham's bag is country": Roger McGuinn to Jerry Hopkins

Chapter 5

1. "Columbia, for some reason...": Gram Parsons to Chuck Casell 1972

2. "Christian Life should have been Gram's vocal": Chris Hillman to Sid Griffin

3. "No. No way.": Chris Hillman to Sid Griffin

4. "Hollywood freaky and it wasn't the time for that": Gram Parsons to Chuck Casell 1972

5. "Roger was edgy that Gram was getting a bit too much": Gary Usher to Johnny Rogan, *Timeless Flight*
6. "Parsons got really mad...": Terry Melcher to Johnny Rogan, *Timeless Flight*
7. "Gram was very ambitious and very charming": Roger McGuinn to Barney Hoskyns
8. "We went down there as a political thing": Roger McGuinn, *When The Music's Over*
9. "Gram was like just like a puppy dog": Chris Hillman, to Barney Hoskyns
10. "Thank you, country music lovers": Roger McGuinn, from Byrds bootleg, *At the Roundhouse*, recorded May 1968
11. "I first heard about the South African tour two months ago": Gram Parsons, statement to *Melody Maker* May 1968
12. "He was let go because he didn't want to go": Roger McGuinn to Barney Hoskyns
13. "Gram wanted to stay in England": Chris Hillman
14. "Gram didn't know much about the situation": Keith Richards to Barney Hoskyns
15. "He agonised to the last minute about going": Author interview with Frank David Murphy, 1996
16. "He wanted a steel guitar...": Carlos Bernal to Johnny Rogan
17. "I was ready to murder Gram": Chris Hillman to Sid Griffin
18. "The Byrds display a good deal of fidelity to the rules of the style": Jon Landau in *Rolling Stone* magazine, August 1968

Chapter 6
1. "Yeah, I wonder if they even appreciate it now...": Author interview with Peter Kleinow, August 2000
2. "It was, it really was...": *ibid*
3. "I hung out with Keith Richards for a while": Gram Parsons to Chuck Casell 1972
4. "I'd met him several times before": *ibid*
5. "I'd been talking with Chris Ethridge": *ibid*
6. "Probably initially at the time": Chris Hillman to *SPIN* magazine, on the occasion of the Byrds induction to the Rock 'n' Roll Hall of Fame in 1991.
7. "He was hard-working – a great guy": Chris Hillman to Sid Griffin

8. "The clubs out in the Valley": Gram Parsons, Fusion magazine, March 26, 1969
9. "Country music is going through its fad": Gram Parsons, *Fusion* magazine, March 26, 1969
10. "Imagine crying over some hillbilly with a crewcut": Mercy Fontagne essay in Sid Griffin's *Gram Parsons* gives a nice insight into how Parsons connected emotionally with country music.
11. "We predicted the rise of fundamentalism": Chris Hillman, liner notes for *Farther Along* A&M Records 1988
12. "When we got together": Gram Parsons, *Fusion* magazine, March 26, 1969
13. "About the only pedal steel player in town": Gram Parsons to Chuck Casell 1972
14. "At that time, I had a regular gig": Author interview with Peter Kleinow, August 2000
15. "Gram and Chris were looking for a steel player": *ibid*
16. "I was never prejudiced against rock and roll at all": *ibid*
17. "In the studio with Chris Ethridge": Peter Kleinow to Chuck Casell 1972
18. "He just wanted the money": Gram Parsons to Chuck Casell 1972
19. "Here they are, both from Florida": Chris Hillman to Ben Fong-Torres *Hickory Wind*
20. "He was doing a real good job": Gram Parsons to Chuck Casell 1972
21. "I kinda knew what they wanted me to do": Author interview with Peter Kleinow, August 2000
22. "There were times during the making of the first album": Gram Parsons to Chuck Casell 1972
23. "That's the only way I record": Author interview with Peter Kleinow, August 2000
24. "To do the album in LA": Gram Parsons, *Fusion* magazine, March 26, 1969
25. "What do I remember about Larry?" Author interview with Peter Kleinow, August 2000
26. "Yeeeeaaahh... some of us more than others": Author interview with Peter Kleinow, August 2000

27. "He was walking around": Chris Hillman to Sid Griffin
28. "It was all unison note parts": Author interview with Peter Kleinow, August 2000
29. "Breaks the old gospel honky-tonk taboo": Stanley Booth, *Rhythm Oil*, Vintage Books
30. "His southern heritage ran through him": Author interview with Ian Dunlop December 1997
31. "I think pure country includes rock'n'roll": Gram Parsons to Chuck Casell 1972
32. "On 'Hippie Boy'...": Gram Parsons, *Fusion* magazine, March 26, 1969
33. "We went through 'Hot Burrito #1'": Gram Parsons, *Fusion* magazine, March 26, 1969
34. "I can't say how long it took": Author interview with Peter Kleinow, August 2000
35. "They have been real good": Gram Parsons, Fusion magazine, March 26, 1969
36. "We are not a negative, put-down group": Gram Parsons, *Fusion* magazine, March 26, 1969
37. "There were other better photographs": Gram Parsons to Chuck Casell 1972
38. "The idea was to create goose bumps": *ibid*
39. "A wild jumble of ideas": Peter Kleinow to Chuck Casell 1972
40. "The Beatles, for instance...": *ibid*
41. "After three years...": Gram Parsons, *Fusion* magazine, March 26, 1969
42. "Jerry Moss pinned it": Gram Parsons to Chuck Casell 1972
43. "Chris is a real bright guy": Author interview with Peter Kleinow, August 2000
44. "Clearly, playing the Grand Ole Opry": Martin C. Strong, *Great Rock Discography* 1999

Chapter 7
1. "In early 1969": Dennis Roger Reed, in an e-mail to author, September 2000
2. "I said, 'Okay, look'": Phil Kaufman in *Road Mangler Deluxe*, White Bouck Publishing
3. "It was like debauchery personified": Phil Kaufman in *Road Mangler Deluxe*, White Bouck Publishing

4. "We were cowboys": Phil Kaufman in *Road Mangler Deluxe*, White Bouck Publishing
5. "Gram seemed to be entranced": Jon Landau, *Rolling Stone* 1969
6. "Things were more difficult than anticipated": Michael Vosse to Ben Fong-Torres *Hickory Wind*
7. "Somehow, I even convinced my psychiatrist": Author interview with Frank David Murphy 1996
8. "Gram was having a great time": *ibid*
9. "I realise the burning question": *ibid*
10. "We weren't very good on stage": Chris Hillman to Ben Fong-Torres *Hickory Wind*
11. "the statement of a young man": Stanley Booth, *Rhythm Oil*, Vintage Books
12. "We're treated great in one way": Gram Parsons, *Fusion* magazine, March 26, 1969
13. "He would turn into a wheelchair person": Chris Hillman to Ben Fong-Torres *Hickory Wind*
14. "They'd see some guy slobbering in a chair": *ibid*
15. "I remember the first time I heard the Flying Burrito Brothers": written by Brian Day, September 2000
16. "Four cosmic kittens": Andee Cohen to Ben Fong-Torres *Hickory Wind*
17. "I don't recall the exact date of the session": Author interview with George Bullfrog September 2000
18. "It was an overwhelming listening experience": *ibid*
19. "Gram was opposed to the idea": *ibid*
20. "Chris wasn't really a country bassplayer": Gram Parsons to Chuck Casell 1972
21. "We had a working group": Bernie Leadon to Ben Fong-Torres *Hickory Wind*
22. "Mick on the couch, leaning over": Stanley Booth, *The True Adventures of the Rolling Stones*
23. "It's the drugs – they keep you healthy": *ibid*
24. "It was on the left, a little roadhouse": *ibid*
25. "There's a lot of things in the last 35 years I don't remember at all": Chris Hillman to Allan Jones, *Uncut* magazine October 2000

26. "the day was dark and depressing": *ibid*
27. "the 'security people' were bouncing full cans of beer": Michelle Phillips *California Dreamin'*
28. "I remember saying to him": Chris Hillman to Allan Jones, *Uncut* magazine October 2000
29. "We got a gentler mood going": *ibid*
30. "moving along, heading down toward to the stage": Stanley Booth, *The True Adventures of the Rolling Stones*
31. "we left as fast as we could": Chris Hillman to Allan Jones, *Uncut* magazine October 2000
32. "I have a phrase that fits what I'm playin'": Stanley Booth, *The True Adventures of the Rolling Stones*
33. "We were just shaking from the whole experience": Gram Parsons to Chuck Casell 1972
34. "After that brief initial burst": I have taken the liberty of pasting two separate statements made by Chris Hillman, one to Sid Griffin in 1980, and "He just went headlong in the direction of physical abuse": to Richard Kingsmill ABC radio 1999. Used by permission.
35. "According to whomever is telling the story": Jeffrey Gold, liner notes to *Farther Along* A&M Records
36. "I'd love to have seen Gram back in the Byrds": Terry Melcher to Johnny Rogan *Timeless Flight*
37. "He wasn't strong enough to hold it all the time:" Chris Hillman to Ben Fong-Torres *Hickory Wind*
38. "John, take me for a long white ride": Gram Parsons, quoted by John Phillips in Ben Fong-Torres' *Hickory Wind*
39. "He wanted it all": Chris Hillman to Richard Kingsmill ABC radio. Used by permission.
40. "I got bored with the Burritos": Gram Parsons to Judith Sims *Rolling Stone* 1973
41. "It didn't get me off": Gram to Chuck Casell
42. "You'll never get out of here": Phil Kaufman in *Road Mangler Deluxe*, White Bouck Publishing
43. "Charlie really, really hated blacks": Phil Kaufman in *Road Mangler Deluxe*, White Bouck Publishing
44. "He was staggering around": Delaney Bramlett *MOJO* 1995
45. "One day Clarence calls me": John Beland, quoted in the *Clarence White Chronicles*, a semi-regular email newsletter. Thanks to Koji Kojihara.
46. "Gram saw himself as a victim": Terry Melcher to Ben Fong-Torres *Hickory Wind*
47. "I didn't know what to do with him": *ibid*
48. "Why don't you leave these fuckers": Bernie Leadon to Ben Fong-Torres *Hickory Wind*
49. "He must be the only guy": Phil Kaufman in *Road Mangler Deluxe*, White Bouck Publishing

Chapter 9

1. "I've always had a dream about doing stuff in England": Gram to Chuck Casell 1972
2. "They were definitely trying to find something on Keith": Gretchen Carpenter to Victor Bockris, *Keith Richards: the Biography*.
3. "really a very nice guy": Charlie Watts to Stanley Booth, *The True Adventures of the Rolling Stones*
4. "He cheered them up in miserly dressing rooms": from Robert Greenfield's account of the Stones 1971 Farewell Britain tour for *Rolling Stone* May 1971
5. "Me, Keith and Gram, with two nurses": Anita Pallenberg to John Perry, *Classic Albums: Exile on Main Street*
6. "Doing a little overdubbing": Perry Richardson to Barney Hoskyns, 'Good Ol' Boy' *MOJO* July 1998
7. "This knife would go whistling through the hall": Anita Pallenberg to John Perry, *Classic Albums: Exile on Main Street*
8. "I was a bit aloof from all these California girls": Anita Pallenberg to Barney Hoskyns, 'Good Ol' Boy' *MOJO* July 1998
9. "We did a lot of recording in the kitchen": Andy Johns to *New York Rocker* 1973
10. "I don't think Gram even went down there": Anita Pallenberg to John Perry, *Classic Albums: Exile on Main Street*
11. "Gram was the other side of the coin": *ibid*
12. "Mick likes to write": *ibid*
13. "Could you please take Gram?": As quoted from Ben Fong-Torres' *Hickory Wind*

14. "I don't know if I can do that": Gram to Keith Richards, as told by Perry Richardson to Barney Hoskyns, 'Good Ol' Boy' *MOJO* July 1998

15. "It was very easy to get caught up": Perry Richardson to Barney Hoskyns, 'Good Ol' Boy' *MOJO* July 1998

16. "There's a history of people getting pulled into that vortex": *ibid*

17. "Who are the Sequins?": Gram to Chuck Casell

18. "He'd almost be over the edge": Dr. Sam Hutt *Hank Wangford, Volume III: the Middle Years*

19. "Gram was always doing stuff like that": Author interview with Frank David Murphy 1997

20. "Here was this bop-a-doo California girl": Eve Babitz to Barney Hoskyns, 'Good Ol' Boy' *MOJO* July 1998

21. "By luck, it turned out that the girl": Emmylou Harris to *Uncut* September 1999

22. "I was just very lucky": Gram Parsons

23. "I was a jaded 25-year old single mother": Emmylou Harris to Allan Jones *Uncut* September 1999

24. "I suggested he take the train": Emmylou Harris to Sid Griffin in *Gram Parsons*

25. "Chris didn't know she was Birmingham, Alabama": Gram to Chuck Casell

26. "I've been looking for someone": Gram Parsons to Chuck Casell

Chapter 10

1. "He had let go of everything": Eve Babitz obituary in *Rolling Stone* November 1973

2. "His mental health became very precarious": Gretchen Carpenter to Barney Hoskyns, 'Good Ol' Boy' *MOJO* July 1998

3. "His pants and shirt wouldn't button": Chris Hillman to Sid Griffin *Gram Parsons*

4. "Gram gave me a call": Eddie Tickner to Phil Kaufman in *Road Mangler Deluxe*, White Bouck Publishing

5. "I think Merle not producing the album": Gretchen Carpenter to Barney Hoskyns, 'Good Ol' Boy' *MOJO* July 1998

6. "He was hopping all round the room": Perry Richardson to Barney Hoskyns,

'Good Ol' Boy' *MOJO* July 1998

7. "Gram had a beautiful humour toward that song": *ibid*

8. "I think Gram wanted a wider audience": *ibid*

9. "Yeah, I got to see Elvis": Author interview with Barry Tashian, 1 November 2000

10. "It just raised the hair on the back of my neck": *ibid*

11. "I knew he was in trouble at the Chateau Marmont": *ibid*

12. "His singing was so extraordinary": Emmylou Harris to CBS 2000

13. "I had never heard the Louvin Brothers before": *ibid*

14. "Aretha was on the jukebox": Author interview with Barry Tashian, 1 November 2000

15. "The funny thing was that I didn't know who these people were": Emmylou Harris to CBS 2000

16. "I really liked the music": Hugh Davies to John M. Delgatto liner notes for *GP/ Grievous Angel* Reprise Records 1990

17. "Gram had a real vivid impression": Al Perkins to John M. Delgatto liner notes for *GP/ Grievous Angel* Reprise Records 1990

18. Lyric from 'A Song For You' by Gram Parsons, 1972 Wait and See Music BMI

19. "I don't know about Gretchen": Author interview with Barry Tashian, 1 November 2000

20. "Just by singing with him": Emmylou Harris to Holly George-Warren *No Depression* July-August 1999

Chapter 11

1. "I had no idea who Gram Parsons was": Author interview with Neil Flanz, July 2000

2. "Phil picked me up at LAX": *ibid*

3. "He said, 'Come on out here'": Author interview with Jon Corneal September 2000

4. "We were supposed to be involved in serious rehearsing": Author interview with Neil Flanz, July 2000

5. "Rehearsal for Gram was just playing": Emmylou Harris to CBS

6. "Right next door to the club": Author interview with Neil Flanz, July 2000

7. "We had our first rehearsal": *ibid*

8. "Gram looked about 50 pounds heavier": Richie Furay to Ben Fong-Torres *Hickory Wind*

9. "Our first gig in Boulder was just a train wreck": Emmylou Harris
10. "We were meant to be there for six nights or so": *ibid*
11. "We set up and played and Jock sat in with us": Author interview with Neil Flanz, July 2000
12. "Hey Gram, Neil doesn't think Jock can't play country worth a shit": *ibid*
13. "Now I guarantee you": *ibid*
14. "Gram said, 'I like Jock'": *ibid*
15. "Man, we really got down to some serious rehearsal": *ibid*
16. "He asked us what we thought about 'progressive' country": Emmylou Harris dialogue from *Gram Parsons and the Fallen Angels: Live* 1973
17. "We had this DJ the other night": Gram Parsons, dialogue from *Gram Parsons and the Fallen Angels: Live* 1973
18. "I wouldn't lie to you": *ibid*
19. "Thanks for the worst interview of my life": Rusty Bell to Gram Parsons, as reported in Ben Fong-Torres' *Hickory Wind*
20. "We literally blew the roof off the place": Author interview with Neil Flanz, July 2000
21. "We ran out of encores": *ibid*
22. "Gram's first solo record": Steve Earle to *Mojo* 1998
23. "The original setting for *McCabe and Mrs Miller*": Emmylou Harris to Ben Fong-Torres *Hickory Wind*
24. "It was a pretty rowdy place": Author interview with Neil Flanz, July 2000
25. "thought that show was a blast": *ibid*
26. "Welcome to Ultrasonic Recording Studios": Ken Kohl dialogue from *Gram Parsons and the Fallen Angels: Live* 1973
27. "We're finally in New York": Gram Parsons
28. "Y'all wanted a Merle Haggard song": *ibid*

Chapter 12
1. "Between sets, I asked a member of Gram's entourage": Author interview with Tom Brown, early 2000
2. "Strange to say": *ibid*
3. "And that was the tour, pretty well": Author interview with Neil Flanz, July 2000

4. "That's when his seizures started": Gretchen Carpenter to Barney Hoskyns, 'Good Ol' Boy' *MOJO* July 1998
5. "Phil, if this happens to me": Gram Parsons to Phil Kaufman as reported in *Road Mangler Deluxe*, White Bouck Publishing
6. "Occasionally, I'd see the dealers coming": *ibid*
7. "Ole Gram's in jail again": *ibid*
8. "Gram spent a lot of time in jail": *ibid*
9. "The first album was not as planned out as the second one": Emmylou Harris
10. "A hotchpotch of old and new": Martin C. Strong, *Great Rock Discography*
11. "Phil and Gram used to come over to my house at night": Glen D. Hardin quoted in *Road Mangler Deluxe*, White Bouck Publishing

Chapter 13
1. "I always thought of Gram": Eve Babitz, GP obituary *Rolling Stone* November 1973
2. "We're never going to let Bob Parsons have his way": Little Avis Parsons to Judson Klinger and Greg Mitchell, 'Gram Finale' *Crawdaddy* October 1976
3. "I was his number one fan": *ibid*
4. "He was always anxious to get there": Eddie Tickner to *Rolling Stone* November 1973
5. "Multiple drug toxicity": Gram Parsons autopsy results, State of California
6. "I was at work in Philadelphia": Author interview with Frank David Murphy 1997
7. Keith and Bobby Keys were "deeply, deeply shocked": Nick Kent, *The Dark Stuff* 1994
8. "No, no, I didn't expect his death to happen": Emmylou Harris to Richard Kingsmill ABC radio 1999, used by permission.
9. "It had gotten to the point": Chris Hillman to Richard Kingsmill ABC radio 1999, used by permission.
10. "I did have contact with Gram": *ibid*
11. "This is it – we're fucked": Phil Kaufman, as related in *Road Mangler Deluxe*, White Bouck Publishing
12. "We looked down.He was very dead": *ibid*

Complete bibliography of magazine articles and books used in research of *God's Own Singer*

No Direction Home: the life and music of Bob Dylan
By Robert Shelton
Penguin Books London UK 1986

The True Adventures of the Rolling Stones
By Stanley Booth
William Heinemann, London UK 1985

Rhythm Oil
By Stanley Booth
Vintage, London UK 1991

Hickory Wind: The Life and Times of Gram Parsons
By Ben Fong-Torres
St. Martin's Griffin Books USA (reprinted 1998)

Classic Rock Albums
Exile on Main Street – the Rolling Stones
By John Perry
Schirmer Books, New York USA 2000

Keith Richards The Biography
By Victor Bockris
Penguin Books, London UK 1992

Are You Ready For the Country?
By Peter Doggett
London UK 2000

Road Mangler Deluxe (2nd edition)
By Phil Kaufman with Colin White
White Boucke Publishing USA 1998

Gram Parsons – A Musical Biography
By Sid Griffin
Sierra Books & Records USA 1985, 1992, 1994

When The Music's Over – Civil Rights From America to South Africa
By?

The Byrds: Timeless Flight Revisited – the Sequel
By Johnny Rogan
Rogan House Books UK 1998

Rock Bottom
By Pamela Des Barres
Omnibus Books USA 1996
I'm With the Band
By Pamela Des Barres
Beech Tree Books USA 1987

You're So Cold, I'm Turning Blue
By Martha Hulme
USA 1985

Who's Who In New Country Music
By Chet Flippo
USA 1980

The Byrds
By Bud Scoppa
USA 1973

Up and Down With the Rolling Stones
By Tony Sanchez
Morrow Quill USA 1979

California Dreamin'
By Michelle Phillips
Warner Books USA 1986

Articles

'Ex-Byrd Gram Parsons Solos: He's No Longer In a Hurry'
Rolling Stone (Aust) Copyright March 1, 1973
Next Publications. All rights reserved. Reprinted with permission.
By Judith Sims

Review of *GP*
Rolling Stone (Aust) Copyright March 1, 1973
Next Publications. All rights reserved. Reprinted with permission.
by Bud Scoppa

'Gram Parsons: The Mysterious Death – and Aftermath'
Rolling Stone (Aust) Copyright November 8th 1973
Next Publications. All rights reserved. Reprinted with permission.
By Patrick Sullivan

Obituary: 'Ashes In the Morning'
Rolling Stone (Aust) Copyright November 8th 1973
Next Publications. All rights reserved. Reprinted with permission.
By Eve Babitz
Review of *Grievous Angel*
Rolling Stone (Aust) Copyright March 28, 1974
Next Publications. All rights reserved. Reprinted with permission.
by Bud Scoppa

'Gram Finale'
Crawdaddy (US) October 1976
By Judson Klinger and Greg Mitchell

'My Dug-Up Buddy: Gram Parsons 1973 – 1993'
New Musical Express (UK) November 1993
By Steve Sutherland

'Gram Parsons: Grievous Angel, Grievously Neglected'
Australian Record Collector (Aust) November 1994
By Jason Walker

Sweep Out the Ashes '71/'72: Gram Parsons interviewed by an unknown A&R guy
[actually a transcription of the Chuck Casell interview of 1972]'
Chemical Imbalance Vol. 3 #1

'Country-Rock'
Record Collector (UK) 1994
By Peter Doggett

'Gram Parsons'
Record Collector (UK) 1994
By Peter Doggett

'One Room At the Inn'
MOJO (UK) September 1996
By Jim Irvin

'Once Upon a Time in the West'
MOJO (UK) April 1997
By Johnny Rogan

'The Fabulous Furry Freak Brothers'
MOJO (UK) April 1997
By Sid Griffin

'The Good Ol' Boy'
MOJO (UK) July 1998
By Barney Hoskyns

'An Angel Outrun by His Demons'
Sydney Morning Herald (Aust) July 1999
From New York Times News Services
By Dave Ferman

'Season of the Witch'
MOJO (UK) September 1999
By Gary Valentine

'Let It Bleed'
UNCUT (UK) September 1999
By Allan Jones

'Emmylou Harris'
CBS Internet article November 2000
By Timothy White

Liner Notes

Gram Parsons – *GP/ Grievous Angel*
Reprise CD 1990
By John Delgatto

Gram Parsons – *GP/ Grievous Angel*
Reprise CD 1990
By Marley Brant

Farther Along
A&M compilation 1988
Liner notes by Jeffrey Gold

Farther Along
A&M compilation 1988
Liner notes by Chris Hillman

Gram Parsons – *Cosmic American Music*
Magnum Music Group
Liner notes by Sid Griffin

Flying Burrito Brothers featuring Gram Parsons & Chris Hillman
A&M Records London 1996
Liner Notes by Sid Griffin

Warm Evenings, Pale Mornings, Bottled Blues
Raven Records Aust. 1992
Liner notes by Glenn A. Baker

Close Up The Honky Tonks
A&M Records USA 1976
Liner notes by Jim Bickhart

Sweetheart of the Rodeo
Columbia/ Sony/ Legacy re-issue
Liner notes by David Fricke

Sweetheart of the Rodeo
Columbia/ Sony/ Legacy re-issue
Liner notes by John Rogan

Last of the Red Hot Burritos
A&M Records 1972
Liner notes by Chuck Casell

Discography
Chapter by Chapter

Chapter 1

Elvis Presley – The Sun Sessions

Chapter 2

The Shilos line-up (1963-1966)
Paul Surratt: banjo, vocals
George Wrigley: vocals, guitar
Joe Kelly: bass, vocals
Gram Parsons: lead vocals, guitar

Album

The Shilos with Gram Parsons: The Early Years 1963-1965

Also recommended listening

The Kingston Trio, Capitol – T*he Best of the Best of the Kingston Trio*
The Cumberland Three – *Folk Scene USA*
The Journeymen – *The Best of the Journeymen*

Chapter 3

International Submarine Band lineup (1966-1967)
Gram Parsons: vocals, guitar
Tom Snow: saxophone
John Nuese: lead/ rhythm guitar
Ian Dunlop: vocals, bass
Mickey Gauvin: drums

Singles

'Sum Up Broke'/ 'One Day Week'
Columbia 4-4395
Released: 1966
International Submarine Band
'The Russians Are Coming (theme)'/ 'Truck Driving Man'
Ascot 2218
Released: 1966

International Submarine Band lineup #2 (1967-1968)
Gram Parsons: lead vocals, guitar
Chris Ethridge: bass
John Nuese: lead guitar, vocals
Jon Corneal: drums, vocals
JD Maness: pedal steel
Earl Ball: piano

Album

Safe At Home
Produced by Suzi Jane Hokom
LHI Records LHI-S-12001
Later reissued as *Gram Parsons* on the Shiloh label, this was the first album as such that Gram Parsons ever released. It was released in 1968, while Gram was in the process of recording *Sweetheart of the Rodeo* with the Byrds. It is a fine, straight-ahead country album, with songs like 'Do You Know How It Feels' and 'Luxury Liner' showcasing his up-and-coming country songwriting talent.
Released: April 1968

Singles

'Luxury Liner'/ 'Blue Eyes'
LHI 45-1205
Released 1968

'Miller's Cave'/ 'I Must Be Somebody Else You've Known'
LHI 45-1217
Released 1968

Chapter 4

The Byrds line-up
Roger McGuinn: lead guitar, vocals
Chris Hillman: bass, mandolin, vocals
Gram Parsons: guitar, keyboards, vocals
Kevin Kelley: drums

Album

The Byrds: *Sweetheart of the Rodeo*
Produced by Gary Usher
Columbia/ CBS CS-9670
Released August 30, 1968
Track listing: You Ain't Going Nowhere/ I Am A Pilgrim/ The Christian Life/ You Don't Miss Your Water/ You're Still On My Mind/ Pretty Boy Floyd/ Hickory Wind/ One Hundred Years From Now/ Blue Canadian Rockies/ Life In Prison/ Nothing Was Delivered
This album is widely considered to be one of the most influential 'non-rock' albums by a major American rock group of the 1960s. Here, you can hear how Parsons rewired all the circuits during his short, sharp tenure with the Byrds. In 1990, the original Parsons lead vocals emerged after nearly thirty years in the CBS vaults. They

had been erased (and presumed lost) from the secondary masters just prior to pressing, due to legal action from Lee Hazlewood, who at the time owned the rights to Gram's vocal performances. Gram got out of that bind by signing over the rights to the practically worthless name of the International Submarine Band (which actually belonged to Ian Dunlop in the first place), just in time to rescue three of his vocal tracks. As for the rest? They were believed to have been completely wiped. Not so, as the uncovering of the original 16-track masters proved. Now, the original Parsons vocals can be heard in all their glory on 1990's *The Byrds* 4-CD box set (Columbia/ Legacy CK46773), and the 1997 Columbia Legacy imprint CD re-issue (Columbia/ Legacy CK65150) of *Sweetheart of the Rodeo*. This serves as a reminder of how good the album was anyway, yet confirms suspicions of just how great it could have been.

Singles

'You Ain't Goin' Nowhere'/ 'Artificial Energy'
Columbia single #44499
Released 1968

'I Am A Pilgrim'/ 'Pretty Boy Floyd'
Columbia single #4-44643
Released 1968

Chapter 5

Also recommended listening

The Rolling Stones: *Beggars Banquet*
Produced by Jimmy Miller
Decca Records UK
Released: 1968

Chapter 6

Flying Burrito Brothers lineup (1968-1969)
Chris Hillman: rhythm guitar, mandolin, lead and harmony vocals
Gram Parsons: rhythm guitar, keyboard instruments, lead and harmony vocals
Sneeky Pete Kleinow: pedal steel
Chris Ethridge: bass, piano
Jon Corneal: drums

Album

The Flying Burrito Brothers: *The Gilded Palace of Sin*
Produced by Larry Marks, Henry Lewy
A&M SP 4175
Released: February 1969

Track listing: Christine's Tune (Devil In Disguise)/ Sin City/ Do Right Woman/ Dark End Of the Street/ My Uncle/ Wheels/ Juanita/ Hot Burrito #1/ Hot Burrito #2/ Do You Know How It Feels/ Hippie Boy
Critics and hardcore fans say this is the sort of album that should have changed popular music at the time it was released, but circumstances conspired against it from the very beginning. Here, we have Parsons' soulful voice matched to Chris Hillman and Chris Ethridge's fine songwriting. This record, although relatively obscure, benefited from several factors; most notably, the Parsons-Hillman and Parsons-Ethridge songwriting teams. It's as much rock and pop as it is country on the surface, but dig a little deeper and you'll discover that this record just about defies description. Essential for anyone who wishes to uncover one of the '60s least-known, best-dressed records.

Also recommended listening

Steve Young: *Rock, Salt and Nails*
Featuring: Gram Parsons, organ and vocals
A&M 4177
Released: 1969

Jesse Davis: *Jesse Davis*
Featuring Gram Parsons: backing vocals
Atco SD 33-346
Released: 1969

Chapter 7

Single

'The Train Song'/ 'Hot Burrito #1'
A&M 1067
Released: 1969
Inspired by a rambling and expensive first US tour, 'The Train Song' can be found on various Flying Burrito Brothers compilations, and is notorious for having been produced by legendary R&B duo Larry Williams and Johnny 'Guitar' Watson. Amid tales of the session's excess, there was the very real dissatisfaction of A&M, who felt they weren't getting a return on what was turning out to be a substantial investment.

Also recommended listening

Delaney & Bonnie: *Motel Shot*
Featuring Gram Parsons: vocals
Atco SD 33-358
Released: 1970
Gram's friends from the early days of the ISB's adventures in the North Hollywood honky-tonks Delaney & Bonnie Bramlett attracted the very best musicians and singers

(George Harrison, Eric Clapton, Gram) with their soulful take on R&B, rock, country and soul. Delaney Bramlett, a Mississippi boy with his roots in every musical stream that flowed from the South had met and married Bonnie, who had once been the only white Ikette, which should give you an idea how soulful they were together. With these like-minded travellers, Gram learned to be himself on record and to be proud of his country music heritage, just as Delaney was.

Chapter 8

The Flying Burrito Brothers line-up (1969-1970)
Chris Hillman: vocals, bass, mandolin,
Gram Parsons: vocals, piano
Sneeky Pete Kleinow: pedal steel
Bernie Leadon: vocals, lead guitar, dobro
Michael Clarke: drums

Album

Flying Burrito Brothers: *Burrito Deluxe*
Produced by Jim Dickson, Henry Lewy
A&M SP 4258
Released: May 1970
Track listing: Lazy Days/ Image Of Me/ High Fashion Queen/ If You Gotta Go/ Man In the Fog/ Farther Along/ Older Guys/ Cody, Cody/ God's Own Singer/ Down In the Churchyard/ Wild Horses
To be polite, this album is a mixed-bag, but it's not as bad as I once thought it was. Produced in 1969 after Chris Ethridge left the group, it was recorded relatively inexpensively with all eyes on the A&M clock, which was ticking over the whole time. Yet it has some charming moments, such as the first version of the Rolling Stones' tune 'Wild Horses' to be released, and two songs from newcomer Bernie Leadon. While it was being made, Parsons was continually distracted by all kinds of things; namely, his new girlfriend Gretchen, his Harley-Davidson and Keith Richards. A&M hated it at first and asked the Burritos for a straight-country record, please. They tried, but didn't get to complete it, and A&M decided to issue *Burrito Deluxe* in the meantime, though not without protest. By the time it was released, Gram had been in a serious motorcycle accident on the aforementioned Harley-Davidson and set about sabotaging what would be his last few live shows with the Burritos as only he could. Chris Hillman and Mike Clarke sacked him.

Singles

'If You Gotta Go'/ 'Cody, Cody'
A&M 1166
Released: May 1970

'Older Guys'/ Down In the Churchyard'
A&M 1189
Released: July 1970

Chapter 9

Gram Parsons solo project #1 (aborted)
Gram Parsons: *Money Honey* or *Sleepless Nights* (mooted titles)
Sessions produced by Terry Melcher and Gram Parsons
A&M Studios/ Olympic studios, London
Released: remains unreleased, master tape whereabouts as yet unknown
Track listing: White Line Fever/ Brass Buttons/ Dream Baby/ Sleepless Nights/ I Fall To Pieces/ She Thinks I Still Care/ Do Right Woman/ $1000 Wedding
Gram Parsons' first attempts at a solo record were produced by Terry Melcher, who had worked miracles for the Byrds and the Beach Boys in the studio. Convening at the A&M studios in late 1970, Gram and Terry lined up the best session musicians they could find – Clarence White, Spooner Oldham, Ry Cooder and Merry Clayton were just some of the artists claimed to have appeared on it. Thanks to a collective lack of discipline, the idea fizzled out at late vocal overdub stage, even though the record was quite close to being finished. Gram took the masters with him to Europe, when he visited Keith in London. Several people insist convincingly that Gram spent quite a lot of time overdubbing piano and vocals onto the tape during 1971, at Olympic Studios in London, where the Stones recorded many of their albums. And where is this record now? The legend, mostly likely true, has it that the tapes were destroyed in a fire that swept through Parsons' Laurel Canyon home in summer 1973.

Also recommended listening

The Rolling Stones: *Exile On Main Street*
Rolling Stone Records COC-2-2900
Produced by Jimmy Miller, assisted by Glyn Johns and Andy Johns
Released: May 1972
Track listing: Rocks Off/ Rip This Joint/ Hip Shake/ Casino Boogie/ Tumbling Dice/ Sweet Virginia/ Torn and Frayed/ Black Angel/ Loving Cup/ Happy/ Turd On the Run/ Ventilator Blues/ I Just Wanna See His Face/ Let It Loose/ All Down the Line/ Stop Breaking Down/ Shine A Light/ Soul Survivor
This is the album which presents the strongest evidence yet that Gram Parsons truly is one of music's most influential characters, and managed to be so even in his own lifetime. *Exile* was recorded in a dirty, filthy basement at Keith's home Nellcote, in the south of France, and while Gram didn't actually sing on the album as has

been claimed, he's still all over it in spirit. While Richards' houseguest, Gram can be felt all over side two of the album; 'Sweet Virginia' and 'Torn and Frayed' are spirited, rocking country-flavoured songs, just what Gram would do if he had Charlie Watts and Keith to fire him up.

Chapter 10

Gram Parsons solo recording line-up #1
Gram Parsons: lead vocals, acoustic guitar
Emmylou Harris: vocals
Rik Grech: bass
Barry Tashian: guitar, harmony vocals
John Conrad: bass
Ronnie Tutt: drums
John Guerin: drums
Sam Goldstein:drums
Glen D. Hardin: piano, organ
James Burton: dobro, electric lead guitar
Al Perkins: pedal steel
Buddy Emmons: pedal steel
Byron Berline: fiddle
Alan Munde: banjo
Hal Battiste: baritone sax

Album

Gram Parsons with Emmylou Harris: *GP*
Produced by Gram Parsons, Rik Grech and Hugh Davies
Reprise Records MS 2123
Recorded: late summer 1972
Released: January 1973
Track listing: Still Feeling Blue/ We'll Sweep Out the Ashes in the Morning/ A Song For You/ Streets of Baltimore/ She/ The New Soft Shoe/ Kiss the Children/ Cry One More Time/ How Much I've Lied/ Big Mouth Blues
If you only get around to purchasing one Gram Parsons album, it should either be this album, or its posthumous follow-up, *Grievous Angel*. The bright, timeless production comes courtesy of Merle Haggard's engineer Hugh Davies, and Parsons' own specific requests that the musicians adhere to more traditional country music conventions. For example, Al Perkins and James Burton duet on pedal steel and twin lead guitar breaks; there are 16-bar solos split up between fiddle, dobro and steel guitar; and as for the positively reverential duet vocals, there is commendable fidelity to the stylistic moves of Conway Twitty and Loretta Lynn or George Jones and Tammy Wynette. Parsons does not put a foot wrong anywhere on this album.

Chapter 11

Gram Parsons and the Fallen Angels line-up #1 (1973) (line-up #2 is the same except for Gerry Mule, who is replaced on lead guitar duties a week into the tour by Jock Bartley: electric lead, rhythm guitar)
Gram Parsons: lead vocals, acoustic guitar
Emmylou Harris: lead vocals, acoustic guitar
Gerry Mule: lead guitar
Neil Flanz: pedal steel
ND Smart II: drums, vocals
Kyle Tullis: bass

Album

Gram Parsons and the Fallen Angels: *Live 1973*
Sierra Records GP 1973 (original vinyl release)
Released: February 1982
This version of the WLIR-FM live radio show was well-edited, but in 1991, former WLIR broadcast producer, the aptly-named Michael Tapes told Sierra Records' John Delgatto that he had located the original, unedited master tapes of this legendary broadcast. It was reissued in a tasteful commemorative box as – *Gram Parsons and the Fallen Angels: Live 1973; Original Unedited Broadcast* Sierra Records OXCD 6003
Produced by Michael Tapes (original, unedited broadcast), John M. Delgatto and Marley Brant
Track listing: We'll Sweep Out the Ashes/ Country Baptizing/ Drug Store Truck Driving Man/ Big Mouth Blues/ The New Soft Shoe/ Cry One More Time/ Streets of Baltimore/ That's All It Took/ Love Hurts/ California Cottonfields/ Six Days on the Road/ Encore medley
It has often been said of Gram that, during this period, was in the process of squandering his talent and among other things, destroying his voice with booze and cocaine. If this was ever truly the case, then his voice must have been able to take some serious punishment. There is nary a trace of a croak in his throat and his vocals soar with ease. As for Emmylou Harris, she is confident throughout this stirring live set, which some spectators say was fairly representative of the quality of the whole tour, barring one very shaky show in Boulder, Colorado, which hastened the departure of guitarist Gerry Mule. As Gram and Emmylou grow together with their singing, there is a hint of the compatibility we can expect from *Grievous Angel*, the recording of which began almost directly following this tour. The incandescent 'Love Hurts' is a highlight of both this live album, and the studio version, which will appear on the shelves of record stores the following year. For what it's worth, the version presented here may well be the superior take.

Chapter 12

Gram Parsons solo recording line-up #2
Gram Parsons: lead vocals, acoustic guitar
Emmylou Harris: vocals
Emory Gordy: bass
Ronnie Tutt: drums
Glen D. Hardin: piano
James Burton: electric lead guitar
Al Perkins: pedal steel
Byron Berline: fiddle, mandolin
Herb Pederson: acoustic rhythm guitar,electric rhythm guitar
Bernie Leadon: acoustic rhythm, electric lead, dobro
N.D Smart II: drums
Steve Snyder: vibes
Linda Ronstadt: backing vocals

Albums

Gram Parsons & Emmylou Harris: *Grievous Angel*
Produced by: Gram Parsons for Tickner-Dickson Productions
Reprise Records MS 2171
Released: January 1974
Track listing: Return of the Grievous Angel/ Hearts On Fire/ I Can't Dance/ Brass Buttons/ $1000 Wedding/ Medley Live From Northern Quebec A) Cash On the Barrelhead B) Hickory Wind/ Love Hurts/ Ooh Las Vegas/ In My Hour of Darkness
Poets, artists and singers have all, through the ages, written at least one piece that may be interpreted as an epitaph, coincidence or not. In this case, Gram Parsons, who was all of 26 when he made this record, certainly did not intend for it to be his last. Nor did he intend it to have the cover that it does. The original artwork, which he approved prior to his death, was vetoed by his wife Gretchen. It showed Gram and Emmylou sitting on Gram's motorcycle. Their comfort with each other is obvious, and they look for all the world like lovers. Whether they were or not is a favoured and endlessly debated topic of conversation among their admirers. Speculation aside, this album is a most fitting goodbye to Gram, who lived well and left us too early. Listen closely to 'In My Hour of Darkness' and discover for yourself how a song that he penned as a tribute to Clarence White, Brandon deWilde and Sid Kaiser became his own moving memorial.

Gram Parsons, Emmylou Harris and the Flying Burrito Brothers: *Sleepless Nights*
A&M SP 3190
Produced by: Hugh Davies, Gram Parsons
Released: May 1976
This record contains a number of tracks recorded by the Flying Burrito Brothers for A&M, which captures them tilting at the honky-tonks and bars with a range of covers, from the Stones to Creedence and Merle Haggard. Furthermore, it gives us three incredibly beautiful songs originating from the *Grievous Angel* sessions in the summer of 1973 – 'Sleepless Nights', 'The Angels Rejoiced' and 'Brand New Heartache'. They didn't make the final cut of the album for a variety of reasons, but they are all equally fine and offer up the possibility of a departure towards an even more stripped-back sound. Thankfully, it also acts as a springboard for the solo career of one Emmylou Harris, who would continue in the same vein as Gram for several albums, then go on to richly-deserved adulation as a true goddess of country music.

Emmylou Harris: *Elite Hotel*
Reprise Records
Released 1975
Track listing: Amarillo/ Together Again/ Feelin' Single – Seein' Double/ Sin City/ One of These Days/ Till I Gain Control Again/ Here, There and Everywhere/ Ooh, Las Vegas/ Sweet Dreams/ Jambalaya/ Satan's Jewel Crown/ Wheels
From the pealing pedal steel of opening track 'Amarillo' to a well-chosen Beatles tune and no less than three Gram Parsons cover versions, Emmylou shows herself to be both the 'keeper of the flame' and more thrillingly, a great artist in her own right. Such was the esteem in which Harris was held by both country and rock music musicians that she was able, as Gram had been, to secure the services of Elvis Presley's TCB showband, which she christened the 'Hot Band'. Never was a group more aptly named.

Emmylou Harris
Wrecking Ball
Released 1995
This Daniel Lanois-produced album showcases Harris's ability not only to choose the best songs for her range, but to keep moving forward constantly. This is not really what you'd call a 'country' record; it is instead, a modern rock record. And in many ways, this is the kind of album we can imagine Gram to have made, were he still with us. Of course, this record shows that, spiritually speaking, he is very much still with us.

Other Titles available from Helter Skelter and Firefly Publishing and SAF.

Calling Out Around the World: A Motown Reader
Edited by Kingsley Abbott £13.99
With a foreword by Martha Reeves, this is a unique collection of articles which tell the story of the rise of a black company in a white industry, and its talented stable of artists, musicians, writers and producers. Included are rare interviews with key figures such as Berry Gordy, Marvin Gaye, Smokey Robinson and Florence Ballard as well as reference sources for collectors and several specially commissioned pieces.

Razor Edge: Bob Dylan and The Never-ending Tour
Andrew Muir £12.99
Respected Dylan expert Andrew Muir documents the ups and downs of this unprecedented trek, and finds time to tell the story of his own curious meeting with Dylan.
   Muir also tries to get to grips with what exactly it all means – both for Dylan and for the Bobcats: dedicated Dylan followers, like himself, who trade tapes of every show and regularly cross the globe to catch up with the latest leg of The Never Ending Tour.

The Beach Boys' *Pet Sounds*: The Greatest Album of the Twentieth Century
By Kingsley Abbott £11.95
Pet Sounds is the 1966 album that saw The Beach Boys graduate from lightweight pop like "Surfin' USA", *et al*, into a vehicle for the mature compositional genius of Brian Wilson. The album was hugely influential, not least on The Beatles. This the full story of the album's background, its composition and recording, its contemporary reception and its enduring legacy.

Ashley Hutchings: The Guvnor and the Rise of Folk Rock – Fairport Convention, Steeleye Span and the Albion Band
By Geoff Wall and Brian Hinton £12.99
As founder of Fairport Convention and Steeleye Span, Ashley Hutchings is the pivotal figure in the history of folk rock. This book draws on hundreds of hours of interviews with Hutchings and other folk-rock artists and paints a vivid picture of the scene that also produced Sandy Denny, Richard Thompson, Nick Drake, John Martyn and Al Stewart.

King Crimson: In The Court of King Crimson
By Sid Smith £14.99
King Crimson's 1969 masterpiece In The Court Of The Crimson King, was a huge U.S. chart hit. The band followed it with 40 further albums of consistently challenging, distinctive and innovative music. Drawing on hours of new interviews, and encouraged by Crimson supremo Robert Fripp, the author traces the band's turbulent history year by year, track by track.

I've Been Everywhere: A Johnny Cash Chronicle
By Peter Lewry £12.99
A complete chronological illustrated diary of Johnny Cash's concerts, TV appearances, record releases, recording sessions and other milestones. From his early days with Sam Phillips in Memphis to international stardom, the wilderness years of the mid-sixties, and on to his legendary prison concerts and his recent creative resurgence with the hugely successful 2000 release, American Recording III: Solitary Man.

Sandy Denny: No More Sad Refrains
By Clinton Heylin £13.99
Paperback edition of the highly acclaimed biography of the greatest female singer-songwriter this country has ever produced.

Emerson Lake and Palmer: The Show That Never Ends
George Forrester, Martin Hanson and Frank Askew £14.00
Prog-rock supergroup Emerson Lake and Palmer, were one the most successful acts of the seventies and, in terms of sound, artistic vision and concept, operated on a scale far in excess of any rivals.
   Drawing on years of research, the authors have produced a gripping and fascinating document of one of the great rock bands of the seventies.

Animal Tracks: The Story of The Animals
Sean Egan £12.99
Sean Egan, author of the acclaimed Verve biography, Starsailor (Omnibus, 1998) has enjoyed full access to surviving Animals and associates and has produced a compelling portrait of a truly distinctive band of survivors.

Like a Bullet of Light: The Films of Bob Dylan
CP Lee £12.99
In studying in-depth an often overlooked part of Dylan's oeuvre, Like A Bullet of Light forms a compelling portrait of an enigmatic artist as keen to challenge perceptions in the visual medium as in his better known career in music.

Rock's Wild Things: The Troggs Files
Alan Clayson and Jacqueline Ryan £12.99
Respected rock writer Alan Clayson has had full access to the band and traces their history from 60s Andover rock roots to 90s covers, collaborations and corn circles. The Troggs Files also features the first ever publication of the full transcript of the legendary "Troggs Tapes," said to have inspired the movie *This is Spinal Tap*, together with an exhaustive discography and many rare photos

Waiting for the Man: The Story of Drugs and Popular Music
by Harry Shapiro UK Price £12.99
Fully revised edition of the classic story of two intertwining billion dollar industries. "Wise and witty." *The Guardian*

The Sharper Word: A Mod Reader
Edited by Paolo Hewitt (available November 1999) UK price:£12.99
Hugely readable collection of articles documenting one of the most misunderstood cultural movements

Dylan's Daemon Lover: The Tangled Tale of a 450-Year Old Pop Ballad
by Clinton Heylin UK price £12.00
Written as a detective story, Heylin unearths the mystery of why Dylan knew enough to return "The House Carpenter" to its 16th century source.

Get Back: The Beatles' *Let It Be* Disaster
by Doug Sulpy & Ray Schweighardt UK price £12.99
No-holds barred account of the power struggles, the bickering, and the bitterness that led to the break-up of the greatest band in the history of rock 'n' roll. "One of the most poignant Beatles books ever." *Mojo*

XTC: Song Stories – The Exclusive & Authorised Story
by XTC and Neville Farmer UK Price £12.99
"A cheerful celebration of the minutiae surrounding XTC's music with the band's musical passion intact … high in setting-the-record-straight anecdotes. Superbright, funny, commanding." *Mojo*

Born in the USA: Bruce Springsteen and the American Tradition
by Jim Cullen UK Price £9.99
"Cullen has written an excellent treatise expressing exactly how and why Springsteen translated his uneducated hicktown American-ness into music and stories that touched hearts and souls around the world." *Q*****

Back to the Beach: A Brian Wilson and the Beach Boys Reader
Ed Kingsley Abbott UK Price £12.99
"A detailed study and comprehensive overview of the BBs' lives and music, even including a foreword from Wilson himself by way of validation. Most impressively, Abbott manages to appeal to both die-hard fans and rather less obsessive newcomers." *Time Out* "Rivetting!" **** *Q* "An essential purchase." *Mojo*

A Journey Through America with the Rolling Stones
by Robert Greenfield UK Price £9.99
Featuring a new foreword by Ian Rankin
   This is the definitive account of their legendary '72 tour.
   "Filled with finely-rendered detail … a fascinating tale of times we shall never see again" *Mojo*

Bob Dylan
by Anthony Scaduto UK Price £9.99
The first and best biography of Dylan. "The best book ever written on Dylan" *Record Collector* "Now in a welcome reprint it's a real treat to read the still-classic Bobography". *Q******

Currently Available from Firefly Publishing:

To Hell and Back with Catatonia
by Brian Wright UK price £12.99
Fronted by the brassy, irrepressible Cerys Matthews, Catatonia exploded onto the British pop scene in 1998. Author Brian Wright has been an ardent Catatonia supporter since their earliest days. Drawing on first hand experience, new interviews and years of research, he charts their struggle from obscure 1993 Cardiff pub gigs to the Top Ten.

U2: The Complete Encyclopedia
by Mark Chatterton UK Price £14.99
Here at last is the book that all completists, fans and U2 reference hounds have been waiting for. Hot on the heels of the huge success of Firefly's ultimate guide to all things Genesis, we can now announce the publication of the complete A to Z of the career of U2. Fully up-to-date, it documents the band's historical details from their early days in Dublin, to the current world tour.

Poison Heart: Surviving The Ramones
by Dee Dee Ramone and Veronica KofmanUK Price £11.95
Dee Dee's crushingly honest account of life as junkie and Ramone. A great rock story!

Minstrels In The Gallery: A History Of Jethro Tull
by David Rees UK Price £12.99
At Last! To coincide with their 30th anniversary, a full history of one of the most popular and inventive British bands.

DANCEMUSICSEXROMANCE: Prince – The First Decade
by Per Nilsen UK Price £12.99
A portrait of Prince's reign as the most exciting black performer to emerge since James Brown and Jimi Hendrix.

Soul Sacrifice: The Santana Story
by Simon Leng UK Price £12.99
In depth study of seventies Latin guitar legend whose career began at Woodstock through to a 1999 number one US album.

Opening The Musical Box: A Genesis Chronicle
by Alan Hewitt UK Price £12.99
Drawing on hours of new interviews and packed with insights, anecdotes and trivia, here is the ultimat compendium to one of the most successful and inventive bands of the modern rock era.

Blowin' Free: Thirty Years Of Wishbone Ash
by Gary Carter and Mark Chatterton UK Price £12.99
Packed with memorabilia, rare photos, a definitive discography and utilising unprecedented access to band members and associates, Gary Carter and Mark Chatterton have charted the long and turbulent career of one of England's premier rock outfits.

Currently available from SAF Publishing:

The Zombies: Hung Up On A Dream
by Claes Johansen UK Price: £16.99 (limited edition hardback)
Formed in 1963, The Zombies featured Rod Argent and Colin Blunstone. Their undenied masterpiece, the album *Odessey & Oracle*, was recorded at Abbey Road during that famous Summer of 1967 and featured the classic "Time Of The Season" and recently made *Mojo*'s best 100 LPs of all time.

Gentle Giant – Acquiring The Taste
by Paul Stump. UK Price: £16.99 (limited edition hardback)
Based around the Shulman brothers, Gentle Giant quickly acquired a large cult following the world over. Their music has endured over time and new generations are as entranced by their intricate sound as were audiences of 30 years ago.

Free At Last: The Story of Free and Bad Company
by Steven Rosen
One of the greatest rock blues outfits of the early seventies, Free peaked with the seminal hit "All Right Now", centred around the gravel-laden voice of Paul Rodgers and the hauntingly resonant guitar playing of troubled soul Paul Kossoff. When Free disbanded, Rodgers and Free drummer Simon Kirke went on to form one of the seventies best-known supergroups – Bad Company.

Steve Rosen's history with both bands goes back a long way – he once drove Paul Rodgers to an Elvis Presley concert in his Triumph Herald, as well as covering Bad Company's formation in *Rolling Stone*. Using old and new interviews with members and associates, here at last is a portrait of two of rock music's treasures.

Necessity Is... The Early Years of Frank Zappa and the Mothers of Invention
by Billy James UK Price: £12.95
No More Mr Nice Guy: The Inside Story of the Alice Cooper Group
By Michael Bruce and Billy James UK Price £11.99
Procol Harum: Beyond The Pale
by Claes Johansen UK Price £12.99
An American Band: The Story of Grand Funk Railroad
By Billy James UK Price £12.99
Wish The World Away: Mark Eitzel and American Music Club
by Sean Body UK Price £12.99
Go Ahead John! The Music of John McLaughlin
by Paul Stump UK Price £12.99
Lunar Notes: Zoot Horn Rollo's Captain Beefheart Experience
by Bill Harkleroad and Billy James UK Price £11.95
Meet The Residents: America's Most Eccentric Band
by Ian Shirley UK Price £11.95
Digital Gothic: A Critical Discography of Tangerine Dream
by Paul Stump UK Price £9.95
The One and Only – Homme Fatale: Peter Perrett & The Only Ones
by Nina Antonia UK Price £11.95
Plunderphonics, 'Pataphysics and Pop Mechanics
The Leading Exponents of Musique Actuelle
By Andrew Jones UK Price £12.95
Kraftwerk: Man, Machine and Music
By Pascal Bussy UK Price £12.95
Wrong Movements: A Robert Wyatt History
by Mike King UK Price £14.95
Wire: Everybody Loves A History
by Kevin Eden UK Price £9.95
Tape Delay: A Documentary of Industrial Music
by Charles Neal UK Price £15.99
Dark Entries: Bauhaus and Beyond
by Ian Shirley UK Price £11.95

Mail Order

All Helter Skelter, Firefly and SAF titles are available by mail order from the world famous Helter Skelter bookshop.

You can either phone or fax your order to Helter Skelter on the following numbers:

Telephone: +44 (0)20 7836 1151 or Fax: +44 (0)20 7240 9880
Office hours: Mon-Fri 10:00am – 7:00pm,
Sat: 10:00am – 6:00pm, Sun: closed.

Postage prices per book worldwide are as follows:

UK & Channel Islands	£1.50
Europe & Eire (air)	£2.95
USA, Canada (air)	£7.50
Australasia, Far East (air)	£9.00
Overseas (surface)	£2.50

You can also write enclosing a cheque, International Money Order, or registered cash. Please include postage. DO NOT send cash. DO NOT send foreign currency, or cheques drawn on an overseas bank. Send to:

Helter Skelter Bookshop,
4 Denmark Street, London, WC2H 8LL, United Kingdom.
If you are in London come and visit us, and browse the titles in person!!

Email: helter@skelter.demon.co.uk
Website: http://www.skelter.demon.co.uk